Corvette 1968-1982
Restoration Guide

Richard Prince

MOTORBOOKS

First published in 1999 by Motorbooks, an imprint of
MBI Publishing Company, Galtier Plaza, Suite 200,
380 Jackson Street, St. Paul, MN 55101-3885 USA

MBI Publishing Company titles are also available at
discounts in bulk quantity for industrial or sales-pro-
motional use. For details write to Special Sales Manager
at MBI Publishing Company, Galtier Plaza, Suite 200,
380 Jackson Street, St. Paul, MN 55101-3885 USA.

ISBN-13: 978-0-7603-0657-4
ISBN-10: 0-7603-0657-5

Printed in the United States of America

Contents

Acknowledgments

I wish to thank the following for their assistance in creating this book: Bill Anderson, Corvette Mike in Anaheim, California, Barbara Donato, John Donato, John Kohronas, William McBrien, Stan Rivera, Bruce Silber, and Ken Silber. I also want to thank the National Corvette Restorers Society for the invaluable work its members and leaders have done in gathering, preserving, and disseminating a wealth of information about the Corvettes we all love so much. Anyone interested in vintage Corvettes is well advised to join this organization by calling (513) 385-8526.

Preface

This book is intended to provide restorers of 1968–1982 "Shark" Corvettes with the technical information needed to return these cars to the same exact configuration they were in at the time of final delivery by Chevrolet Motor Division. This is not, however, a how-to manual. Rather, it is a compendium of information about how the cars were originally built, including available options, exterior and interior colors and materials, correct components and their respective factory finishes, part numbers, casting numbers, date codes, and the like. It will not tell you how to do a restoration procedure, but it will tell you where and how to read original part numbers and date codes, what parts your restoration procedures should be done with, and how those parts should look when you are finished.

Owing to the explosive popularity of the 1968–1982 models, there is an ever-expanding body of published information available to assist the restorer. To obtain the greatest benefit from this restoration guide, it should be used in conjunction with some of these other valuable resources. Among them are the *Chevrolet Chassis Service, Chassis Overhaul,* and *Shop Manuals*. These provide detailed instructions, diagrams, and specifications for component service, repair, and overhaul.

Though it does not provide "how-to" instructions per se, another invaluable companion to this restoration guide is *Chevrolet's Corvette Assembly Instruction Manual*. Available for each year of production, these comprehensive manuals are exact reprints of the same assembly instructions the production line workers used to build the cars. They contain hundreds of exploded drawings showing how virtually every part of a Corvette goes together.

All of the above referenced materials, as well as many others, are readily available from any of the major Corvette restoration parts suppliers. They complement this restoration guide because they show you how to do many of the procedures commonly performed during a comprehensive restoration.

Introduction

In January 1953, 38,000 fortunate individuals had the privilege of walking into the grand ballroom of New York's Waldorf Astoria Hotel to view the GM Motorama. Reflecting the postwar feelings of American invincibility and unparalleled ingenuity, this extravaganza was designed to showcase the company's creative talent in ways that would leave a lasting impression. At a cost in excess of 5 million 1953 dollars, the Motorama was the epitome of showmanship and marketing genius. Incredibly ornate displays, beautiful women, and elaborate stage productions orchestrated by the best choreographers and dancers Broadway had to offer certainly contributed to the desired effect, but it was the cars that really stirred people's emotions.

This was the golden era of the dream cars, fantastically styled and engineered vehicles designed to demonstrate the company's prowess while at the same time thrilling spectators. Among the more notable dream machines, which included the LeSabre and Buick XP-300, there was one car that really stood out from the others. Called Corvette, this little white two-seat sports car, perched on a revolving turntable in front of a panoramic image of the Manhattan skyline, was the sensation of the 1953 Motorama. Public reaction was so strong, in fact, that GM decided to actually put the car into production, something that had never before been done with a dream car.

In June 1953, a scant six months after it made its debut on the Waldorf Astoria stage, production of the Corvette began on a pilot assembly line in Flint, Michigan. By year's end, only 300 of the cars were built, though plans were underway to substantially increase production capacity for the following year. But unfortunately, the public's reaction, which was so hot at the Motorama, had cooled considerably when the cars actually came to market, and by the end of 1954, as many as one-third of that year's 3,640 Corvettes remained unsold.

What was it that caused this apparent turn-around in the public's attitude? Quality control problems, mediocre performance emanating from the car's six-cylinder/two-speed Powerglide automatic combination, as well as a relatively high component cost, certainly all played a role. Perhaps the most important factor, however, was inadequate marketing. In 1953, Chevrolet was the largest division of the largest automobile manufacturer in the world. It had a well-deserved reputation for building economical and reliable transportation for the masses. The decision makers at Chevy, who were more accustomed to producing hundreds of thousands of ordinary passenger cars at a time, knew virtually nothing about selling low-volume, largely handmade sports cars to a few thousand devoted enthusiasts.

As a result of poor sales performance and mounting losses, the Corvette "experiment" came perilously close to ending as quickly as it had begun. But to their everlasting credit, a small, intensely dedicated group of individuals within Chevrolet simply would not allow this to happen. They recognized and systematically addressed the car's shortcomings and turned an apparent loser into a surefire winner. The 1955 model year saw the introduction of the legendary small-block V-8 and, at the end of the year, a manual three-speed transmission. The following year, 1956, marked the beginning of Corvette's racing legacy, and the following year brought such high-performance options as fuel injection, a heavy-duty brake and suspension package, and four-speed transmission.

With the introduction of the awesome Sting Ray in 1963, the Corvette's reputation for world-class performance was upheld with features such as independent rear suspension, fuel injection, racing brakes and suspension, and the Positraction rear axle. In addition, 1963 marked the beginning of the car's development as a true GT machine. Options such as air conditioning, power steering and brakes, and leather seat covers gave buyers great latitude in equipping their cars just as they wanted them.

By 1968, when the sensational third-generation Corvette was introduced, the car had really reached maturity. Four-wheel disc brakes and four-wheel independent suspension were standard. Buyers had a choice of no less than seven different engines, five different transmissions, and a wide variety of performance options. By simply checking off the correct boxes on the order form, a race-ready Corvette could be ordered directly from Chevrolet. And for those more interested in luxurious motoring, a bevy of grand touring and luxury features were also available. Corvettes equipped with full power, air conditioning, leather seats, AM-FM stereo, and all the other comfort and convenience goodies were perfect long-distance cruisers.

Third-generation Corvettes, commonly referred to as "Stingrays" or "Sharks," remained in production until 1982, longer than any other Corvette model. In their 15 years of production, more than 542,861 Sharks were built, a staggering number when you consider the marque's near demise for lack of interest 20 years earlier.

The period between 1968 and 1982 was a fascinating and tumultuous time in the automotive industry. The beginning of this stretch marked the end of the golden era of Detroit muscle machines. Appropriately equipped Corvettes, such as those sporting the potent L88 or exotic ZL1 option packages, were the undisputed kings of the musclecar epoch.

As the 1960s turned into the 1970s, unrestrained power and speed fell victim to increasingly stringent insurance industry demands, governmental regulations, and market considerations. Research and development dollars that had previously been directed toward enhancing performance were now targeted at meeting fuel economy, exhaust emissions, and safety requirements. As a result, all cars, including Corvettes, got heavier, clumsier looking, more expensive, and slower. But the Corvette, unlike many other cars, weathered the storm with dignity and managed to emerge from this rather gloomy era with its character and place in history still intact.

As the 1970s came to a close and the 1980s dawned, a transformation in the automobile building business began to emerge. Science had finally caught up with the mandates from Washington and elsewhere and was on the brink of surging ahead. Through the application of very sophisticated com-

puter technology, superior manufacturing techniques and materials, and high-tech electronics, Corvettes met all of the safety, emissions, and economy demands imposed upon them and were performing admirably at the same time.

In the nearly two decades since their production came to an end, collector interest in third-generation Corvettes has grown steadily. The sheer number of cars produced, as well as the great variety of offerings during the Stingray's 15-year model run, including incredibly high-horsepower big blocks, efficient and powerful computer-directed small blocks, convertibles, and special offerings such as the 1978 Indy Pace Car Replicas and 1982 Collector Editions, mean there is something of interest for just about everyone.

In addition to the selection and variety of third-generation Corvettes available, collector interest in these cars has also been generated as a result of their recognition by the major Corvette show organizations, most notably Bloomington Gold and the National Corvette Restorers Society. Recognition has fostered interest in showing the cars at the highest levels, and this in turn has encouraged their restoration. In the great free market tradition, the resultant demand for correct restoration parts has induced manufacturers and suppliers to make available just about anything needed for the restoration of a Shark Corvette.

Concurrent with the emergence and maturation of the Shark restoration hobby is a need for increasingly detailed and accurate information about the cars. To succeed at the highest levels of judging, realize the maximum economic return from the investment in restoration, and for many people, to derive the greatest feelings of accomplishment and happiness from their efforts, an intensely detailed and factory correct restoration is essential.

This book is intended to provide restorers of 1968 to 1982 Corvettes with the technical information needed to return these cars to the same exact configuration they were in at the time of final delivery by Chevrolet Motor Division. This is not, however, a how-to manual. Rather, it is a compendium of information about how the cars were originally built, including available options and their permissible combinations, exterior and interior colors and materials, correct components and their respective factory finishes, part numbers, casting numbers, date codes, and the like. It will not tell you how to do a restoration procedure but it will tell you what parts the procedure should be done with and how they should look when you are finished.

As you utilize the information contained herein and traverse the road to restoration, you will experience the full range of human emotions. At one end of the spectrum is the pain of scraped knuckles and the depression that inevitably results from feelings that your car will never go back together again. At the other end, and of far greater importance, are the intense feelings of accomplishment derived from a job well done and the unmitigated delight you will take in the finished product.

As you travel the road to restoration, experiencing the agony of a thousand small setbacks and the ecstasy of a million small victories, I urge you to remember one thing above all else: Your Corvette and, in fact, all of the Corvettes in all of the world are not worth losing the use of one finger on one hand, your eyesight, or your life. Automotive repair and restoration is an inherently dangerous pursuit. By consistently practicing safe habits you can, however, reduce the probability of injury to an absolute minimum. Common sense and overcoming the lazy tendencies inherent in all of us account for 99 percent of the safety steps in an automotive shop. Do not, under any circumstances, fail to use goggles, a breathing mask, hearing protection, and all the other proper safety gear necessary for the task you are performing and the tools you are employing. If you have any doubt concerning your personal safety, consult an applicable shop manual and seek professional advice. Remember, regardless of how much you love your Corvette and how special it is and how important it is to complete what you are doing as quickly as possible, it is still just a car. And a car is just a conglomeration of metal, plastic, rubber, and glass that together is not worth one single cell in your body.

After personal safety, the second most important thing for practitioners of the restoration art is to have fun. General Motors has always built Corvettes to realize a profit for its shareholders. That, after all, is the purpose of GM's and every other corporation's existence. In contrast, the magnificent men and women within Chevrolet who transformed what would have been little more than a footnote in automotive history into a respected and beloved automotive icon the world over had something even more important than corporate profits in mind. They had feelings of excitement and passion in their hearts, for they knew they were creating far more than just another car. The Corvette transcends mere transportation, and the people who built it recognized it as an expression of the American ideal, the near-perfect melding of art and science, the creation of a legacy that would endure long after they were forgotten. For these people, the Corvette was far more than the source of their livelihood; it was also a major source of joy in their lives.

As you delve into the restoration hobby you too will feel what the car's creators felt, for you too will be playing a role in preserving and perpetuating the Corvette legend. It is my sincere hope that you find the information in this book useful and that it plays a role in enhancing your enjoyment of the Corvette restoration hobby.

Chapter 1

1968–1969

1968–1969 Exterior
Body Fiberglass
The 1968 model was the first car to have what is now commonly called the shark body style. With the exception of the door skins, which differ due to the different door opening mechanisms, 1968 and 1969 body panels are functionally interchangeable. There are, however, various minor differences between some 1968 body parts and their 1969 counterparts. For example, the rear lower filler panel differs in that 1968s have rectangular backup lamps mounted in them and 1969s do not. Another example is the top surround panel, which was strengthened in 1969 with the enlargement of the lip in the front corners adjacent to the hood opening.

All 1968 and 1969 body panels are made from press molded fiberglass. The panels are smooth on both sides and are very dark gray in color.

Body Paint
All 1968–1969 cars were painted with acrylic lacquer. Factory paint is generally smooth and shiny, though some orange peel is evident throughout. Roughness and poor coverage is fairly typical along the very bottom edges of the body panels and in less conspicuous areas such as edges of the wiper doors, inside the front fender vents, and so on. The factory did not use clear coat, even with metallic colors. Because clear coat was not used, metallics may tend to be slightly mottled or blotchy.

A right-side front grille assembly for 1969s made after approximately January 1969. Note that the grille is black with the front edge of each horizontal slat painted silver.

Left-side front grille assemblies for 1968s and those 1969s made before approximately January 1969 are all black, including the front edge of each horizontal slat. Later 1969s are painted silver on the front edges of each slat.

In 1968 the two black Phillips head screws above and below the park light housing help retain the grille. In 1969s the holes for these screws are present in the grilles but the screws are not used.

Front Bumpers

Front bumpers are chrome plated and held to the car with semi-gloss painted steel brackets. Cadmium-plated hex head bolts are used to retain the bumper to the brackets and cadmium and/or black oxide hex head bolts hold the brackets to the chassis. Unpainted or silver cadmium–plated shims are sometimes used between the outer bumper mounts and the body.

Front Grille Area and Parking Lamps

The front grille assembly is made from three pieces of black molded plastic, each of which has horizontal slats. The grilles remain all black for 1968 and for those 1969 cars assembled through approximately January 1969. Grilles in cars assembled after approximately January 1969 are black with the front edge of each horizontal slat painted silver. In 1968 there are two black Phillips head screws in each of the outer grilles. One is above and one is below the park light housing. In 1969 cars the holes are present in the grilles for these screws but the screws are not used.

The front parking lamp housings are inset into the outer front grilles. In 1968 and 1969 they get clear plastic lenses with amber-colored bulbs. A very light gray gasket seals the lens to the housing. The lenses are held by chrome Phillips head screws. A fiber-optic cable is inserted into the top of each parking light housing.

Rectangular-shaped side marker lamps are used at all four corners in 1968 and 1969. The lamp housings, which can only be seen from behind the body panels, are made from white plastic. Very light gray gaskets seal the lenses to the lamp housings. In 1968 front side marker lamps have clear lenses with amber bulbs. In 1969 the lamps have amber lenses and clear bulbs.

Front License Plate Bracket

The front license plate brackets for 1968 and 1969 are painted semi-gloss black and are held on by two cadmium-plated hex head bolts. A small rubber bumper is inserted in a hole toward the bottom center, and two white plastic nuts insert into square holes in the upper corners. A small brown paper bag marked "LICENSE ATTACHING" on one side, "REAR PLATE PARTS" on the other, and "UNIT NUMBER 3875313" along the top came in the car originally. In it were four large cadmium-plated, slotted pan head screws for the front and rear license plates.

Front Headlamps and Headlamp Bezels

All four headlamp bulbs in 1968 and 1969 were made by Guide and feature a Guide T-3 logo in the glass. All bulbs have a centered triangle with "T-3" surrounded by vertical bars. Headlamp bezels are diecast aluminum and painted body color. Paint on the bezels is usually not as shiny or smooth as it is on the body. The 1968 cars do not have any headlight washer nozzles or nozzle holes in the bezels. The 1969s have two chrome-plated headlamp washer nozzles in each bezel. Both nozzles are pointed at the low beam (outer) bulb, one from above and one from below.

A semi-gloss black plastic shield is behind each front grille to shield the headlamps from view when the light assemblies are in the down position. The shields are each held to the body by three self-tapping, black phosphate Phillips pan head screws with integral flat washers. A cadmium dichromate vacuum actuator is mounted behind each headlamp assembly. A red-striped hose connects to the back of each actuator and a green-striped hose connects to the front.

Front Fenders

Front fenders on 1968s and 1969s are functionally interchangeable. Front fender louver trim molding is optional for 1969s, but not for 1968s. The chrome and metallic-silver-painted louver trim moldings are each held by two chrome-plated Phillips head screws. In 1969 both front fenders had an emblem reading "Stingray" above their louvers. The 1968s did not have these emblems. The 1969-only Stingray emblems are chrome with the thin stepped edge surrounding each letter painted black. Emblems are held onto the body by a thick, black adhesive strip that is visible and each has four long studs that were used for positioning only and therefore do not get nuts. Original emblems feature an "i" without a dot whereas later replacements have a small groove cut into the "i" to simulate the dot.

Corvettes from 1968 through late 1971 came equipped with this style Guide T3 headlamp. Later 1971s and 1972s have the T3 logo in squares and rectangles located at the bottom of the bulb rather than in a centered triangle as shown here.

Hood

All 1968 and 1969 cars originally equipped with a small-block engine have a low-profile hood with a single wind split down the middle. There are no emblems, decals, or other markings on these hoods. Hoods on all cars equipped with a 427 engine (except optional L88 and ZL1 engines) have a raised area with twin simulated vents in the center for added engine compartment clearance. The leading edge of each simulated vent has a cast-metal piece of chrome trim (except on its inside where it is painted semi-gloss black).

L88- and ZL1-equipped cars utilize a special hood with a higher bulge than the hood used for

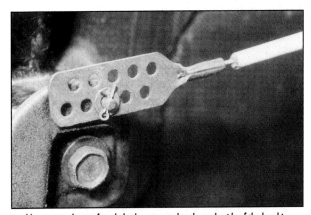

A cable connects the two female latches mounted to the underside of the hood in 1968–1976. In very early 1968 this cable is inside a wound metal sheath. This changes to a black nylon sheath for mid-production 1968s and then to a white nylon sheath for later 1968s and all 1969s. The example shown is from a 1969.

other 427-powered cars. These have a functional cold air induction feature that directs outside air to the carburetor. All 427-equipped cars, including L88s and ZL1s, have a "427" emblem on each side of the hood bulge. The emblems are comprised of three separate numerals, each of which is chrome plated with painted black recesses.

Windshield Vent Grille, Wiper Door, and Wipers

The windshield vent grille is painted body color and is retained by black oxide, recessed Phillips flat head screws with fine threads. The area beneath the vent grille is painted semi-gloss black. The windshield wiper door, like the vent grille, is painted body color. A stainless-steel trim strip is on the rear edge of the wiper door. The strip is painted body color except for an unpainted polished bead that runs adjacent to the windshield. The strip is attached to the wiper door with small, round head rivets. Wiper arms and blade holders are dull black in color and each holder says "TRICO" on one of its ends. Wiper blade inserts are 16 inches long and also say "TRICO." They have various patent numbers molded in and two raised ribs are present below all of the writing.

Windshield Washers

In 1968 two flat-black metal tubes are each welded to L-shaped brackets. The brackets in turn are attached to the underside of the windshield vent grille with a hex head screw in very early cars and a Phillips head screw thereafter. 1969 Corvettes assembled through approximately December 1968 use the same washer nozzles as 1968 cars. 1969s assembled after approximately December 1968 have a different configuration.

In these cars the two short lengths of flat-black tubing are each welded to a metal block that is screwed to the body at the base of the windshield. Late 1969s have yet another washer nozzle configuration. In these cars a length of metal tubing is welded to a small tab at the end of each wiper arm and is further retained to the arm by one to four black plastic clips.

Windshield, Door Glass, and Back Glass

All 1968 and 1969 Corvette windshields were manufactured by Libby-Owens-Ford (LOF) utilizing Safety Plate glass. The LOF logo, the words "SAFETY PLATE," and a two letter manufacturing date code are etched into the lower right side of the windshield. In the date code, one letter represents the month and the other denotes the year. There is no discernible pattern to the letter usage so you must refer to the glass date codes in Appendix R.

The letters "ASI" are present in the upper right portion of the windshield. These letters are white and sandwiched between the laminates of glass, not etched into the surface like the LOF logo and date code. Both side windows are made from LOF Safety Flo Lite glass that has the manufacturer's logo and a two-letter date code etched in just like the windshield. If the glass is tinted, the words "Soft-Ray" or "Soft-Ray Tinted" are also etched in. In addition, the words "Astro Ventilation" are present in white silk-screened letters in the lower forward corner of each window. Back windows in 1968 and 1969 coupes, like the windshields and side glass, have the LOF logo and manufacturing date code etched in.

Door Mirror, Handles, and Locks

All 1968 and 1969 Corvettes have one chrome-plated outside rearview mirror that is mounted on

Windshield wiper doors have a stainless-steel trim strip on their rear edge. The strip is painted body color except for an unpainted, polished bead that runs adjacent to the windshield. As seen here, the strip is attached to the wiper door with a small, round head rivet on either side.

All 1968 and 1969 Corvettes have one outside rearview mirror on the driver door. The mirror glass bears a date code and manufacturer's logo. This example indicates that Donnelly Mirror, Inc. made the mirror in November 1968.

A door release button with an integral lock cylinder was unique to 1968. The flapper above the button served only as a grab. In subsequent years the flapper also functioned as the release mechanism.

the driver's door. A mounting base is held to the door by two screws and the mirror goes over the base and is held on by a black oxide Allen head screw. A thin gasket goes between the base and door and is visible when the mirror is installed.

The mirrors on early 1968s were mounted about four inches farther forward than they were on later 1968 and 1969s. This change occurred in approximately March 1968. The mirror's head is rectangular and measures 3-7/8-inches high by 5-3/8-inches wide. The glass is coded with the manufacturer's symbol and a date code. Mirrors supplied by Donnelly Mirror, Inc. have "DMI" in the code and those supplied by Ajax Mirror have "AX" in it. For example, the code in a Donnelly-supplied mirror manufactured in April 1968 would read "4-DMI-8" whereas the code for an Ajax-supplied mirror manufactured in February 1969 would read "2-AX-69."

All 1968 door handles consist of a spring-loaded, press-flap design grab and a push-button release. The door lock is incorporated into the push-button release, which sits in a recess molded into the fiberglass door skin. In all 1969s, the door release mechanism is incorporated into the spring-loaded, press flap grab. The door locks in 1969, which are positioned below the door handles, feature a polished stainless-steel bezel. Original bezels are retained to the cylinders by means of a continuous crimp around their entire circumference. Incorrect replacement locks may have bezels retained by four tangs. A thin, black rubber gasket is visible between the lock and door. On original 1968 and 1969 press flap handles the spring action is provided by a coil spring on the hinge shaft. A butterfly spring covering a coil spring is incorrect. When the flap is depressed the spring is

visible. A thin, black rubber gasket is visible between the handle and door.

Side Rocker Molding and Optional Side Exhaust

Side rocker molding for all 1968 and 1969 Corvettes is comprised of two sections: the larger piece is semi-gloss black-painted fiberglass and the smaller piece is brushed aluminum that is polished along the top and painted semi-gloss black along the bottom. The smaller piece goes on top of the larger one and seven black oxide Phillips oval head screws pass through both to attach them to the body. In addition, the larger piece has two mounting tabs on the bottom underside toward the front.

Front fenders for 1968 and 1969 are the same, but the Stingray emblem and optional louver trim shown here were available in 1969 only.

Two black oxide Phillips fillister head screws pass through these into J-nuts affixed to the lower edge of the body.

Side-mounted exhaust was an option for 1969 cars only. The pipe covers replace the standard rocker molding. The side pipe covers are made from chrome-plated metal with a fiberglass insulator bonded to the inside. The covers have horizontal ridges in the middle. The covers are painted semi-gloss black between the ridges and along the top edge. Six black oxide Phillips oval head screws retain each cover to the car's body.

Radio Antenna

A radio was still an option for Corvettes in 1968 and 1969, and according to published production figures 1,423 cars were built without one during the two years. On those cars no radio antenna was installed, but on all others a fixed-height antenna was mounted on the driver-side rear deck. A black plastic gasket goes between the antenna base and

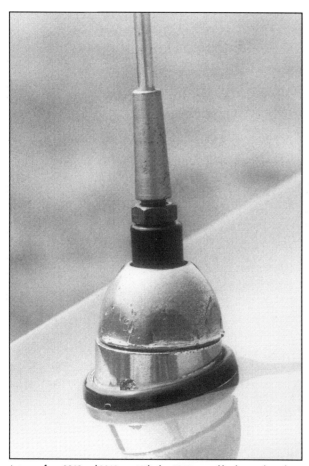

Antennas from 1968 and 1969 are similar but 1968 masts, like the one shown here, thread into the base, while 1969 masts sit in an additional black insulator and are held by a metal collar with two flat areas for tightening.

the car's body. The base is also made of black plastic beneath a chrome bezel. The base, along with the portion of the antenna assembly beneath the body, is retained by a chrome cap with two flat areas for a wrench to grab. 1968 masts thread into the base while 1969 masts sit in an additional black insulator and are held by a metal collar with two flat areas for tightening. For both 1968 and 1969 antennas the mast ball is .300-inch in diameter, not .250-inch as seen on some later replacements.

Rear Deck Vent Grilles and Gas Fill Door

Two vent grilles are installed on the rear deck behind the back window (or behind the convertible top deck on convertibles). The vent grilles are painted body color and are each retained by four black oxide Phillips flat head screws. The lips in the body the grilles sit on and the vent channel below are sprayed with flat black paint in varying degrees of coverage. Gas lid doors are painted body color and feature a chrome and painted crossed flags emblem. For 1968s assembled through approximately late April 1968 spin rivets retain the emblem. For the remainder of 1968 models either these same rivets or chrome-plated acorn nuts are utilized. For all of 1969 the acorn nuts are utilized.

For 1968s assembled through approximately late April 1968, four spin rivets hold the gas door to its hinge. Starting in May 1968 the rivets were replaced with four chrome-plated Phillips fillister head screws. For the remainder of 1968 models either spin rivets or chrome-plated screws are utilized. For all of 1969 the screws are utilized.

In both 1968 and 1969 a latch that is part of the hinge assembly holds the door in the open position. A tab peened to the underside of the door inserts into a receptacle in the gas door bezel to hold the door closed. The receptacle is formed from two white, spring-loaded pieces of nylon to hold the door closed. For both 1968 and 1969 the polished gas door bezel is held to the body with chrome-plated Phillips oval head screws. In both years doors don't use any rubber bumpers to cushion the door when it is closed.

All 1968 and 1969 Corvettes came with a twist-on gas cap, not a locking cap. The locking caps, which are usually flat and chrome plated, were dealer installed or aftermarket. All correct caps are silver cadmium–plated and only have the word "VENTED" stamped in. Later caps have additional words such as "SEALED" and "OPEN SLOWLY CAUTION" stamped into them.

For 1968 and 1969 the gas cap has a handle for twisting it on and off. The handle is attached by two ears that are bent over and spot welded onto the cap. On original caps the ears face down when the word "VENTED" is upright.

A black rubber boot surrounds the gas filler neck in both years. The boot has a plastic nipple facing the rear of the car and a rubber drain hose attaches to it. The hose, which has a metal spring inside to prevent it from collapsing, runs down behind the gas tank and exits the body through a hole adjacent to one of the rear bumper braces. A black plastic tie wrap holds the hose to the bumper brace.

Rear Fascia, Taillamps, Bumpers, and Related Parts

The rear fascia has "CORVETTE" spelled out in eight individual letters centered between the taillamps. Each letter is chrome plated with silver paint in its recessed face. An audio alarm was optional beginning in May 1968. All cars so equipped have a lock cylinder switch on the rear body panel between the taillamps and above the Corvette letters. All 1968s and 1969s use an open-style lock cylinder that does not have a spring-loaded face plate and crimped-over bezel like the door lock cylinders. No gasket is used between the alarm lock cylinder and body.

The recessed area of the body where the rear license plate mounts is covered by a diecast surround trim that is chrome plated. A lamp assembly mounts at the top of the recess behind the rear body panel and illuminates the rear license plate. A fiber-optic cable inserts into the license lamp housing. A black rubber bumper is inserted into the rear valance panel centered toward the lower edge of the license plate. Two white plastic push nuts insert into square

Gas lid doors are painted body color in 1968 and 1969. Original crossed flags emblems have the pattern shown here for the black-and-white checkered flag. Some replacements have the pattern reversed.

The underside of the gas lid door from an early 1968. Note the use of spin rivets to hold the door to its hinge. Some later 1968s and all 1969s use chrome-plated Phillips head screws.

The underside of the gas lid door from a 1969. The two chrome-plated acorn nuts retain the crossed flags emblem on the top of the door. Acorn nuts or spin rivets hold the emblem in late 1968s and spin rivets only were used in early 1968s.

Corvettes produced in 1969 through early 1971 utilize taillamp lenses with a distinct conical shape and concentric lines molded in as shown in this 1969 example. Black oxide Phillips pan head screws hold each lens in place.

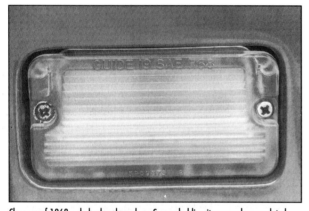

Close-up of 1968-only backup lamp lens. Screws holding it on are chrome plated.

In 1968 only the backup lights are in the rear lower valance panel beneath the bumpers. Beginning in 1969 they are incorporated into the inboard taillamps.

cutouts in the rear body panel for the license plate retaining screws.

1968s all utilize four rear lamps, each of which has a red, conical-shaped lens. Three chrome-plated Phillips head screws retain the lenses.

1968s have a rectangular backup lamp assembly mounted beneath each rear bumper. Each lamp has a clear lens held by two chrome Phillips head screws. A black rubber gasket seals each lens to its housing. 1969s utilize four rear lamps, but the lenses on the two inner lamps are different than in 1968. The two outer ones utilize red, conical-shaped lenses that function as taillamps, stop lamps, and turn signals. The two inner ones utilize red lenses with clear plastic centers that function as back-up lamps. These are conical shaped with concentric grooves on the inside. Rear bumpers are chrome plated and are attached to the body with semi-gloss black painted brackets. As with the front bumpers, cadmium-plated hex head bolts retain the bumpers to the brackets and cadmium- and/or black oxide–plated hex head bolts hold the brackets to the chassis.

The rear valance panel is painted body color but often shows poor paint quality including runs or sparse coverage along the bottom edge. It is retained to the body by four cadmium-plated indented hex head bolts. The two outer ones utilize integral washers while the two inners have separate flat washers.

Cars equipped with optional side exhaust do not have the exhaust tip cutouts in the rear valence panel or rear quarter panels. Cars with undercar exhaust have rounded cutouts in the body. The cutouts are trimmed with chromed, diecast bezels that are round in shape but with open bottoms. The bezels are retained by chrome Phillips oval head screws.

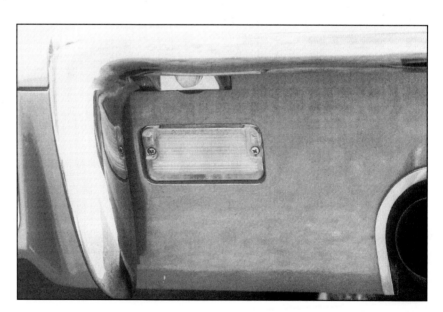

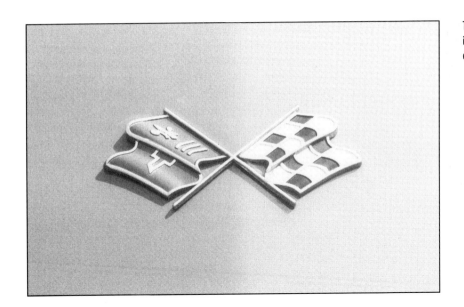

The correct 1968 and 1969 front nose emblem. Some incorrect later replacements have the colors in the checkered flag reversed.

Convertible Tops

Convertible tops are made from vinyl with a woven pattern. The convertible top is available in either white, beige, or black, regardless of exterior body color. The front header roll and tack strip cover are also vinyl but have a grained rather than a woven pattern. Two small, stainless-steel trim pieces cover the ends of the tack strip. The trim pieces are flared around their perimeter and attach with one small, bright Phillips flat head screw. The convertible top is clear vinyl and is heat sealed, not sewn, to the top.

The convertible top back window contains a manufacturer's logo, manufacturing date, and the words "VINYLITE, TRADE MARK, AS-6," and "DO NOT RUB DRY WASH WITH WATER SOAKED CLOTH" heat stamped in the driver-side lower corner. The date code is normally three or four numbers, with the first one or two representing the month and the second two representing the year. For example, a convertible top manufactured in April of 1968 would have a date code of 468. A paper caution label is sewn into the top in the corner below the heat-stamped logo and date in the window.

When a convertible was purchased, the buyer could choose either a soft top or a hardtop. As an extra cost option both tops could be purchased.

The hardtop is painted body color unless vinyl covered. All vinyl-covered hardtops are black. Beginning in approximately December 1968 stainless-steel tips were installed on the lower rear points of the top to protect them from damage. The hardtop rear window contains the LOF manufacturing logo and is date coded with two letters like the remainder of the body glass. The first letter represents the month of production and the second represents the year of production. (See Appendix R for glass date codes.)

Tires, Wheels, and Wheel Covers

1968 and 1969 Corvettes have either Goodyear, Firestone, or Uniroyal F70x15 bias-ply nylon cord tires. The standard tire for all three years is a blackwall. Whitewalls and red lines are optional both years. Raised white letter tires are available as an extra cost option beginning in approximately September 1969. Whitewalls and red lines are either Firestone Super Sport Wide Ovals, Goodyear Speedway Wide Treads, or Uniroyal Tiger Paws. The Firestones have a 3/8-inch white stripe that is 1-7/8 inches from the bead edge. The Goodyears have a 5/16-inch white stripe that is 1 inch from the bead edge. The Uniroyals have a 5/16-inch stripe that is 1-3/8 inches from the

Original convertible soft tops have the manufacturer's logo, washing instructions, and a date code heat stamped into the lower driver-side corner of the rear window. This example was manufactured August 1, 1968.

This is an example of an original valve stem cap from a 1968. It is typical of correct caps for most 1968–1982 cars. "DILL" (shown upside down in this photo) was the manufacturer.

bead edge. Raised white letter tires are believed to be Goodyears or Firestones, not Uniroyals. Raised white letter Goodyears say "Goodyear Wide Tread F70-15" in block letters. Raised white letter Firestones say "Firestone Wide O Oval" in block letters.

All 1968 and 1969 Corvettes are equipped with steel Rally wheels. For 1968s they are 15x7 inches and for 1969s they are 15x8 inches. The front sides of Rally wheels are a color called Argent Silver. This color is predominantly silver but it has a slight greenish hue. The back sides of the wheels are painted semi-flat black and always have silver overspray since the front side was painted silver after the black was applied to the rear. All wheels are stamped with a date code, manufacturer's logo, and size code on the front face.

All 1968 Corvette wheels are 15x7 inches and have the code "AG" stamped in to indicate this. All 1969 Corvette wheels are 15x8 inches and have the code "AZ" stamped in to indicate this. The "AG" or "AZ" is adjacent to the valve stem hole. Also adjacent to the valve stem hole is the manufacturer's logo and date code stamping. On one side of the hole it says "K" for the wheel manufacturer, Kelsey Hayes. This is followed by a dash and a "1" that represents Chevrolet. Next comes another dash and either a "7," "8," or a "9" to denote the last digit of the year of manufacture. This is followed by a space and one or two numbers to indicate the month of manufacture. On the other side of the valve stem hole are one or two more numbers that represent the day of manufacture.

Stainless-steel trim rings and chrome center caps are standard for all cars. Original trim rings are held to the wheel by four steel clips. Center caps should read "Chevrolet Motor Division" in black painted letters. A full wheel cover is available as an extra cost option for all 1968 and 1969 Corvettes. Called option PO2, this cover has a stainless-steel outer rim and

closely spaced radial fins that converge outward toward a protruding ornamental disc in the center. The disc is chrome around its edge, black in the middle, and contains the Corvette crossed flags emblem. Other Chevrolet products use a similar wheel cover but those have a flat center disc instead of the protruding disc utilized for Corvettes. Wheels on cars equipped with standard trim rings and center caps utilize black rubber valve stems that measure approximately 1-\1/4 inches long. These are fitted with caps that come to a point and have longitudinal ridges around their entire perimeter.

Wheels on cars equipped with optional full wheel covers have extensions threaded onto the standard valve stems. The extensions have a white color inner shaft that is visible because they are not fitted with caps.

To ease the balancing process, wheels are sometimes marked with a tiny weld drop or paint dot at their highest point. This mark is lined up with an orange dot on the tire. Balance weights are the type that clamp onto the edge of the rim and are placed on the inside of the wheel only. Original balance weights usually have the letters *OEM* molded into their face. There is usually a small white or colored dot of paint on the tire adjacent to each balance weight.

All cars have a full-size spare tire and wheel that is identical to the other four tires and wheels. The spare wheel is not fitted with a wheel covering like the other four.

The spare tire and wheel are housed in a carrier bolted to the rear underbody area. The carrier is fiberglass with steel supports. The fiberglass is unpainted and the steel support is painted semi-gloss black. The tire tub portion of the carrier has a fair amount of flat to semi-gloss black paint on its outside surface applied during the blackout process. A lock covered by a black rubber boot goes over the spare tire carrier access bolt.

1968–1969 Interior
Trim Tag

Interior trim color and material, as well as exterior body color and body assembly date, are stamped into an unpainted stainless-steel plate attached to the driver's door hinge pillar by two aluminum Pop Rivets. This plate is commonly called a trim plate or trim tag. Trim color and material are indicated in the plate by a three-number code. For example, in 1968 trim code 408 indicates red color interior with leather seat covers. Exterior body paint is likewise indicated by a three-number code stamped in the trim plate. For example, in 1969 code 980 indicates Riverside Gold. (See Appendix T for paint and trim codes.)

The body build date represents the date when the painted and partially assembled body reached that point on the assembly line where the trim plate was installed. The car's final assembly date is typically one to several days after the body build date. A letter indicating the month followed by two numbers indicating the day represents the body build date. The letter "A" was assigned to the first month of production, which was August 1967 for 1968 cars and August 1968 for 1969 cars. The second month of production was assigned "B" and so on. A body assembled on the sixth day of August 1967 would have "A06" stamped into the trim plate, for example, and a body built on the eleventh day of May 1969 would have "J11" stamped into its plate. (See Appendix S for body build date codes.)

Seats

Standard seat upholstery for 1968 cars (and some early 1969s) is a combination of very slightly grained, flat vinyl with Chevrolet's "Basket-weave" vinyl inserts sewn into the seat bottoms and backs. Standard seat upholstery for 1969 cars is a combination of very slightly grained, flat vinyl with Chevrolet's "Comfort-weave" vinyl inserts sewn into the seat bottoms and backs. The difference between the Basket-weave and Comfort-weave inserts is the texture and pattern orientation. Basket-weave is somewhat coarser and the pattern is in an over/under crisscross that resembles a woven basket. Regardless of which weave is used, all seats have vertical insert panels. Leather seat covers were available as an extra cost option for all interior colors except Gunmetal in 1968. Leather seat covers have vertical panels just like their vinyl counterparts.

Each seat rests on two seat tracks, which allow for forward and rearward adjustment of the seat's position. The tracks are painted semi-gloss black in early 1968s and plated black phosphate in later 1968s and all 1969s. Each track is held to the floor by one black phosphate indented hex head bolt at either end for a total of four per seat. The front bolts are covered by a flap of carpet that was cut away while the rear bolts simply pass through the carpet.

The seat adjust lever is painted semi-gloss black in early 1968s and plated black phosphate in later 1968s and all 1969s. All levers are fitted with a chrome ball screwed onto their ends.

Headrests were an extra cost option for all 1968 Corvettes. They were a mandatory option for all 1969s assembled through approximately January 1969 and were standard equipment thereafter. All headrests are covered with a smooth, faintly patterned vinyl.

The seat backs are made of molded plastic and match interior color. They are retained by two chrome-plated Phillips head screws at the bottom. In 1968s assembled through approximately mid-November 1967 the seat back is released by means of a chrome-plated lever surrounded by a chrome-plated bezel positioned near the bottom of the seat. 1968s assembled after approximately mid-November 1967 do not have the bezel around the release lever.

In 1968s assembled after approximately early July, and in all 1969s, the seat release lever is positioned higher than it was previously.

In 1968 and 1969 the seat back position is adjustable. The adjustment mechanism consists of a black plastic stop positioned on the seat back and a pad located on the seat bottom. The pad is silver cadmium–plated metal on 1968s assembled through approximately mid-July 1968. The pads on 1968s assembled thereafter and on all 1969s are made from black rubber.

Lap and Shoulder Belts

All 1968 and 1969 coupes were equipped with lap and shoulder belts while convertibles came with lap belts as standard and shoulder belts as an extra cost option. All belts were manufactured by a company called Hamill and a tag bearing that name is sewn to them. The tag also bears the date that particular belt was manufactured. This date is indicated by an ink stamping with a number representing the week of the year, a letter representing the day of the week ("A" being Monday, "B" being Tuesday, and so on,) and another number representing the year. For example, a stamping of "16 D 68" means April 20, 1968—"16" representing the 16th week of the year, which was the week of April 14th–20th, "D" representing the fourth work day of the week, which was Thursday, April 18th, and "68" representing the year 1968.

In addition to the tag bearing the manufacturer's name and date code there are other, smaller tags sewn to the belts. 1968s have tags sewn into both the male and female lap belts. These tags read "THIS BELT CONFORMS TO SAE 14C FEDERAL MOTOR VEHICLE SAFETY STANDARDS HAMILL MODEL C11."

In 1968 another label is sewn into the male lap belt on the side opposite the above described label. This second label reads "IMPORTANT, READ OWNER'S MANUAL, WEAR LAP BELT AT ALL TIMES, ADJUST LOW AND SNUG, EXTEND BELT COMPLETELY FROM ANY RETRACTOR, SHOULDER BELT MUST NOT BE USED WITHOUT LAP BELT."

In 1968 the shoulder harness has two labels sewn in as well. In addition to the tag bearing the manufacturer's name and date code, there is a tag that reads "IMPORTANT, DO NOT USE WITHOUT A LAP BELT, LEAVE ENOUGH SLACK TO INSERT HAND WIDTH BETWEEN BELT AND CHEST, DO NOT USE IF LESS THAN 4 FEET 7 INCHES TALL, WHEN NOT IN USE SECURE SHOULDER BELTS IN RETAINERS." In 1969 the lap belts have a sewn-in label that reads "IMPORTANT, WEAR LAP BELT AT ALL TIMES, ADJUST SNUGLY." In 1969 the shoulder belts have a sewn-in label that reads "IMPORTANT, ATTACH SHOULDER HARNESS SECURELY TO LAP BELTS, DO NOT USE IF LESS THAN 4 FEET 7 INCHES TALL, DO NOT USE WITHOUT A LAP BELT."

All belts are made from a three-row webbing material and are the same color as the carpet. The material used for lap belts is slightly thicker than that used for shoulder belts. In 1968 the inboard lap belts each rest in a receptacle in the center console when they are not in use. In 1969 there is a chrome clip attached to the front of each seat bottom to hold the outboard lap belts when they are not in use.

In 1968 the female lap belt latch is comprised of a stainless-steel housing fitted with a chrome-plated back. Release of the belt is accomplished by means of a square push button adorned with the GM logo on the latch's front. In 1969 the female lap belt latch is encased in a semi-rigid plastic color-matched to the interior. In early 1969s the female latch has a square, plastic cover with a round release button adorned with the GM logo. In later 1969s the female latch is made from stainless steel with a brushed silver finish. In the center is a square black release button with a rigid metallic sticker that says "GM" in silver letters on a blue background.

Door Panels and Door Hardware

All door panels are made from molded vinyl and match the interior color. Door panels utilized in

1968s assembled through approximately April 1968 have an integral door pull molded in. In 1968s assembled after this a separate vinyl grab pull is added below the molded-in pull. All 1969s have a separate, vertically mounted door pull anchored with a silver cadmium–plated Phillips pan head screw. The 1969 vertical pull is vinyl-covered steel matched to the interior color. 1969 door panels have an insert fastened to them. This insert is covered with the same Comfort-weave-pattern vinyl as the seat upholstery. In both 1968 and 1969, side window felts are fastened to the top edges of each door panel with heavy metal staples.

Door panels are attached to the doors by means of chrome Phillips oval head screws that go through the face of each panel at the upper front and rear corners. These screws have a separate finishing washer. Inside door release handles are chrome with black paint in the center knurled area. A round black emblem glued to each handle features the crossed flags logo. In early 1968s the back of the door release lever is smooth. In later 1968s it has two ridges and in

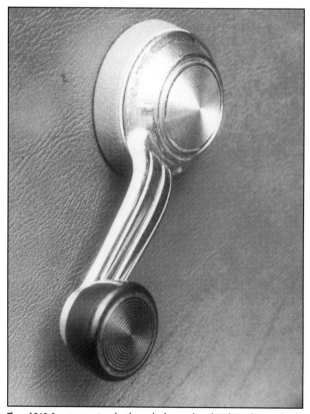

The federal government required that all vehicles assembled after September 1, 1969, have a "Vehicle Certification Label" glued toward the top of the rear portion of the driver's door. The date the vehicle was assembled, in this case November 1971, is indicated by the numbers in the upper right corner.

Those 1968 Corvettes equipped with standard manual windows have chrome-plated window cranks with plastic knobs that match interior color. 1969 and newer cars with manual windows utilize chrome cranks with opaque or black plastic knobs as shown here. Note how the knob on this original crank is about 1 inch away from the door panel's surface. Some later replacement knobs are farther away.

Door panels in 1968s assembled through approximately April 1968 have an integral door pull molded in near the top as shown here. In 1968s assembled after this, a separate vinyl grab pull is added below the molded-in pull. All 1969s have a separate, vinyl-covered steel door pull mounted vertically.

1969s it has four ridges. The inside lock knob is chrome with a black stripe painted in the center indent. There is a light beige–colored, plastic washer between the lock knob and door panel.

1968 Corvettes equipped with standard manual windows have chrome-plated window cranks with plastic knobs that match interior color. 1969 models utilize chrome cranks with opaque or black plastic knobs. Unlike some later replacements, the knobs on original cranks are about 1 inch away from the door panel's surface. There is a light beige–colored, plastic washer between the window crank and door panel.

Door Jambs and Door Perimeters

The door jamb and perimeter of each door are painted body color. Early 1968s are usually painted body color around the entire perimeter of each door. Later 1968s and all 1969s are painted body color around the entire perimeter with the exception of the top front area, which is painted semi-gloss black. The door striker, which is the large pin threaded into the door post, and its corresponding receiver in the door, are both cadmium plated. The striker is a special

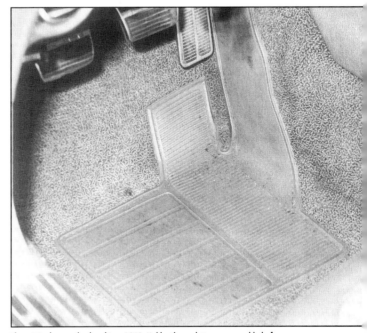

The original carpet heel pad in a 1969. Unlike the pads in cars assembled after about March 1971, the horizontal ribs in the middle section continue up to the top, very close to the stitching

Pedals in 1968 and 1969 cars utilize stainless trim to separate the areas of rubber as shown here. Later pedals are all black without this stainless trim.

indented hex head bolt, and should not have any body paint overspray.

The courtesy light pin switches and door ajar warning light/alarm system pin switches are cadmium plated and should not have any paint overspray. All pin switches have *SX,* the manufacturer's logo, stamped into the head of their plunger. As with the pin switches, door strikers, and door striker receivers, door alignment blocks and the door weather strip were added after the body was painted and should not have any body paint overspray. The main door weather stripping is two separate pieces and typically shows a gap in the center on the bottom of the door.

Early 1968 cars do not have water-deflecting strips attached to each door post near the door ajar warning light/alarm system pin switches. These strips are present in later 1968s. They are unpainted black rubber pieces that are glued to the body. 1969 cars have plastic water-deflecting strips that are painted body color. The strips in early 1969s are glued onto the body. In 1969s assembled after approximately mid-September 1969 the strips are Pop Riveted in place. Door hinges, bolts, and return springs (there should be one spring in each top hinge) are painted body color in both 1968 and 1969.

The federal government required that all vehicles assembled after September 1, 1969, have a "Vehicle Certification Label" glued toward the top of the rear portion of the driver's door. It contains the VIN as well as the month and year the vehicle was produced. The label was placed on after the body was painted and therefore should not have any paint overspray. Door sills are bright aluminum with black painted ribs. Each sill is held on with four black phosphate Phillips oval head screws.

Kick Panels, Quarter Trim Panels, Pedals, and Carpet

The kick panels beneath the dash just forward of the doors are molded plastic and are interior color. On air-conditioned cars the passenger-side panel was cut by hand for increased clearance and the cut is frequently rough. One chrome Phillips oval head screw in the forward, upper corner of each panel holds it in place. The panels have a bevy of small holes for the speakers that mount behind them. Speakers were mounted behind these panels in 1968 but not in 1969. Some replacement kick panels have a slot in the speaker grille area and others have a solid rectangular area in the middle of the speaker grille holes. Neither style is original for 1968 or 1969.

The quarter trim panels just rearward of the doors are vinyl-covered plastic in 1968 and molded plastic in 1969. For both years they match the interior color. They are each held in place by a piece of metal trim retained by four chrome Phillips oval head screws. The quarter trim panels on coupes also have one chrome Phillips oval head screw with a trim washer at their top.

For all 1968s and 1969s, accelerator, brake, and clutch pedals have black rubber pads with horizontal ribs. Correct pedals do not have a polished metal surround like some later pedals. The accelerator pedal measures 5-5/8 inches high by 2 inches wide and does not taper like some later accelerators.

All 1968 and 1969 Corvettes are fitted with carpet made from an 80/20 loop pile molded material dyed to match interior color. Three rubber plugs in the driver's foot well and three more in the passenger's foot well help hold the carpet in place. The plugs pass through the carpet near its upper front edge.

Carpet covers the bulkhead behind the seats and does not have sewn-on binding on the lower edge where it overlaps the front floor carpet behind the seats. Rather, it has an unfinished cut edge.

Rear storage compartment doors each have carpet under their frames. One piece of carpet covers the rear storage area floor and extends up the rear bulkhead. The edge at the top of the bulkhead is trimmed with sewn-on binding and is held by three rubber plugs. Separate pieces of untrimmed carpet cover the two wheelwells. Front carpet has a molded vinyl accelerator heel pad sewn into the corner of the driver's foot well adjacent to the accelerator pedal. Heel pads have horizontal ribs that extend to within 1/4 inch of the top stitching holding the pad to the carpet. Carpeting in 1968 and those 1969 Corvettes assembled through approximately mid-September does not have a dimmer switch pad. Carpet in 1969s assembled after approximately mid-September 1969 may have a sewn-in, molded vinyl dimmer switch pad.

Dash Pad and Dash Panels

The upper dash pad, as well as the driver's and passenger's dash panels, are made of soft vinyl and match interior color. The two vertical panels are attached to the upper pad by means of six Phillips oval head screws with conical washers. The screw heads are painted to match interior color except in some cars fitted with black interiors. In those cases the screws are finished in a black oxide plating. Dash pads do not have white stitching across their tops as is seen in 1970 and later cars. An interior color hard plastic grille is located in the defroster opening of the upper pad.

1968 Corvettes do not have a pocket storage area inset into the passenger-side dash panel. Instead, the panel is simply smooth. A three-pocket storage area is inset into the passenger-side dash panel in 1969 Corvettes. The storage pocket assembly is made from vinyl and is the same color as the interior. The pockets each have two rows of horizontal stitching along their top edge. The two smaller, outboard pockets are retained to the larger one with a single chrome-plated snap. A spring-loaded retainer behind the dash holds the three-pocket assembly tight against the dash panel.

Interior Switches, Controls, and Related Parts

All 1968s and 1969s have a headlamp switch mounted in the upper left corner of the driver-side dash pad. For 1968s and 1969s assembled through

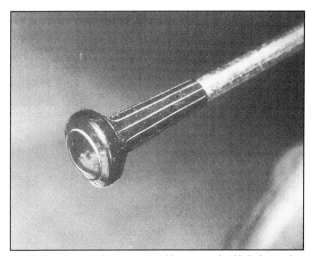

All 1968 through very early 1970 turn signal levers use a gloss-black plastic end with molded-in grooves parallel to the chrome shaft. Later 1970s and very early 1971s use either this design or the subsequent-design lever, which features a different end.

An example of the chrome-plated, short-style flasher switch used in all 1968 through late 1971 standard columns, as well as all 1968 telescopic columns.

approximately mid-December the headlamp switch knob is made from smooth gloss-black plastic and is relatively short in length. It has a white circle on the face and radial grooves around the circle.

In 1969s assembled after approximately mid-December 1969 the headlamp knobs are made from grained gloss-black plastic with a chrome disc in the center. This second-design knob is about 1 inch longer than the first. A black plastic bezel behind the knob has the word *LIGHTS* in white letters.

All 1968 and 1969 Corvettes have air vents on both sides of the dash toward the lower, outboard corner. The vent mechanisms are chrome spheres that rotate to change the direction of air flow. There is no mechanism for controlling the flow of air in

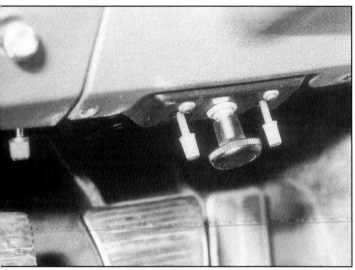

The knobs below the dash in this 1969 are, from left to right, the trip odometer reset knob, wiper door override switch, wiper arm override switch, and headlamp door override switch. Those 1968s assembled prior to about mid-January 1968 that are equipped with air conditioning, all 1968s assembled after approximately mid-January, and all 1969s have these override controls mounted under the dash directly beneath the steering column as seen here. Those 1968s that were assembled prior to approximately mid-January 1968, and that are not equipped with air conditioning, have these controls mounted under the dash between the steering column and center console.

Original door pin switches seen through at least 1976 typically have "SX" stamped into the head to represent the switch's manufacturer.

1968. In 1969 a chrome-plated push/pull knob next to each sphere controls the flow of air.

In 1968 only the ignition switch is located in the upper right driver-side dash panel. The switch is integrated into the steering column for 1969.

A small black T-handle pull mechanism beneath the driver-side dash on the left side releases the hood latch. The handle is black with the words "HOOD RELEASE" in white painted block letters across its face. The hood release cable is in a spiral-wound metal sheathing.

A semi-gloss black bracket mounts the trip odometer reset knob, wiper door override switch, wiper arm override switch, and headlamp door override switch. Those 1968s that were assembled prior to approximately mid-January 1968, and that are not equipped with air conditioning, have these controls mounted under the dash between the steering column and center console. 1968 Corvettes assembled prior to approximately mid-January 1968 that are equipped with air conditioning, all 1968s assembled after approximately mid-January, and all 1969s have these override controls mounted under the dash directly beneath the steering column.

The trip odometer reset knob has a grooved black rubber cover. The wiper door override switch has a

All 1968 and 1969 Corvettes utilize chrome-plated spheres for air vents on both sides of the dash toward the lower, outboard corner. There is no mechanism for controlling the flow of air in 1968, but in 1969 a chrome-plated push/pull knob next to each sphere controls the flow of air.

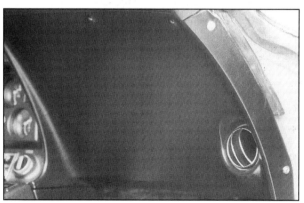

In 1968 only the passenger-side dash panel is blank. Starting in 1969 this panel includes a sewn-in three-pocket storage receptacle.

Those 1968s and 1969s assembled through approximately mid-December 1968 have a headlamp switch knob made from smooth, gloss-black plastic with a white circle on the face and radial grooves around the circle. Those 1969s assembled after approximately mid-December 1969 use this style knob, which has a chrome disc in the center.

An example of a 1968–1976 windshield wiper/washer control switch. The switch knob is hard, black plastic with the words "WASHER-PUSH" painted in block letters on its face. In 1968s assembled prior to mid-December 1967 the letters are light blue. In all subsequent cars the letters are white.

Most 1969 steering columns have a caution sticker on their left side pertaining to the ignition switch/column interlock mechanism. This is the second-design sticker, which was used on cars assembled in approximately July and August 1969. Steering column design was changed toward the end of 1969 production, eliminating the rotating mast jacket shift bowl and the need for the caution sticker.

large, round, shiny black knob with grooved edges. The wiper door override switch and headlamp door override switch are both vacuum switches that mount to either side of the wiper arm switch. The two vacuum switches have dull black plastic push/pull knobs.

Steering Wheel and Steering Column

All 1968 steering wheels have a simulated wood rim made from plastic that is molded to a brushed stainless-steel three-spoke center with a pattern of parallel lines extending from the center of the wheel to the outer rim. 1968 steering wheels are 16 inches in diameter. All 1969 steering wheels are black regardless of interior color. They have grained vinyl rims molded to a three-spoke stainless-steel hub. Each of the spokes has a brushed finish with a pattern of parallel lines extending from the center of the wheel to the outer rim.

The standard steering columns and optional columns in 1968 and 1969 are painted whatever the interior color is in a semi-gloss finish. With a telescopic column, the locking ring is painted the same color as the rest of the column. The optional column in 1968 is telescopic but does not tilt. A thick, locking ring below the steering wheel controls the telescoping function. Twisting the lever on the ring counterclockwise releases the locking mechanism and allows the column to telescope. The optional column in 1969 is a combination tilt and telescoping unit. This tilt-telescoping column has a thick, locking ring below the steering wheel to control the telescoping function. The ring is painted to match the rest of the column. Twisting the lever on the ring releases the locking mechanism and allows the column to telescope. A lever similar to but shorter than the turn signal lever controls the tilt function of the optional steering column. This lever has a chrome-plated stem and smooth black plastic knob. It is located

In 1968 only a 16-inch-diameter simulated wood, plastic steering wheel was used. Beginning in 1969 a wheel with a grained black vinyl rim was used.

between the turn signal lever and dash, and threads into its mount.

Most 1969 steering columns have a caution sticker on their left side. This sticker pertains to the ignition switch/column interlock mechanism. Two versions of the sticker are utilized: The first, which was used on cars assembled through approximately July 1969, has a white background and reads "AS PART OF THE NEW LOCKING COLUMN FEATURE, IT IS NORMAL FOR THE MAST JACKET SHIFT BOWL TO ROTATE WHEN SHIFTING THE TRANSMISSION. HOWEVER DO NOT ATTEMPT TO ROTATE THE SHIFT BOWL BY ITSELF AS DAMAGE TO THE SHIFT LINKAGE WILL RESULT." The second design caution sticker, which was used on cars assembled in approximately July and August 1969, has a clear background and reads "THIS IS A ROTATING INTERLOCK — DO NOT MANIPULATE — DAMAGE MAY RESULT."

The horn buttons for 1968s and 1969s have a pebble grain texture and are painted around the perimeter to match interior color. The crossed flags emblem should have a white square in the upper right corner of the checkered flag as shown here. Some incorrect replacements have the checkered pattern reversed.

The steering column design was changed toward the end of 1969 production, eliminating the rotating mast jacket shift bowl. This eliminated the need for the caution sticker, so late production cars do not have it.

All columns have a four-way flasher switch mounted on the right side. All 1968 and 1969 standard columns, as well as all 1968 telescopic columns, utilize a short switch with a one-piece chrome-plated knob that has black painted, debossed letters in the head spelling the word "FLASHER."

1969 tilt-telescopic columns are fitted with a flasher switch that is longer than the above described switch. In addition, this switch differs in that its head is concave and has no writing in it.

1968 and 1969 Corvettes use the same turn signal lever. It is comprised of a chrome-plated shaft with a gloss-black plastic end. The end has molded-in grooves that are parallel to the chrome shaft.

All 1968 and 1969 models use a textured metal horn button painted to match the interior. A crossed flags emblem is in the center of the button. The upper right square in the flag in the horn button's emblem is white in cars assembled through approximately January 1968. In later 1968s and in 1969s this same square is black.

Interior Windshield Moldings, Sun Visors, and Rearview Mirror

Three pieces of vinyl-covered molding matched to the interior color cover the inside of the windshield frame for all 1968 and 1969 Corvettes. The two side pieces are held on by plastic retainers attached to the reverse side. The plastic retainers are not visible when the moldings are installed. In addition, each side molding has one chrome Phillips head screw retaining it at the top. Very early 1968s sometimes have two chrome-plated Phillips oval head screws retaining each side piece of molding. The top

In 1968 only the ignition switch is in the dash as seen here. Beginning in 1969 it is in the steering column.

piece of molding is retained by four chrome, recess head Phillips screws.

Sun visors utilized in 1968 cars are covered with padded soft vinyl that has the same "Madrid" pattern as the vinyl covers on the optional headrests. Each sun visor is held to the windshield frame with chrome, recess head Phillips screws. The brackets mounting 1968 visors have 1/8-inch-diameter holes and have a more pronounced offset that results in the visors mounting farther from the windshield frame.

Sun visors utilized in 1969 cars are covered with padded soft vinyl that has the same comfort-weave pattern as the vinyl seat covers. Each sun visor is held to the windshield frame with chrome, recess head Phillips screws. The brackets mounting 1969 visors have 3/16-inch-diameter holes and have a less pronounced offset that results in the visors mounting

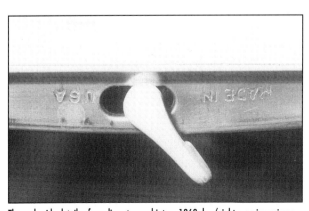

The underside details of wording stamped into a 1969 day/night rearview mirror.

The underside of this 1968 rearview mirror has "GUIDE" and "GLARE-PROOF" stamped in.

Two different designs of radio knobs are used in 1968. Both designs are painted silver around the outer ring and semi-gloss black in the concave face. The raised rectangle in the face is painted silver in the first design and chrome plated in the second. Knobs used in 1969 are shiny black plastic with convex faces and a chrome-plated ring around the perimeter.

closer to the windshield frame than they do in 1968.

Some 1969 Corvettes were originally equipped with a card describing the operation of the ignition lock and engine starting procedures. This card was wrapped around the driver-side sun visor.

All 1968 and 1969 Corvettes have an interior day/night rearview mirror mounted to the center of the upper windshield frame. The mirror is 8 inches wide and is held to its mount with a slotted oval head screw. A piece of trim covered with interior-color vinyl is mounted over the base of the mirror mount at the windshield frame. All interior mirrors have stainless-steel housings with gray rubber trim around the perimeter. A gray lever at the bottom center moves the mirror between its "day" and "night" position.

Instruments and Radio

The center console instrument cluster housing is cast metal painted semi-gloss black. In 1968s the painted surface is smooth and in 1969s it is textured. In the upper left portion of the center console instrument cluster housing there is a solid bar separating the seatbelt warning light from the button below it. Later replacement housings don't have this bar.

There is space for two more warning lights in the upper right portion of the housing. In 1968s assembled through approximately early March 1968 the additional squares say "DOOR AJAR" and "LOW FUEL." Some 1968s assembled in this time frame have a square that says either "DOOR AJAR" or "LOW FUEL," with the other square being blank.

In 1968 cars assembled after mid-March 1968, the upper right light reads "DOOR AJAR" and the lower reads "WIPER O'RIDE." In 1969 cars the upper right light reads "DOOR AJAR" and the lower reads "HEAD LAMPS."

The windshield wiper/washer control switch is mounted above the center console instrument cluster housing. The switch knob is hard black plastic with the words "WASHER-PUSH" painted in block letters on its face. In cars assembled prior to mid-December 1967 the letters are light blue. In 1968s assembled thereafter and in all 1969s the letters are white.

All gauges, including the speedometer and tachometer, have a semi-flat black background. All gauge needles are straight. With the exception of the needle for the optional speed warning, which is pale yellow, all gauge needles are red. Gauge numerals are slightly greenish white.

Tachometer redlines vary according to the engine. The high beam indicator light, which is in the speedometer face, is red in all cars and reads "BRIGHT."

All 1968 and 1969 Corvettes came standard without a radio, and if the purchaser elected not to buy one of the optional radios the car was delivered without one. For those cars not equipped with a radio a block-off plate is fitted to the cutout where the radio would otherwise go. The block-off plate for both years is painted semi-gloss black and has a flat face with a thin, raised chrome border around its perimeter near the edge.

As an extra cost option one of two different Delco radios could be ordered. The first is an AM/FM push-button and the second is an AM/FM push-button with stereo reception. Both radios have a small slide bar above the dial that changes reception between AM and FM and both have "Delco" written in script lettering across the lens face in a greenish-white color. 1968 stereo radios have the word "STEREO" in script while 1969 stereo radios have the word "STEREO" in block letters.

All 1968 and 1969 stereo radios have an indicator light that comes on when FM stereo is being received. The light illuminates the word "STEREO" in green.

In 1968s assembled through approximately late May 1968 two different designs of radio knobs are used interchangeably. The first design knob is painted silver around its outer ring and has a concave face painted semi-gloss black. A raised rectangle in the face is painted silver.

The second design 1968 radio knob is very similar to the first design except the areas painted silver in the first design are chrome plated in the second. The second design knob is used exclusively in 1968s assembled after approximately early June 1968.

Interiors for 1968 feature a lot of one-year-only parts, including a plastic simulated wood steering wheel, seatbelt receptacles in the park brake surround, and a dash-mounted ignition switch. Headrests were an extra cost option for all 1968s, and this car does not have them. They were a mandatory option for all 1969s assembled through approximately January 1969 and were standard equipment thereafter.

Radio knobs used in 1969 Corvettes are shiny black plastic with convex faces and a chrome-plated ring around the perimeter.

Beneath the main radio knobs on all 1968s and 1969s is a secondary control, which is chrome plated. The one on the left controls tone and the one on the right, which is functional only on stereo-equipped cars, controls balance.

Center Console, Shifter, and Park Brake

All 1968 and 1969 center consoles are made from molded vinyl in the same color as the interior. Park brake lever consoles are made from rigid molded plastic and also match interior color.

The insert in the top of the center console is painted semi-gloss black both years. In 1968 it is smooth and in 1969 it has a pebble grain texture. Four black oxide–plated Phillips oval head screws retain the insert.

In 1969s, engine specifications are debossed into a rectangular-shaped insert that is located below the lower fiber-optic indicators. The specifications

Passenger-side view of a 1968 interior. As seen here, standard seat upholstery for 1968 cars (and some early 1969s) is a combination of very slightly grained flat vinyl with Chevrolet's "Basket-weave" vinyl inserts. Standard seat upholstery for 1969 cars is a combination of very slightly grained flat vinyl with Chevrolet's "Comfort-weave" vinyl inserts. The Basket-weave inserts are coarser than the Comfort-weave inserts.

The air-conditioning/heater control for 1969. Because this car has air conditioning, the fan switch has four positions instead of three.

This is a 1968 heater/defroster control assembly. It differs slightly from 1969 assemblies, which read "OFF," "AIR," "DE-FOG," and "DE-ICE" on the left and "L" and "H" on the right.

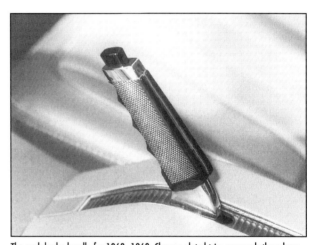

The park brake handle for 1968–1969. Chrome-plated trim surrounds the release button on the top.

stamped into the insert include horsepower, torque, compression ratio, and engine displacement.

No 1968s have the above described engine data plate. Instead, they have a crossed flags emblem in the area below the lower fiber-optic indicators.

In manual transmission–equipped cars the shift pattern is indicated next to the shifter. The shift pattern area is semi-gloss black and the letters and numbers are chrome, as is a border around the pattern.

The shifter boot for all 1968 and 1969 manual transmission cars is made from black rubber. In 1968s the boot has a single bellows and in 1969 it has a double bellows.

Manual shifters for all years have a chrome shaft and threaded-on ball. In 1968 this ball is silver chrome–plated and in 1969 it is plated with a black chrome. Four-speed shifters for both years have a "T" handle integral to the shaft to control the reverse lock-out. Three-speed manual shifters do not have a T-handle.

On those Corvettes equipped with an automatic transmission, the shift pattern is also next to the shifter. Chrome letters are used to indicate shifter position.

Rather than a boot, automatic transmission shifters are surrounded by a two-piece gloss-black plastic seal that slides back and forth as the shifter is moved.

Automatic shifters for all 1968s and 1969s are made from a chrome shaft topped by a black plastic ball. The ball has a chrome, spring-loaded button in the top to release the detent and allow the shifter to be moved.

Heater/air-conditioning control assemblies used in 1968 and 1969 differ slightly from one another. For example, in 1968 the left thumbwheel indicator positions for non-air-conditioned cars read "OFF," "AIR," and "DE-ICE." The right indicator positions read "COLD" and "HOT." In 1969 the left indicator positions read "OFF," "AIR," "DE-FOG," and "DE-ICE." The 1969 right indicator positions read "L" and "H."

Both styles of control assemblies utilize green letters and a separate fan switch plate that is inset into the larger assembly. A chrome lever is used to set fan speed. Fan switches in all 1968 cars and non-air-conditioned 1969 cars have three positions in addition to off. All air-conditioned 1969 cars use a switch with four positions in addition to off.

Whether the car is equipped with air conditioning or not, its control assembly employs two large black plastic rotary thumbwheels on either side. The left-side thumbwheel controls temperature and the right-side thumbwheel controls the system setting.

All non-air-conditioned cars have two fresh air vent controls on the center console. In all 1968s and those 1969s assembled through approximately January 1969, the controls are sliding levers with chrome-plated rectangular knobs. The faces of the knobs are painted semi-gloss black and have raised chrome block letters reading "OPEN" and "VENT."

1969s assembled after approximately January 1969 use a different style of fresh air vent control. This second design has a smooth, shiny black plastic ball with a flat area mounted to a black oxide metal arm. On their flat faces the balls say "CLOSE" in white painted letters and have a white arrow.

All 1968s and 1969s have an ashtray inset into the center console insert next to the heater/air-conditioning control assembly. The ashtray door is semi-gloss black and slides back and forth with slight resistance. The ashtray is chrome plated and can be removed for cleaning.

All cars are equipped with a cigarette lighter. The lighter uses a shiny black plastic knob that has a white circle and white concentric grooves in its face. Each lighter has "63 CASCO 12V" stamped in its element.

On those 1968 and 1969 Corvettes equipped with the optional rear window defogger a control switch is mounted on the left-side trim panel forward of the center console. The switch uses a large, round, chrome-plated knob.

All 1968 and 1969 Corvettes have a park brake lever mounted between the seats. The lever's handle is made from hard, shiny black plastic with a cross-hatch pattern to enhance grip. Chrome trim separates the black plastic grips in all cars with the possible exception of some very early 1968s. A release button on the top of the lever is made from hard, shiny black plastic also. The slotted opening in the park brake lever console is covered by a rippled, black plastic cover that slides along with the movement of the lever.

Rear Storage Compartments and Their Contents, Battery, Rear Window Storage Tray

All 1968 and 1969 Corvettes feature three enclosed storage compartments behind the seats. The lids for these compartments are made from press-board and are covered with carpet that matches the interior carpet. The underside of each lid

In 1968 only the park brake surround has receptacles for the female seatbelt latches.

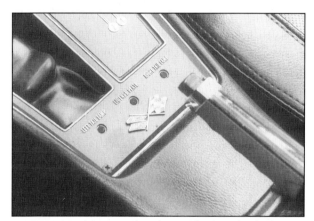

For 1968, a unique shifter surround console was used. It is smooth rather than textured like 1969 and later ones. Also, it has a crossed flags emblem beneath the fiber-optic indicators rather than the engine data plate found on later cars.

is usually painted flat black, though some 1968 lids are unpainted.

Stickers for tire pressure, jacking instructions, and the limited-slip differential are on the underside of the passenger-side compartment lid. Limited-slip was still an option in 1968 and 1969, so some cars are not equipped with it. Nonetheless, most such cars still received the limited-slip differential sticker under the passenger compartment lid.

Each lid is surrounded by a molded plastic border that is painted to match interior color. The entire assembly of all three lids is also surrounded by a color-matched molded plastic border.

Each lid is hinged and latches with a spring-loaded mechanism. Each lid has a chrome button to release its latch. Starting with 1969s assembled after approximately mid-January 1969 a vinyl hoop was

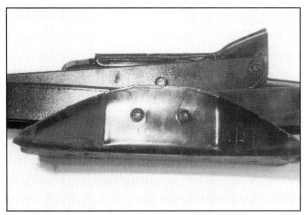

This is a 1969 jack. It differs from 1968 jacks in the dimension of the base. The 1968s measure 6x4 inches while 1969s measure 9x5 inches.

The date code stamping in the side arm of a 1969 jack; "9 B" indicates that the jack was made in February 1969. Note the blotchy paint coverage on this unrestored, original example.

added to each door to help pull it open. The vinyl hoop is stitched together and is the same color as the interior. It is retained to the lid by a chrome Phillips head machine screw secured with a 3/8-inch nut on the underside of the lid.

Each molded plastic border is held to its lid by chrome, flat head Phillips screws. Each lid is held to its hinge by black oxide round head Phillips screws fitted with integral black oxide flat washers. Each hinge is held to the compartment surround by rivets. The whole assembly is held to the body by black oxide, silver cadmium, or chrome-plated flat head Phillips screws.

The center compartment is fitted with a locking chrome release button. The same key operates the storage compartment lid lock and the spare tire compartment lock, but a different key operates the anti-theft alarm switch on those cars equipped with the optional anti-theft burglar alarm.

The compartment directly behind the driver's seat holds the vehicle's battery. It has a thin foam seal around the perimeter of the door opening to help keep battery fumes from entering the passenger compartment. This seal is not one continuous piece of foam but instead has a seam where the two ends of the strip meet.

Beginning with those 1968s assembled after approximately mid-January 1968, aluminum foil–backed fiberglass matting is used for insulation in the two large storage compartments. Use of this insulation continues in 1969.

All 1968 Corvettes and those 1969s assembled through approximately mid-June 1969 use a top-post-design model R59S Delco battery. Small-block-engine-equipped 1969s assembled after mid-June 1969 use a model R79S side terminal battery. Big-block-engine-equipped 1969s assembled after mid-

June 1969 use a model R79W side terminal battery. In either case, the side terminals face toward the front of the car when the battery is correctly installed.

All of the batteries used in 1968 and 1969 have six cells that are covered by two plastic caps, each of which covers three cells. Each cap has three of the Delco "split circle" logos molded into its top. The split circles are painted dark orange. A black rubber vent hose runs from each of the caps through a hole in the underbody.

Battery cables for all 1968s and those 1969s assembled through approximately mid-June 1969 are the Delco spring ring design. A gray felt washer impregnated with an anti-corrosive chemical is found beneath the positive terminal end on the positive battery post.

All 1969s assembled after approximately mid-June 1969 have side terminal–style battery cables. This style cable has red positive ends and black negative ends, each of which has a raised, Delco split circle logo. Both terminals are fastened to the battery with a 7/16-inch hex head bolt.

The passenger-side storage compartment contains a removable insert. The insert, which is like a squared-off bucket, is made from grayish-black fiberboard and measures -1/4 inches deep.

For 1968 and 1969 convertibles only, the fiberboard insert contains a 1/2-inch open-ended wrench for installation and removal of the hardtop.

Also inside the fiberboard insert is an off-white cotton pouch that has a yellow drawstring. The drawstring is held on by an encasement stitched with red thread. The pouch contains four silver washers and four oblong-shaped, gray phosphate shims that are to be used to adjust the seat backs to the occupants' preferred positions.

In addition to the hardtop wrench and seat hardware pouch, there are a number of other items in the storage insert. A small, white paper envelope with the "GM mark of excellence" logo and instructions printed in black letters contains the car's keys and the key knock-outs.

A small, brown paper envelope contains license plate screws. "LICENSE SCREWS" is written in black ink on the outside of this envelope.

Another small, brown paper envelope is included with those Corvettes equipped with the optional P02 Deluxe Wheel Covers. This envelope contains four extensions for the valve stems.

The final item in the storage insert is the owner's packet. In 1968 this packet is contained in a clear vinyl envelope with a yellow hex head key and "DON'T INVITE CAR THEFT!" printed in blue on the outside. Part No. 3955549 is printed on the outside of this envelope. Included in the envelope are an owner's manual, warranty folder, Protect-o-plate, air pollution control system information booklet, trim ring installation instruction card, override control instruction sheet, and radio instruction sheet if the car is equipped with a radio.

In 1969 the owner's packet is contained in a clear vinyl envelope with a yellow rectangular head key and "DON'T INVITE CAR THEFT!" printed in blue on the outside. Part No. 3950779 is printed on the outside of this envelope. Included in the envelope are an owner's manual, warranty folder, Protect-o-plate, consumer information booklet, trim ring installation instruction card, and radio instruction sheet if the car is equipped with a radio.

Two different designs of owner's manuals are used in 1969. The first edition is found in cars assembled through approximately early February 1969 and the second edition is found in cars assembled thereafter.

The fiberboard insert in the passenger-side rear storage compartment lifts out to reveal an additional storage area beneath. A jack and jack handle are mounted to the bottom of the compartment (to the car's floor panel) with a black spring that latches onto a black hook riveted to the floor.

1968 and 1969 jacks differ in the size of their bases. The 1968 jacks have a base that measures 6 by 4 inches while 1969 jacks have a base that measures 9 by 5 inches.

All jacks are painted semi-gloss to gloss black and have the letter "A" stamped in their chassis contact pad. This letter is the logo for Auto Specialties Manufacturing, the company that made the jacks.

In addition to the manufacturer's logo, all jacks contain a date code stamping. The stamping is on the jack's large side arm and contains a number for the year followed by a letter for the month, with "A" representing January, "B" representing February, and so on. For example, the date code stamping for a jack manufactured in June 1968 would say "8 F."

All jack handles are painted semi-gloss black and include a pivoting 3/4-inch boxed hex-wrench on the end to remove and install the car's lug nuts. A thick rubber ring is fitted around the hex-wrench end to prevent rattling.

In addition to the jack and jack handle, electrical relays and a flasher unit are mounted in the area underneath the fiberboard insert on those cars equipped with the audio anti-theft alarm system.

All 1968 and 1969 coupes have two storage bags to hold the T-tops when they are removed. Some cars have bags dyed to match interior color while others

The rear compartment storage area in a 1969.

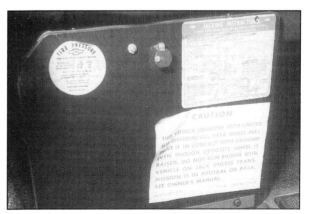

The underside of the rear storage compartment door behind the passenger's seat in a 1969. The storage compartment storage assemblies were made from fragile plastic and fiberboard components that are usually broken and warped.

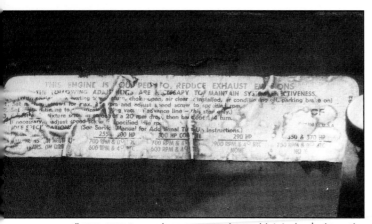

All 1968–1979 Corvettes have an emissions/tune-up label glued to the driver-side firewall. This example is from a 1969 L46.

have black bags regardless of interior color. Earlier cars for each year are more likely to have a color-matched bag and later cars are more likely to have black bags.

All bags have a date code stamped inside in ink. Typical date stampings contain a month and year designation. For example, bags manufactured in October 1968 read "10-68." In addition to the date stamping, bags may also contain a logo stamping representing the manufacturer. The most common logo seen is "TEX."

All T-top storage bags have a flap that closes over the opening. Bags found in all 1968s and in those 1969s assembled through approximately October 1969 utilize Velcro to hold the flap closed. Bags found in 1969s assembled after approximately October 1969 use three chrome-plated snaps to hold the flap shut.

All 1968 and 1969 coupes have adjustable T-top hold down straps. As with the T-top bags, early cars tend to have straps dyed to match interior color and later cars tend to have black straps regardless of interior color.

All coupes have two straps that attach to chrome-plated anchors. The anchors are fastened to the floor of the rear luggage area. The anchors are secured by chrome-plated Phillips oval head screws. The adjustment clips on the straps have the manufacturer's logo stamped in. The manufacturer for the straps is the Irving Air Chute Company.

All 1968 and 1969 coupes have molded vinyl trim mounted to the underside of the T-tops. The vinyl is the same color as the interior.

All 1968 and 1969 coupes have a rear window storage tray mounted above the rear luggage area. Trays in 1968s have a black vinyl-coated spring clip to hold them up. Trays in 1969s have a gloss-black painted rectangular cast handle to hold them up. These cast handles contain the words "BACK WINDOW STORAGE" in raised, chrome block letters.

The rear window storage tray is made from black fiberboard. Each tray has nine slots and a metal strip riveted on toward the front of the car. In 1968 this metal strip is painted gloss black or left unpainted. In 1969 it is unpainted and polished to a high luster. The tray contains two riveted-on spring clips to hold the rear window securely.

Convertible Top Frames

For all 1968 and 1969 convertibles, top frames are painted semi-gloss black. A black fiberglass header panel is secured to the front underside of the top frame. Three chrome-plated latches secure the front top header to the windshield frame. Black rubber coats the latch levers and each latch is accompanied by an adjustable tensioning bolt. In 1969 only the tensioning bolt is rubber tipped.

The convertible-top frame's rear bow is secured to the body deck lid with two chrome-plated pins that insert into chrome-plated receptacles affixed to the body. Chrome Phillips oval head screws hold the pins to the rear bow. In 1968 the pins are 1/4 inch in diameter. In 1969 they are enlarged to 5/16 inch.

The underside of the convertible top, including the top material itself and the pads, is always black regardless of interior color.

The optional removable hardtop on those convertibles so equipped has a padded vinyl headliner color matched to the interior. Front latches for the hardtop are chrome plated but unlike the soft top, the levers on these latches are not rubber coated. The hardtop latches each have a tensioning bolt and, as with the soft top, the tensioning bolts are rubber tipped in 1969 only.

All 1968 and most 1969 hardtops have two mounting bolts in the rear. Very late 1969s have a third mounting bolt in the center of the hardtop beneath the rear window.

The underside of the convertible deck lid is painted body color. Deck lid release levers, release cables, and lock mechanisms were all mounted prior to painting and should therefore also be painted body color.

The latch receptacles mounted underneath the rear deck, which receive the pins in the rear bow of the convertible top, are black and not body color. The rods that control the receptacles are also black. Deck lid rubber bumpers are black, as are their brackets. The receptacles attached to the body that receive the convertible deck lid's front locating guides have white nylon bushings.

1968–1969 Mechanical

Engine Blocks

Engine-block casting numbers for all 1968 and 1969 engines are located on the top rear driver side of the block, on the flange that mates to the transmission bell housing. (Refer to Appendix F for engine block casting numbers.)

Engine-block casting dates for all 1968 and 1969 small blocks, and those 1969 big blocks in cars assembled after approximately March 1969, are located on the top rear passenger side of the block, on the flange that mates to the transmission bell housing. The casting date for 1968 big blocks, as well as 1969 big blocks in cars assembled prior to approximately March 1969, is located on the passenger side of the block adjacent to the engine mount area.

The engine-block casting date for all blocks consists of a letter for the month, one or two numbers for the day, and one number for the year. For example, a block cast on June 17, 1968, would have a casting date of "F 17 8." As is typical of cast numbers (but not stamped-in numbers), the letter "I" is used to denote the month of September.

All 1968 and 1969 engines contain two distinct stampings on a machined pad located on the top of the passenger side between the cylinder head and water pump. One stamping is commonly referred to as the assembly stamping, and the other is commonly called the VIN derivative stamping.

The assembly stamping begins with a prefix letter to indicate the engine assembly plant. *V* indicates the Flint plant, where all small blocks were assembled, and *T* designates the Tonawanda plant, where all big blocks were assembled. Following the prefix letter are four numbers indicating the month and day of assembly. After the numbers indicating the assembly date are three suffix letters denoting the particular engine. This suffix code is often referred to as the engine broadcast code, or simply the engine code. (Refer to Appendix C for engine suffix codes.)

To illustrate what a typical engine assembly stamping looks like, consider the following 1968 combination: a base 327/300-horsepower engine

The passenger-side view of a 1969 L88 engine. This power plant, in conjunction with all the other high-performance options that were required along with it, makes L88 Corvettes the undisputed kings of the musclecar era.

The driver-side view of a 1969 L88 engine compartment. Only 116 cars were sold with this aluminum-headed 427. Approximately 17 were automatics and the remainder were four-speeds.

built on May 5 and coupled to an automatic transmission. The assembly stamping for such an engine would read "V0505HO."

Most big blocks have the assembly stamping on the outboard side of the pad and the VIN derivative stamping on the inboard side. Most small-block engines have their two stamp sequences reversed, with the assembly stamping on the inboard side and the VIN derivative stamping on the outboard side.

Always remember that the engine assembly date must come after the engine-block casting date (you can't assemble an engine before the block is cast!) and

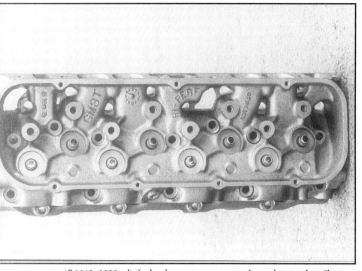

All 1968–1982 cylinder heads contain a casting number and casting date. This is a 1969 L71 427/435 head (casting No. 3919840) that was manufactured on February 19, 1969 (casting date B 19 9).

both the casting date and assembly date must precede the final assembly date of the car (you can't finish assembling a car before the engine has been cast and assembled!). The great majority of engines were cast and assembled within a couple of weeks prior to the car's assembly date. Some engines, however, were cast and/or assembled months prior to installation in a car. Six months is generally accepted as the outer limit for the difference between an engine assembly or casting date and the final assembly date of the car it is installed into.

The VIN derivative stamping, as the name implies, is a stamping containing a portion or a derivative of the car's vehicle identification number. For example, the VIN derivative stamping for the very first 1969 assembled would read "19S700001," for the second car it would read "19S700002," and so on.

All 1968 and 1969 engine blocks, with the exception of 1969 ZL1s, are cast-iron that is painted Chevrolet Engine Orange. 1969 ZL1 blocks are cast aluminum.

Some blocks were originally painted before exhaust manifolds were installed, and therefore coverage on the sides of the block behind the manifolds is good. Other blocks apparently had the exhaust manifolds installed when they were painted and therefore the manifolds got painted as well. The engine stamp pad was normally covered up when the engine was painted, and therefore it normally appears unpainted.

Cylinder Heads

As with engine blocks, all 1968 and 1969 cylinder heads have both a casting number and a casting date. As with blocks and other cast parts, the cylinder head casting date typically has a letter to indicate month, one or two numbers to indicate the day of the month, and one number to indicate the year. (Refer to Appendix G for a comprehensive list of cylinder head casting numbers.)

All 1968 and 1969 small-block engines utilize cast-iron cylinder heads. All big-block engines, with the exception of the optional L88s, L89s, and ZL1s, also utilize cast-iron heads. The above three optional engines all have aluminum cylinder heads.

All cylinder heads and head bolts, with the exception of the aluminum heads, are painted Chevrolet Engine Orange. Aluminum heads remain unpainted, though they often have orange overspray around the bottom.

Intake Manifolds

All 1968 and 1969 small-block intake manifolds are cast-iron and all 1968 and 1969 big-block manifolds are cast aluminum. As with engine blocks and cylinder heads, intake manifolds contain casting numbers and casting dates. As is typical of cast engine parts, the casting date consists of a letter designating the month, one or two numbers designating the day of the month, and a number denoting the year.

Casting numbers for all manifolds are on the top surface, as are casting dates for cast-iron manifolds. For aluminum manifolds, casting dates are on the underside and are therefore not visible when the manifold is installed on an engine. (Refer to Appendix H for intake manifold casting numbers.)

1968 Corvette intake manifolds have a machined opening at their forward edge for an oil fill tube. 1969 intakes do not have this opening. In 1968 the oil fill tube and its cap are painted Chevrolet Engine Orange with base engines. With optional L79 327/350 engines the tube is still painted orange but the cap is chrome plated.

All 1968 and 1969 engines, except L88s and ZL1s, utilize a cast-aluminum thermostat housing. L88s and ZL1s utilize a cast-iron housing. Housings on Chevrolet Engine Orange–painted intake manifolds are painted orange as well. Housings on aluminum intakes are unpainted. No 1968 or 1969 thermostat housings have a hole for a temperature sending unit. Housings used on certain other Chevrolets and some replacement housings have a tapped hole.

Thermostat housings on big-block engines are fastened with two hex head bolts. Housings on small-block engines are fastened with a tall hex head bolt and a short double-sided stud that has a hex in its center. Nothing attaches to the stud that sticks up on the short side of the housing.

With original 1968 and 1969 intake manifold side gaskets, but not with later GM replacements, semicircular tabs are visible sticking up between the runners for cylinders No. three and six, and the exhaust heat crossover passage. Also, original front and rear intake gaskets do not have side tabs to locate the gaskets on the block's rail-like later replacements.

All intake manifolds are held on by 9/16-inch hex head bolts. The bolts do not get any type of washer.

Engine lifting brackets are attached to most 1968 and 1969 Corvettes. On small blocks one bracket is attached to the second intake manifold bolt from the front on the driver side. If the car has a manual transmission the other bracket is attached to a bellhousing bolt on the passenger side. If the car has an automatic there is no rear lifting bracket.

On all big-block engines, except for those fitted with tri-power, the front lifting bracket is attached to the two front intake bolts on the driver side. Tri-power engines do not have a front lifting bracket. The rear lifting bracket on all big-block engines is attached to the rear of the passenger-side cylinder head.

Regardless of engine size, if a lifting bracket is attached to a part painted Chevrolet Engine Orange it is also painted that color. If it is attached to an unpainted aluminum part it is left unpainted or painted silver.

All intake manifolds, including aluminum examples, were installed before engines were painted. Therefore, on those engines with cast-iron intakes, hold down bolts as well as any exposed portions of gaskets are painted Chevrolet Engine Orange.

Aluminum intakes were crudely masked off prior to the engine being painted. Therefore, engines with aluminum intakes may have orange paint over-

All 1968–1982 intake manifolds have a casting number and a casting date. This example is from a 1969 L46. Just visible in the background is the casting date, "B 20 9," which translates to February 20, 1969.

The front engine lift bracket on this 1969 L88 is painted silver because the intake manifold is aluminum. If the manifold was cast-iron and thus painted Chevrolet Engine Orange, the bracket would also be orange. Note the Winters Foundry logo (a "W" in a snowflake) cast into the intake manifold.

spray on edges, bolts, and gaskets. If orange over-spray was excessive the factory sometimes sprayed the area along the edges of the manifold silver, resulting in silver overspray on bolts, gaskets, and sometimes even the cylinder heads.

Distributor and Ignition Coil

All 1968 and 1969 Corvettes use a mechanical tach drive Delco Remy distributor. All distributors have a thin aluminum identification band secured around the housing in a recess just above where the distributor hold down clamp rests.

The identification band is natural on one side and colored on the other with a pinkish-red dye. While the majority of cars have the dye on the outside of the band, some have it on the inside, making it difficult to see when the band is installed on the distributor.

The identification band has the words "DELCO REMY" stamped into it. This is followed by a seven-character part number and a date code. (See Appendix K for distributor part numbers.)

The date code, which represents the day the distributor was assembled, consists of a number representing the year, a letter representing the month, and one or two numbers representing the day of the month. For 1968 and 1969 distributor date codes the letter "A" represents January, "B" represents February, and so on. As is typical of stamped-in date codes, the letter "I" is skipped, so the month of September is represented by "J." The date code on a distributor assembled March 17, 1969, for example, would read "9 C 17," and one assembled November 21, 1968, would read "8 L 21."

Although most distributors were made several weeks before the engine was assembled, it is entirely possible that several months can separate the two. As with most other components, six months is the generally accepted maximum for all distributors except those installed into L88s and ZL1s. Distributors for these engines may have assembly dates more than six months prior to the engine assembly date.

All 1968 and 1969 Corvettes utilize a distributor housing without a small hole opposite the tachometer drive gear. Later distributor housings, beginning in mid-1970, do have this small hole and are therefore not correct for 1968 or 1969 cars.

Distributor housings are painted semi-gloss black and have one of several color daubs of paint just below the distributor cap on the passenger side toward the front of the car.

All distributors, including those for L88s and ZL1s, are fitted with a vacuum advance unit. Vacuum advances have part numbers stamped into them in the bracket that mounts the vacuum canister to the distributor.

All 1968 and 1969 Corvettes, except for those equipped with an L88 or ZL1, use a black Delco Remy distributor cap that has the words "Delco Remy Patent 2769047 R." molded into the top between the towers. Cars equipped with an L88 or ZL1 utilize a dark brown Delco cap.

All 1968s and 1969s use a Delco Remy ignition coil. All coils are held by a silver cadmium–plated, stamped steel bracket. The coil is clamped into the bracket with a slotted round head machine screw, and the bracket is held to the intake manifold by two hex head bolts. If the car is equipped with a radio there is a capacitor held to the coil bracket with a clamp retained by a single screw.

Coils are painted gloss black and have the last three numbers of their Chevrolet part number embossed in the housing from the inside out so they are raised up. (See Appendix L for coil numbers and applications.)

In addition to the final three numbers of the part number, some ignition coils (coils No. 270 and No. 263) also have "B-R" embossed in their cases. Coils utilized with the optional transistor ignition system have a red, black, and silver foil sticker that reads "Delco Remy Ignition Coil for Transistor Ignition" affixed to them.

Transistor ignition was a required option with L71s, L88s, L89s, and ZL1s. It was optional on other engines.

Transistor ignition includes a different distributor, a special wire harness, a different ignition coil, and a pulse amplification box. The amplification box is mounted to the driver-side front inner wheelwell. It is visible if you look in the area between the driver-side front inner wheelwell and the driver-side front corner of the body with the hood in the raised position.

The correct 1968 pulse amplification box has a plug to receive a mating plug in the transistor ignition wire harness. The correct 1969 amplification box has a three-wire pigtail coming out of it and terminating in a plug connector. The plug connector is mated with a corresponding plug connector in the transistor ignition harness.

Original 1968 and 1969 pulse amplification boxes have a part number stamped into the base. For 1968 the part number is 1115005 and for 1969 it is 1115438. Later boxes sometimes have the part number stamped into the amplifier's housing rather than its base.

Ignition Shielding

All 1968 and 1969 Corvettes equipped with a radio are outfitted with ignition shielding. All pieces of shielding are plated with flash chrome. As such, quality and appearance of the chrome is not very good.

All small-block and big-block cars have a two-section main ignition shield. It consists of a surround that completely encapsulates the distributor and coil, and a lid for the surround.

The surround for 1968s and 1969s assembled through approximately the spring of 1969 is held together by three spot welds. Later 1969s have two small Phillips head screws at the seam in addition to the spot welds.

A translucent, white plastic shield is held to the underside of the top lid by four plastic rivets. Three chrome-plated wing bolts retain the lid to the surround.

The main shield, or top shield as it is sometimes called, attaches to support brackets with two chrome wing bolts on each side. The support brackets are painted Chevrolet Engine Orange and attach to the intake manifold bolts.

Small blocks have a vertical ignition shield on each side of the main shield. The vertical shields encase the ignition wires. These vertical shields are not used on big blocks.

All small blocks also use a pair of boomerang or V-shaped sections of chrome-plated shielding to encapsulate the spark plug wires. The boomerang shielding runs from the bottom of the vertical shields to the area beneath the spark plugs.

All small blocks have four silver cadmium–plated spark plug heat shields, each of which covers two plugs. These shields are each fastened to the cylinder block with a single indented hex head bolt. The bolts pass through brackets attached to the heat shields. The brackets, like the shields, are cadmium plated.

Small blocks also have four chrome-plated spark plug ignition shields. The spark plug shields are retained to brackets with chrome-plated wing bolts. The brackets have "FPM" stamped in to represent the manufacturer. Later, incorrect GM replacement brackets have the letters "CNI" stamped in.

Small-block cars not originally equipped with a radio still have the two main shield support brackets on the back of the intake manifold and the cadmium-plated spark plug heat shields. They do not, however, have any of the chrome shielding.

Rather than spark plug wire and spark plug shields like small blocks have, big blocks have special spark plug wires covered with braided stainless-steel wire. Toward the end of each wire the braid ends in a hoop that gets fastened to the valve cover bolts to provide a ground. The hoops on the right side attach in pairs to the forward-most bolt and the third bolt back. On the left side of the engine they attach to the second and fourth bolts back.

Big-block cars not originally equipped with a radio do not have the main shield support brackets or braided steel spark plug wires.

This chrome-plated steel main ignition shield top cover has a plastic insulator riveted to the underside with plastic rivets. The example shown is from a 1969.

Spark Plug Wires

All 1968 and 1969 Corvettes, except those equipped with an L88 or ZL1 engine, use black spark plug wires manufactured by Packard Electric. Wires for L88s and ZL1s are made by Packard Electric but they are brown in color.

All wires are ink stamped every few inches with the words "Packard T V R Suppression" and a date code. The date code indicates the quarter and the year of manufacture. For example, wires labeled "2Q-69" were made in the second quarter of 1969.

Wires for small-block engines have black boots with 90-degree bends at the spark plug end and straight black boots at the distributor end.

On those 1968 and 1969 big blocks equipped with a radio, wires have gray boots with 135-degree bends at the spark plug ends and black boots with 90-degree bends at the distributor ends. On those big blocks not equipped with a radio the wires are the same except the boots are straight at the distributor ends.

Carburetors and Choke

All 1968 and 1969 Corvettes are carbureted. Original carburetors come from either Rochester, Holley, or Carter. Carter was at times contracted to manufacture Rochester Quadrajet carburetors for General Motors, so the Carter-built Quadrajets are almost identical to the Rochester-built ones. Carter-built Quadrajets are identified as being manufactured by

Those 1968 and 1969 big-block cars equipped with a radio use spark plug wires covered with a woven stainless-steel sheathing to shield the radio from interference that emanates from the wires. As seen here, big blocks not equipped with a radio use ignition wires without this sheathing. L88 engines, like the one shown, all got special ignition wires that were brown in color rather than black. Since L88s could not be had with a radio, L88 wires do not have the steel sheathing. Note the lack of a nipple on the vacuum advance, a characteristic unique to L88s, which did not utilize the advance mechanism.

Carter and use Carter's system of date coding rather than Rochester's system.

Rochester-built Quadrajets contain an alphanumeric sequence stamped into a flat, vertical area of the main body on the rear of the driver side. Either the full seven digit GM part number or the final five digits of the part number are stamped in. Several letters, which identify the specific plant where the carburetor was made, may be stamped here as well. And finally, four numbers denoting the date of manufacture are also stamped into this area.

Rochester utilized the Julian calendar for date coding its carburetors. With this system of dating, the first three numbers represent the day of the year and the final number is the last digit of the specific year. For example, the Julian date code for a carburetor

A close-up of the fuel filter mounting in a 1969. The cadmium-plated bracket mounts to the pivot for the A.I.R. pump. Note that the short piece of rubber hose connecting the fuel return line to the top, left of the filter, has two small spring clamps holding it in place. This is correct for 1969. 1968s use tower clamps in this position.

made on January 1, 1968, would read "0018." The first three digits, "001," represent the first day of the year, and the final digit, "8," represents 1968.

One tricky element to figuring out the exact day a Julian calendar date corresponds to is remembering that leap years have an extra day. For example, the Julian date code for a carburetor made on December 31, 1968, would read "3668" since 1968 was a leap year. The first three digits, "366," represent the 366th day of the year, which in 1968 was December 31. The final digit, "8," represents 1968.

Carter-built Quadrajets don't use a Julian calendar date coding system. Instead, they use a single letter and a single number. The letter denotes the month, with "A" indicating January, "B" indicating February, and so on. The letter "I" is not used, so September is represented by "J."

The number in the date code for Carter-built Quadrajets is the last digit for the year of manufacture. For example, a date code of C8 indicates the carburetor was made in March 1968.

Holley carburetors have three distinct stampings on the front driver side of the air horn. The top stamping is the seven-digit GM part number, which may be followed by one or two letters.

Below the GM part number is what is called the Holley list number. The list number corresponds to Holley's part number. This stamping says "LIST" followed by four numbers and then an additional number, a letter, or a combination of numbers and letters.

Below the Holley list number is the date code. Holley date codes in 1968 and 1969 utilize three characters. The first is a number representing the last digit of the year, the second is either a number or a letter representing the month of production, and the third is a number representing the week of production.

For the month of production the numbers "1" through "9" denote January through September, "O" denotes October, "A" denotes November, and "B" denotes December.

A Holley carburetor manufactured on April 3, 1969, would have a date code of 941, with "9" representing 1969, "4" representing April, and "1" representing the first week of April, which includes April 3.

(For charts showing 1968 and 1969 carburetor numbers see Appendix J.)

All 1968 and 1969 carburetors are plated gold dichromate. Rochester carburetors tend to be darker and more uniform in color than Holleys.

All engines equipped with a single carburetor use a single accelerator return spring. It is black phosphate–plated and mounts from the primary shaft bell crank to the accelerator cable mount.

Accelerator return spring usage varies on those engines equipped with tri-power. Earlier cars appear to utilize a single spring attached to the center carburetor throttle lever and the linkage clip to the front carburetor. A second, smaller spring was later added. This second spring was attached to the bottom of the center carburetor throttle lever and the bracket holding the accelerator cable. Later 1969 tri-power cars appear to have only the second, smaller spring and not the first.

All 1968 and 1969 Corvettes, except those equipped with an L88 or ZL1 engine, utilize a mechanical carburetor choke controlled by a thermostatic coil. The coil is mounted in a recess on the passenger side of the intake manifold and is covered by a cadmium-plated steel housing. A rod links the coil to the choke linkage on the carburetor.

Air Cleaner

L88 and ZL1 engines utilize a unique air cleaner arrangement. A gloss-black painted base rests on the carburetor, with a thin gasket between the two. A dark gray foam ring sits in the outer lip of the base. A 5-1/2-inch-diameter circular metal screen sits in a recess in the inner lip of the base. A small, semi-gloss painted lid goes over this metal screen and is retained by a silver cadmium–plated wing nut.

The remainder of the L88 and ZL1 air cleaner system is housed in the hood. The underside of the hood has a unique fiberglass housing bonded on. A foam and metal air cleaner element resides in the underhood fiberglass housing. When the hood is shut the foam ring in the outer lip of the air cleaner base seals against the underhood housing. Fresh air is drawn in from the area at the base of the windshield, travels through the underhood housing, passes through the

All Corvettes between 1968 and about 1976, including both small and big blocks, were originally fitted with this style AC Delco spin-on-type oil filter. The filter is white with a red AC logo, blue circumferential stripes, and blue lettering reading "FULL FLOW" and "TYPE PF-25."

This unique air-cleaner assembly was used on 1968 and 1969 L88 engines only. The base seals against a duct bonded to the underside of the hood. Fresh air is drawn into the duct through an opening at the base of the windshield.

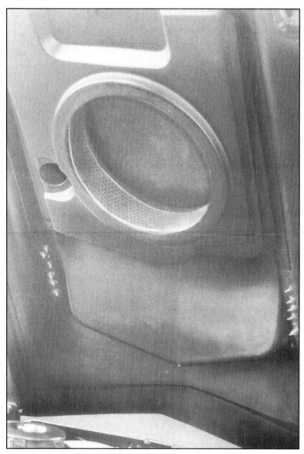
The underside of an L88 hood, showing the ductwork that channeled outside air from the base of the windshield to the engine's air cleaner.

air cleaner element and small metal screen, and enters the carburetor.

All 1968 and 1969 Corvettes not equipped with an L88 or ZL1 use an open element air cleaner assembly. The assembly is comprised of a base, an element, and a lid.

All air cleaner bases are painted gloss black and have a fitting for a breather tube that connects to the right side valve cover.

All single carburetor engines use an air cleaner with a 14-inch-diameter chrome-plated lid. Tri-power engines have chrome-plated triangular lids. All lids have red and silver foil decals identifying engine displacement and horsepower rating. In addition, all lids have service instructions and the replacement filter part number silk screened on the underside.

Original air filter elements have "BEST WAY TO PROTECT YOUR ENGINE — REPLACE WITH TYPE A 212 CW" silk screened in white around the horizontal lip. Furthermore, original elements, unlike later replacements, have a fine wire screen around the outside. Most replacements use a noticeably heavier

wire. Earlier cars probably utilize an element with the wire screen in a diagonal pattern. Later cars probably use an element with the wire screen in a horizontal pattern. With a horizontal pattern, the wire forms rectangles with the longer measurement running vertical when the element is installed.

Valve Covers

All 1968 and 1969 base engines are fitted with stamped steel valve covers painted Chevrolet Engine Orange. They have a raised area that spans their width but do not have "Chevrolet" stamped in like earlier covers. They are held on with hex head bolts and metal tabs that are also painted orange. Original valve covers have more rounded corners than later replacements. Also, original covers do not have spark plug wire brackets or oil drip rails welded to them.

A PCV valve inserts into a rubber grommet in the driver-side valve cover. A hose connects the PCV valve to the carburetor. The intake for the PCV system is in the passenger-side valve cover.

1968 covers do not have an oil fill since 1968 intake manifolds have an oil fill tube pressed in. 1969 covers do have a steel twist-on oil fill cap in the driver-side valve cover. The oil cap is painted orange on base engines, and has an "S" (for Stant, the manufacturer) stamped into the rivet in the center.

In 1968 the optional L79 327/350 engine is equipped with the same stamped steel valve cover as base engines except it is chrome plated instead of painted.

In 1969 the optional L46 350/350 engine is equipped with natural-finish cast-aluminum valve covers. These covers have seven ribs running from end to end on top. Both the driver- and passenger-side covers have holes for the PCV system and the driver side only has a hole for the oil fill. The oil fill cap is the same as the one used for base engines except it is chrome plated. The passenger-side cover has a rigid black disc with a crossed flags emblem in a circle glued in the spot where the oil fill cap is located on the other cover. As with the painted steel covers, a vent hose connects the passenger-side valve cover to the air cleaner base and a PCV valve is in the driver-side valve cover. Aluminum valve covers are retained by silver cadmium–plated, indented hex head bolts.

All 1968 and 1969 big-block valve covers are plated with low-quality chrome. They all have internal drippers that are spot welded on and the spot welds show as irregular indents on the outside of the cover. A foil decal reading "Tonawanda #1 Team" is on the top of the passenger-side cover toward the front. A twist-on-style chrome-plated oil fill cap is located on the passenger-side cover.

The oil fill cap used on 1968 and 1969 big blocks. Like the big-block valve cover it twisted into, the cap is chrome plated. The stamped-in "S" in the middle of the center rivet is for the manufacturer, Stant.

All cars have a Positive Crankcase Valve in the driver-side valve cover. As seen here, a paper ring with the valve's part number and other information was slipped over the valve's nipple before the hose was put on. This valve, part No. CV736C, is in a 1969 L88.

All 1968 and 1969 big blocks were fitted with chrome-plated valve covers. The quality of the plating was generally poor and the spot welds that held the oil drippers on the underside showed up as blemishes on the top side. This foil decal reading "Tonawanda #1 Team" is on the front of each passenger-side cover. It honored the people who built all Corvette big-block engines at Chevrolet's Tonawanda, New York, foundry and assembly plant.

A number of changes were made in big-block valve cover design in 1968 and 1969. The first style covers are the same as those used on 1967 big-block Corvettes. The passenger- and driver-side covers each have two welded-on brackets to hold plastic spark plug wire looms, and two clips on the intake side of the cover to hold wires. The rear of the driver-side cover has a large depression to clear the power brake booster. This cover is used on both power and non-power brake cars.

A second design big-block valve cover came into use in approximately January 1968. With this design, the L-shaped bracket for the forward spark plug wire loom on the passenger side is moved back so it is no longer centered between the cover ends. Instead, it just about lines up with the cover's breather hose opening. The deep depression in the rear of the driver-side cover is eliminated and a much smaller depression is substituted. And finally, the two welded-on clips on the intake side of the cover are replaced with a single clip centered on the bottom of the exhaust side.

In approximately July 1969 another change in big valve covers appeared. The rearmost welded-on spark plug wire loom bracket on the driver side is moved forward about 2 inches. This change places it forward of the rear intake manifold bolt rather than rearward of it.

A final change is incorporated beginning in approximately December 1969. The small clearance depression first seen in approximately January 1968 is eliminated.

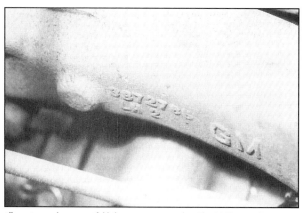

All cast-iron exhaust manifolds have a casting number. This 1968 example is casting number 3872765. This same manifold was used on the left side for all small blocks in 1968 and 1969 and some small blocks in 1970 and 1971.

Exhaust Manifolds

All 1968 and 1969 exhaust manifolds are cast-iron. They contain a casting number that is normally on the side facing away from the engine, and a casting date that is normally on the side facing toward the engine. (Refer to Appendix I for exhaust manifold casting numbers.)

Small-block exhaust manifold casting dates normally include a letter denoting the month and one or two numbers denoting the day of the month. Big-block exhaust manifolds normally include a letter denoting the month, one or two numbers denoting the day of the month, and one or two numbers denoting the year.

Small-block exhaust manifolds were not yet installed when engines were originally painted, so they show no signs of overspray. Big-block manifolds may or may not have Chevrolet Engine Orange paint overspray.

No 1968 or 1969 exhaust manifolds use a gasket where they mount to the cylinder head.

Small-block manifolds use 9/16-inch hex head bolts that have two concentric rings on their heads. The front two bolts and rear two bolts on both sides of the engine get French locks with one of the two tabs bent over to prevent the bolts from loosening. In addition, the same front and rear bolts on each side get thick, flat washers that sit between the French lock and manifold. If, however, the exhaust manifold bolt also retains a bracket (such as an air-conditioning bracket), the flat washer is usually not used.

Bolts holding big-block manifolds on have been observed with three different styles of heads. The most prevalent has two concentric rings like small-block manifold bolts. A second design bolt, with an integral washer, recessed hex head, and the letter *A*

(the manufacturer's logo) in the center of the head, is also utilized. A third variety that is sometimes seen is a simple hex head with no markings at all.

1968 and 1969 big-block exhaust manifolds do not have French locks or any type of washers used with the bolts.

Starter Motor

All 1968 and 1969 Corvettes have a Delco-Remy starter motor. Automatic transmission–equipped cars utilize starters with aluminum noses whereas starters for manual transmission–equipped cars have a cast-iron nose. The only exception to this is 1969s equipped with big blocks and automatics, which have cast-iron starter noses.

On 1968 starter motors, field coils as well as the solenoid are retained by slotted head screws. On 1969 starter motors, field coils as well as the solenoid are retained by Phillips head screws. Motor housings and both aluminum and cast-iron noses are painted semi-gloss black.

The starter's part number and assembly date are stamped into the side of the motor housing. The date code contains a number representing the last digit of the year, a letter denoting the month with "A" representing January, "B" representing February, and so on. As is typical of stamped-in date codes, the letter "I" is skipped so the month of September is represented by "J." One or two numbers indicating the day follow the letter denoting the month. For example, a date code of 9B14 indicates the starter was made February 14, 1969. (See Appendix N for starter motor part numbers.)

Starter solenoids have a black Bakelite cover for the electrical connections. Solenoid housings may be painted semi-gloss black or silver cadmium plated.

A black phosphate–plated spring clip clamps around the starter solenoid in all cars. A protrusion on top of this clip holds the starter motor wires away from the engine and exhaust system.

All cars use a stamped steel brace to support the forward end (the end facing toward the front of the car when the starter is installed). The brace mounts to a stud on the starter's end plate and to a threaded boss in the engine block. The brace is painted semi-gloss black.

Late 1968s and all 1969s have a heat shield to protect the starter motor from exhaust system heat. Small-block engines are fitted with a rectangular-shaped shield while big blocks get a larger, irregularly shaped shield. Small-block shields are painted semi-gloss black and big-block shields are plated with poor-quality flash chrome. Heat shields attach to the solenoid screws with barrel nuts.

The alternator from an unrestored 1969. The upper mount bolt with both an external tooth lock washer and a thick flat washer is typical of factory configuration. The "NS" ink stamping is a broadcast code. The raised ridges on the original black rubber boot at the bottom center of the photo distinguish it from the boot found on most reproduction wire harnesses.

Oil Filter

All 1968 and 1969 engines, including both small and big blocks, utilize an AC Delco spin-on-type oil filter. Original filters are white with a red AC logo, blue circumferential stripes, and blue lettering reading "FULL FLOW" and "TYPE PF-25."

Alternator and Voltage Regulator

All engines are fitted with a Delco-Remy alternator mounted on the driver side. Alternator housings are made from cast aluminum and are not painted or coated with anything.

The front half of the housing has the unit's part number, amperage rating, and assembly date code stamped in. The date code contains a number for the year, and a letter for the month, with "A" representing January, "B" representing February, and so on. As is typical of stamped-in codes, the letter "I" is skipped, so the month of September is represented by "J." The letter denoting the month is followed by one or two numbers for the day. For example, an alternator stamped "8F17" was assembled June 17, 1968.

The alternator pulley on all L88s, L89s, ZL1s, and L71s is machined from solid material and is silver cadmium–plated. While this high-performance pulley is randomly seen on other engines, most other applications used a zinc-plated, stamped steel pulley.

The lower alternator bracket on 1968 and 1969 small blocks is stamped steel that is painted Chevrolet Engine Orange. The upper brace is stamped steel that is painted semi-gloss black.

The lower alternator bracket on all 1968 and 1969 big blocks without power steering is cast and painted semi-gloss black. The lower bracket for big-block cars equipped with power steering is stamped steel that is painted semi-gloss black. The upper brace for all big-block engines is stamped steel that is painted semi-gloss black.

External voltage regulators are utilized in 1968 only. In 1969 the regulator is integral to the alternator.

The 1968 external voltage regulator is mounted on the left side inner wheelwell adjacent to the alternator. "DELCO REMY" is stamped into the gloss-black painted regulator cover from the inside, so the letters

All Corvette alternators have a part number, amp rating, and date code stamped into their case. This example shows a number 1100882 61-amp alternator that was assembled February 17, 1969 (9 B 17). The broadcast code is "NS." The head marking on the bolt (NAT) is correct.

Original fuel pumps typically have "AC" cast into the housing. The part number is stamped into the underside of the edge of the flange that mounts the pump to the engine block.

are raised up. "DELCO" and "REMY" are not lined up on original covers but are on later replacements.

The regulator cover is secured to the base with two silver cadmium–plated hex head bolts. Bolts on those cars assembled through approximately November 1968 have a slot in their head. Bolts used in cars assembled thereafter do not have these slots.

The voltage regulator base is zinc plated and has a part number and date code stamped in. The part number for all 1968s is 1119519. The date code contains a single number denoting the year and a letter indicating the month. The letter "I" is not used, so "J" represents the month of September.

Power Steering Pump and Fuel Pump

Small-block 1968 and 1969 cars equipped with power steering use a semi-gloss black painted power steering pump with a neck that is the same diameter from top to bottom. The necks on big-block pumps, in contrast, widen toward the bottom.

Two different power steering pump caps are used in 1968 and 1969. The first, which is used in 1968 through mid-1969, is stamped steel and says "CHECK OIL HOT, USE AUTOMATIC TRANSMISSION FLUID TYPE A" in the top. The second design is black plastic and says "FILL TO PROPER LEVEL, USE APPROVED FLUID" in the top.

Small-block cars usually use a semi-gloss black painted, stamped steel pulley for the power steering pump. All big-block-equipped cars use an open spoke, cast pulley for the power steering pump. Cast pulleys are painted semi-gloss black or are black phosphate plated.

All 1968 and 1969 power steering pumps, regardless of engine, use a semi-gloss painted, stamped steel support bracket.

All 1968 and 1969 Corvettes use an AC brand mechanical fuel pump. The pumps have "AC" cast into the top or side of the upper housing and a five-character part number stamped into the underside of the mounting flange. Pumps are natural dull silver in color.

Only those 1968 and 1969 Corvettes equipped with a Rochester carburetor utilize an external fuel filter. When so equipped, the filter is a metal body design manufactured by AC. It is silver colored with an AC logo and "GF432" silk screened on in red ink.

The filter is located on the front right side of the engine above the fuel pump. It is held by a silver cadmium–plated stamped steel bracket. The bracket is secured to the pivot for the A.I.R. pump. Two steel lines come out of the top of the filter. The larger of the two is the fuel feed to the carburetor and the smaller is the fuel return line to the tank. The fuel return line has a short length of rubber hose connecting it to the chassis fuel return line. In 1968 small tower clamps secure the hose and in 1969 spring clamps hold it.

Water Pump, Engine Fan, and Fan Clutch

1968 and 1969 small blocks use casting No. 3782608 water pumps. With this pump the snout does not have reinforcing ribs and the top of the pump housing does not have a boss for a bypass hose fitting.

1968 and 1969 big-block engines use casting No. 385624 water pumps. All big-block pumps utilize a bypass hose connected to a fitting on top of the pump housing. The bypass hose is 3/4-inch inside diameter and has a molded 90-degree bend. It connects to a fitting in the front of the intake manifold and is secured at both ends by SAE Type D screw-type clamps. The clamps are stamped with the number "10."

All solid lifter engines utilize a deep-groove water pump pulley while pulleys on hydraulic lifter engines have a shallower groove. Most water pump pulleys are painted semi-gloss black, though some originals have been observed with a black phosphate finish.

All 1968 and 1969 Corvettes use a thermostatically controlled, viscous coupled fan clutch. The thermostatic control is via a rectangular bi-metal strip on the front face of the clutch. The front face remains unpainted but the remainder is sometimes seen with dull aluminum paint.

Original clutches usually have a date code stamped in the flange that goes against the water pump pulley. The code contains one or two numbers indicating the month, one or two numbers indicating the day, and two numbers denoting the last two digits of the year. Thus, a clutch manufactured on May 11, 1969, would have a date stamping that reads "5 11 69." The date code stamping is often followed by the letters "SC," which represent the manufacturer, Sweitzer Clutch.

On all 1968 and those 1969 cars assembled through approximately April 1969 fan clutches (as well as water pump pulleys) are retained by silver cadmium–plated grade-eight hex head bolts. These bolts are frequently seen with "AP," "RSC," or "WB" head markings. Each bolt gets a split ring lock washer.

Fan clutches in 1969 cars assembled after approximately April 1969 are retained by studs and nuts that thread into the water pump's front hub. Regardless of whether bolts or studs are utilized to retain the fan clutch and water pump pulleys, the clutch hub has holes, not slots.

All 1968 and 1969 Corvettes use a gloss-black painted cooling fan that is mounted to the fan clutch.

Cars equipped with air conditioning usually use a seven-blade fan that has a part number and date code stamped into the edge of one or more of the blades. The date code contains a letter for the month, with "A" designating January, "B" designating February, and so on. As is typical of stamped-in date codes, the letter "I" is skipped, so the month of September is represented by "J." Following the letter indicating the month are two numbers to denote the year.

Small-block air-conditioned cars use a seven-blade fan that is essentially flat along the outer edge of each blade. In contrast, the ends of the blades on big-block air-conditioned cars are irregularly shaped and come to an off-center point.

Cars not equipped with air conditioning use a five-blade fan. Five-blade fans do not have a part number or date code stamped in.

A minority of air-conditioned cars have a five-blade fan instead of the more commonly seen seven-blade unit. This five-blade fan differs from the one seen in non-air-conditioned cars in that its blades are pitched at a more severe angle.

Radiator, Hoses, and Related Parts

1968 and 1969 Corvettes use either a copper or an aluminum radiator, depending on the engine and transmission choice, and whether the car is equipped with air conditioning.

Aluminum radiators have a part number and date code stamped into the top left side. The date code consists of two numbers to denote the year and a letter to indicate the month, with "A" representing January, "B" representing February, and so on. To the right of the stamping is a rectangular foil sticker with "HARRISON," which is the manufacturer, printed on

Those 1968–1969 cars not equipped with an expansion tank, and 1970–1972 cars not equipped with an aluminum expansion tank, use this RC-15 radiator cap.

it. Aluminum radiators are painted semi-gloss to gloss black.

1968 and 1969 Corvettes equipped with L88 engines utilize a unique aluminum radiator. It resembles the aluminum radiator used in other Corvettes but is slightly larger. Also, its top neck is long and curved instead of short and straight.

Copper radiators were also manufactured by Harrison and have that name embossed in the passenger-side radiator tank. In addition, there is a stamped steel tag containing a two-letter broadcast code and a part number attached to the passenger side of copper radiators. As with aluminum, the copper radiators are painted semi gloss to gloss black.

1969 Corvettes equipped with an L88 coupled to an automatic transmission utilize a fiberglass shroud. No other L88- (or ZL1) equipped cars use a fan shroud.

Most 1968 and 1969 cars with copper radiators use an unpainted black or very dark gray two-piece plastic

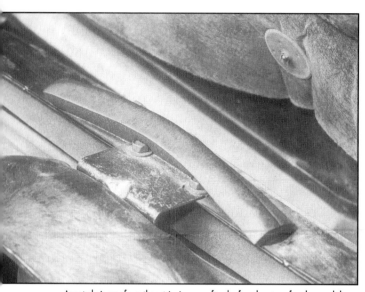

Assorted pieces of weather stripping can often be found on top of and around the radiator support. This example is from an unrestored 1969 small block with air conditioning.

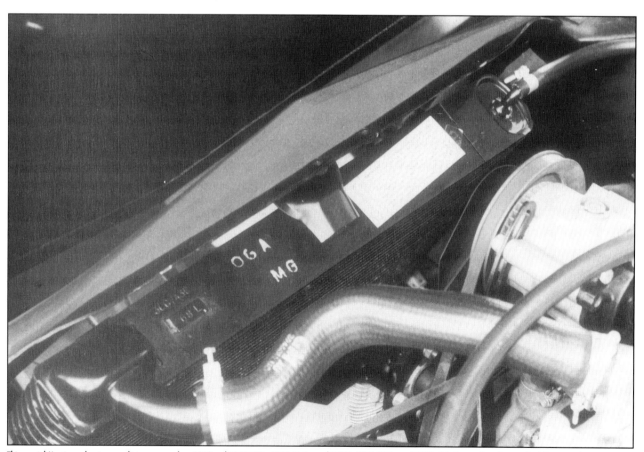

This special Harrison aluminum radiator was used on 1968 and 1969 L88s, 1969 ZL-1s, and 1970–1972 ZR-1s and ZR-2s. It is larger than the standard Harrison aluminum radiator used on some small-block cars and has a curved top neck rather than the standard radiator's straight neck. Toward the left-side top of the radiator you can see a rectangular, welded-on plate stamped "68L." This is the assembly date for this radiator. For an unknown reason some radiators have the date code stamped directly into the top plate while others, including this one, have it stamped into a separate plate that is welded on.

shroud that has a bolt-on extension on the bottom. Very early 1968 cars fitted with copper radiators are sometimes seen with semi-gloss painted steel fan shrouds.

All cars fitted with aluminum radiators, except L88s and ZL1s as noted above, use a semi-gloss painted, stamped steel shroud.

In 1968 a strip of rubber is utilized to seal the top of the radiator support to the hood. In 1969 a thick, black foam rubber seal replaces the rubber flap. In both years, black foam rubber strips seal the shroud to the radiator.

Some 1968 and 1969 Corvettes are fitted with an aluminum expansion tank, some are fitted with a brass tank, and some don't have a tank at all.

Aluminum tanks are unpainted and have the Harrison logo embossed in the side. 1968 and 1969 aluminum expansion tanks differ from earlier ones in that earlier ones have one outlet on the bottom and 1968–1969 units have two outlets.

In addition to the Harrison logo, the part No. 3016340, the words "FILL 1/2 WHEN COLD," and a manufacturing date code are also embossed in the face of aluminum tanks. The date code contains two numbers to denote the year and a letter to indicate the month, with "A" representing January, "B" representing February, and so on.

Brass expansion tanks are longer and thinner than their aluminum counterparts. They are approximately 3 inches in diameter and 20 inches long. A thin brass tag with "Harrison," a part number, and a date code stamped in is soldered to the side of the tank. The whole tank is painted gloss black.

Cars that don't have an expansion tank use an RC-15 radiator cap rated at 15 psi installed directly on the radiator. Cars with a brass expansion tank use the same cap installed on the tank. Cars with an aluminum expansion tank use an RC-26 cap, also rated at 15 psi, installed on the tank.

Both the RC-15 and RC-26 caps have the AC logo and the words "TURN TIGHT" and "REMOVE SLOWLY" stamped in them. On the RC-15 cap "RC-15" and "15#" are stamped inside of a stamped circle. On the RC-26 cap "RC-26" and "15#" are stamped, but not inside a circle.

All radiator and heater hoses are molded black rubber. Stamped on radiator hoses in white ink are a part number, GM logo, and several letters that are believed to be manufacturer's codes. In addition, there is usually a blue-colored line running the length of the hose.

Heater hoses usually contain a GM logo in white ink. They sometimes have the letters "DL" or "U" stamped on them also. Most original hoses are smooth (not textured) and have three or four thin ridges running lengthwise.

All 1968 and those 1969 Corvettes assembled through approximately September 1969 use tower-style clamps made by the Wittek Manufacturing Company. These clamps have a galvanized finish and contain the size, the words "WITTEK MFG. CO. CHICAGO U.S.A.," and a date code stamped into the band. The first number of the date code denotes the quarter and the following two numbers indicate the year.

Those 1969 cars assembled after approximately September 1969 use SURE-TITE brand stainless-steel worm drive clamps for the radiator hoses. All applications use size 28 clamps except air-conditioned big blocks, which use size 32 on the lower hose only. Original clamps have "SURE-TITE" in italics stamped into the band along their circumference. In addition, "WITTEK MFG. CO. CHI. U.S.A." is stamped into the worm screw's housing.

All cars use tower-style clamps for the heater hoses. The 5/8-inch heater hoses use 1-1/16-inch clamps. This size clamp has a galvanized finish and contains the size, the words "WITTEK MFG. CO. CHICAGO U.S.A.," and a date code stamped into the band. The first number of the date code denotes the quarter and the following two numbers indicate the year.

The 3/4-inch heater hose uses 1-1/4-inch clamps. These clamps have a cadmium dichromate finish that results in a translucent goldish tint as opposed to the smaller clamps' dull silver color4

The larger 1-1/4-inch clamps contain the manufacturer's logo and size designation but do not have a date code. Instead, they have the letters "DCM" stamped into the band.

Brake Master Cylinder and Related Components

All 1968 and 1969 Corvette master cylinders are manufactured by Delco and contain a casting

Master cylinders for all 1968–1982 Corvettes have a casting number on their side. This example, numbered 5455509, is from a non-power brake 1968.

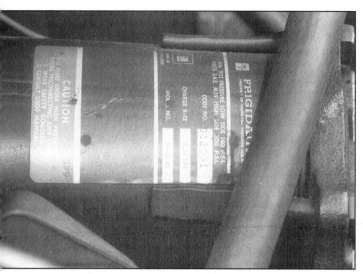

Air-conditioning compressors have a green, black, and silver foil sticker as shown. In this example the model number 5910645 identifies it as a 1968 or early 1969 unit. The code number is actually a manufacturing date code that translates to January 20, 1969, first shift.

number and the Delco split ring logo on the inboard side. Non–power assist master cylinders are casting No. 5455509 and power assist masters are casting No. 5480346.

In addition to the casting number, each master also contains a two-letter application code stamped into a flat machined boss on the top front of the unit. Most cars with power assist brakes have "PG" stamped into the master cylinder and most without power assist have "DC" stamped in. The entire master cylinder is semi-gloss black except for machined areas, which are natural.

All masters contain two bleeder screws above the brake line ports, and two steel wire bails that hold the cover on. A small vinyl sticker with two letters is folded around one of the bail wires. This sticker is white with red letters, which are "TG" for power brake cars, "YA" for manual brake cars.

All master cylinders use a stamped steel, cadmium dichromate–plated cover fitted with a rubber gasket. The cover has two domes that are not connected by a small ridge like later units. "SERVICE WITH DELCO PARTS" is stamped into one dome, while "USE DELCO SAE J 1703 BRAKE FLUID" or "SERVICE WITH SAE J 1703 BRAKE FLUID" is stamped into the other dome.

Power brake boosters, on cars so equipped, are painted gloss black and frequently have a spot of yellow paint somewhere. The yellow is thought to be an inspection mark or an application code.

Some boosters have a Julian date code stamped in on top opposite the vacuum valve. The code contains a number corresponding to the final number of the year and then three numbers denoting the day of the year. For example, a booster stamped "9134" was manufactured on the 134th day of 1969.

Air Conditioning and Heating System Components

All 1968 and 1969 Corvettes equipped with air conditioning utilize a model A-6 Frigidaire compressor. Compressors are painted semi-gloss black and have a green, black, and silver foil sticker on the top of the housing. The sticker usually contains a date code and model number.

The date code normally consists of two numbers for the month, two numbers for the day, and one number corresponding to the last digit of the year. The final number indicates the shift during which the unit was assembled.

For all 1968 small- and big-block-equipped cars, and some of those 1969 small-block cars assembled through approximately November 1968, the model number is 5910645. For some early 1969 and all later 1969 small blocks the model number is 5910741. For all 1969 big-block-equipped cars the model number is 5910740.

The air-conditioning system for all cars includes a POA valve assembly that is natural aluminum in color. Likewise, the thermostatic expansion valve, the tubing crimped onto the ends of the hoses, and the manifold block that connects the hoses to the back of the compressor are also unpainted.

An unpainted, dark gray fiberglass housing covers the evaporator. There is a Harrison foil sticker on the housing, as well as a fan relay. The relay has a gloss-black painted cover that has "DELCO REMY" stamped in from the inside. The relay mounts by means of a silver cadmium–plated bracket that has "881" stamped in it.

1968 and 1969 Corvettes with air conditioning have a vacuum actuated valve spliced into the heater hose. Tower-style clamps are used to retain the heater hose to the valve. When the air conditioning is on this valve shuts off the flow of engine coolant to the heater core.

The blower motors for both air-conditioned and non-air-conditioned cars are painted gloss black. Motors on air-conditioned cars have a rubber tube that extends from the motor housing to the evaporator housing. Motors on non-air-conditioned cars do not have this tube. Motors have a part number and date code stamped into their mounting flange, as well as the words "DELCO REMY DAYTON OHIO USA." The date code contains one or two numbers to denote the month and two numbers to indicate the year.

An aluminum expansion tank was used in 1968 on small blocks without air conditioning and L88s, and in 1969 on small blocks without air conditioning, big blocks with air conditioning, L88s, and L71s. At the very bottom of this example is the date code "68H," which is August 1968. The sticker with the number "7" is believed to be an inspection code.

Air conditioning was available as an extra cost option on all cars except those equipped with an L88, L89, L71, or ZL1 engine.

Windshield Wiper Door Mechanism, Wiper Motor, and Related Components

All 1968 and 1969 Corvettes have a vacuum actuated wiper door. The door is moved up and down by a vacuum motor mounted on the upper right side of the firewall. In all 1968 Corvettes, as well as early 1969 cars, the vacuum actuator is cylindrical in shape. Later 1969s use a different design of actuator that resembles two pie tins joined together. All vacuum actuators are cadmium dichromate plated.

The vacuum motor is controlled by a cadmium dichromate–plated vacuum valve. The body of the valve has two ridges extending into the depressed center. Later replacement valves only have one ridge.

In 1968 to mid-1969 cars the valve is mounted on the rear of the right front inner wheelwell housing. In those cars assembled after mid-1969 it is on the upper left side of the firewall near the emissions sticker. As with the vacuum motor, the valve is plated cadmium dichromate.

All 1968 and 1969 Corvettes utilize wiper motors that are natural diecast silver in color. A black plastic cover goes over the wiper motor.

In 1969 only the wiper motor has a sticker indicating the unit's part number and date code. All motors are part No. 5044731. The date code utilizes the Julian calendar, with three numbers for the day of the year and a single number representing the last digit of the year.

The washer pump utilized for 1968 has three ports. A three-port pump is again used in 1969, but with the addition of a valve containing an additional two ports. These two extra ports are for the headlamp washer system.

For 1968 and 1969 Corvettes without air conditioning the windshield washer fluid reservoir is mounted on the rear of the passenger-side inner wheelwell housing. The reservoir is rigid black plastic and has marks indicating fluid level.

All air-conditioned cars use a flexible plastic bag to hold washer fluid. The front of the bag is clear and the rear is very dark gray. For 1968s this bag is mounted

This long, cylindrical brass expansion tank was used in 1969–1972s equipped with both a big block and air conditioning. It was originally painted semi-gloss black but as demonstrated here the paint did not typically adhere well to the brass.

1968s and those 1971s assembled after mid-March, and newer cars, use a three-port washer pump. However, 1969s, 1970s, and early 1971s use a five-port pump, with the two extra ports supplying the headlamp washers.

on the passenger-side front inner wheelwell housing. For 1969s it mounts on the lower left-side firewall.

Air Injection Reactor System and other Emissions Components

Air Injection Reactors (A.I.R.) are installed in all 1968 and 1969 Corvettes, including L88s and ZL1s. The A.I.R. system includes black cadmium–plated tubes (they tend to be black on small blocks and brownish on big blocks) that thread into each of the four runners on both exhaust manifolds. All A.I.R.-equipped cars therefore have four holes drilled and tapped into each manifold.

The A.I.R. pump body is diecast aluminum and natural in color. A semi-gloss black painted, rough-textured, sand-cast plate covers the back of the pump.

All pumps contain a centrifugal filter (this is the piece that looks like a fan) behind the pulley. It is made from opaque white plastic and has squared-off fins. A white filter with rounded-off fins or a black plastic filter is not correct.

Small-block engines use a steel spacer between the front pump pulley and centrifugal filter. Big

Driver-side details of a windshield wiper motor in a 1969.

blocks do not use a spacer. The spacer is unplated or silver cadmium–plated and the pulley is gray phosphate–plated or semi-gloss black painted.

Pulleys used on all small blocks in 1968, and the base engine in 1969, have part No. 3917234 stamped in. Pulleys found on 1969 L46 engines have part No. 3932458 stamped in. A.I.R. pumps on all 1968 and 1969 big-block engines use a pulley with part No. 3925522 stamped in.

Most pumps are date coded, though the date can be difficult to see with the pump installed. It is stamped into a boss on the rear underside of the body. The sequence may begin with a letter to indicate the assembly plant or specific line. Then there are one or three numbers to indicate the day of the year on the Julian calendar. Earlier dates (prior to the 100th day) may start with two zeros or they may not. For example, a pump assembled on the fifth day of the year may be stamped "005" or simply "5." A fourth (or second) number follows to denote the last digit of the year. This is followed by a number indicating the shift, and a letter indicating the model of the pump.

The lower pump bracket is painted Chevrolet Engine Orange and the upper bracket is semi-gloss black. For small blocks, the lower bracket is cast and contains the number 3923214. For big blocks the lower bracket is stamped steel.

The diverter valve body is natural in color, while the diaphragm cover and check valves are cadmium dichromate. The diaphragm cover has a round sticker with a two-letter broadcast code printed on it. The diverter valve muffler is plated gray phosphate. The diverter valve part number is stamped into the valve below the muffler. Check valves have a part number stamped into their center ridge.

Hoses connecting the various parts of the A.I.R. system are molded black and hose clamps are tower style. Clamps have a galvanized finish and contain the size, the words "WITTEK MFG. CO. CHICAGO U.S.A.," and a date code stamped into the band. The first number of the date code denotes the quarter and the following two numbers indicate the year.

All 1968 and 1969 Corvettes have a PCV valve located in the left-side valve cover. The valve has a part number stamped into it. For those engines

Driver-side view of the A.I.R. pump on a 1969 L46.

Even ultra-high-performance L88 engines were equipped with Air Injection Reactor pumps. This example is from a 1969.

equipped with a Holley carburetor the PCV valve is part No. CV746C and for those equipped with a Rochester carburetor it is No. CV736C.

All 1968 and 1969 Corvettes equipped with automatic transmission or air conditioning have an anti-diesel/fast idle solenoid that is mounted with a bracket to the front of the carburetor. The bracket is cadmium dichromate–plated and the solenoid housing is silver cadmium–plated and has a white sticker that reads "CAUTION NEVER USE TO SET IDLE SEE SERVICE MANUAL FOR ADJUSTMENT" in red letters.

On non-air-conditioned cars equipped with an automatic transmission, a pinkish wire runs along the driver-side valve cover and plugs into the solenoid. The wire is secured by clips attached to the valve cover.

On air-conditioned cars a single green wire in a black fabric-like protective tube comes out of the air-conditioning compressor harness and plugs into the solenoid.

All 1968 and 1969 Corvettes have what is commonly called an emissions label glued in the engine compartment. On early 1968 cars it is found on the top of the radiator on the driver side. On later 1968s and

Passenger-side view of the A.I.R. pump on a 1969 L46. Squared-off fins on the centrifugal filter are correct. Later filters sometimes have rounded-off fins.

Passenger-side view of the A.I.R. pump on a 1969 L88 engine. Big-block and small-block A.I.R. pumps differ significantly.

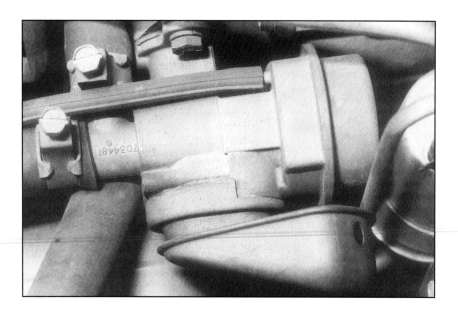

A close-up of an Air Injection Reactor system diverter valve from a 1969. Note the color stripe on the vacuum hose and top screw-style hose clamps.

all 1969s it is glued to the left upper area of the fire-wall. These labels are white in color and contain engine tune-up specifications as well as information about the emission control systems installed in the car.

Engine Compartment Brackets, Latches, Wiring, and Related Components

The firewall, underside of the hood, and engine compartment side of the inner wheelwells are painted semi-gloss black. The wheel side of the front and rear inner wheelwells are also painted semi-gloss black, though coverage is usually sparse. In addition, the rear areas of the wheel sides normally have some undercoating.

Some 1969 Corvettes have a section of very dark gray insulation fastened to the forward underside of the hood. It is held in place with glue and three black discs that lock onto pins imbedded in the hood. This insulation is seen more frequently in cars equipped with big-block engines though there appears to be no consistency in its use.

All 1968 and 1969 big blocks have a small oil pressure line bracket on the left side of the engine block. In 1968 a steel tube goes from the block fitting to a junction at this bracket. Another steel tube continues up to the oil pressure gauge.

In 1969 a steel tube extends from the block fitting up to a junction on the bracket. Then a black plastic tube continues up to the oil pressure gauge.

All 1968 and 1969 small blocks utilize black plastic tubing that goes directly from the engine block fitting to the oil pressure gauge. The plastic line has tiny white lettering and is fastened at both ends with brass fittings.

Engine compartment wiring harnesses and vacuum hoses are bundled together in a circle. Vacuum hoses are fastened to each other with pieces of non-adhesive black plastic tape used as ties. The electrical harnesses and vacuum hoses are held to each other with black plastic tie wraps.

All vacuum hose is color coded with an ink stripe that runs the length of the hose. Larger hoses have a green, red, or yellow stripe while smaller hoses usually have a white stripe.

All cars have a horn relay mounted to the inner wheelwell. The relays have a zinc-plated cover with "DELCO REMY" and four letters stamped in from the inside out. The cover sits on a white plastic base for 1968 models and on a black plastic base for 1969 models.

A silver cadmium–plated metal bracket attached to the horn relay mounts it to the left-side inner wheelwell housing. The bracket has "12V" and the last three digits of the relay's part number stamped in it. In 1968 the stamping is "862" and in 1969 it is "890."

All 1968 and 1969 Corvettes have two horns, a high and a low note. The high note is part No. 9000246 and it mounts on the passenger side. The low note is part No. 9000245 and it mounts on the driver side.

Horns have the last three digits of the part number and a manufacturing date code stamped into flat areas near the sound opening. The date code contains a number denoting the year, a letter denoting the month (with "A" representing January, "B" representing February, and so on), and another number indicating the week. For example, a horn stamped "8B2" was made the second week of February 1968.

Each horn is spot welded to a mounting bracket and the whole assembly is painted semi-gloss black.

Hood hinges are silver cadmium–plated and usually have both body color and underhood black overspray on them. Hinges are usually fastened by black phosphate–plated, indented hex head bolts.

The hood support for 1968 and 1969 is silver cadmium plated and has two sections that telescope together as the hood is lowered. Early 1968s utilize two bolts to secure the bottom of the support to the inner wheelwell housing. Later 1968s and all 1969s use a third bolt that passes through the fender's drip rail.

The hood latches are black phosphate plated and mount with black phosphate–plated hardware. The driver-side male latch has the hood release cable attached with a brass barrel cable stop that utilizes a hex bolt to lock the stop to the cable. The cable is inside a spiral-wound metal sheath.

The male latches mounted to the firewall each have a pin that engages the female latches on the underside of the hood. The male latches in all 1968 and those 1969 cars assembled through approximately September 1969 use cone-shaped pins. 1969 cars assembled thereafter use pyramid-shaped pins.

Another cable connects the two female latches mounted to the underside of the hood. In very early 1968 this cable is inside a wound metal sheath. This changes to a black nylon sheath for mid-production 1968s and then to a white nylon sheath for later 1968s and all 1969s.

In 1968 this underhood crossover cable is fastened at its ends with small brass cylinders and silver cadmium–plated hex head set screws. In 1969 flat tabs of metal containing multiple holes are attached to the cable's ends. The flat tabs are secured to the hood latches with small clevis pins fitted with flat washers and cotter pins.

In 1968 and early 1969 two clips held by indented hex head bolts fasten the cable to the underside of the hood. Beginning in approximately September 1969 the two clips are replaced with a single clip centered under the hood.

1968–1969 Chassis

Chassis

1968 and 1969 Corvette chassis are painted semigloss black. Chassis for automatic transmission–equipped cars have a removable, bolt-on center crossmember while standard transmission– equipped cars have a welded-on center cross-member. Also, cars with automatics do not have a clutch cross shaft tower welded on top of the chassis behind the left front wheel as standard transmission cars do.

A pair of 1-inch-high chassis' part number sequences is painted in white on the frame with a sten-

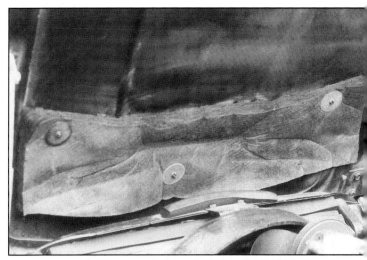

This dark gray layer of insulating material is fastened to the forward underside of the hood on some 1969s. It is held in place with glue and three black discs that lock onto pins imbedded in the hood. Though more frequently seen in big-block cars, there appears to be no consistency in its use. This example is in a small block.

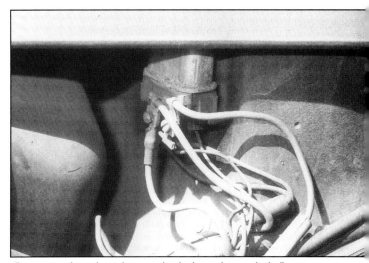

All 1968–1973s have a horn relay mounted to the driver-side inner wheelwell. Through 1971 the relay has a zinc-plated cover with "DELCO REMY" and four letters stamped into the top from the inside out. In 1972 the cover is shorter and squared off and does not have anything stamped in. Note the rough texture on the fiberglass inner wheelwell. The large item to the left is the vacuum storage tank.

cil. One sequence is the A.O. Smith part number (this is the company that fabricated the chassis for GM) and the other sequence is the Chevrolet part number.

A manufacturing date code is stenciled on the rail as well. The date contains one or two numbers representing the month, one or two numbers indicating the day, and two numbers denoting the year.

The stencil numbers and date code usually appear on the outside of the right frame rail and are usually upside down.

All 1968–1969 Corvettes have a vacuum storage tank mounted underneath the driver-side fender. As seen here, the horn relay is mounted forward of the storage tank.

All 1968–1972 Corvettes have a vacuum-actuated wiper door that is moved up and down by a vacuum motor mounted on the upper right side of the firewall. In all 1968 Corvettes, as well as early 1969 cars, the vacuum actuator is cylindrical-shaped as shown here. Later cars use a different design of actuator that resembles two pie tins joined together. All vacuum actuators are cadmium dichromate plated. The plunger switch mounted behind the actuator is for the optional UA6 anti-theft alarm system.

This is the second-design windshield wiper door actuator used from late 1969 through 1972. Note the color code stripe on the vacuum hose and the absence of a hose clamp on the end, both of which are correct.

All 1968 and 1969 Corvettes have their serial number stamped into their chassis in two locations. It is typically found in the left-side rail slightly forward of the No. 4 body mount bracket. It is also typically found on the left-side rear kick up above the wheel area slightly forward of the No. 3 body mount bracket.

1968 and 1969 body mounts are not made from rubber as in 1967 and older Corvettes. Instead they are thick aluminum discs that get sandwiched between the body and the chassis' body mount bracket.

Steel shims are frequently utilized at body mount points to make up for irregularities in fit. If present, shims are usually taped to the body mount bracket with 1 1/2-inch masking tape. The number of shims needed at each body mount bracket is typically written on the chassis adjacent to the bracket with a green or white grease crayon. Unlike earlier cars, this number is usually an actual number rather than slash marks.

Front Suspension

Upper and lower front control arms are painted semi-gloss to gloss black. Ball joints are installed after the arms are painted and are therefore not painted. Crushed steel rivets (not bolts) hold ball joints on and are also natural in finish.

Control arm cross shafts are painted semi-gloss black on some cars and unpainted on others. Cars with painted cross shafts typically have control arm bushing retention washers and bolts that are also painted semi-gloss black. Cars with unpainted cross shafts typically have retention washers that are gray phosphate plated, and bolts that are black phosphate plated.

Front coil springs are natural in finish and sometimes have an irregular bluish cast from the manufacturing process. A green paper sticker contains two black letters indicating the spring's broadcast code (i.e., their application) as well as a black GM part number.

Front shock absorbers are manufactured by Delco and are oil hydraulic, not gas filled. They are painted semi-gloss gray and have the words "DELCO REMY PLIACELL" and a date code stamped in around the bottom. The Julian date code contains three numbers indicating the day and two numbers denoting the year. In addition, there is a small paper sticker with a two-letter broadcast code on the side of the shock.

The upper shock-mount rubber bushings are unpainted black rubber. The top upper bushing is larger in diameter than the bottom upper bushing and the upper shock washer is gray phosphate plated.

The lower shock-mount rubber bushings are integral to the shock and are therefore painted along with the shock.

All 1968 and 1969 big-block Corvettes and all small-block-equipped cars with optional F-41 suspension utilize a 15/16-inch front sway bar. All small blocks not equipped with F-41 utilize a 3/4-inch bar. Some cars have a semi-gloss black painted sway bar while others have a natural, unpainted finish bar.

Bushings mounting the front sway bar to the chassis, as well as bushings in the end links, are unpainted black rubber. Semi-gloss black painted, stamped steel brackets hold the bar to the chassis.

End link bolts are zinc-plated 5/16-24 SAE fine thread and have the manufacturer's logo, "WB," on their heads. End link spacers are zinc plated, have a split seam, and typically have a "K" or a "C" stamped in.

Steering Box and Steering Linkage

1968 and 1969 Corvettes use a cast steering gear that is usually natural in color though some are painted semi-gloss black. The steering box cover is aluminum and does not have any symbols or writing in it. A daub of yellow paint is frequently seen on top of the box.

A forged pitman arm links the steering box to the relay rod. The pitman arm is natural in color and is often seen with a blue or green daub of paint.

The steering relay rod and idler arm are typically natural finish. Both parts are forged and tend to have a bluish-gray tint. Original idler arms do not have grease fittings.

Tie rod ends are natural finish and also typically have a bluish-gray color cast. Daubs of yellow paint are often seen on tie rod ends.

Tie rod end sleeves are painted semi-gloss black. Tie rod end clamps have two reinforcing ridges around their circumference and are sometimes painted semi-gloss black and sometimes left unpainted.

Outer tie rod ends can install into either of two holes in the steering knuckles. Cars equipped with standard, non-power steering have the outer tie rod ends installed into the rear holes while cars equipped with power steering, and cars equipped with an L88 or ZL1 engine, have them in the forward holes. On those cars equipped with power steering the unused steering knuckle hole is plugged with an aluminum plug inserted from the bottom.

On those cars so equipped, the power steering control valve and hydraulic cylinder are both painted semi-gloss black. The nut and washers retaining the hydraulic cylinder's ram to the frame bracket are both zinc plated. The frame bracket may be painted semi-gloss black or unpainted. Original power steering hoses typically have longitudinal ridges around their entire circumference while later replacements don't.

Rear Suspension

All 1968 and 1969 Corvettes equipped with standard suspension utilize a nine-leaf rear spring. Cars equipped with optional F-41 suspension utilize a seven-leaf spring. All springs are painted light gray

For all 1968–1982 Corvettes, original upper and lower ball joints were held to their control arm by crushed steel rivets, not bolts and nuts as with replacements.

and have black plastic liners between the leaves. Nine-leaf springs do not have a liner between leaf No. 6 and leaf No. 7 (with the bottom leaf being No. 1).

The center rear spring mount bracket is painted semi-gloss black. The four bolts retaining the spring to the differential typically have the manufacturer's logo, "WB," on their heads and are either black phosphate or zinc plated. The outer spring bolts and nuts are usually black phosphate plated and the washers are typically silver cadmium plated or natural.

Rear trailing arms are painted semi-gloss to gloss black. Rear wheel bearing carriers (also called spindle supports) are natural and have a part number and date code cast in. The date code has a letter representing the month, with "A" for January, "B" for February, and so on, one or two numbers for the day, and one number for the final digit of the year. The date code for a rear bearing carrier made on August 18, 1969, for example, would read "H 18 9."

All 1968 and 1969 Corvettes equipped with F41 suspension or a big-block engine have a rear stabilizer bar. The bar is 9/16-inch diameter and may be painted semi-gloss black or unpainted. It mounts to the chassis with semi-gloss black painted, stamped steel brackets. At each end the bar has a semi-gloss black painted link bracket that attaches to brackets bolted to the trailing arms. The brackets on the trailing arms have a plating that is sometimes called "pickling." It results in a brownish olive color. These brackets attach to the trailing arm via bolts that thread into small, unpainted steel plates that slip into the rear of the arms.

Rear camber adjustment rods (also called strut rods) are usually natural and often have a bluish-gray tint. Some rods are painted semi-gloss black or are partially painted during the undercarriage "black-out" process. Original rods have 1-1/2-inch-diameter ends while 1974 and newer rods have 1-3/4-inch-diameter ends.

The outboard ends of the camber adjustment rods are held to the rear wheel bearing carriers with forged L-shaped pins that also serve as the lower mounts for the rear shock absorbers. These pins, which are sometimes referred to as rear shock brackets, contain a raised part number. Originally, there was a left and a right pin, with each having a slight bend to angle it upward when installed. Later GM replacements are not angled, so the left and right side interchange.

The inboard ends of the camber adjustment rods attach to a semi-gloss black painted bracket with special bolts. These bolts have integral off-center washers that, when rotated, move the rods in or out and thus allow for rear wheel camber adjustment. The camber adjustment bolts are usually silver cadmium plated

Rear sway bar ends are mounted to trailing arms as shown here. Unusually thin nuts (seen on the top) are used in this application.

though they may be black phosphate plated instead.

Rear wheel toe adjustment is set with the use of shims placed on either side of the trailing arms where they mount to the chassis. The adjusting shims are unpainted rectangular pieces of steel of varying thickness. Correct shims have equal-size holes at each end, and when installed one end protrudes from the chassis pocket where the end of the trailing arm resides. Later cars use a different style of shim that has a slot in one end that slips over the trailing arm mount bolt.

Rear axle shafts (often called "half shafts") are made from forged ends welded to extruded steel tubes. The axle shafts are natural, with the tube being shiny silver and the ends being a dull gray. Original axle shaft tubes are approximately 2-1/2 inches in diameter. Later tubes are considerably larger than this.

U-joints do not have grease fittings and do have a raised part number on the body. They are natural and tend to have that faint bluish tint that is characteristic of forged parts.

The outboard axle shaft U-joints are pressed into a flange that is natural in color. The flange is held to the rear wheel bearing carrier by four bolts that are usually black phosphate plated. The bolts are prevented from turning out by two pairs of French locks, the tabs of which are bent over to contact the bolt heads. The French locks are zinc plated and typically have only one of the two tabs adjacent to each bolt bent over.

The inboard axle shaft U-joints are held to the differential output yokes by one of two methods: Forged caps retained by hex head bolts are used on Corvettes equipped with a big-block engine, and U-shaped strap clamps with nuts are used on cars equipped with a small-block engine.

Front Wheel Assemblies

Front spindles and steering knuckles are natural and tend to have a bluish tint to their gray color. In addition, the lower portions of the spindles are frequently seen with orange or white paint as though the bottoms of the spindles were dipped into it.

Original front brake backing plates are zinc plated and then chromate dipped. This results in varying finishes ranging from gold with a faint rainbow of other colors throughout to a dull silver with only a trace of the yellowish chromate coloring. Well-preserved original backing plates typically appear dull silver, probably because the chromate dip deteriorates over time.

Front brake caliper support brackets are plated silver cadmium or cadmium dichromate, which results in a translucent gold color with varying degrees of other colors present in a rainbow-like pattern.

Cars equipped with J56, the heavy-duty brake option, have a number of special components. These include front calipers that use two pins to hold the pads instead of the standard one, extra front caliper supports, semi-metallic brake pads, heat insulators on the face of all caliper pistons, and a proportioning valve mounted beneath the master cylinder.

The J56 proportioning valve was made by Kelsey-Hayes and has "K-H" cast into its side. The body is painted semi-gloss black and the front adjusting nut and its shaft are silver cadmium plated. The stamped steel bracket that mounts it below the master cylinder is painted semi-gloss black.

Front brake calipers are painted semi-gloss black and frequently have blue or while daubs of paint on the side. Painting is done before the caliper halves are machined and therefore machined surfaces are unpainted. Bleeder screws are zinc plated and remain unpainted.

Caliper hoses are black rubber with gold irridite–plated end hardware. Federally mandated DOT specifications are written on the hose in red ink. In addition, there is a red longitudinal stripe put there to make it easier to see if the hose is twisted. Original hoses typically have raised longitudinal ridges around their entire circumference while later replacements are typically smooth.

Front brake rotors are natural in finish. The front wheel bearing carrier (also called a hub) is riveted to the rotor disc.

Rear Wheel Assemblies

As with the fronts, original rear brake backing plates were zinc plated and then chromate dipped. This resulted in varying finishes ranging from gold with a faint rainbow of other colors throughout to a dull silver with only a trace of the yellowish chromate coloring. Well-preserved original backing plates typically appear dull silver, probably because the chromate dip deteriorates over time.

Rear brake caliper support brackets are natural, and hence a dull gray, or on occasion painted flat to semi-flat black.

Rear brake calipers are painted semi-gloss black and frequently have blue or while daubs of paint on the side. Painting is done before the caliper halves are machined and therefore machined surfaces are unpainted. Bleeder screws are zinc plated and remain unpainted.

Rear brake rotors are natural in finish. They are riveted to the rear spindle, which is pressed into the rear wheel bearing carrier. In order to service the park brake assembly or the rear wheel bearings, the rivets are often drilled out. The wheel lug nuts retain the rotor in the absence of the rivets.

Transmission

Automatic-equipped 1968 and 1969 Corvettes utilize a Turbo-Hydra-Matic 400 transmission. The main case and the tail housing are both cast aluminum with a natural finish. The fluid pan is stamped steel and is also natural.

Automatic transmissions contain an identification plate on the right side. The plate has two alpha-numeric sequences stamped in. The bottom sequence is the car's serial number and the top sequence is referred to as a production code. The first two numbers of this code indicate the model year. Next comes a letter that denotes the car model (in our case Corvette) and the engine. This is followed by three numbers that represent the day the transmission was assembled.

The transmission assembly date is a modified version of the Julian calendar system. The three numbers represent the day of the year, but unlike most applications of the Julian calendar system in dating Corvette components, with transmissions the count does not begin with the first day of the year. Instead, for 1968 Corvettes it begins with January 1, 1967, and continues sequentially through calendar year 1968. Similarly, for 1969 models it begins January 1, 1968, and continues through calendar year 1969.

This dating system sounds confusing, but it's easy once you get the hang of it. For example, in the production code "68K018," the "68" represents the 1968 model year, "K" represents the application code (which is 1968 and 1969 small block), and "018" represents the eighteenth day from when the count begins. Remember, the count begins January 1st of the preceding year, so this transmission was assembled January 18, 1968. Had that same transmission been assembled January 17, 1969, the code would read "69K383," with January 17, 1969, being 383 days after the count for the 1968 model year began (factoring in that 1968 was a leap year).

The application codes for 1968 and 1969 Corvettes include "K" for all small blocks, "S" for hydraulic lifter big blocks, and "Y" for solid lifter big blocks.

Four-speed manual transmissions have cast-aluminum main cases, side covers, and tail housings that are natural in color. A steel tag with a part number is affixed to the transmission with one of the side cover bolts.

Two alpha-numeric sequences are stamped into the main case on a vertical surface at the front of the right side. One of these sequences is the car's serial number. The other is a production code and the date the transmission was originally assembled.

The production code begins with a letter to indicate the source for the transmission. All Corvette four-speeds were obtained from Muncie which is represented by the letter "P." This is followed by a number representing the last digit of the model year. Next, there is a letter indicating the month of production, followed by two numbers denoting the day of the month. Various letters are not used in denoting the month, so refer to this chart when determining assembly date:

A   January
B   February
C   March
D   April
E   May
H   June
K   July
M   August
P   September
R   October
S   November
T   December

The final character in the production code is a letter commonly called a suffix code. This letter indicates which of the three available four-speeds the unit is. For the suffix code, "A" indicates a wide-ratio M-20 with 2.52:1 first gear ratio; "B" indicates a close-ratio M-21 with a 2.20:1 first gear ratio; and "C" denotes a close-ratio M-22 "heavy-duty" transmission, which also has a 2.20:1 first gear ratio.

An example of a four-speed transmission code is "P9M24A." This identifies an M-20 wide-ratio Muncie four-speed assembled August 24, 1969.

Differential and Driveshaft

All 1968 and 1969 Corvettes are equipped with a non-limited-slip differential as standard. A Positraction limited-slip differential is available both years as an extra cost option. The differential case and cover are both natural-colored castings and as such are a dull silvery gray.

A plastic triangular tag is attached to Positraction differentials by means of the square-head oil fill plug. The tag is red with white lettering that says "USE LIMITED SLIP DIFF. LUBRICANT ONLY." The fill plug is natural and has a large "W" cast into the square. Even though the tag is specific to Positraction differentials, it is often seen on non-Positraction units as well.

The front input yoke and side output yokes are forgings that are natural in color. Because they are forged they have a somewhat smoother surface than the case and cover, and they tend to have a slight bluish tint to their dull gray color.

Differential cases and covers both have casting numbers and a casting date that includes a letter for the month (with "A" representing January, "B" representing February, and so on), one or two numbers indicating the day of the month, and one number indicating the last digit of the year.

In addition to the cast-in dates, all cases also have a stamped-in production code. The code begins with a number that indicates the assembly shift that built the unit. This is followed by a two- or three-letter code indicating the gear ratio. Next comes a date code that includes one or two numbers for the month, one or two numbers for the day, and two numbers for the year. The final character in the production code is a letter that indicates the specific plant that built the differential.

(See Appendix E for differential gear ratio codes.)

The transmission and differential are connected by a drive shaft made from extruded steel tubing welded at each end to a forged universal joint coupling. As with the axle shafts, the drive shaft is natural in color. The center tube portion is bright silver with longitudinal extrusion lines sometimes visible, and the ends are a dull silvery gray with a slight bluish hue at times.

A part number stenciled on the drive shaft tube in yellow or white paint is sometimes seen. One or two green circumferential stripes on the tube and daubs of various colors of paint on the forged ends are sometimes seen as well.

Exhaust System

All 1968 and most 1969 Corvettes use an undercar, carbon steel exhaust system manufactured by Walker for Chevrolet. Side-mount exhaust was available as an option in 1969 only.

All 1968 cars equipped with either a big-block engine or the optional N11 off-road exhaust utilize 2 1/2-inch exhaust pipes. All other cars utilize 2-inch pipes. All 1969 cars with undercar exhaust systems, including those equipped with big blocks, utilize 2-inch pipes.

All cars except those equipped with an L88 or ZL1 engine use a heat riser valve at the base of the passenger-side exhaust manifold. The manifold studs are longer to accommodate the valve, and the exhaust pipe is correspondingly shorter. L88 and ZL1 engines use a spacer in place of the valve. The spacer resembles a valve without the butterfly or counterbalance weight.

Mufflers are galvanized on the exterior and have an embossed "W" to represent the manufacturer. At the rear of each muffler there is one welded-on bracket to which the rear hangar bolts. Mufflers are welded to the intermediate exhaust pipe, not clamped. On those 1968 Corvettes so equipped, 2 1/2-inch intermediate pipes are flattened somewhat where they pass underneath the rear camber adjustment rod bracket for additional ground clearance. 2-inch pipes are not flattened.

In 1968 and 1969 a round, chrome-plated steel exhaust tip is clamped to each muffler. The tips are the same both years.

Fuel Lines, Brake Lines, and Miscellaneous Chassis and Underbody Components.

All 1968 and 1969 fuel lines run along, and at times through, the right-side chassis rail. All cars except those equipped with an L88, L89, L71, or ZL1 engine have two fuel lines. One supplies fuel from the tank to the carburetor and the other is a return line. The two lines run parallel to one another.

Fuel lines are galvanized carbon steel. Black rubber fuel hose connects the lines to the tank and the fuel pump. Galvanized tower clamps are used to secure the hose to its line in 1968. Zinc chromate–plated spring clamps are usually used in 1969. Exceptions to this include the hoses on the fuel return line, which may use small, galvanized tower-style clamps.

Brake lines are galvanized carbon steel. Brake line end fittings are brass. Fittings at the master cylinder are often seen with red or blue dye, which was probably used to denote the two different sizes. In addition, daubs of yellow paint are sometimes seen on the fittings at junction blocks.

Various heat shields are affixed to the underside of the body to help insulate the passenger compartment from engine and exhaust system heat.

All cars are fitted with transmission tunnel insulation. A semi-rigid foil-wrapped blanket in the shape of the tunnel is fastened above the transmission with clips riveted to the underbody.

Early 1968s have an aluminum foil–backed fiberglass insulation pad at the base of the firewall. Later 1968s use a white plastic shield in this area instead. Early 1968s also utilize a semi-gloss painted triangular steel shield on each side underneath the firewall area.

On late 1968s and all 1969s, the previously used foil-backed insulation and triangular steel heat shield are replaced with a large, rectangular steel shield. This shield, which is gray phosphate plated, is mounted on the lower vertical area of the firewall on both sides.

All cars, with the possible exception of some earlier 1968s, have a thick, black foam insulating pad attached to the underbody above the engine's bellhousing. Also, a thick, white foam pad is fastened to the underbody on each side of the car just forward of the doors. 1969s equipped with side-mount exhaust do not have these pads.

A variety of steel plates are fastened to the underbody to mount components in the passenger compartment. These components include the battery, seats, jack hold down clips, and so on. All of these plates are painted semi-gloss black and are retained by unpainted, aluminum rivets.

Chapter 2

1970–1972

1970–1972 Exterior

In 1970 the Corvette's body was modified in subtle but easily recognizable ways. The front fender and rear quarter panel areas behind each of the four wheels are flared out rather than tucked under as they had previously been. The flares are intended to catch stones and other road debris kicked up by the wheels, and in fact they work quite well, preventing the paint chips so prevalent on 1968 and 1969 models. The flares in the fenders and quarter panels continued unchanged for 1971 and 1972.

All 1970–1972 cars were painted with acrylic lacquer. Factory paint is generally smooth and shiny, though some orange peel is evident throughout. Roughness and poor coverage are fairly typical along the very bottom edges of body panels. Clear coat was not used by the factory, even with metallic colors. Because clear coat was not used, metallics tend to be slightly mottled or blotchy.

Front bumpers are chrome plated and held to the car with semi-gloss painted steel brackets. Cadmium-plated hex head bolts are used to retain the bumper to the brackets and cadmium and/or black oxide hex head bolts hold the brackets to the chassis.

The two front grille assemblies are made from cast metal that is silver gray in color with chrome trim. In 1970 they are retained by one chrome Phillips oval head screw in the upper outside corner and three studs that are not readily seen when they are installed on the car. They are retained by three of these screws for 1971–1972. There is, however, overlap and late 1970s (assembled in June or July of 1970) may have the later grilles while early 1971s (assembled in December 1970 or earlier) may have the earlier units.

The front parking lamp housings are part of the front grilles. In 1970–1971 they get clear plastic lenses with amber-colored bulbs. In 1972 they get amber lenses with clear bulbs. Chrome Phillips head screws hold the lenses in. Both 1970s and 1971s, assembled through the end of June 1971, have a fiber-optic cable inserted into the top of each parking light housing. The 1971s built in July 1971 and all the 1972s have no fiber optics and have no holes for the cables in the parking light housings.

Rectangular-shaped side marker lamps are used at all four corners in 1970–1972. The lamp housings, which can only be seen from behind the body panels, are made from diecast aluminum. Later replacements have plastic bodies. Front side marker lamps have amber lenses while rears have red lenses.

The 1970–1972 front license plate brackets are painted semi-gloss black and are held on by two cadmium-plated hex head bolts. A small rubber bumper is inserted in a hole toward the bottom center, and two white plastic nuts insert into square holes in the upper corners. A small, brown paper bag marked "LICENSE PLATE SCREWS" came in the car originally. In it were four large, cadmium-plated, slotted pan head screws for the front and rear license plates.

All four headlamp bulbs in 1970–1972 were made by Guide and feature a Guide T-3 logo in the glass. The 1970–1971 bulbs have a centered triangle with "T-3" surrounded by vertical bars. Some late 1971s (assembled May and June of 1971) and 1972s have the "T-3" enclosed in squares and rectangles centered at the bottom of the bulb's face.

Headlamp bezels are diecast aluminum and painted body color. Paint on the bezels is usually not as shiny or smooth as it is on the body. The 1970s and early 1971s have two headlamp washer nozzles in the bezels. Both nozzles are pointed at the low beam (outer) bulb, one from above and one from below.

The 1971s assembled after December 1970 do not have the headlamp washer system, though cars assembled through at least March 1971 may have bezels with nozzle holes but no nozzles, nozzles, or nozzles on one bezel and just holes on the other.

A semi-gloss black plastic shield is behind each front grille to shield the headlamps from view when the light assemblies are in the down position. The shields are each held to the body by three self-tapping, black phosphate Phillips pan head screws with integral flat washers.

A cadmium dichromate vacuum actuator is mounted behind each headlamp assembly. A red-striped hose connects to the back of each actuator and a green-striped hose connects to the front.

The 1970–1972 front fenders got a redesigned vent area, which features a cast-metal grille fastened into a recess in the fiberglass. Each grill is held in place by two recessed Phillips flat head screws at the top and a stud and nut on the bottom. Because the grilles were already mounted when the car was painted, the screw heads are body color, and the underside of the rectangular boxes formed in the grille frequently show poor paint coverage. For 1970s and early 1971s (cars assembled up to about the first week of September 1970), fender grilles have chrome edges on horizontal surfaces only. Later 1971s and 1972s have chrome on vertical and horizontal surfaces.

Both fenders have an emblem reading "Stingray" above their grilles. The emblems are chrome with a thin stepped edge that surrounds each letter and is painted black. Emblems are held onto the body by a thick, black adhesive strip that is visible, and each has four long studs that were used for positioning only and therefore do not get nuts. Original emblems feature the letter "i" without a dot while later replacements have a small groove cut into the "i" to simulate the dot.

All 1970–1972 cars originally equipped with a small-block engine, except those with the optional LT-1, have a low-profile hood with a single wind split down the middle. There are no emblems, decals, or other markings on these hoods. LT-1- and 454-ci equipped cars have a raised area with twin simulated vents in the center of their hoods for added engine clearance. The leading edge of each simulated vent has a cast-metal piece of trim that is chrome, except on its inside, where it is painted semi-gloss black.

Hood Graphics

The 454-ci-equipped cars have a 454 emblem on each side of the hood's bulge. The emblems are

The side fender emblem used in 1969–1976. Emblems used on later cars (this example is from a 1972) have a distinct dot over the "i" whereas those used on earlier cars do not.

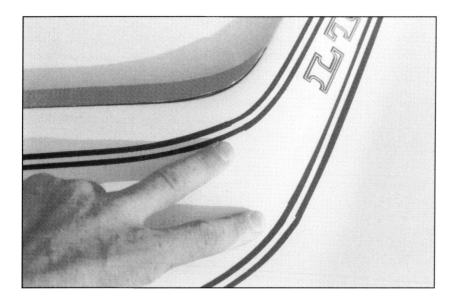

LT-1 hood stripes were painted on 1970–1972 cars using an adhesive-backed mask. Original stripes, like the example shown, tend to be slightly misaligned where the mask sections met one another. In addition, the edges of the stripes are normally not razor sharp along their entire length.

The "LT-1" decals are placed between the two stripes on each side of the hood bulge. 1970 Corvettes assembled through approximately mid-May 1970 have silver decals outlined in black whereas later cars have white decals outlined in black.

chrome with painted black recesses. LT-1-powered cars have special paint striping and LT-1 hood decals. There are two bands of striping, each consisting of two thin stripes. The stripes are either black or white depending on what color the car is painted. In 1970, the individual thin stripes that compose each of the two larger stripes differ in width in their front portion only. The front portion of the two inside thin stripes measures 1/4 inch wide while the front portion of the two outside thin stripes measures 1/8 inch wide. As the two 1/4-inch thin stripes curve around the hood bulge and extend rearward they taper down to 1/8 inch. The 1970 LT-1s assembled from mid- to late July 1970 had these unequal stripes, whereas on very late 1970 through 1972 models all four thin stripes are 1/8 inch wide

all the way around. The gaps between the two thin stripes in each band of striping are 1/8 inch for all 1970–1972 LT-1s.

Hood Stripes

The 1970 hood stripes were originally applied with a four-piece mask that resulted in a sharp point where the stripes met in the middle of the hood. The mask was changed in 1971–1972 to three pieces, and the point was rounded instead of sharp. Whether created from the earlier four-piece or later three-piece mask, the stripes tend to be slightly misaligned where the mask sections meet. In addition, the edges of the stripes are normally not razor sharp along their entire length. The LT-1 decals are placed between the two stripes on each side of the hood bulge. Earlier 1970 cars assembled through mid-May 1970 have silver decals outlined in black, while later cars all had white decals outlined in black.

Windshield Vent Grille

The windshield vent grille is painted body color and is retained by black oxide recessed Phillips flat head screws with fine threads. The windshield wiper door is also painted body color. A stainless-steel trim strip is on the windshield edge of the wiper door. The strip is painted body color except for an unpainted polished bead that runs adjacent to the windshield. The strip is attached to the wiper door with small round head rivets on either end in 1970 and part of 1971. Later 1971s and 1972s use small Phillips flat head screws.

Wiper Arms

Wiper arms and blade holders are dull black in color and each holder says "TRICO" on one of its ends. A length of washer tubing is soldered to a small tab at the end of each wiper arm and is further retained by between one and four black plastic clips. (According to Chevrolet's Assembly Instruction Manual three clips should hold the left tube while four were to be used for the right, but in reality the number varies from car to car.)

Wiper blade inserts say "TRICO" and have various patent numbers molded in. Two raised ribs are present below all of the writing.

Windshields and Windows

All 1970–1972 Corvette windshields were manufactured by Libby-Owens-Ford (LOF) utilizing Safety Plate glass. The LOF logo, the words "SAFETY PLATE," and a two-letter manufacturing date code

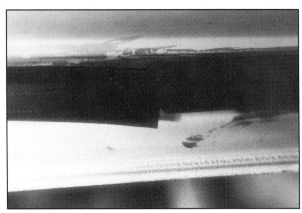

As shown in this 1972 example, main door weather stripping is two separate pieces that shows a gap in the center on the bottom of the door. Note the sloppy application of weather strip adhesive that is typical of all Corvettes.

are etched into the lower right side of the windshield. In the date code, one letter represents the month and the other denotes the year, There is no discernible pattern to the letter usage, so you must refer to the glass date codes in Appendix R.

The letters "ASI" are present in the upper right portion of the windshield. These letters are white and sandwiched between the laminates of glass, not etched into the surface like the logo and date code.

Both side windows are made from tinted LOF Safety Flo Lite glass that has the manufacturer's logo and a two-letter date code etched in, just like the windshield. The words "Astro Ventilation" are present in white silk-screened letters in the lower forward corner of each window.

Back windows in 1970–1972 coupes, like the windshields and side glass, have the LOF logo and manufacturing date code etched in. All 1970–1972 Corvettes have one outside rearview mirror that is mounted on the driver's door. A mounting base is held to the door by two screws, and the mirror goes over the base and is held on by a black oxide Allen head screw. A thin gasket goes between the base and door and is visible when the mirror is installed.

The mirror's head is rectangular and measures 3-7/8 inches high by 5-3/8 inches wide. The glass is coded with the manufacturer's symbol and a date code. Mirrors supplied by Donnelly Mirror, Inc. have "DMI" in the code, and those supplied by Ajax Mirror have "AX" in it. For example, the code in a Donnelly-supplied mirror manufactured in April 1971 would read "4-DMI-1" while the code for an Ajax-supplied mirror manufactured in February 1970 would read "2-AX-70."

Door Handles and Locks

All 1970–1972 door handles are a spring-loaded, press flap design. On original handles the spring action is provided by a coil spring on the hinge shaft. A butterfly spring covering a coil spring is incorrect. When the flap is depressed, the spring is visible. A thin, black rubber gasket is visible between the handle and door.

The door locks, which are positioned below the door handles, feature a polished stainless-steel bezel. Original bezels are retained to the cylinders by means of a continuous crimp around their entire circumference. Incorrect replacement locks may have bezels retained by four tangs. A thin, black rubber gasket is visible between the lock and door.

Side rocker moldings for all 1970–1972s are brushed aluminum with a painted 3/8-inch-wide flat black stripe along their length. In 1970–1971s they attach to the body with six black oxide Phillips oval

All door locks, as well as audio alarm key switches utilized after mid-June 1970, feature a polished stainless-steel bezel that is retained by means of a continuous crimp around its entire circumference as shown here. Incorrect replacements have bezels retained by four tangs. The thin, black rubber gasket visible beneath the lock is correct.

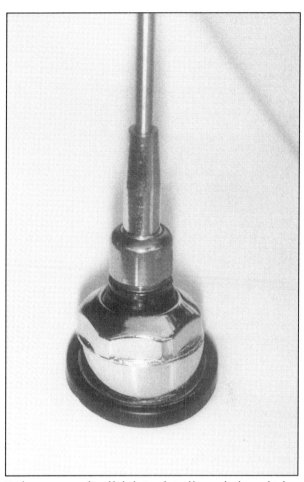

Fixed-mast antennas utilize a black plastic gasket and base, and a chrome-plated spacer, hex nut, and mast nut.

head screws. On 1972s the forward two and rearmost screws are often pan head instead of oval head.

In addition to the six screws that go through the face toward the top edge, original rocker moldings also have a single vertical fastener that goes through a tab on the molding's lower lip near the front and into a J-nut on the body. In 1970 and part of 1971 a black oxide fillister head screw is used here while later 1971s and 1972s usually use a black oxide hex head screw.

Radio Antennas and Vent Grilles

A radio was still an option for Corvettes in 1970–1972 and several hundred cars were built without one. On those cars no radio antenna was installed, but on all others an antenna was mounted on the driver-side rear deck. Most antennas utilize a fixed-height mast, though some originals have telescoping masts. Either way, the antenna ball is .300 inch in diameter, not .250 inch as seen on later replacements. A black plastic gasket goes between the antenna base and the car's body. The base is also made of black plastic and it, along with the portion of the antenna assembly beneath the body, is retained by a chrome hex nut. A chrome cap with two flat areas for a wrench to grab holds the mast to the base.

Two vent grilles are installed on the rear deck behind the back window (or behind the convertible top deck on convertibles). The vent grilles are painted

Front fender vent grilles on 1970-1972s were all painted body color. The grilles in cars made before mid-September 1970 have chrome edges on the horizontal ridges only. Subsequent cars have chrome edges on the vertical ridges as well.

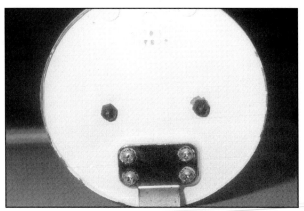

The underside of the gas lid door from an unrestored 1972. Chrome-plated Phillips head screws hold the door to a chrome-plated hinge.

Two different twist-on gas caps were used in 1970–1972. 1970 and early 1971 caps are cadmium plated, whereas later 1971 and 1972 caps are gold irridite plated. The 1970-style caps have only "SEALED" stamped into them whereas the 1971- and 1972-style, shown here, has "OPEN SLOWLY CAUTION" in addition to "SEALED." Some early 1971s have a separate red plate attached with "OPEN SLOWLY CAUTION" in white letters.

body color and are each retained by four black oxide Phillips flat head screws. The grilles sit on lips in the body, and the vent channels below are sprayed with flat black paint in varying degrees of coverage.

Gas Lid Doors

Gas lid doors are painted body color and feature a chrome and painted crossed flags emblem that is held on by cadmium acorn nuts visible with the door open. In 1970 a latch that is part of the hinge assembly holds the door in the open position. A tab riveted to the underside of the door inserts into a receptacle in the body bezel formed from two white pieces of nylon to hold the door closed. In 1971–1972 an over-center spring integral to the hinge holds the door both open and closed. For all years, gas lid door hinges are chrome plated and the door is held to the hinge with chrome-plated Phillips fillister head screws. The polished door bezel is held to the body with black oxide Phillips flat head screws. The1970 doors don't use any rubber bumpers while 1971 and 1972 doors have two bumpers that insert into the bezel toward the rear of the car.

Gas Caps

All 1970–1972s came with a twist-on gas cap, not a locking cap. The locking caps, which are usually flat and chrome plated, were dealer installed or aftermarket. 1970 and early 1971 caps are cadmium plated while later 1971 and 1972 caps are gold irridite plated. The 1970 caps have "SEALED" stamped into them while 1971–1972s have "OPEN SLOWLY CAUTION" in addition to "SEALED." Some early 1971s have a plate attached with "OPEN SLOWLY CAUTION" in white letters. For all years, the cap has a handle for twisting it on and off. The handle is attached by two ears that are bent over and spot welded onto the cap. On original

1970 and early 1971 caps, the ears face down when the word "SEALED" is upright. With later 1971 and all 1972 caps, the ears face down when "SEALED" is upside down, and "OPEN SLOWLY CAUTION" is upright.

A black rubber boot surrounds the gas filler neck on all 1970–1972s. The boot has a plastic nipple facing the rear of the car, and a rubber drain hose attaches to it. The hose, which has a metal spring inside to prevent it from collapsing, runs down behind the gas tank and exits the body through a hole adjacent to one of the rear bumper braces. A black plastic tie wrap holds the hose to the bumper brace.

Rear Fascia, Taillamps, Bumpers, and Related Parts

The rear body panel has "CORVETTE" spelled out in eight individual letters centered between the taillamps. Each letter is chrome plated with silver paint in its recessed face. An audio alarm was optional in 1970–1971 and standard equipment in 1972. All cars so equipped have a lock cylinder switch on the rear body panel between the taillamps and above the Corvette letters. The1970s, assembled until some time in June 1970, use an open-style lock cylinder while subsequent cars use cylinders with spring-loaded face plates and crimped-over bezels like the door locks. As with the door locks, the bezel should be crimped over around its full circumference. Incorrect replacement locks have bezels with four tabs that bend over.

The recessed area of the body, where the rear license plate mounts, is covered by a diecast surround trim that is chrome plated. A lamp assembly mounts at the top of the recess behind the rear body panel and illuminates the rear license plate. For

Early 1971s and previous cars utilize taillamp lenses that have concentric lines and come to a subtle point in the center. Later 1971s and subsequent cars all have a lens that is more rounded with a checkerboard pattern on the inside as shown. Through 1973, lenses are retained with three black oxide Phillips pan head screws. Starting in 1974, lenses were integral to the housing, and therefore no screws were needed.

1970–1973 Corvettes utilize chrome-plated rectangular exhaust tips. The bezel trimming the opening in the body is also chrome plated.

1970–1971s a fiber-optic cable inserts into the license lamp housing. A black rubber bumper is inserted into the rear valance panel centered toward the lower edge of the license plate. Two white plastic push nuts insert into square cutouts in the rear body panel for the license plate retaining screws.

The 1970–1972s all utilize four rear lamps. The two outer ones utilize red lenses that function as taillamps, stop lamps, and turn signals. The two inner ones utilize red lenses with clear plastic centers that function as back-up lamps. The 1970s and early 1971s (through January 1971 production) use a conical-shaped back-up lens with concentric grooves on the inside. Later

1971s and 1972s have a rounded lens with a checkerboard pattern on the inside. All lenses are retained with three black oxide Phillips pan head screws.

Rear bumpers are chrome plated and are attached to the body with semi-gloss black painted brackets. As with the front bumpers, cadmium-plated hex head bolts retain the bumpers to the brackets and cadmium- and/or black oxide–plated hex head bolts hold the brackets to the chassis.

The rear valance panel is painted body color but often shows poor paint quality including runs or sparse coverage along the bottom edge. It is retained to the body by four cadmium-plated indented hex

Optional P02 deluxe wheel covers were available from 1969–1973. The covers utilized on Corvettes are the same as those used on other Chevrolet products with the exception of the ornamental disc in the center, which protrudes on Corvettes but is flat on other cars.

head bolts. The two outer ones utilize integral washers while the two inners have separate flat washers.

Exhaust Systems

All 1970–1972s originally came with undercar exhaust systems, not side pipes. The exhaust tips exit the rear of the car through rectangular cutouts in the body. The cutouts are trimmed with chromed diecast bezels that are rectangular in shape but with open bottoms. The bezels are retained by chrome Phillips oval head screws.

Convertible Tops

Convertible tops are made from vinyl with a woven pattern. The convertible top is available in either white or black regardless of exterior body color. The front header roll and tack strip cover are also vinyl but have a grained rather than woven pattern. Two small stainless-steel trim pieces cover the ends of the tack strip. The trim pieces are flared around their perimeter and attach with one small, bright Phillips flat head screw. The back window is clear vinyl and is heat sealed, not sewn, to the top.

The convertible top back window contains a manufacturer's logo, manufacturing date, and the words "VINYLITE, TRADE MARK, AS-6" and "DO NOT RUB DRY WASH WITH WATER SOAKED CLOTH" heat stamped in the driver-side lower cor-

ner. The date code is normally three or four numbers, with the first one or two representing the month and the second two representing the year. For example, a convertible top manufactured in April 1971 would have a date code of "471." A paper label is sewn into the top in the corner below the heat-stamped logo and date in the window.

As an extra cost option, a removable hardtop was available for convertibles in addition to the standard soft top. The hardtop is painted body color unless vinyl covered. All vinyl-covered hardtops are black. The hardtop rear window contains the LOF manufacturing logo and is date coded with two letters like the remainder of the body glass. The first letter represents the month of production and the second represents the year of production. (See Appendix R for glass date codes.)

Tires, Wheels, and Wheel Covers

The majority of 1970–1972 Corvettes have either Goodyear or Firestone F70x15 bias-ply nylon cord tires with raised white letter, US Royal tires are believed correct for 1972 only.

The standard tire for all three years is a blackwall. Whitewalls and raised white letter tires are available as extra cost options. Whitewalls are either Firestone Super Sport Wide Ovals or Goodyear Speedway Wide Treads. The Firestones have a 3/8-inch white stripe that is 1-7/8 inches from the bead edge. The

Optional PO2 deluxe wheel covers require valve stem extensions, which were included in a brown envelope placed in the car. The extensions, which thread onto the standard stems, have a white inner shaft that is visible because they are not fitted with caps.

Goodyears have a 5/16-inch white stripe that is 1 inch from the bead edge.

Raised white letter Goodyears say "Wide Tread F70-15" in block letters. Raised white letter Firestones say "Firestone Wide Oval" in block letters. Raised white letter US Royals say "Uniroyal Tiger Paw" in block letters.

All 1970–1972s are equipped with steel Rally wheels. They are painted a color called Argent Silver for all three years, but actually two different colors are used. The 1970 Argent Silver has a slight greenish hue while 1971–1972 Argent Silver is a noticeably brighter, more silvery color. The back sides of the Rally wheels are painted semi-flat black and always have silver overspray, since the front side was painted silver after the black was applied to the rear.

All wheels are stamped with a date code, manufacturer's logo, and size code on the front face. All 1970–1972 Corvette wheels are 15x8 inches and have the code "AZ" stamped in to indicate this. The "AZ" is adjacent to the valve stem hole.

Also adjacent to the valve stem hole is the manufacturer's logo and date code stamping. On one side of the hole it says "K" for the wheel manufacturer, Kelsey Hayes. This is followed by a dash and a "1" that represents Chevrolet. Next comes another dash and either a "0," "1," or a "2" to denote the last digit of the year of manufacture. This is followed by a space and one or two numbers to indicate the month of manufacture. On the other side of the valve stem hole are one or two more numbers that represent the day of manufacture. Stainless-steel trim rings and chrome center caps are standard for all cars. Original trim rings are held to the wheel by four steel clips.

All Corvette Rally wheels are stamped with a date code, manufacturer's logo, and size code on the front face. "K" represents the wheel manufacturer, Kelsey Hayes; the "1" represents Chevrolet; the "2" denotes 1972, the year of manufacture; and the "4," which happens to be a weak stamping in this particular wheel, indicates April, the month of manufacture. On the other side of the valve stem is "13," representing the day of manufacture. The final stamping, which is also rather weak, is "AZ," which indicates that this is a 15x8-inch Corvette wheel.

Center caps should read "Chevrolet Motor Division" in black painted letters.

A full wheel cover is available as an extra cost option for all 1970–1972 Corvettes. Called option PO2, this cover has a stainless-steel outer rim and closely spaced radial fins that converge outward toward a protruding ornamental disc in the center. The disc is chrome around its edge, black in the middle, and contains the Corvette crossed flags emblem. Other Chevrolet products use a similar wheel cover, but those have a flat center disc instead of the protruding disc utilized for Corvettes.

Leather seat upholstery was part of the Custom Interior Trim offered in 1970–1976. The black insert at the top of the seatback was used from 1970 through 1975. The horizontal stitching first appeared late in the 1971 model year and continued through 1977. Seats from 1974 and earlier have eight stitched seams in the lower cushion, whereas 1975 and newer cars have six.

Wheels on cars equipped with standard trim rings and center caps utilize black rubber valve stems that measure approximately 1-1/4 inches long. These are fitted with caps that come to a point and have longitudinal ridges around their entire perimeter.

Wheels on cars equipped with optional full wheel covers have extensions threaded onto the standard valve stems. The extensions have a white color inner shaft that is visible because they are not fitted with caps.

To ease the balancing process, wheels are sometimes marked with a tiny weld drop or paint dot at their highest point. This mark is lined up with an orange dot on the tire. Balance weights are the type that clamp onto the edge of the rim and are placed on the inside of the wheel only. Original balance weights usually have the letters "OEM" molded into their face. There is usually a small white or colored dot of paint on the tire adjacent to each balance weight.

All cars have a full-size spare tire and wheel that is identical to the other four tires and wheels. The spare wheel is not fitted with a wheel cover like the other four.

The spare tire and wheel are housed in a carrier bolted to the rear underbody area. The carrier is fiberglass with steel supports. The fiberglass is unpainted, and the steel support is painted semi-gloss black. The tire tub portion of the carrier has a fair amount of flat to semi-gloss black paint on its outside surface applied during the blackout process. A lock covered by a black rubber boot goes over the spare tire carrier access bolt.

1970–1972 Interior

Interior trim color and material, as well as exterior body color and body assembly date, are stamped into an unpainted stainless-steel plate attached to the dri-

Shoulder belts have an instructional/caution tag sewn to them. Like seatbelts, they are made from a three-row webbing material and are the same color as the carpet. Shoulder belt material is slightly thinner than that used for lap belts. The plastic casing around the buckle discourages it from scratching the metal trim piece it passes through and prevents the spring-loaded belt from pulling through the seatback. The example shown is from a 1972 model.

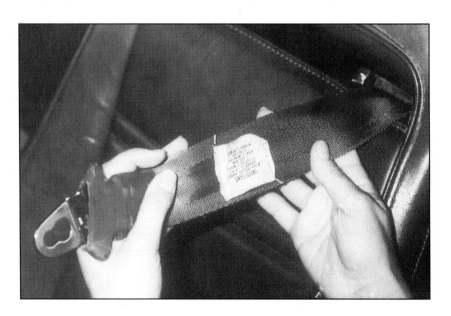

All 1968–1982 lap belts have a tag with the manufacturer's name and a date code sewn on. Hamill was the manufacturer through 1974 and Firestone, which purchased Hamill, was the manufacturer thereafter. On this example, "44 E 71" is a date code that translates to the 44th week of 1971. The letter between the numbers may represent the day of the week, with "A" being Monday, "B" being Tuesday, and so on, but since the vast majority of tags contain an "E," there is some doubt about this. After all, it is unlikely that nearly all belts were made on just Fridays.

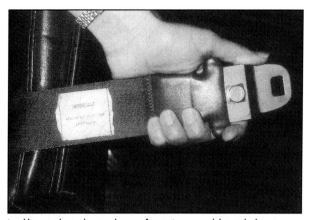

In addition to the tag bearing the manufacturer's name and date code there is a second tag containing safety instructions sewn to all lap belts. Note the correct three-row webbing material and color-matched plastic sheath covering part of the metal buckle on this 1972 example.

ver's door hinge pillar by two aluminum Pop Rivets. This plate is commonly called a trim plate or trim tag.

Trim color and material is indicated in the plate by a three-number code. For example, in 1970 trim code 424 indicates saddle color with leather seat covers. Exterior body paint is likewise indicated by a three-number code stamped in the trim plate. For example, in 1972 code 946 indicates Elkhart Green. (See Appendix T for paint and interior trim codes.)

The body build date represents the date when the painted and partially assembled body reached that point on the assembly line where the trim plate was installed. The car's final assembly date is typically one to several days after the body build date. A letter indicating the month followed by two numbers indicating the day represents the body build date. The letter "A" was assigned to the first month of production, which was January in 1970 and August in 1971 and 1972. The second month of production (September) was assigned "B," and so on. A body assembled on the sixth day of August 1971 would have "A06" stamped into the trim plate, for example, and a body built on the 11th day of May 1970 would have "E11" stamped into its plate. (See Appendix S for body build dates.)

Standard seat upholstery was a combination of very slightly grained flat vinyl with Chevrolet's "comfort-weave" vinyl inserts sewn into the seat bottoms and backs. Vinyl seats for 1970–1972 all had vertical insert panels. Leather was available as an extra cost option but only in black or saddle. From 1970 through late 1971, leather seats had vertical panels, while late 1971s and all 1972s had horizontal panels.

Each seat rests on two seat tracks, which allow for forward and rearward adjustment of the seat's position. The tracks are black phosphate and each is held to the floor by one black phosphate, indented hex head bolt at each end for a total of four per seat. The front bolts are covered by a flap of carpet that was cut away, while the rear bolts simply pass through the carpet. The seat adjust lever is black phosphate with a chrome ball screwed onto its end.

The seat backs are made of molded plastic and match interior color. The seat back release button and its bezel are both chrome plated. Two bolts that allow for the adjustment of seat back position are bright silver and have a rubber cushion over their heads. The 1970s assembled prior to April 1970 do not have plastic washers under the seat back release bezel or adjustment bolts. Later 1970s and all 1971s and 1972s do have them in these places.

All 1970–1972 coupes were equipped with lap and shoulder belts while convertibles came with standard lap belts and optional shoulder belts as an extra cost option. All belts were manufactured by a company called Hamill, and a tag bearing that name is sewn to them. The tag also bears the date that particular belt was manufactured. This date is indicated by an ink stamping with a number representing the week of the year, a letter representing the day of the week ("A" being Monday, "B" being Tuesday, and so on,) and another number representing the year. For example, a stamping of "16 D 72" means April 20, 1972. The "16" representing the 16th week of the year,

This 1972 door panel illustrates some of what was included with the Custom Interior Trim option. Plush-cut pile carpet is added along the bottom of the panels, a strip of chrome trim covers the gap where the carpet meets the vinyl, and a band of veneered walnut wood trim is added to the area behind the door pull.

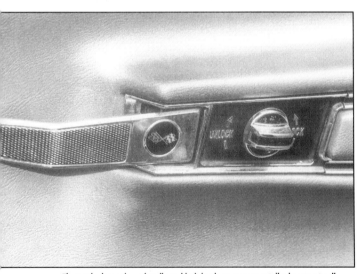

The inside door release handle and lock knob appear essentially the same in all years, but release handles differ on their underside. In early 1968s the back of the handle is smooth, in later 1968s it has two ridges, and in 1969 and subsequent cars it has four ridges.

which was the week of April 17th–21st, "D" representing the fourth day of the week, which was Thursday, April 20th, and "72" representing the year 1972.

In addition to the tag bearing the manufacturer's name and date code there is another, smaller tag sewn to the outboard lap belts close to the male latch. This tag reads "IMPORTANT wear lap belt at all times. Adjust snugly." A similar tag is sewn at the same position on each of the shoulder harness belts. This tag reads "IMPORTANT Attach shoulder harness securely to lap belts. Do not use if wearer is less than 4 feet 7 inches tall. Do not use without a lap belt." All belts are made from a three-row webbing material and are the same color as the carpet. The material used for lap belts is slightly thicker than that used for shoulder belts.

In 1970 and 1971 there is a chrome clip attached to the front of each seat bottom to hold the outboard lap belts when they are not in use. Also for these two years, there is a plastic collar around each outboard belt and its tail (the loose end or slack in the belt used for adjustment) to keep the tail from flapping around. The plastic collar is the same color as the belts.

In 1972 the outboard belts are on a spring-loaded retractable coil, so the retaining clips on the seat bottoms and plastic tail collars are eliminated. The retractor for 1972 also includes an integral switch that controls the seatbelt alarm buzzer. The retractors are beneath each seat under a plastic cover.

Inboard portions of the seatbelts are encased in a semi-rigid plastic that goes over part of the female buckles. The buckles are brushed silver in color, and the black release buttons each have a rigid metallic sticker that says "GM" in silver letters on a blue background.

All door panels are made from molded vinyl and match the interior color. With standard interiors (i.e., interiors with vinyl seat covers), the door panels are plain with no trim. Custom interiors include, in addition to either saddle or black leather seat covers, fancier door panels. A piece of plush-cut pile carpet is added along the bottom of the panels, and a strip of chrome trim covers the gap where the carpet meets the vinyl. In addition, custom door panels include a band of veneered walnut wood trim in the middle of the panel. With both standard and custom interiors, inside window felts are attached to the upper edge of the door panels with heavy staples, not Pop Rivets.

Door Panels, Door Handles, Door Jambs, and Door Hardware

Door panels are attached to the doors by means of black phosphate clips along the front, bottom, and rear. The clips insert into a cutout in the back of the panel and then get fastened to the door with black phosphate Phillips pan head screws. In addition, a chrome Phillips oval head screw goes through the face of each panel at the upper front and rear corners. In 1970 and part of 1971 these screws had a separate finishing washer, and from part of 1971 and all of 1972 the screws utilized an integral finishing washer.

Inside door release handles are chrome with black paint in the center knurled area. A round, black emblem features the crossed flags logo. The inside lock knob is chrome with a black stripe painted in the center indent. The inside door pull is a grained vinyl handle that matches interior color. Cars equipped with standard manual windows have chrome window cranks with opaque plastic knobs. Unlike some later replacements, the knobs on original cranks are about 1 inch away from the door panel's surface.

The door jambs and perimeter of each door are painted body color with the exception of the top front of each door, which is painted semi-gloss black. The door striker, which is the large pin threaded into the door post, and its corresponding receiver in the door are both cadmium plated. The striker is a special indented hex head bolt on 1970s built through Janu-

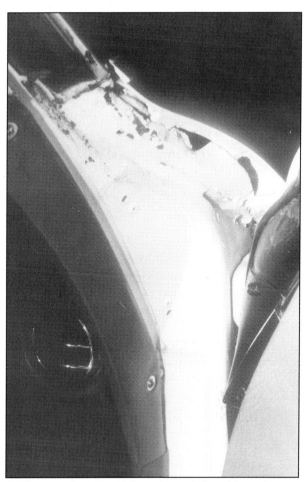

Though it improved as time passed, this roughness in the forward door jamb area is characteristic of 1968–1982 Corvettes. Note the large washers under the screws holding the trim on, and the blacked-out area on the forward surface of the door.

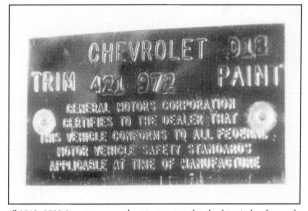

All 1968–1982 Corvettes came with a trim tag riveted to the driver's-door hinge pillar. This example, from a 1972, indicates Saddle leather interior trim (code 421), Classic White exterior paint (code 972), and a body build date of November 18 (code D18). The body build date codes for all St. Louis cars start with "A" for the first month of production, which was August for all years except 1970 (January), 1975 (October), 1978 (September), and 1980 (October).

ary 1970. In early February 1970 they changed to an indented star head design. The courtesy light pin switches and door ajar warning light/alarm system pin switches are cadmium plated and should not have any paint overspray. All pin switches have "SX," the manufacturer's logo, stamped into the head of their plunger.

As with the pin switches, door strikers, and door striker receivers, door alignment blocks and the door weather strip were added after the body was painted and should not have any body paint overspray. The main door weather stripping is two separate pieces and typically shows a gap in the center on the bottom of the door.

In 1970 and 1971 the water-deflecting strips, Pop Riveted to each door post near the door ajar warning light/alarm system pin switches, are painted body color since they were already installed when the body was painted. These strips were not used in 1972. Likewise, door hinges, bolts, and return springs (there

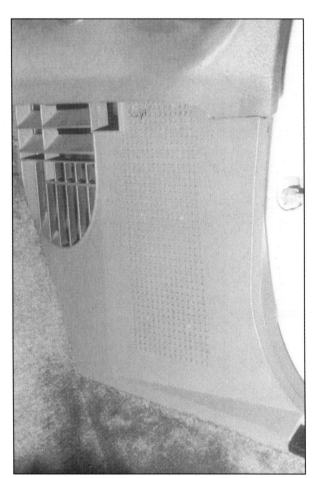

The original passenger-side kick panel from a 1972 without air conditioning. The panel would be crudely cut if the car had air conditioning. Replacement panels frequently have a slot cut in the dimples or a flat, rectangular area in the middle of the dimples.

should be one spring in each top hinge) are also painted body color.

The blue vehicle certification label, glued toward the top of the rear portion of the driver's door, is unpainted. It contains the VIN and month and year the vehicle was produced. At the end of calendar year 1971 (during early 1972 production) axle loading and gross vehicle weight ratings were added to the labels. Door sills are bright aluminum with black painted ribs. Each sill is held on with four black phosphate Phillips oval head screws.

The kick panels beneath the dash just forward of the doors are molded plastic and are interior color. On air-conditioned cars the passenger-side panel was cut by hand for increased clearance, and the cut is frequently rough. One chrome Phillips head oval screw in the forward, upper corner of each panel holds it in place. The panels have a bevy of small holes for the speakers that mount behind them. Speakers were never mounted in the kick panels. Some replacement kick panels have a slot in the speaker grille area and others have a solid rectangular area in the middle of the speaker grille holes. Neither style is original for 1970–1972.

The quarter trim panels just rearward of the doors are molded plastic to match the interior color. They are each held in place by a piece of metal trim retained by four chrome Phillips oval head screws. The quarter trim panels on coupes also have one chrome Phillips oval head screw with a trim washer at their top.

Carpet

In standard interiors carpet is made from an 80/20 loop pile molded material. In custom interiors it is made from plush-cut pile material. In all cases it matches interior color. Three rubber plugs in the driver's foot well and three more in the passenger's foot well help hold the carpet in place. The plugs pass through the carpet near its upper front edge.

Carpet covers the bulkhead behind the seats and has sewn-on binding on the lower edge where it overlaps the front floor carpet behind the seats. Rear storage compartment doors each have carpet under their frames. One piece of carpet covers the rear storage area floor and extends up the rear bulkhead. The edge at the top of the bulkhead is trimmed with sewn-on binding and is held by three rubber plugs. Separate pieces of untrimmed carpet cover the two wheelwells.

Carpet has a molded vinyl accelerator heel pad in the corner of the driver's foot well adjacent to the accelerator pedal. Heel pads in 1970s and 1971s assembled through approximately March 1971 have

This molded vinyl pad is sewn into the carpet above the headlamp dimmer switch. It is typical of what is found in cars made after approximately March 1971. The pads found in earlier 1971s and some 1970s have the manufacturer's logo, "IMCO," molded in. Most 1970s did not have any pad over the dimmer switch.

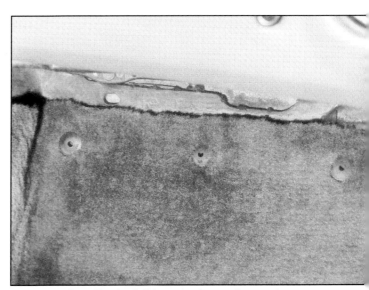

In 1968–1972, three rubber plugs hold the carpet in place near the upper edge in both foot wells. Later cars use a rubber flap attached to the firewall insulation to hold the carpet.

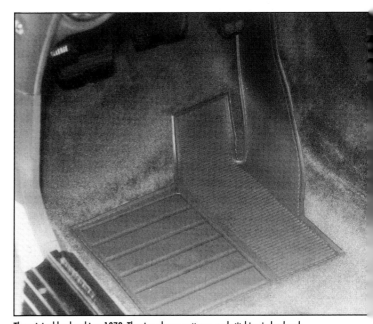

The original heel pad in a 1972. The size, shape, patterns, and stitching in heel pads found in replacement carpet often differ from originals.

horizontal ribs that extend right up to the top stitching holding the pad to the carpet. Pads for later 1971s and 1972s have ribs that stop about 3/8 inch from the stitching. The earlier-style pads have "IMCo," the Interstate Manufacturing Company's logo, molded in.

Some 1970s had a sewn-in, molded vinyl dimmer switch pad but most did not. Early 1971s with the first design heel pad have a dimmer switch pad which also bears the IMCo logo.

Dash Pad, Dash Panel

Upper dash pads, as well as driver's and passenger's dash panels, are made of soft vinyl and match interior color. The two vertical panels are attached to the upper pad by means of six Phillips oval head screws with conical washers. The screw heads are painted to match interior color, except in 1970 and early 1971s fitted with black interiors. In that case the screws are finished in a black oxide plating. Later 1971s and 1972s with black interiors use black painted screws. Dash pads have white stitching across their tops regardless of interior color. An interior color hard plastic grille is located in the defroster opening of the upper pad.

A three-pocket storage area is inset into the passenger-side dash panel. The storage pocket assembly is made from vinyl and is the same color as the interior. The dash panel has stitching around the opening

In this close-up of the top of the center section of an original 1972 carpet heel pad, notice how the closely spaced, molded-in horizontal ribs do not extend all the way up close to the stitched edge as they do on cars assembled prior to about April 1971. Also notice that the very top rib is rounded off on the top corners while all the others are squared off in this area.

for the storage pockets. The two smaller, outboard pockets are retained to the larger one with a single chrome-plated snap. A spring-loaded retainer behind the dash holds the three-pocket assembly tight against the dash panel.

Instrument Panel

All 1970–1972s have a headlamp switch mounted in the upper left corner of the driver-side dash pad. 1970–1971 headlight knobs are gloss-black grained plastic with a chrome disc in the center. A black plastic bezel behind the knob has the word "LIGHTS" in white letters.

1972 headlight knobs are gloss-black grained plastic like the earlier knobs, but instead of a chrome center they have an image of a headlamp with light rays coming out of it in their centers.

All 1970–1972 Corvettes have air vents on both sides of the dash toward the lower, outboard corner. The vent mechanisms are chrome spheres that rotate to change the direction of air flow. A push/pull knob next to each sphere controls the flow of air. In 1970–1971 the knob is chrome and in 1972 it is black.

The passenger-side dash pad in all 1969–1977 Corvettes features this three-pocket storage insert. Original inserts are stitched as shown.

A small, black T-handle pull mechanism beneath the driver-side dash on the left side releases the hood latch. The handle is black with the words "HOOD RELEASE" in white painted block letters across its face. The hood release cable is in a spiral-wound metal sheathing.

A semi-gloss black bracket beneath the steering column mounts the trip odometer reset knob, wiper door override switch, wiper arm override switch, and headlamp door override switch. The trip odometer reset knob has a grooved black rubber cover. The wiper door override switch has a large, round, shiny black knob with grooved edges. The wiper door override switch and headlamp door override switch are both vacuum switches that mount to either side of the wiper arm switch. The two vacuum switches have dull black plastic push/pull knobs.

Steering Wheel, Steering Column

All 1970–1972 steering wheels are black regardless of interior color. All wheels have grained vinyl rims molded to a three-spoke stainless-steel hub. Each of the spokes has a brushed finish with a pattern of parallel lines extending from the center of the wheel to the outer rim.

The standard steering column and optional tilt-telescoping column in 1970–1972 are painted whatever the interior color is in a semi-gloss finish. The tilt-telescoping column has a thick locking ring below the steering wheel to control the telescoping function. The ring is painted to match the rest of the column. Twisting the lever on the ring releases the locking mechanism and allows the column to telescope.

A lever similar to but shorter than the turn signal lever controls the tilt function of the optional steering column. The tilt lever is located between the turn signal lever and dash.

All columns have a four-way flasher switch mounted on the right side. All 1970 and 1971s built through approximately February 1971 equipped with a standard steering column use a switch with a one-piece chrome-plated knob that has black painted, debossed letters in the head spelling the word "FLASHER."

Later 1971s with a standard steering column use a black metal knob on the flasher switch instead of chrome. As in earlier cars the word "FLASHER" is debossed in the top of the knob only in later 1971s; the letters are painted white instead of black.

All 1970s and 1971s built through about March 1971 and equipped with the optional tilt-telescoping steering column use a different style chrome flasher knob than cars with standard columns. The knob has a longer shaft and the word "FLASHER" is pressed

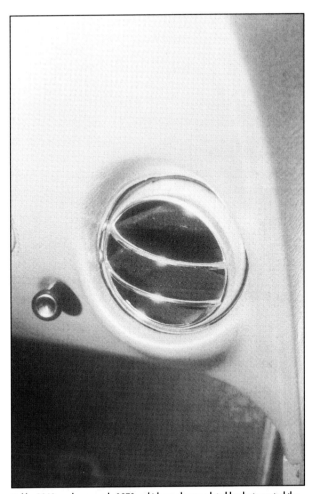

Unlike 1969s and some early 1970s, which use chrome-plated knobs to control the flow of air from the two dash-mounted vents, most 1970s and later cars use black plastic knobs.

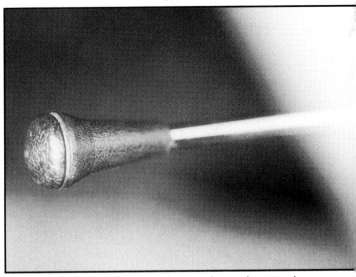

This is the second design of turn signal lever end. It was used on some late 1970 and early 1971 cars and on all subsequent cars through 1976. Rather than grooved, hard black plastic this second design is made from pliable, grained black rubber.

into the shaft rather than into the head. As with the standard column, the letters are painted black.

In 1972 the same flasher switch knob is used for both the standard steering column and the optional tilt-telescoping column. The knob is black with white lettering but is made of plastic rather than metal as it previously was. And unlike earlier versions, the 1972 knob has a black Phillips head screw through its center holding it on.

Turn Signal Levers

1970 and 1971 models used two different styles of turn signal levers. Both have a chrome-plated shaft, but the molded-on plastic ends differ. Very early 1970s use a gloss-black plastic end with molded-in grooves parallel to the chrome shaft. For the remainder of 1970 and 1971s built through approximately September 1970 this first design end continues to be used but a second design is added as well. The second design is similar to the first but does not have grooves in the gloss-black plastic end. Instead, the end is grained. Later 1971s, built from approximately September 1970 onward, use the lever with a grained end.

1972 (and possibly some late-1971) models use a third design turn signal lever. This third design has a dull black rubber end with a single concentric groove near the tip.

Cars equipped with standard steering columns and tilt-telescoping columns use the same design turn signal levers but the method of attachment differs slightly. On standard columns the lever is attached with a screw while on tilt-telescoping columns the lever threads in.

All 1970–1972 models use a textured metal horn button painted to match the interior. A crossed flag emblem is in the center of the button. In 1970 and 1972 the upper right-side square of the flag in the emblem is black, while in 1971 this same square is white.

Three pieces of vinyl-covered molding matched to the interior color cover the inside of the windshield frame for all 1970–1972 Corvettes. The two side pieces are held on by plastic retainers attached to the reverse side. The plastic retainers are not visible when the moldings are installed. In addition, each side molding has one chrome Phillips head screw retaining it at the top. The top piece of molding is retained by chrome recess head Phillips screws.

Sun Visors, Rearview Mirrors, Interior Mirrors

Sun visors are covered with padded soft vinyl that has the same Comfort-weave pattern as the vinyl seat covers. Each sun visor is held to the windshield frame with chrome recess head Phillips screws.

Beginning in approximately January 1972 a sticker describing the proper engine starting procedure is glued to the top of the driver-side sun visor. The sticker is white with black lettering and is made of nylon cloth.

All 1970–1972 Corvettes have an interior day/night rearview mirror mounted to the center of the upper windshield frame. The mirror is eight inches wide and is held to its mount with a slotted oval head screw. A piece of trim covered with interior-color vinyl is mounted over the base of the mirror mount at the windshield frame.

1970–1971 and some early 1972 interior mirrors have a stainless-steel housing with gray rubber trim around the perimeter. A gray lever at the bottom center moves the mirror between its "day" and "night" position.

1972 interior mirrors, with the exception of some early cars, have black vinyl with a grain pattern covering their housing. The vinyl-backed mirrors have black rubber trim around their perimeter but still use a gray day/night lever like the earlier stainless, housed mirrors.

Center Console, Instruments

The center console instrument cluster housing is cast metal painted semi-gloss black. In 1970 and 1971 there is a solid bar separating the seatbelt warning light from the button below it. Later replacement housings don't have this bar. 1972s have the seatbelt warning light and a buzzer but don't have a button below it to turn it off. Early 1972s have a timer that shuts both the light and buzzer off after about 15 seconds. In later 1972s the light and buzzer go off only after the seatbelt is extended or the parking brake is applied.

The windshield wiper/washer control switch is mounted above the center console instrument cluster housing. The switch knob is hard black plastic with the words "WASHER-PUSH" in white painted block letters on its face.

All gauges, including the speedometer and tachometer, have a flat black background and a straight red needle. Gauge numerals are slightly greenish in 1970 and 1971 and white in 1972. Tachometer redlines vary according to the engine. The high beam indicator light is red in cars assembled during January 1970 and blue in all cars thereafter.

Stereo

All 1970–1972 Corvettes came standard without a radio. For those cars not equipped with a radio a block-off plate is fitted to the cutout where the radio would otherwise go. The block-off plate for all three years is painted semi-gloss black and has a flat face with a thin, raised chrome border around its perimeter near the edge.

As an extra cost option one of two different Delco radios could be ordered. The first is an AM/FM push-button and the second is an AM/FM push-button with stereo reception. Both radios have a small slide bar above the dial that changes reception between AM and FM and both have "Delco" written in script lettering across the lens face.

All 1970–1972 stereo radios have indicator lights that come on when FM stereo is being received. In 1970 and 1971 the word "STEREO" appears in green and in 1972 an orange circle lights up.

In 1970–1971, radio knobs are shiny black plastic with silver accents. In 1972 the knobs are dull black rubber with white-colored pictorial inserts. The on/off volume knob on the left has a musical note while the tuning knob on the right has an antenna with a radiating signal.

Beneath the main radio knobs on all 1970–1972s is a secondary control, which is chrome plated. The one on the left controls tone and the one on the right, which is functional only on stereo-equipped cars, controls balance.

All 1970–1972 center consoles are made from molded vinyl in the same color as the interior. Park brake lever consoles are made from rigid molded plastic and also match interior color.

The insert in the top of the center console is painted semi-gloss black. Engine specifications are stamped into the insert that is located below the shifter. In 1970 and 1971, horsepower, torque, compression ratio, and engine displacement are indicated. In 1972 the horsepower designation was dropped and only torque, compression ratio, and engine size are specified.

Shifters

In manual transmission–equipped cars the shift pattern is indicated next to the shifter. The shift pattern area is semi-gloss black and the letters and numbers are chrome, as is a border around the pattern.

The shifter boot for all 1970–1972 manual transmission cars is made from black leather and has a sewn seam toward the passenger side of the car.

Optional Custom Interior Trim, offered in 1970–1976, included this walnut-veneer insert around the center console. Note the fresh-air vent levers, found on non-air-conditioned cars only. This style, with the black plastic ball on the end, was used from approximately January 1969 through 1976. Cars made before January 1969 use chrome-plated rectangular knobs.

Park brake consoles on 1968–1976 Corvettes are made from rigid plastic that matches interior color. Screws that hold it on (one can be seen toward the lower right) are chrome-plated Phillips head fitted with conical trim washers.

Manual shifters for all years have a chrome shaft and threaded-on black chrome ball. A T-handle integral to the shaft controls the reverse lock-out.

On those Corvettes equipped with an automatic transmission, the shift pattern is also next to the shifter. Chrome letters are used to indicate shifter position in 1970s built through approximately June 1970. 1970s built after approximately June 1970, as well as 1971s and 1972s, use a plastic lighted band with painted letters. The letters are painted to match the instrument faces; slightly greenish in 1970 and 1971 and white in 1972.

Rather than a boot, automatic transmission shifters are surrounded by a gloss-black plastic seal that slides back and forth as the shifter is moved.

Automatic shifters for all 1970–1972s are made from a chrome shaft topped by a black plastic ball. The ball has a chrome, spring-loaded button in the top to release the detent and allow the shifter to be moved.

Heating/Air Conditioning

Two types of heater/air-conditioning control assemblies are used in 1970–1972. The first, which is used in 1970–1971, has green letters and a separate fan switch plate that is inset into the larger assembly. In 1972 the letters are white and the fan switch is mounted directly behind the larger assembly, not in a separate small rectangle. With both style control assemblies, a chrome lever is used to set fan speed. All air-conditioned cars use a switch with four positions in addition to "off." Switches in non-air-conditioned cars only have three positions in addition to "off."

Whether the car is equipped with air conditioning or not, its control assembly employs two large black plastic rotary thumbwheels on either side. The left-side thumbwheel controls temperature and the right-side thumbwheel controls the system setting.

1970–1972 non-air-conditioned cars only have two fresh air vent controls on the center console. The controls are sliding levers made from small, black plastic balls with a flat area mounted to black oxide metal arms. In 1970–1971 the balls are smooth and shiny on their rounded portion and on their flat face. In 1972 the balls are still shiny black on the flat face but change to dull black with a grained pattern on the rounded portion only. All three years say "CLOSE" in white painted letters and have a white arrow on the balls' flat faces.

Ashtray, Cigarette Lighter

All 1970–1972s have an ashtray inset into the center console insert next to the heater/air-conditioning control assembly. The ashtray door is semi-gloss black and slides back and forth with slight resistance. The ashtray is chrome plated and can be removed for cleaning.

All cars are equipped with a cigarette lighter. All 1970–1971s and most 1972s use a lighter with a shiny black plastic knob that has a white circle and white concentric grooves in its face. Some 72s use a lighter with a chrome knob.

The lighters with black knobs have "63 CASCO 12V" stamped in the element while the lighters with chrome knobs have "72 CASCO 12V" stamped in.

On those 1970–1972 Corvettes equipped with the optional rear window defogger, a control switch is mounted on the left-side trim panel forward of the center console. The switch uses a large, round chrome-plated knob.

All 1970–1972 Corvettes have a park brake lever mounted between the seats. The lever's handle is made from hard, shiny black plastic with a crosshatch pattern to enhance grip. Chrome trim separates the black plastic grips. A release button on the top of the lever is made from hard, shiny black plastic also. The slotted opening in the park brake lever console is covered by a rippled, black plastic cover that slides along with the movement of the lever.

For all 1970–1972s, accelerator, brake, and clutch pedals have black rubber pads with horizontal ribs. 1970–1971 pedals have a polished metal surround while 1972 pedals do not.

In 1970–1971s the accelerator pedal measures 5-5/8 inches high by 2 inches wide. In 1972 the pedal is 4 inches high, 1-7/8 inches wide at the top and 1-5/8 inches wide at the bottom.

Storage Compartment

All 1970–1972s feature three enclosed storage compartments behind the seats. The lids for these compartments are made from press-board and are covered with carpet that matches the interior carpet. The underside of each lid is painted flat black. A white vehicle-maintenance sticker is on the underside of the center compartment lid for 1971s manufactured starting in mid-March 1971 and all 1972s. Stickers for tire pressure, jacking instructions, and the limited-slip differential are on the underside of the passenger-side compartment lid.

Each lid is surrounded by a molded plastic border that is painted to match interior color. The entire assembly of all three lids is also surrounded by a color-matched molded plastic border.

Each lid is hinged and latches with a spring-loaded mechanism. Each lid has a chrome button to release its latch and a vinyl hoop to pull it open. The vinyl hoop is the same color as the interior and is retained to the lid by a chrome Phillips head screw.

In 1970–1971 the center compartment is fitted with a locking chrome release button. In 1972 the center compartment does not have a locking button but the passenger-side compartment does.

For 1970s built through mid-June 1970 the same key operates the storage compartment lid lock and the spare tire compartment lock, but a different key operates the anti-theft alarm switch on those cars equipped with the optional anti-theft burglar alarm.

For 1970s built after mid-June 1970, as well as 1971–1972s, the key for the storage compartment lid lock is the same as the keys for the anti-theft alarm and spare tire storage compartment.

Each molded plastic border is held to its lid by chrome flat head Phillips screws. Each lid is held to its hinge by black oxide round head Phillips screws fitted with integral black oxide flat washers. Each hinge is held to the compartment surround by rivets. The whole assembly is held to the body by chrome flat head Phillips screws. The screws holding the rear of the assembly have chrome, countersunk integral washers.

The compartment directly behind the driver's seat holds the vehicle's battery. It has a thin foam seal around the perimeter of the door opening to help keep battery fumes from entering the passenger compartment.

Battery, Battery Cables

All 1970–1972 Corvettes use a side terminal Delco Battery. 1970s manufactured through approximately early June 1970 use two different model batteries.

Big-block-equipped cars or those with the heavy-duty battery option (option T60) use Delco model R 79W. Delco Model R 79S is standard for all small-block cars not equipped with the optional battery.

1970s assembled after early June 1970, as well as 1971–1972s, use Delco battery model R 89S for small blocks and model R 89W for big blocks and cars equipped with the heavy-duty battery option.

All of the batteries used in 1970–1972 have six cells that are covered by two plastic caps, each of which covers three cells. Each cap has three of the Delco split circle logos molded into its top. The split circles are painted dark orange. A black rubber vent hose runs from each of the caps through a hole in the underbody.

All 1970–1972 battery cables are side terminal–style and have red positive ends and black negative ends.

For 1970s assembled through approximately the end of March 1970, battery cables have a raised Delco split circle logo on both cable terminals. Both terminals are fastened to the battery with a 7/16-inch hex head bolt.

For 1970s assembled from approximately April 1970 through early June 1970 the Delco split circle logo disappears from the battery cable terminals. Instead, the positive cable terminal has a "+" sign and the negative terminal has a "-" sign. The cables are still retained with 7/16-inch hex head bolts.

1970s made from approximately mid-June onward may utilize 5/16-inch hex head retention bolts instead of the previously used 7/16-inch bolts. It is possible that some 1970s made after mid-June use a 5/16-inch hex head bolt for one cable and a 7/16-inch bolt for the other cable. The later a 1970 is, the more likely it is to use the smaller bolts. It is believed that all 1971s as well as all 1972s use the smaller 5/6-inch hex head bolts.

The battery cable itself changes in 1972. Each of the cables is thicker and the insulation has "COPPER CLAD ALUMINUM" written on it in white block letters.

Passenger Side Storage Compartment

The passenger side storage compartment contains a removable insert. The insert, which is like a squared-off bucket, is made from grayish-black fiberboard and measures 6-1/4 inches deep.

For 1970–1972 convertibles only, the fiberboard insert contains a 1/2-inch open-ended wrench for installation and removal of the hardtop.

Also inside the fiberboard insert is an off-white cotton pouch that has a yellow drawstring. The drawstring is held on by an encasement stitched with red thread. The pouch contains eight silver washers and four oblong-shaped gray phosphate shims that are to be used to adjust the seat backs to the occupants' preferred positions.

In addition to the hardtop wrench and seat hardware pouch, there are a number of other items in the storage insert. A small, white paper envelope with the "GM mark of excellence" logo and instructions printed in black letters contains the car's keys and the key knock-outs.

A small, brown paper envelope contains license plate screws. "LICENSE SCREWS" is written in black ink on the outside of this envelope.

Another small, brown paper envelope is included with those Corvettes equipped with the optional P02 Deluxe Wheel Covers. This envelope contains four extensions for the valve stems.

The final item in the storage insert is the owner's packet. This packet included an owner's manual, warranty folder, Protect-o-plate, consumer information booklet, trim ring installation instruction card, and radio instruction sheet. 1970s equipped with the optional stereo radio also have a stereo instruction sheet. Some 1971–1972s have this stereo sheet and some do not. Cars that did not come with a radio did not have the radio instruction sheet or the stereo instruction sheet. In 1972 only an emissions control systems booklet is also included in the packet.

The above described contents of the owner's packet are in a clear vinyl envelope. In 1970–1971 the same envelope, which carries the part number 3950779, is used. It has a yellow key with blue letters reading "Don't invite car theft" printed on it. 1972s use a similar envelope but without the yellow key or blue writing on it.

The fiberboard insert in the passenger-side rear storage compartment lifts out to reveal an additional storage area beneath. A jack and jack handle are mounted to the bottom of the compartment (to the car's floor panel) with a black spring that latches onto a black hook riveted to the floor.

All jacks are painted semi-gloss black and have the letter "A" stamped in their chassis contact pad. This letter is the logo for Auto Specialties Manufacturing, the company that made the jacks.

In addition to the manufacturer's logo, all jacks contain a date code stamping. The stamping is on the jack's large side arm and contains a number for the year followed by a letter for the month, with "A" representing January, "B" representing February, and so on. For example, the date code stamping for a jack manufactured in June 1971 would say "1 F".

All jack handles are painted semi-gloss black and include a pivoting 3/4-inch boxed hex-wrench on the end to remove and install the car's lug nuts. A thick

rubber ring is fitted around the hex-wrench end to prevent rattling.

In addition to the jack and jack handle, electrical relays and a flasher unit are mounted in the area underneath the fiberboard insert on those cars equipped with the audio anti-theft alarm system.

T-Top Storage Bags

All 1970–1972 coupes have two storage bags to hold the T-tops when they are removed. Some cars have bags dyed to match interior color while others have black bags regardless of interior color. Earlier cars for each year are more likely to have a color-matched bag and later cars are more likely to have black bags.

All bags have a date code stamped inside in ink. Typical date stampings contain a month and year designation. For example, bags manufactured in October 1970 read "10-70." In addition to the date stamping, bags may also contain a logo stamping representing the manufacturer. The most common logo seen is "TEX."

All bags have a flap that closes over the opening and is retained by three chrome-plated snaps.

All 1970–1972 coupes have adjustable T-top hold down straps. As with the T-top bags, early cars tend to have straps dyed to match interior color and later cars tend to have black straps regardless of interior color.

1970 coupes have two straps that are attached to chrome-plated anchors. The anchors are fastened to the floor of the rear luggage area. 1971–1972 coupes use only a single-strap harness that is attached to the rear bulkhead in the luggage area and extends to a chrome-plated anchor attached to the front bulkhead between the seats.

All 1970–1972 coupes have molded vinyl trim mounted to the underside of the T-tops. The vinyl is the same color as the interior.

All 1970–1972 coupes have a rear window storage tray mounted above the rear luggage area. Trays in 1970–1971s assembled through approximately mid-March 1971 have a thin steel latch marked "Rear Window Storage." This latch holds the hinged storage tray up and releasing the latch allows the tray to drop down. Most 1971s assembled from mid-March 1971 forward and all 1972s utilize a push-button release instead of the spring steel latch to drop the storage tray down. The push-button release has no writing or markings on it.

Some 1970 and early 1971 coupes have latches mounted on the inside of the window storage tray to hold the window in place while it is being stored. These inside hold down latches are not used at all after early-1971 production.

Convertible Top Frame

For all 1970–1972 convertibles, top frames are painted semi-gloss black. A black fiberglass header panel is secured to the front underside of the top frame. Three chrome-plated latches secure the front top header to the windshield frame. Black rubber coats the latch levers and each latch is accompanied by an adjustable rubber-tipped tensioning bolt.

The convertible top frame's rear bow is secured to the body deck lid with two chrome-plated pins that insert into chrome-plated receptacles affixed to the body. Chrome Phillips oval head screws hold the pins to the rear bow.

The underside of the convertible top, including the top material itself and the pads, is always black regardless of interior color.

The optional removable hardtop on those convertibles so equipped has a padded vinyl headliner color matched to the interior. Front latches for the hardtop are chrome plated, but unlike the soft top, the levers on these latches are not rubber coated.

The underside of the convertible deck lid is painted body color. Deck lid release levers, release cables, and lock mechanisms were all mounted prior to painting and should therefore also be painted body color.

The latch receptacles for the pins in the rear bow of the convertible top, as well as the rods that control the receptacles, are black. Deck lid rubber bumpers are black, as are their brackets.

1970 convertibles assembled through approximately July 1970 have two round rubber bumpers mounted to the underside of the deck lid. When the soft top is down in its storage compartment and the lid is closed, these rubber bumpers contact the black fiberglass header panel mounted to the front underside of the top frame. Most very late 1970s, as well as most 1971s and early to mid-1972s, have only one such bumper. Most late 1972s again have two bumpers.

1970–1972 Mechanical

Engine Blocks

Engine-block casting numbers for all 1970–1972 engines are located on the top rear driver side of the block, on the flange that mates to the transmission bellhousing.

All 1970–1971 and most 1972 small-block cars use No. 3970010 blocks. Some 1972s assembled beginning in March 1972 use a No. 3970014 block.

All 1970–1971 big-block cars use No. 3963512 blocks. All 1972 big blocks use No. 3999289 blocks.

Engine-block casting dates for all 1970–1972 small- and big-block Corvettes, with the exception of small blocks utilizing the No. 3970014 blocks, are located on the top rear passenger side of the block, on the flange that mates to the transmission bellhousing. The casting date for the No. 3970014 cast block is on the top rear driver-side flange adjacent to the casting number.

The engine-block casting date for No. 3970010 small blocks and all big blocks consists of a letter for the month, one or two numbers for the day, and one number for the year. For example, a No. 3970010 block cast on June 17, 1972, would have a casting date of F 17 2.

No. 3970014 cast small blocks found in some late 1972s uses a similar date code system except the year is designated by two numbers rather than one. For example, a No. 3970014 block cast on June 17, 1972, would have a casting date of F 17 72.

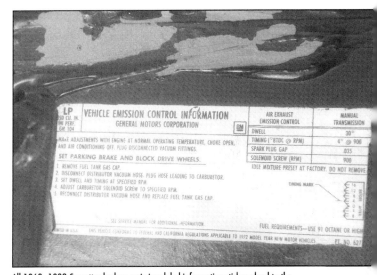

All 1968–1982 Corvettes had an emissions label information sticker glued to the upper, driver side of the firewall. This sticker is on a 1972 LT-1.

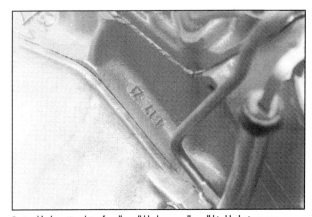

Engine-block casting dates for all small blocks, as well as all big blocks in cars assembled after approximately March 1969, are located on the top, rear passenger side of the block, on the flange that mates to the transmission bellhousing. The date for 1968 and pre–March 1969 big blocks is located on the passenger side of the block adjacent to the engine mount area. This 1971 454 block was cast May 17, 1971 (E 17 71).

Engine-block casting numbers can be found on the flange that mates the block to the transmission bellhousing just behind the driver-side cylinder head.

All 1970–1972 engines contain two distinct stampings on a machined pad located on the top of the passenger side between the cylinder head and water pump. One stamping is commonly referred to as the assembly stamping and the other is commonly called the VIN derivative stamping.

The assembly stamping begins with a prefix letter to indicate the engine assembly plant. "V" indicates the Flint plant, where all small blocks were assembled, and "T" designates the Tonawanda plant, where all big blocks were assembled. Following the prefix letter are four numbers indicating the month and day of assembly. After the numbers indicating the assembly date are three suffix letters denoting the particular engine. This suffix code is often referred to as the engine broadcast code, or simply the engine code. (Refer to Appendix C for 1970–1972 engine suffix codes.)

To illustrate what a typical engine assembly stamping looks like, consider the following 1971 combination: a base 350/270-horsepower engine built on April 5 and coupled to a four-speed transmission. The assembly stamping for such an engine would read "V0405CJL."

Passenger-side details of a 1972 LT-1 engine compartment.

Driver-side details of a 1972 LT-1 engine compartment.

Always remember that the engine assembly date must come after the engine-block casting date (you can't assemble an engine before the block is cast!), and both the casting date and assembly date must precede the final assembly date of the car (you can't final assemble a car before the engine has been cast and assembled!). The great majority of engines were cast and assembled within a couple of weeks prior to the car's assembly date. Some engines, however, were cast and/or assembled months prior to installation in a car. Six months is generally accepted as the outer limit for the difference between an engine assembly or casting date and the final assembly date of the car it is installed into.

The VIN derivative stamping, as the name implies, is a stamping containing a portion or a derivative of the car's vehicle identification number. For 1970 Corvettes this stamping begins with "70" for model year 1970. This is followed by the letter "S" for St. Louis, where all 1970–1972 Corvettes were built. The "S" is in turn followed by the final six digits of the particular car's VIN. For example, the VIN derivative stamping for the very first 1970 assembled would read "70S400001," for the second car it would

read "70S400002," and so on.

VIN derivative stampings in early 1971s built in August and very early September 1970 follow the same pattern as the stampings used in all of 1970. The very first 1971, for example, would have a VIN derivative stamping that reads "71S100001." After early September 1970, however, the beginning of the stamping is changed, with "C11" replacing the two-number designation for the year. So the 4,000th 1971 built, for example, would have a VIN derivative stamping that reads "C11S104000." The "C" represents Chevrolet, the first "1" designates the Chevrolet car line, and the second "1" designates the 1971 model year.

For model year 1972 the VIN derivative stamping was again changed. The "C" was dropped but the "1" immediately following it was retained to designate the Chevrolet car line. So the VIN derivative stamping in the 4,000th 1972 built would read "12S504000."

On big-block engines the assembly stamping is normally on the left and toward the rear of the pad when viewing it to read the stamping. The VIN derivative stamping is to the right and toward the front of the pad.

All Corvette engines were stamped with an assembly code and a portion of the car's VIN. This example is from a 1971 big block. The "T" is for Tonawanda, the city in northern New York where the engine plant is located; "0525" indicates that the engine was assembled on May 25 and "CPJ" translates to a 454/365 coupled to an automatic transmission.

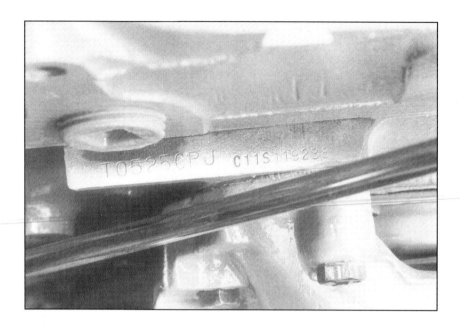

Driver-side engine details shown here are from a 1972 LT-1 engine. Most engines with aluminum valve covers came with chrome-plated twist-in oil fill caps, but this completely original car appears to have come with a rubber plug-in-style cap.

On small-block engines this positioning is reversed.

A notable exception to the location of the engine stampings occurred in the first few days of 1970 production. Very-early-1970 engines have been observed with the VIN derivative stamping on the bottom driver side of the block above the oil filter.

All 1970–1972 engine blocks are cast-iron and all are painted Chevrolet Engine Orange. Blocks were originally painted before exhaust manifolds were installed and therefore coverage on the sides of the block behind the manifolds is good. The engine stamp pad was normally covered up when the engine was painted and therefore it normally appears unpainted.

Cylinder Heads

As with engine blocks, all 1970–1972 cylinder heads have both a casting number and a casting date. As with blocks and other cast parts, the cylinder head casting date typically has a letter to indicate month, one or two numbers to indicate the day of the month, and one number to indicate the year. (Refer to Appendix G for a comprehensive list of cylinder head casting numbers.)

All 1970–1972 engines utilize cast-iron cylinder heads with the exception of the optional 1971 LS6 engine, which has aluminum cylinder heads.

All cylinder heads and head bolts, with the exception of the aluminum heads installed on 1971 LS6 engines, are painted Chevrolet Engine Orange.

Intake Manifolds

All 1970–1972 intake manifolds are cast-iron except for those on optional LT1 small blocks and LS6 big blocks, which are cast-aluminum.

As with engine blocks and cylinder heads, intake manifolds contain casting numbers and casting dates. As with other cast engine parts, the casting date consists of a letter designating the month, one or two numbers designating the day of the month, and a number denoting the year.

Casting numbers for all manifolds are on the top surface, as are casting dates for cast-iron manifolds. For aluminum manifolds, casting dates are on the underside and are therefore not visible when the manifold is installed on an engine. (Refer to Appendix H for intake manifold casting numbers.)

No original 1970–1972 Corvette intakes have a machined opening at their forward edge for an oil fill tube as is seen on earlier intakes and some later replacements.

All 1970–1972 Corvette engines utilize an aluminum thermostat housing that does not have a hole for a temperature sending unit. Housings used on certain other Chevrolets and some replacement housings have a tapped hole.

Aluminum thermostat housings are painted orange when mounted to cast-iron intakes and left unpainted when mounted to aluminum intakes.

With original 1970–1972 intake manifold side gaskets, but not with later GM replacements, semicircular tabs are visible sticking up between the runners for cylinders number three and six and the exhaust heat crossover passage. Also, original front and rear intake gaskets do not have side tabs to locate the gaskets on the block's rail like later replacements.

All intake manifolds are held on by 9/16-inch hex head bolts. The bolts do not get any type of washer when used for any cast-iron intakes and 1970–1971 aluminum intakes. For aluminum intakes in 1972, however, those intake bolts not also used to hold a bracket in place received flat washers.

Engine lifting brackets are attached to most 1970–1972 Corvettes. In 1970 all small blocks have one bracket attached to the second intake manifold bolt from the front on the driver side.

All 1971–1972 small blocks and all 1970–1972 big blocks have a front bracket that attaches to the first and second intake manifold bolts from the front on the driver side.

A second bracket attaches to the upper bolt holding the bellhousing to the block on the passenger side for all 1970–1972 small blocks except those mated to an automatic transmission. Small blocks mated to automatics did not get a rear lift bracket at all.

A second bracket attaches to the rear of the passenger-side cylinder head for all 1970–1972 big blocks.

The front bracket is painted orange on those 1970–1972 engines equipped with cast-iron intake manifolds and silver on 1970 LT1s. Brackets on 1971–1972 LT1s are typically unpainted toward the

Cast-iron intake manifolds contain a casting date near the area where the ignition coil mounts. This manifold was cast May 21, 1971 (E 2171).

All Corvette intake manifolds contain a casting number on their top surface. This late 1971 and 1972 LS5 manifold bears the casting number "6263753" to the rear of where the carburetor mounts.

bottom and painted orange toward the top. The rear bracket is painted orange for all 1970–1972 engines except LS6s. LS6 rear brackets are unpainted, as are LS6 front brackets.

All cast-iron intake manifolds are painted Chevrolet Engine Orange. Some small-block aluminum intakes are painted with a dull aluminum paint, while others are unpainted. LS6 aluminum intakes are unpainted

All intake manifolds, including aluminum examples, were installed before engines were painted. Therefore, on those engines with cast-iron intakes, hold down bolts as well as any exposed portions of gaskets are painted Chevrolet Engine Orange.

Aluminum intakes were crudely masked off prior to the engine being painted. Therefore, engines with aluminum intakes may have orange paint overspray on edges, bolts, and gaskets. If orange overspray was excessive the factory sometimes sprayed the area along the edges of the manifold silver, resulting in silver overspray on bolts, gaskets, and sometimes even the cylinder heads.

Distributor and Ignition Coil

All 1970–1972 Corvettes use a mechanical tach drive Delco Remy distributor. All distributors have a thin aluminum identification band secured around the housing in a recess just above where the distributor hold down clamp rests.

The identification band is natural on one side and colored on the other with a pinkish-red dye. While the majority of cars have the dye on the outside of the

band some have it on the inside, making it difficult to see when the band is installed on the distributor.

The identification band has the words "DELCO REMY" stamped into it. This is followed by a seven-character part number and a date code. (See Appendix K for distributor part numbers.)

The date code, which represents the day the distributor was assembled, consists of a number representing the year, a letter representing the month, and one or two numbers representing the day of the month. For 1970–1972 distributor date codes the letter "A" represents January, "B" represents February, and so on. As is typical of stamped-in date codes, the letter "I" is skipped so the month of September is represented by "J." The date code on a distributor assembled March 17, 1972, for example, would read "2 C 17," and one assembled November 21, 1970, would read "0 L 21."

While most distributors were made several weeks before the engine was assembled it is entirely possible that several months can separate the two. As with most other components, six months is the generally accepted maximum.

1970 Corvettes assembled through approximately the middle of the model year utilize a distributor housing without a small hole opposite the tachometer drive gear. Mid-1970 and 1971–1972 housings do have this small hole.

Distributor housings are painted semi-gloss black and have one of several color daubs of paint just below the distributor cap on the passenger side toward the front of the car.

All distributors are fitted with a vacuum advance unit. Vacuum advances have part numbers stamped into them in the bracket that mounts the vacuum canister to the distributor.

All 1970–1972 Corvettes use a black Delco Remy distributor cap that has the words "Delco Remy Pat. Pend. R." molded into the top between the towers.

All 1970–1972s use a Delco Remy ignition coil. All coils are held by a silver cadmium–plated, stamped steel bracket. The coil is clamped into the bracket with a slotted round head machine screw, and the bracket is held to the intake manifold by two hex head bolts. If the car is equipped with a radio there is a capacitor held to the coil bracket with a clamp retained by a single screw.

Coils are painted gloss black and have the last three numbers of their Chevrolet part number embossed in the housing from the inside out so they are raised up. (See Appendix L for coil numbers and applications.)

In addition to the final three numbers of the part number, some ignition coils also have "B-R" embossed in their cases. Coils utilized with the optional transistor ignition system have a red, black, and silver foil sticker that reads "Delco Remy Ignition Coil for Transistor Ignition" affixed to them.

Transistor ignition was a distinct option in 1970, was available only with LT1 and LS6 in 1971 as part of those options, and was not available at all in 1972.

Transistor ignition includes a different distributor, a special wire harness, a different ignition coil, and a pulse amplification box. The amplification box is mounted to the front of the driver-side front inner wheelwell. It is visible if you look in the area between the driver-side front inner wheelwell and the driver-side front corner of the body with the hood in the raised position.

The correct 1970–1971 pulse amplification box has a three-wire pigtail coming out of it and terminating in a plug connector. The plug connector is mated with a corresponding plug connector in the transistor ignition harness. Earlier versions of the amplification box have a female plug directly on the box rather than a short pigtail of wire with a plug on the end.

Ignition Shielding

All 1970–1972 Corvettes equipped with a radio are outfitted with ignition shielding. All pieces of shielding are plated with flash chrome. As such, the quality and appearance of the chrome is not very good.

All 1970 small-block cars assembled through approximately early July 1970 have a two-section main ignition shield. It consists of a surround that completely encapsulates the distributor and coil, and a lid for the surround.

The surround for 1970s assembled through approximately the end of February 1970 is actually two pieces held together by two small Phillips head screws. The two halves in cars assembled after approximately the end of February 1970 are spot welded together rather than screwed.

A translucent plastic shield is held to the underside of the top lid by four plastic rivets. Three chrome-plated wing bolts retain the lid to the surround.

The main shield, or top shield as it is sometimes called, attaches to support brackets with two chrome wing bolts on each side. The support brackets are painted Chevrolet Engine Orange and attach to the intake manifold bolts.

1970 small blocks assembled after approximately early July 1970 and all 1971–1972 small blocks utilize a one-piece top ignition shield. The one-piece shield is held to the support brackets by one chrome-plated wing bolt on each side.

All 1970–1972s small blocks have four cadmium-plated spark plug heat shields, each of

Main ignition shield support brackets were painted the same color as the engine. The brackets were still used on cars without shielding (non-radio-equipped cars) because they also served to support the spark plug wires. Note the raised ridge on the original vacuum hose going to the distributor advance on this 1971.

which covers two plugs. Each of these heat shields is retained to the engine block by means of a single silver cadmium–plated indented hex head bolt.

Small-block-equipped 1970s assembled through approximately June 1970 (these are the cars with two-section top shields) have four chrome-plated spark plug shields, each of which covers two plugs. The spark plug shields are retained to cadmium-plated brackets with chrome-plated wing bolts. The brackets are cadmium plated and have "FPM" stamped in to represent the manufacturer. Later, incorrect GM replacement brackets have the letters "CNI" stamped in.

After approximately June 1970, more or less concurrent with the change to a one-piece top shield, use of the two forward spark plug shields was discontinued. The rearward two shields remained, covering the plugs in cylinders number five, seven, six, and eight.

All 1970–1972 small blocks use a pair of boomerang or V-shaped sections of chrome-plated shielding to encapsulate the spark plug wires. The boomerang shielding runs from the bottom of the vertical shields to the area beneath the spark plugs.

Small-block cars not originally equipped with a radio still have the two main shield support brackets on the back of the intake manifold and the cadmium-plated spark plug heat shields. They do not, however, have any of the chrome shielding.

1970 big blocks assembled through approximately early July 1970 have a two-section main ignition shield just like small-block-equipped cars. Very late 1970 and all 1971–1972 big blocks have the second style shielding. This is the one-piece shield that is held to the support brackets by one chrome-plated wing bolt on each side.

Rather than spark plug wire and spark plug shields like small blocks, big blocks have special spark plug wires covered with braided stainless-steel wire. The braid toward the end of each wire ends in a hoop that gets fastened to the valve cover bolts to provide a ground. In 1970–1971 the hoops on the right side attach in pairs to the forward-most bolt and

the third bolt back. On the left side of the engine they attach to the second and fourth bolts back. In 1972 the left side is also attached in pairs to the second and fourth bolts back, but the right side has a single wire on the first and second bolts, and a pair of wires on the third bolt back.

Beginning some time in the 1971 model year, big-block engines were fitted with spark plug heat shields. Each heat shield is a cadmium-plated steel tube with a welded-on tab. The tab allows each shield to be mounted to an exhaust manifold bolt.

Big-block cars not originally equipped with a radio do not have the main shield support brackets or braided steel spark plug wires, but do have the heat shields.

In addition to the external ignition shielding fitted to all 1970–1972 Corvettes equipped with a radio, some cars had an additional shield covering the ignition points beneath the distributor cap. Called a Radio Frequency Interference (RFI) shield, it was used on standard ignition distributors (i.e., non-transistor ignition distributors) in 1971–1972, and in 1970s

Big-block cars with radios use spark plug wires covered with braided stainless steel to reduce radio interference from the ignition system. The hoop on each wire gets fastened to the valve cover bolts to provide a ground. In 1970 and 1971 the hoops on the right side attach in pairs to the forward-most bolt and the third bolt back as shown here. Beginning in 1972 the right side has a single wire on the first and second bolts, and a pair of wires on the third bolt back.

assembled after approximately August 1970 onward. Its use in 1970 appears to correlate to the use of the 1971-style external shielding, which was also installed on 1970 models assembled from approximately August 1970 onward.

Spark Plug Wires

All 1970–1972 Corvettes use black spark plug wires manufactured by Packard Electric. All wires are ink stamped every few inches with the words "Packard T V R Suppression" and a date code. The date code indicates the quarter and the year of manufacture. For example, wires labeled "2Q-71" were made in the second quarter of 1971.

Wires for small-block engines have black boots with 90-degree bends at the spark plug end and straight black boots at the distributor end.

1970–1971 big-block wires have gray boots with 135-degree bends at the spark plug ends and gray boots with 90-degree bends at the distributor ends. 1972 big-block wires are the same except that the boots at the spark plug ends are straight.

Carburetors

All 1970–1972 Corvettes are carbureted. Original carburetors come from either Rochester, Holley, or Carter. Carter was at times contracted to manufacture Rochester Quadrajet carburetors for General Motors, so the Carter-built Quadrajets are almost identical to the Rochester-built ones. Carter-built Quadrajets are identified as being manufactured by Carter and use Carter's system of date coding rather than Rochester's system.

Rochester-built Quadrajets contain an alphanumeric sequence stamped into a flat, vertical area of the main body on the rear of the driver side. Either the full seven-digit GM part number or the final five digits of the part number are stamped in. Several letters, which identify the specific plant where the carburetor was made, may be stamped here as well. And finally, four numbers denoting the date of manufacture are also stamped into this area.

Rochester utilized the Julian calendar for date coding its carburetors. With this system of dating, the first three numbers represent the day of the year and the final number is the last digit of the specific year. For example, the Julian date code for a carburetor made on January 1, 1972, would read "0012." The first three digits, "001," represent the first day of the year, and the final digit, "2," represents 1972.

The Julian date code for a carburetor made on December 31, 1971, would read "3651." The first three digits, "365," represent the 365th day of the year, which in 1971 was December 31st. The final digit, "1," represents 1971.

All Rochester Quadrajet carburetors contain a part number and date code stamped into a vertical boss in the body toward the rear of the driver side. The part number for a 1971 LS5 automatic is 7041204. "FC" denotes the plant where this carburetor was made, and "0681" indicates that it was assembled the 68th day of 1971.

One tricky element to figuring out the exact day a Julian calendar date corresponds to is remembering that leap years have an extra day.

Carter-built Quadrajets don't use a Julian calendar date coding system. Instead, they use a single letter and a single number. The letter denotes the month, with "A" indicating January, "B" indicating February, and so on. The letter "I" is not used, so September is represented by "J."

The number in the date code for Carter-built Quadrajets is the last digit for the year of manufacture. For example, a date code of "C1" indicates the carburetor was made in March 1971.

Holley carburetors have three distinct stampings on the front driver side of the air horn. The top stamping is the seven-digit GM part number, which may be followed by one or two letters.

Below the GM part number is what is called the Holley list number. The list number corresponds to Holley's part number. This stamping says "LIST" followed by four numbers and then an additional number, a letter, or a combination of numbers and letters.

Below the Holley list number is the date code. Holley date codes in 1970–1972 utilize three numbers. The first is the last digit of the year, the second is the month of production, and the third is the week of production.

For the month of production the numbers one through nine denote January through September, "O" denotes October, "A" denotes November, and "B" denotes December.

A Holley carburetor manufactured on April 3, 1970, would have a date code of "041," with "0" representing 1970, "4" representing April, and "1" representing the first week of April, which includes April 3rd.

(For charts showing production codes for 1970–1972 carburetors see Appendix J.)

All 1970–1972 carburetors are plated gold dichromate. Rochester carburetors tend to be darker and more uniform in color than Holleys.

All carburetors have an insulator separating them from the intake manifold. 1970 Corvettes equipped with a Rochester carburetor and sold new in all states except California utilize a 1/16-inch-thick insulator. 1970 Rochester-equipped cars delivered new in California have a 3/16-inch-thick insulator.

All 1970–1972 Holley-equipped Corvettes, as well as all 1971–1972 Rochester-equipped ones, have 1/4-inch-thick insulators.

1970 Corvettes sold new in California were required to have option NA9, which was called "Evaporative Emissions System." NA9 includes a thin, brushed aluminum heat shield that goes beneath the carburetor. In addition to the aluminum shield, NA9 also includes heat insulating inserts that go over the carburetor mounting bolts to discourage heat transfer through the bolts into the carburetor.

All 1970–1972 carburetors use a single accelerator return spring. It is black phosphate–plated and mounts from the primary shaft bell crank to the accelerator cable mount.

All 1970–1972 Corvettes utilize a mechanical carburetor choke controlled by a thermostatic coil. The coil is mounted in a recess on the passenger side of the intake manifold and is covered by a cadmium-plated steel housing. A rod links the coil to the choke linkage on the carburetor. In 1970 the rod is secured to the linkage with a clip that locks back on the choke rod. In 1971–1972 it is secured with a clip that locks over a groove in the end of the rod.

Air Cleaner

The majority of 1970 Corvettes use an open element air cleaner assembly. 1970s assembled after approximately mid-June 1970, except for LT1-equipped cars, use the 1971–1972 closed element air cleaner. LT1s continue to use an open element design.

All 1971–1972s use a closed element design except for LT1s and LS6s, which continue to use the open element air cleaner. The closed element design uses a housing that is enclosed except for two forward-facing snorkels that allow air to enter. The housing is painted gloss black.

All air cleaners, including both open and closed element designs, have chrome-plated lids. All 1970–1971 lids have a decal identifying engine displacement and horsepower rating. 1972 lids do not have a decal.

All open element air cleaner lids have service instructions and the replacement filter part number silk screened on the underside.

Closed element air cleaner assemblies do not have anything on the underside of the lid. Instead, the replacement filter number and other information is on a sticker affixed to the outside of the air cleaner housing. The sticker is white, and has the letters "CR" and the number "6485887" on it.

Original 1970–1972 air filter elements for both open and closed element air cleaner assemblies are AC Delco number A 212 CW. Original elements, unlike later replacements, have a fine wire screen around the outside in a vertical (and not diagonal) pattern. The horizontal and vertical wires form rectangles with the longer measurement running vertical when the element is installed.

Valve Covers

All 1970–1972 base engines are fitted with stamped steel valve covers painted Chevrolet Engine Orange. These are held on with hex head bolts and metal tabs that are also painted orange. Original valve covers have more rounded corners than later replacements. Also, original covers do not have spark plug wire brackets welded to them. Stamped steel valve covers do, however, have small tabs welded to the side to hold electrical wires. In 1970 small blocks have one tab welded on the passenger side while big blocks have two welded on the passenger side. In 1971 and 1972 all engines

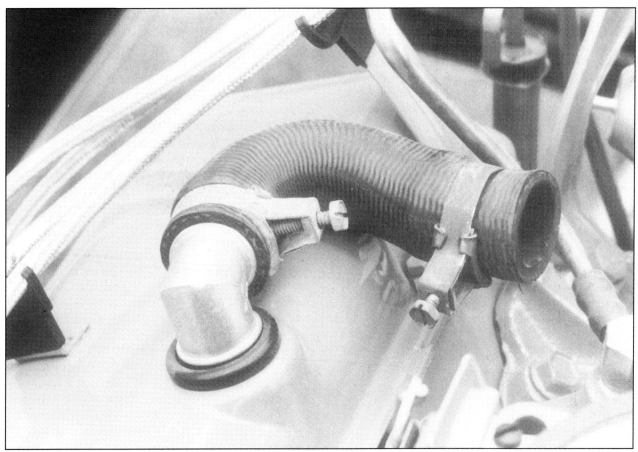

A breather hose with a 90-degree bend connected the passenger-side valve cover to the air cleaner base on this 1972 big block. Note the pronounced ridges on the surface of this original hose, as well as the original tower-style clamps.

with steel valve covers have two tabs welded on the driver side.

A PCV valve inserts into a rubber grommet in the driver-side valve cover. A hose connects the PCV valve to the carburetor. A crankcase vent intake hose connects from a nipple in the passenger-side valve cover to a nipple on the air cleaner base.

1970 base engines use a steel twist-on oil fill cap in the driver-side valve cover. The oil cap has a square rivet in its center and is painted orange.

1971 and most 1972 base engines use a push-in black rubber plug with the word "OIL" molded into the top. Some late 1972 base engines use a steel twist-on oil cap that is the same as the 1970-style except it has the words "ENGINE OIL FILL AC-FC2" stamped in a circle around the center rivet.

1970 L46 (350/350 horsepower) and 1970–1972 LT1s have cast-aluminum valve covers with longitudinal ribs. As with the painted steel covers, a vent hose connects the passenger-side valve cover to the air cleaner base and a PCV valve is in the driver-side valve cover. Aluminum valve covers are

retained by silver cadmium–plated, indented hex head bolts.

All 1970 aluminum valve covers had chrome-plated twist-in-style oil fill caps on the driver side. A large "S" for Stant, the manufacturer of the caps, is stamped into the center rivet.

1971 and most 1972s use a rubber push-in-style oil fill plug that has the word "OIL" molded into the top.

Both passenger- and driver-side aluminum valve covers are made from the same mold. The only difference between the two is that the driver-side cover has a hole for the oil fill cap that the passenger side does not have. On the passenger side, where the hole would go, there is a rigid disc with the crossed flag emblem glued on.

1970 big-block valve covers are plated with low-quality chrome. They have internal drippers that are spot welded on and the spot welds show as irregular indents on the outside of the cover. The passenger- and driver-side covers each have two welded-on brackets to hold plastic spark plug wire looms. The rear of the driver-side cover has a large depression to clear the power brake booster. This cover is used on both power and non-power brake cars. A foil decal reading "Tonawanda #1 Team" is on the top of the passenger-side cover toward the front. A twist-on-style chrome-plated oil fill cap is located on the passenger side.

1971 big-block valve covers are the same as those used in 1970 except they are painted with Chevrolet Engine Orange paint instead of chrome plated. Also, only very early 1971s have the "Tonawanda #1 Team" decals on the valve cover. As with 1971 small-block covers, a rubber push-in plug with "OIL" molded into the top is used for the oil fill. It is located on the passenger side.

1972 big-block valve covers are the same as those used in 1971 except for the spark plug wire brackets. Instead of the two brackets seen in 1970–1971, the 1972 covers each have one bracket welded toward the middle rear that holds a four-wire plastic loom. In addition, 1972-only covers have four single wire retainers welded along the bottom edge. A rubber

push-in plug with "OIL" molded into the top is located on the passenger side for oil fill.

Exhaust Manifolds

All 1970–1972 exhaust manifolds are cast-iron. They contain a casting number that is normally on the side facing away from the engine, and a casting date that is normally on the side facing toward the engine. (Refer to Appendix I for exhaust manifold casting numbers.)

Small-block exhaust manifold casting dates normally include a letter denoting the month and one or two numbers denoting the day of the month. Big-block exhaust manifolds normally include a letter denoting the month, one or two numbers denoting the day of the month, and two numbers denoting the year.

Small-block exhaust manifolds were not yet installed when engines were originally painted so they show no signs of overspray. Big-block manifolds may or may not have Chevrolet Engine Orange paint overspray.

No 1970–1972 exhaust manifolds use a gasket where they mount to the cylinder head.

Small-block manifolds use 9/16-inch hex head bolts that have two concentric rings on their heads. The front two bolts and rear two bolts on both sides of the engine get French locks with one of the two tabs bent over to prevent the bolts from loosening. In addition, the same front and rear bolts on each side get thick flat washers that sit between the French lock and manifold. If, however, the exhaust manifold bolt also retains a bracket (such as an air-conditioning bracket) the flat washer is not used.

Bolts holding big-block manifolds have been observed with three different styles of heads. The most prevalent has two concentric rings like small-block manifold bolts. A second design bolt, with an integral washer, recessed hex head, and the letter "A" (the manufacturer's logo) in the center of the head, is also utilized. A third variety that is sometimes seen is a simple hex head with no markings at all.

1970 big-block exhaust manifolds do not have French locks or any type of washers used with the bolts. Some 1971 big blocks have French locks, and all 1972 big blocks have them.

Starter Motor

All 1970–1972 Corvettes have a Delco-Remy starter motor. Automatic transmission–equipped cars utilize starters with aluminum noses while starters for manual transmission–equipped cars have a cast-iron nose.

Motor housings and cast-iron noses are painted semi-gloss black. Aluminum noses are unpainted.

The starter's part number and assembly date are stamped into the side of the motor housing. The date

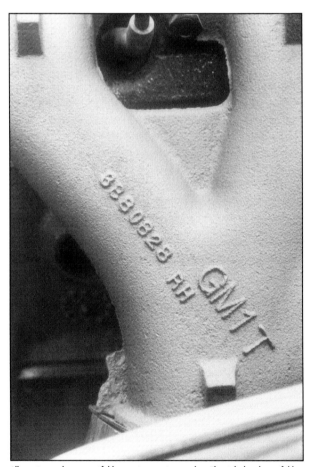

All cast-iron exhaust manifolds contain a casting number. The right-hand manifold used on all 1968-74 big blocks is No. 3880828. A casting date is found on the opposite side of the manifold, facing inward toward the engine block.

code contains a number representing the last digit of the year, and a letter denoting the month, with "A" representing January, "B" representing February, and so on. As is typical of stamped-in date codes, the letter "I" is skipped, so the month of September is represented by "J." One or two numbers indicating the day follow the letter denoting the month. For example, a date code of 2B14 indicates the starter was made February 14, 1972. (See Appendix N for starter motor part numbers.)

Starter solenoids have a black Bakelite cover for the electrical connections. Solenoid housings may be painted semi-gloss black or silver cadmium plated.

All starters use a stamped steel brace to support the forward end (the end facing toward the front of the car when the starter is installed). The brace mounts to a stud on the starter's end plate and to a threaded boss in the engine block. The brace is painted semi-gloss black.

Every starter has a heat shield to protect it from exhaust system heat. Small-block engines are fitted with a rectangular-shaped shield while big blocks get a larger, irregularly shaped shield. Small-block shields are painted semi-gloss black and big-block shields are plated with poor quality flash chrome. Heat shields attach to the solenoid screws with barrel nuts.

Oil Filter

All 1970–1972 engines, including both small and big blocks, utilize an AC Delco spin-on-type oil filter. Original filters are white with a red AC logo, blue circumferential stripes, and blue lettering reading "FULL FLOW" and "TYPE PF-25."

Alternator, Power Steering Pump, and Fuel Pump

All engines are fitted with a Delco-Remy alternator mounted on the driver side. Alternator housings are made from cast aluminum and are not painted or coated with anything.

The front half of the housing has the unit's part number, amperage rating, and assembly date code stamped in. The date code contains a number for the year, and a letter for the month, with "A" representing January, "B" representing February, and so on. As is typical of stamped-in date codes, the letter "I" is skipped, so the month of September is represented by "J." The letter denoting the month is followed by one or two numbers for the day. For example, an alternator stamped "2D17" was assembled April 17, 1972.

The alternator pulley on all LT1s without air conditioning and all LS6s was machined from solid material and is silver cadmium plated. While this high-performance pulley is randomly seen on other

This plastic power steering pump cap was used from mid-1969 forward. Prior to mid-1969 Corvettes used a stamped steel cap that says "CHECK OIL HOT, USE AUTOMATIC TRANSMISSION FLUID TYPE A" in the top.

engines, most other applications used a zinc-plated, stamped steel pulley.

The lower alternator bracket on 1970 and 1971 small blocks is stamped steel that is painted Chevrolet Engine Orange. 1972 small blocks use a cast lower bracket that is painted semi-gloss black.

The lower alternator bracket on all 1970–1972 big blocks without power steering is cast and painted semi-gloss black. The bracket for big-block cars equipped with power steering is stamped steel that is painted semi-gloss black.

All 1970–1972 Corvettes utilize a stamped steel upper alternator bracket. This bracket is painted semi-gloss black.

Small-block 1970–1972 cars equipped with power steering use a semi-gloss black painted power steering pump with a neck that is the same diameter from top to bottom. The necks on big-block pumps, in contrast, widen toward the bottom. Small-block pumps have a semi-gloss black, stamped steel belt guard bolted to the body.

Small-block cars equipped with air conditioning usually use a semi-gloss black painted, stamped steel pulley for the power steering pump. Non-air-conditioned small blocks usually use a cast pulley with open spokes.

All big-block-equipped cars use a double groove, open spoke, cast pulley for the power steering pump.

All 1970–1972 power steering pumps, regardless of engine, use a semi-gloss painted, stamped steel support bracket.

All 1970–1972 Corvettes use an AC brand fuel pump. The pumps have "AC" cast into the top or

As with most cast-iron components, Corvette water pumps typically contain a casting date. This big-block pump housing was cast on February 3, 1970.

side of the upper housing and a five-character part number stamped into the underside of the mounting flange. Pumps are natural dull silver in color.

Water Pump, Radiator, Hoses, and Related Parts

1970 small blocks use casting No. 3782608 water pumps. These have a smaller-diameter front bearing than 1971 and newer pumps so the snout of the housing is smaller. Also, the snout does not have reinforcing ribs and the top of the pump housing does not have a boss for a bypass hose fitting.

All 1971 and those 1972 small blocks assembled through approximately the end of May 1972 use casting No. 3991399 water pumps. These have reinforcing ribs on the snout and larger-diameter front bearings than 1970 pumps. As in 1970, these do not have a boss for a bypass hose fitting on the top.

1972 small blocks assembled after approximately the end of May 1972 use casting No. 330813 water pumps. These pumps have large-diameter front bearings and reinforcing ribs on the snout. They also have flat bosses on the top for bypass hose fittings, though the bosses are not drilled and tapped.

The engine compartment of a 1972 LS5. Note the texture and markings in the original upper radiator hose.

Passenger-side details of a 1972 LS5 engine compartment.

1970 big blocks assembled through at least January 1970 use casting No. 3992077 water pumps. Later 1970s and those 1971 big blocks assembled through approximately the end of August 1970 use casting No. 3856284 water pumps. Most 1971s and 1972s use casting No. 386100 water pumps. All big-block pumps utilize a bypass hose connected to a screwed-in fitting on top of the housing.

All solid lifter engines utilize a deep groove water pump pulley while pulleys on hydraulic lifter engines have a shallower groove. Most water pump pulleys are painted semi-gloss black, though some originals have been observed with a black phosphate finish.

All 1970–1972 Corvettes use a thermostatically controlled, viscous coupled fan clutch. Original clutches usually have a date code stamped in the flange that goes against the water pump pulley. Clutches (as well as water pump pulleys) are retained by studs and nuts that thread into the pump's front hub.

All 1970–1972s use a gloss-black painted cooling fan that is mounted to the fan clutch. Cars equipped with air conditioning use a seven-blade fan that has a part number and date code stamped into the edge of

one or more of the blades. The date code contains a letter for the month, with "A" designating January, "B" designating February, and so on. As is typical of stamped-in date codes, the letter "I" is skipped, so the month of September is represented by "J." Following the letter indicating the month are two numbers to denote the year.

Small-block air-conditioned cars use a seven-blade fan that is essentially flat along the outer edge of each blade. In contrast, the ends of the blades on big-block air-conditioned cars are irregularly shaped and come to an off-center point.

Cars not equipped with air conditioning use a five-blade fan. Five-blade fans do not have a part number or date code stamped in.

A minority of air-conditioned cars have a five-blade fan instead of the more commonly seen seven-blade unit. This five-blade fan differs from the one seen in non-air-conditioned cars in that its blades are pitched at a more severe angle.

1970–1972 Corvettes use either a copper or an aluminum radiator, depending on the engine and transmission choice, and whether the car is equipped with air conditioning.

Aluminum radiators have a part number and date code stamped into the top left side. The date code consists of two numbers to denote the year and a letter to indicate the month, with "A" representing January, "B" representing February, and so on. To the right of the stamping is a rectangular foil sticker with "HARRISON," which is the manufacturer, printed on it. Aluminum radiators are painted semi-gloss to gloss black.

1970–1972 Corvettes equipped with option ZR1 or the combination of an LT1 and M22 transmission, and 1971s with option ZR2, utilize a unique aluminum radiator. It resembles the aluminum radiator used in other Corvettes but is slightly larger. Also, its top neck is long and curved instead of short and straight.

Copper radiators were also manufactured by Harrison and have that name embossed in the passenger-side radiator tank. In addition, there is a stamped steel tag containing a two-letter broadcast code and a part number attached to the passenger side of copper radiators. As with aluminum, the copper radiators are painted semi-gloss to gloss black.

All cars except 1971s with option ZR2 and 1972s with option ZR1 use a fan shroud. Most cars with copper radiators use an unpainted black or very dark gray plastic shroud, though some 1970 big-block cars have been observed with light gray plastic shrouds.

All cars fitted with aluminum radiators use a semi-gloss painted, stamped steel shroud.

Some 1970–1972 Corvettes are fitted with an aluminum expansion tank, some are fitted with a brass tank, and some don't have a tank at all. Generally speaking, cars with aluminum radiators got aluminum expansion tanks and cars with copper radiators did not get any tank. The exception to the latter is LS5-equipped cars, which had copper radiators and brass tanks.

Aluminum tanks are unpainted and have the Harrison logo stamped in the side. Embossed in the same side is a part number, the words "FILL 1/2 WHEN COLD," and a manufacturing date code. The date code contains two numbers to denote the year and a letter to indicate the month, with "A" representing January, "B" representing February, and so on. Unlike earlier aluminum tanks that have only one outlet in the bottom, the tanks used in 1970–1972 have two outlets.

Brass expansion tanks are longer and thinner than their aluminum counterparts. They measure approximately 3 inches in diameter by 20 inches long. A thin brass tag with "Harrison," a part number, and a date code stamped in is soldered to the side of the tank. The whole tank is painted semi-gloss to gloss black.

Cars that don't have an expansion tank use an RC-15 radiator cap rated at 15 psi installed directly on the radiator. Cars with a brass expansion tank use the same cap installed on the tank. Cars with an aluminum expansion tank use an RC-26 cap, also rated at 15 psi, installed on the tank.

All radiator and heater hoses are molded black rubber. Stamped on radiator hoses in white ink are a part number, GM logo, and several letters that are believed to be manufacturer's codes. In addition, there is usually a colored line running the length of the hose. On air-conditioned big-block cars, the lower radiator hose is two pieces joined by a steel tube in the middle.

Heater hoses usually contain a GM logo in white ink. They sometimes have the letters "DL" or "U" stamped on them also. Most original hoses have three or four thin ridges running lengthwise.

All cars use SURE-TITE brand stainless-steel worm drive clamps for the radiator hoses. All applications use size 28 clamps except air-conditioned big blocks, which use size 32 on the lower hose only. Original clamps have "SURE-TITE" in italics stamped into the band along their circumference. In addition, "WITTEK MFG. CO. CHI. U.S.A." is stamped into the worm screw's housing.

All cars use tower-style clamps for the heater hoses. The 5/8-inch heater hoses use 1 1/16-inch clamps. This size clamp has a galvanized finish and contains the size, the words "WITTEK MFG. CO. CHICAGO U.S.A.," and a date code stamped into the band. The first number of the date code denotes the quarter and the following two numbers indicate the year.

The 3/4-inch heater hose uses 1 1/4-inch clamps. These clamps have a cadmium dichromate finish that results in a translucent goldish tint as opposed to the smaller clamps' dull silver color. The larger 1 1/4-inch clamps contain the manufacturer's logo and size designation but do not have a date code. Instead, they have the letters "DCM" stamped into the band.

Brake Master Cylinder and Related Components

All master cylinders are manufactured by Delco and contain a casting number and the Delco split ring logo on the inboard side. Non–power assist master cylinders are casting No. 5455509 and power assist masters are casting No. 5480346.

In addition to the casting number, each master also contains a two-letter application code stamped in. For 1970–1972 cars assembled through approximately mid-June 1970, this code was stamped into a flat machined boss on the top front of the unit. Later 1972s were stamped on a flat surface by the front brake line fitting.

Most cars with power assist brakes have "PG" stamped into the master cylinder and most without power assist have "DC" stamped in. Some 1972s use "MK" for power assist masters and "HC" or "ZC" for non–power assist. Very late 1972s with the stamping by the front brake line fitting use the code "TG."

The entire master cylinder is semi-gloss black except for machined areas, which are natural.

All masters contain two bleeder screws above the brake line ports, and two steel wire bails that hold the cover on. A small vinyl sticker with two letters is folded around one of the bail wires. This sticker is white with red letters, which are "TG" for power brake cars, "YA" for 1970 through early 1972 manual brake cars, and "HC" for later 1972 manual brake cars.

All master cylinders use a stamped steel, cadmium dichromate–plated cover and rubber gasket. The cover has two domes that are not connected by a small ridge like later units. "SERVICE WITH DELCO PARTS" is stamped into one dome, while "USE DELCO SAE J 1703 BRAKE FLUID" or "SERVICE WITH SAE J 1703 BRAKE FLUID" is stamped into the other dome.

Power brake boosters, on cars so equipped, are painted gloss black and frequently have a spot of yellow paint somewhere. The yellow is thought to be an inspection mark or an application code.

Some boosters have a Julian date code stamped in on top opposite the vacuum valve. The code contains a number corresponding to the final number of the year and then three numbers denoting the day of the year. For example, a booster stamped "1134" was manufactured on the 134th day of 1971.

Original Corvette fan clutches are usually date coded with a stamping on the edge of the flange that mounts against the water pump pulley. This clutch was made on April 16, 1971. Barely visible after the date code are the letters "SC," for the manufacturer Sweitzer Clutch. Clutches in cars assembled after approximately April 1969 are retained by studs and nuts as shown. Prior to that they were retained by hex head bolts.

Air Conditioning and Heating System Components

All 1970–1972 Corvettes equipped with air conditioning utilize a model A-6 Frigidaire compressor. Compressors are painted semi-gloss black and have a green, black, and silver foil sticker on the top of the housing. The sticker contains, among other things, the compressor's model number. For 1970 and 1971 454s the model number is 5910740 and for 1972 454s

This fan clutch is typical of those found on cars built from 1968 through July 1973. After July 1973 the bi-metallic thermostat seen here was replaced with a thermostatic coil.

Big-block air-conditioned cars use seven-blade engine cooling fans with irregularly shaped pointy tips. Most air-conditioned small blocks use seven-blade fans with regular, slightly rounded ends. Some small blocks with air conditioning use a five-blade fan.

Engine cooling fans used on big blocks with air conditioning usually have a part number and date code stamped into each blade. This fan is dated August 1970 (H70) in the lower right corner.

it's 5910797. For 1970 and early 1971 350s the model number is 5910741; for later 1971s it's 5910778; and for 1972s it's 1131002.

The air-conditioning system for all cars includes a POA valve assembly that is natural aluminum in color. Likewise, the thermostatic expansion valve, the tubing crimped onto the ends of the hoses, and the manifold block that connects the hoses to the back of the compressor are also unpainted.

An unpainted, dark gray fiberglass housing covers the evaporator. There is a Harrison foil sticker on the housing, as well as a fan relay. In 1970 and 1971 the relay has a gloss-black painted cover that has "DELCO REMY" stamped in from the inside. In 1972 the cover is zinc or cadmium plated and does not have any words stamped in it.

1970–1971 Corvettes with air conditioning have a vacuum-actuated valve spliced into the heater hose. When the air conditioning is on this valve shuts off the flow of engine coolant to the heater core. The valve was not used in 1972.

The blower motors for both air-conditioned and non-air-conditioned cars are painted gloss

This aluminum expansion tank is in a 1972 LS5 without air conditioning. It is dated February 1972. Note that the overflow hose does not have a clamp.

black. Motors on air-conditioned cars have a rubber tube that extends from the motor housing to the evaporator housing. Motors on non-air-conditioned cars do not have this tube. Motors have a part number and date code stamped into their mounting flange. The date code contains one or two numbers to denote the month and two numbers to indicate the year.

Windshield Wiper Door Mechanism, Wiper Motor, and Related Components

All 1970–1972 Corvettes have a vacuum-actuated wiper door. The door is moved up and down by a vacuum motor mounted on the upper right side of the firewall. In 1970 the vacuum connection nipple protruding from the front of the motor is straight while in 1971–1972 it has a 90-degree bend. All vacuum motors are cadmium dichromate plated.

The vacuum motor is controlled by a vacuum valve mounted to the upper left side of the firewall for all 1970 and some 1971 cars. For some 1971 and all 1972 cars this valve is mounted on the right-side inner wheelwell. As with the vacuum motor, the valve is plated cadmium dichromate.

The wiper motor and windshield washer pump are an integral assembly for all 1970–1972 Corvettes. The motors are natural diecast silver in color and the washer pump is white plastic. A black plastic cover goes over the wiper motor.

The washer pump utilized for 1970 and 1971 models assembled through approximately mid-March 1971 has five ports. Cars assembled after mid-March 1971 use pumps with three ports. The two additional ports found on the earlier pumps are for

Passenger-side firewall details from a 1972. The wiper door vacuum motor that looks as though it is formed from two pie tins put together was used from mid-1969 through 1972. Earlier 1969s and all 1968s use a cylindrical vacuum motor.

the headlight washer nozzles. 1971s assembled after December 1970 do not have the headlamp washer system, so from approximately December 1970 to mid-March 1971 there are two unused ports on the washer pumps. The two ports are connected to each other with a short length of hose.

For 1970 Corvettes without air conditioning the windshield washer fluid reservoir is mounted on the rear, engine compartment side of the right inner wheelwell. The reservoir is rigid white plastic and does not have any writing on it.

Passenger-side view of the A.I.R. pump on a 1972 LT-1. The pump body is diecast aluminum and natural in color. The cast cover on the back of the pump is painted semi-gloss black.

Driver-side view of the A.I.R. pump on a 1972 LT-1. Because this is a later 1972 the centrifugal filter behind the pulley (the item with the radial fins) is made from black plastic. An opaque white plastic filter was used for 1968 through early 1972 cars. Note also the steel spacer between the pulley and centrifugal filter, which was used on small blocks only, and the heat-stamped part numbers and codes in the belt.

1971 and 1972 cars have a similar reservoir mounted in the same location, but these include a long fill neck that extends up slightly below the fender lip.

All air-conditioned cars use an off-white-color flexible plastic bag to hold washer fluid. This bag is mounted on the lower left-side firewall.

Air Injection Reactor System and other Emissions Components

Air Injection Reactors (A.I.R.) were in fairly widespread use by 1970 and many, but not all, 1970–1972 Corvettes are equipped with them. The A.I.R. system includes black cadmium–plated tubes that thread into each of the four runners on both exhaust manifolds. All A.I.R.-equipped cars, therefore, have four holes drilled and tapped into each manifold.

Corvettes not originally equipped with A.I.R. systems have exhaust manifolds that are not drilled and tapped. Possible exceptions to this are 1970 LS5s made in approximately the last three weeks of March 1970. Exhaust manifolds on LS5s made during this time may have drilled and tapped holes closed off with steel pipe thread plugs having recessed squares for a driving tool.

The A.I.R. pump body is diecast aluminum and natural in color. A semi-gloss black painted, rough textured, sand cast plate covers the back of the pump. Original covers have the numbers "7801149" cast in.

All pumps contain a centrifugal filter behind the pulley. A white plastic filter was used for 1970 through early 1972 cars and a black plastic filter was utilized thereafter.

Small-block engines use a steel spacer between the front pump pulley and centrifugal filter. Big blocks do not use a spacer. The spacer is zinc or silver cadmium plated and the pulley is gray phosphate plated or semi-gloss black painted. Pulleys used on small blocks have part No. 3917234 stamped in while those used on big blocks have part No. 3925522 stamped in.

Most pumps are date coded, though the date can be difficult to see with the pump installed. It is stamped into a boss on the rear underside of the body. The sequence may begin with a letter to indicate the assembly plant or specific line. Then there are one or three numbers to indicate the day of the year on the Julian calendar. Earlier dates (prior to the 100th day) may start with two zeros or they may not. For example, a pump assembled on the fifth day of the year may be stamped "005" or simply "5." A fourth (or second) number follows to denote the last digit of the year. This is followed by a number indicating the shift, and a letter indicating the model of the pump.

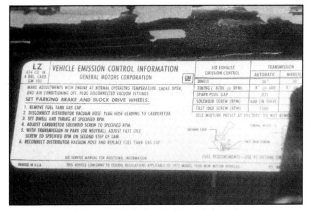

Emission control information label glued to the driver-side firewall in a 1972 LS5.

Passenger-side details of an Air Injection Reactor pump in a 1972 LS5. Note how close the pulley is to the pump body. Small-block pumps used a spacer between the body and pulley, but big block pumps did not.

Driver-side details of an Air Injection Reactor pump in a 1972 LS5. Note that the filter behind the pulley is white and has squared-off fins. This is correct for early 1972 cars.

The lower pump bracket is painted Chevrolet Engine Orange and the upper bracket is semi-gloss black. For small blocks, the lower bracket is cast and contains the number "3923214." For big blocks the lower bracket is stamped steel.

The diverter valve body is natural in color, while the diaphragm cover and check valves are cadmium dichromate. The diaphragm cover has a round sticker with a two-letter broadcast code printed on it. The diverter valve muffler is plated gray phosphate. The diverter valve part number is stamped into the valve below the muffler. Check valves have a part number stamped into their center ridge.

Hoses connecting the various parts of the A.I.R. system are molded black and hose clamps are tower style. Clamps have a galvanized finish and contain the size, the words "WITTEK MFG. CO. CHICAGO U.S.A.," and a date code stamped into the band. The first number of the date code denotes the quarter and the following two numbers indicate the year.

The following 1970–1972 Corvettes were originally equipped with an A.I.R. system: all LS6s, all LT1s, all 1972 LS5s, and all 1972 ZQ3 base engine cars fitted with option NB2 (Exhaust Emission Control), which was required on all cars delivered new in California. All other 1970–1972 Corvettes do not have an A.I.R. system.

1970 Corvettes equipped with option NA9 (California Emissions Equipment) and all 1971–1972 Corvettes are fitted with an Evaporative Control System. This system includes a black carbon-filled canister mounted to the lower left-side inner wheelwell. One hose runs from the canister to a fitting on the Positive Crankcase Ventilation (PCV) valve and another goes to a steel line attached to the chassis.

All 1970–1972 Corvettes have a PCV valve located in the left-side valve cover. The valve has a part number stamped into it. For those engines equipped with a Holley carburetor the PCV valve is part No. CV746C, and for those equipped with a Rochester carburetor it is No. CV736C.

All 1970–1972 Corvettes have a Transmission Controlled Spark (TCS) solenoid. On 1970 and 1972 small-block engines it is attached to an intake manifold stud toward the passenger-side rear of the carburetor. On 1970 big blocks it is on a stud toward the passenger-side front of the carburetor, and on 1972 big blocks it is mounted to the right-side coil bracket bolt.

All 1971s have the TCS integrated into a throttle position solenoid and the two together are called a Combined Emissions Control (CEC). The CEC is mounted with a bracket to the forward driver side of the carburetor base.

All 1972s have an anti-diesel solenoid that is mounted with a bracket to the carburetor base. The bracket is cadmium dichromate plated and the solenoid housing is silver cadmium plated.

All 1970–1972 Corvettes have what is commonly called an emissions label glued to the left upper area of the firewall. These labels are either white or yellow in color, and contain engine tune-up specifications as well as information about the emission control systems installed in the car.

Engine Compartment Brackets, Latches, Wiring, and Related Components

The firewall, underside of the hood, and engine compartment side of the inner wheelwells are painted semi-gloss black. The wheel side of the front and rear inner wheelwells are also painted semi-gloss black, though coverage is usually sparse. In addition, the rear areas of the wheel sides normally have some undercoating.

1970s and some 1971s have engine compartment wiring harnesses and vacuum hoses bundled together in a circle. Some 1971s and all 1972s have the harnesses and adjacent hoses bundled together in a row, so rather than forming a circle they are flat. The harnesses and hoses are held to each other with black plastic tie wraps.

All vacuum hose is color coded with an ink stripe that runs the length of the hose. Larger hoses have a green, red, or yellow stripe while smaller hoses usually have a white stripe.

All 1970–1972 Corvettes equipped with a big block have a small oil pressure line bracket on the left side of the engine block. A steel tube goes from the brass block fitting to a junction at this bracket. Then a black plastic tube continues up to the oil pressure gauge.

All 1970–1972 small-block-equipped cars utilize black plastic tubing that goes directly from the engine

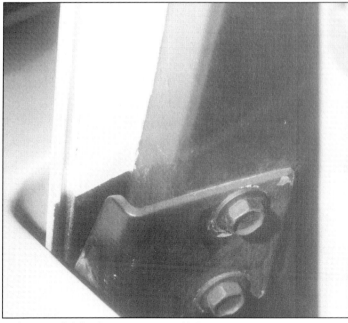

Hoods were installed when the engine compartment blackout operation was performed. The underside of the hood lip was masked only to the area that was easily accessible, leaving black overspray on the bottom of the hood and on the hinge.

Most 1970–1982 Corvettes have a Transmission Controlled Spark (TCS) system. In 1971 the TCS was integrated into a throttle position solenoid (shown here with the caution sticker on it), and the two together are called a Combined Emissions Control (CEC).

This type of plastic tie, shown here on a 1972, was used throughout the engine compartment to hold wires and vacuum hoses in place. Tape reinforced with a woven fabric (a deteriorating piece of which can be seen in the lower center of the photo) was used to bind vacuum hoses to each other at junctions.

block fitting to the oil pressure gauge. The plastic line has tiny white lettering and is fastened at both ends with brass fittings.

All cars have a horn relay mounted to the inner wheelwell. 1970 relays have a zinc-plated cover with "DELCO REMY, MADE IN THE USA," and four letters stamped in from the inside out. The cover sits on a black plastic base that has a silver cadmium–plated metal bracket attached for mounting.

1971 horn relays are the same as 1970 units except that the mounting bracket is black plastic and is part of the base rather than being a separate, metal piece.

The 1972 horn relay has a short, squared-off silver cadmium cover that has nothing stamped in. The plain cover sits on a black plastic base and relies on a black plastic tab that is formed as part of the black plastic base for mounting.

1970 Corvettes have two horns, a high and a low note. The high note is part No. 9000246 and it mounts on the driver side. The low note is part No. 9000245 and it mounts on the passenger side.

In 1971 and 1972 only one horn is installed. It is part No. 9000245 in 1971 and part No. 9000032 in 1972.

Horns have the last three digits of the part number and a manufacturing date code stamped into flat areas near the sound opening. The date code contains a number denoting the year, a letter denoting the

All big-block valve covers are equipped with welded-on brackets to hold spark plug wire looms. This is the rear bracket on a late 1971. The positions of the brackets changed over time.

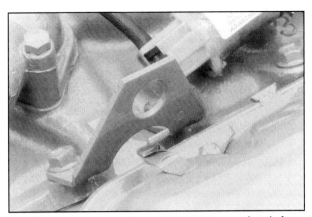

Engine lifting brackets are attached to most 1970–1972 Corvettes. This is the forward bracket on a 1971 454 engine. It is painted engine color, as is the intake manifold. A second bracket attaches to the rear of the passenger-side cylinder head for all 1970–1972 big blocks. Note the little horseshoe-shaped stamping in the bracket. This was the manufacturer's logo.

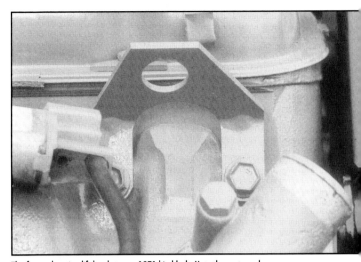

The forward engine lift bracket on a 1971 big block. Note the part number "3994055" stamped into the bracket on this side.

month (with "A" representing January, "B" representing February, and so on), and another number indicating the week. For example, a horn stamped "1D2" was made the second week of April 1971.

Each horn is spot welded to a mounting bracket and the whole assembly is painted semi-gloss black.

Hood hinges are silver cadmium plated and usually have both body color and underhood black overspray on them. Hinges are usually fastened by black phosphate–plated, indented hex head bolts.

The hood support is silver cadmium plated. 1970 and 1971 supports have two sections that telescope together as the hood is lowered. 1972 supports have two sections that are hinged and they fold as the hood is lowered.

The hood latches are black phosphate plated and mount with black phosphate–plated hardware. The driver-side male latch has the hood release cable attached with a brass barrel cable stop that utilizes a hex bolt to lock the stop to the cable. The cable is inside a spiral-wound metal sheath.

Another cable connects the two female latches mounted to the underside of the hood. This cable is inside a black nylon sheath and its ends are secured to the latches with small clevis pins fitted with flat washers and cotter pins.

1970–1972 Chassis
Chassis

1970–1972 Corvette chassis are painted semi-gloss black. Chassis for automatic transmission–equipped cars have a removable, bolt-on center cross-member, whereas standard transmission–equipped cars have a welded-on center cross-member. Also,

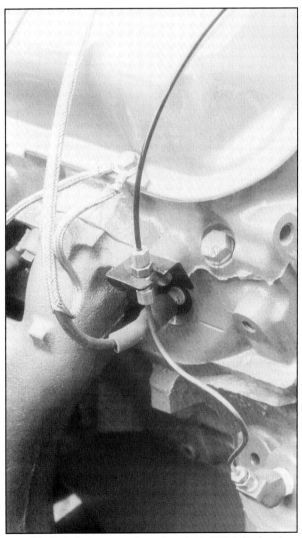

A typical big-block oil pressure gauge line configuration. In 1968 the line from the bracket to the gauge was steel. Beginning in 1969 this line was black plastic.

Certain things are much easier to see with the body removed from this 1971! The fuel filler neck boot and drain hose were common to all years. The steel line on the left chassis rail, as well as the hoses on the left side of the tank, are part of the vapor recovery system. The hose going into the top of the right side of the tank is the fuel return line.

cars with automatics do not have a clutch cross shaft tower welded on top of the chassis behind the left front wheel as standard transmission cars do.

A pair of 1-inch-high chassis part number sequences is painted in white on the frame with a stencil. One sequence is the A.O. Smith part number (this is the company that fabricated the chassis for GM), and the other sequence is the Chevrolet part number.

A manufacturing date code is stenciled on the rail as well. The date contains one or two numbers representing the month, one or two numbers indicating the day, and two numbers denoting the year.

The stencil numbers and date code usually appear on the outside of the right frame rail and are usually upside down.

All 1970–1972 Corvettes have their serial number stamped into their chassis in two locations. It is typically found in the left-side rail slightly forward of the No. 4 body mount bracket. It is also typically found on the left-side rear kick up above the wheel area slightly forward of the No. 3 body mount bracket.

Steel shims are frequently utilized at body mount points to make up for irregularities in fit. If present, shims are usually taped to the body mount bracket with 1 1/2-inch masking tape. The number of shims needed at each body mount bracket is typically written on the chassis adjacent to the bracket with a green or white grease crayon. Unlike earlier cars, this number is usually an actual number rather than slash marks.

Body mounts are not made from rubber as in 1967 and older Corvettes. Instead they are thick aluminum discs that get sandwiched between the body and the chassis' body mount bracket.

Front Suspension

Upper and lower front control arms are painted semi-gloss to gloss black. Ball joints are installed after the arms are painted and are not painted. Crushed steel rivets (not bolts) hold ball joints on and are also natural in finish.

Control arm cross shafts are painted semi-gloss black on some cars and unpainted on others. Cars with painted cross shafts typically have control arm

All Corvettes have their serial number stamped into their chassis in at least two locations. The number is typically found in the left-side rail slightly forward of the No. 4 body mount bracket and, as shown here, on the left-side rear kick up above the wheel area slightly forward of the No. 3 body mount bracket.

All Corvette chassis received a stenciled-on part number and date code. The date, in this case May 6, 1971, represents when the chassis was pulled from the stack and fed into the assembly system for build up into a car. Since the stencils were applied with the chassis stacked upside down, the stencil reads upside down with the chassis right side up.

bushing retention washers and bolts that are also painted semi-gloss black. Cars with unpainted cross shafts typically have retention washers that are gray phosphate plated, and bolts that are black phosphate plated.

Front coil springs are natural in finish and sometimes have an irregular bluish cast from the manufacturing process. A green paper sticker contains two black letters indicating the spring's broadcast code (i.e., their application) as well as a black GM part number.

Front shock absorbers are manufactured by Delco and are oil hydraulic, not gas filled. They are painted semi-gloss gray and have the words "DELCO REMY PLIACELL" and a date code stamped in around the bottom. The Julian date code

contains three numbers indicating the day and two numbers denoting the year. In addition, there is a small paper sticker with a two-letter broadcast code on the side of the shock.

The upper shock mount rubber bushings are unpainted black rubber. The top upper bushing is larger in diameter than the bottom upper bushing and the upper shock washer is gray phosphate plated.

The lower shock mount rubber bushings are integral to the shock and are therefore painted along with the shock.

All 1970–1972 big-block Corvettes and all small-block-equipped cars with optional F-41 suspension utilize a 15/16-inch front sway bar. All small blocks not equipped with F-41 utilize a 3/4-inch bar. Some

Steering gear boxes contain the Saginaw logo and a part number cast into the side as shown here. Some boxes were painted semi-gloss black while others were unpainted.

With standard steering the outer tie rod ends install into the rear holes in the steering knuckles. With power steering, and cars equipped with an L88 or ZL1 engine, the tie rods are in the forward holes. When the tie rod ends are in the forward hole as shown here, the unused hole is closed off with an aluminum plug.

cars have a semi-gloss black painted sway bar while others have a natural, unpainted finish bar.

Bushings mounting the front sway bar to the chassis, as well as bushings in the end links, are unpainted black rubber. Semi-gloss black painted, stamped steel brackets hold the bar to the chassis.

End link bolts are zinc plated 5/16-24 SAE fine thread and have the manufacturer's logo "WB" in their heads. End link spacers are zinc plated, have a split seam, and typically have a "K" or a "C" stamped in.

Steering Box and Steering Linkage

1970–1972 Corvettes use a cast steering gear that is usually natural in color though some are painted semi-gloss black. A daub of yellow or blue paint is frequently seen on top of the box.

A forged pitman arm links the steering box to the relay rod. The pitman arm is natural in color and is often seen with a blue or green daub of paint.

The steering relay rod and idler arm are typically natural finish. Both parts are forged and tend to have a blue-gray tint. Original idler arms do not have grease fittings.

Tie rod ends are natural finish and also typically have a bluish-gray color cast. Daubs of yellow paint are often seen on tie rod ends.

Tie rod end sleeves are painted semi-gloss black. Tie rod end clamps have two reinforcing ridges around their circumference and are sometimes painted semi-gloss black and sometimes left unpainted.

Outer tie rod ends can install into either of two holes in the steering knuckles. Cars equipped with

standard, non-power steering have the outer tie rod ends installed into the rear holes while cars equipped with power steering have them in the forward holes. On those cars equipped with power steering the unused steering knuckle hole is plugged with an aluminum plug inserted from the bottom.

On those cars so equipped, the power steering control valve and hydraulic cylinder are painted semi-gloss black. The nut and washers retaining the hydraulic cylinder's ram to the frame bracket are zinc plated. The frame bracket may be painted semi-gloss black or unpainted. Original power steering hoses typically have longitudinal ridges around their entire circumference while later replacements don't.

Rear Suspension

All 1970–1972 Corvettes equipped with standard suspension utilize a nine-leaf rear spring. Cars equipped with optional F-41 suspension utilize a seven-leaf spring. All springs are painted light gray and have black plastic liners between the leaves. Nine-leaf springs do not have a liner between leaf No. 6 and leaf No. 7 (with the bottom leaf being No. 1).

The center rear spring mount bracket is painted semi-gloss black. The four bolts retaining the spring to the differential typically have the manufacturer's logo "WB" on their heads and are either black phosphate or zinc plated. The outer spring bolts and nuts are usually black phosphate plated and the washers are typically natural.

Rear trailing arms are painted semi-gloss to gloss black. Rear wheel bearing carriers (also called spindle supports) are natural and have a part number and date code cast in. The date code has a letter

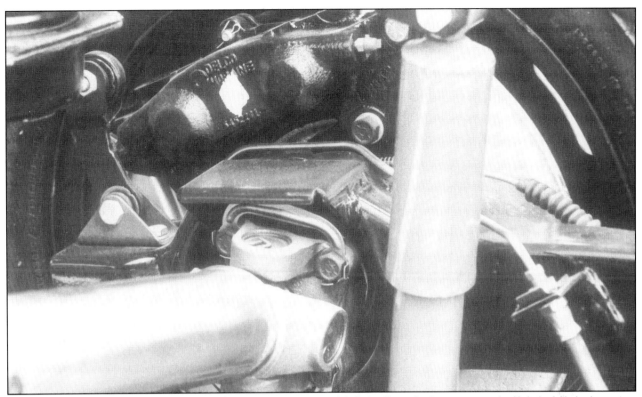

This rear wheel assembly is typical for 1968–1982. The half shaft and its flange are unpainted, the brake caliper and trailing arm are semi-gloss black, the shock absorber is gray, and the brake line, emergency brake cable, and brake hose are all unpainted.

Drive shaft and half shafts were not painted or coated at the factory. The tube should be smooth, shiny steel and the welded-on ends should have a dull gray cast.

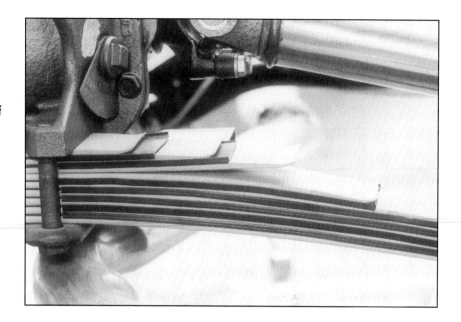

Steel rear springs, used on all 1969–1982s except 1981 automatics and 1982s with standard suspension (not FE7), use leaves that are painted light gray. All cars through 1977 have unpainted black plastic liners between the leaves. Beginning in 1978 the liners are painted gray. Nine-leaf springs do not have a liner between leaf No. 6 and leaf No. 7 (with the bottom leaf being No. 1).

representing the month, with "A" for January, "B" for February, and so on, one or two numbers for the day, and one number for the final digit of the year. The date code for a rear bearing carrier made on April 18, 1971, for example, would read "D 18 1."

All 1970–1972 big blocks have a rear stabilizer bar. The bar is 9/16 inch in diameter and may be painted semi-gloss black or unpainted. It mounts to the chassis with semi-gloss black painted, stamped steel brackets. At each end the bar has a semi-gloss black painted link bracket that attaches to brackets bolted to the trailing arms. The brackets on the trailing arms have a plating that is sometimes called a "pickling." It results in a brownish-olive color. These brackets attach to the trailing arm via bolts that thread into small, unpainted steel plates that slip into the rear of the arms.

Rear camber adjustment rods (also called strut rods) are usually natural and often have a bluish-gray tint. Some rods are painted semi-gloss black or are partially painted during the undercarriage "black-out" process. Original rods have 1-1/2-inch-diameter ends while 1974 and newer rods have 1-3/4-inch-diameter ends.

The outboard ends of the camber adjustment rods are held to the rear wheel bearing carriers with forged L-shaped pins that also serve as the lower mounts for the rear shock absorbers. These pins, which are sometimes referred to as rear shock brackets, contain a raised part number.

The inboard ends of the camber adjustment rods attach to a semi-gloss black painted bracket with special bolts. These bolts have integral off-center washers that, when rotated, move the rods in or out and thus allow for rear wheel camber adjustment. The camber adjustment bolts are usually silver cadmium plated though they may be black phosphate plated instead.

Rear wheel toe adjustment is set with the use of shims placed on either side of the trailing arms where they mount to the chassis. The adjusting shims are unpainted rectangular pieces of steel of varying thicknesses. In 1970 the shims have equal-size holes at each end, and when installed one end protrudes from the chassis pocket where the end of the trailing arm resides. The last few hundred 1970s produced and all 1971–1972 cars use a different style of shim. This second design has a slot in one end that slips over the trailing arm mount bolt. Rather than protruding from the chassis pocket the other ends of all the shims are rotated upward so their holes all align with a corresponding hole in the chassis. A long cotter pin passes through the stacks of shims on both sides of the trailing arm and through the hole in the chassis.

Rear axle shafts (often called "half shafts") are made from forged ends welded to extruded steel tubes. The axle shafts are natural, with the tube being shiny silver and the ends being a dull gray. 1972-only shafts sometimes have a faint alligator-type pattern in the tube. Slashes, or green, blue, or white paint are sometimes seen on axle shaft tubes.

U-joints do not have grease fittings and do have a raised part number on the body. They are natural and tend to have that faint bluish tint that is characteristic of forged parts.

The outboard axle shaft U-joints are pressed into a flange that is natural in color. The flange is held to the rear wheel bearing carrier by four bolts that are usually black phosphate plated. The bolts are prevented from turning out by two pairs of French locks, the tabs of which are bent over to contact the bolt heads. The French locks are zinc plated and typically have only one of the two tabs adjacent to each bolt bent over.

The inboard axle shaft U-joints are held to the differential output yokes by one of two methods. Forged caps and bolts are used on Corvettes equipped with a 454 engine, and U-shaped strap clamps with nuts are used on cars equipped with a 350 engine.

Front Wheel Assemblies

Front spindles and steering knuckles are natural and tend to have a bluish tint to their gray color. In addition, the lower portions of the spindles are frequently seen with orange or white paint as though the bottoms of the spindles were dipped into it.

Original front brake backing plates are zinc plated and then chromate dipped. This results in varying finishes ranging from gold with a faint rainbow of other colors throughout to a dull silver with only a trace of the yellowish chromate coloring. Well-preserved original backing plates typically appear dull silver, probably because the chromate dip deteriorates over time.

Front brake caliper support brackets are plated silver cadmium or cadmium dichromate, which results in a translucent gold color with varying degrees of other colors present in a rainbow-like pattern.

Cars equipped with option ZR1 or ZR2 have a heavy-duty brake package. This package includes front calipers that use two pins to hold the pads instead of the standard one, extra front caliper supports, semi-metallic brake pads, heat insulators on the face of all caliper pistons, and a proportioning valve mounted beneath the master cylinder.

Front brake calipers are painted semi-gloss black and frequently have blue or white daubs of paint on the side. Painting is done before the caliper halves are machined, and therefore machined surfaces are unpainted. Bleeder screws are zinc plated and remain unpainted.

Caliper hoses are black rubber with gold irridite–plated end hardware. Federally mandated DOT specifications are written on the hose in red ink. In addition, there is a red longitudinal stripe put there to make it easier to see if the hose is twisted. Original hoses typically have raised longitudinal ridges around their entire circumference while later replacements are typically smooth.

Front brake rotors are natural in finish. The front wheel bearing carrier (also called a "hub") is riveted to the rotor disc.

Rear Wheel Assemblies

As with the fronts, original rear brake backing plates were zinc plated and then chromate dipped. This resulted in varying finishes ranging from gold with a faint rainbow of other colors throughout to a dull silver with only a trace of the yellowish chromate coloring. Well-preserved original backing plates typically appear dull silver, probably because the chromate dip deteriorates over time.

Rear brake caliper support brackets are natural, and hence a dull gray, or on occasion painted flat to semi-flat black.

Rear brake calipers are painted semi-gloss black and frequently have blue or white daubs of paint on the side. Painting is done before the caliper halves are machined and therefore machined surfaces are unpainted. Bleeder screws are zinc plated and remain unpainted.

Rear brake rotors are natural in finish. They are riveted to the rear spindle, which is pressed into the rear wheel bearing carrier. In order to service the park brake assembly or the rear wheel bearings, the rivets are often drilled out. The wheel lug nuts retain the rotor in the absence of the rivets.

Transmission

Automatic-equipped 1970–1972 Corvettes utilize a Turbo-Hydra-Matic 400 transmission. The main case and the tail housing are both cast aluminum with a natural finish. The fluid pan is stamped steel and is also natural.

Automatic transmissions contain an identification plate on the right side. The plate has two alphanumeric sequences stamped in. The bottom sequence is the car's serial number and the top sequence is referred to as a production code. The first

Automatic transmissions were stamped with the VIN of the car they were originally installed into. This 1971 Turbo-Hydra-Matic 400 was stamped on the driver side near the bottom where the fluid pan mounts.

This is the identification plate mounted to the right side of a 1971 Turbo-Hydra-Matic 400 transmission. The top sequence, "71S 505," translates as follows: "71" indicates the model year 1971; "S" indicates it's a Turbo 400 in a 454 Corvette ("Y" is the 1971 Corvette 454 application code and "S" is the 1972 code, but since this transmission is in a very late 1971 car it got the 1972 code); and "505" indicates it was assembled February 17, 1971 (the 505th day from January 1, 1970, which is when the count began for the 1971 model year). The bottom sequence indicates the model year, application, and unit number.

two numbers of this code indicate the model year. Next comes a letter that denotes the car model (in our case Corvette) and the engine. This is followed by three numbers that represent the day the transmission was assembled.

The transmission assembly date is a modified version of the Julian calendar system. The three numbers represent the day of the year, but unlike most applications of the Julian calendar system in dating Corvette components, with transmissions the count does not begin with the first day of the year. Instead, for 1970 model Corvettes it begins with January 1, 1969, and continues sequentially through calendar year 1970. Similarly, for 1971 models it begins January 1, 1970, and continues through calendar year 1971. And for 1972 models it begins January 1, 1971, and continues through calendar year 1972.

This dating system sounds confusing, but it's easy once you get the hang of it. For example, in the production code "71Y018," the "71" represents the 1971 model year, "Y" represents the application code (which is 1971 Corvette with 454 engine), and "018" represents the 18th day from when the count begins. Remember, the count begins January 1st of the preceding year, so this transmission was assembled January 18, 1970. Had that same transmission been assembled January 18, 1971, the code would read "71Y383," with January 18, 1971, being 383 days after the count for the 1971 model year began.

The application codes for 1970–1972 Corvettes include "K" for all small blocks, "S" for 1972s with a

454 engine, and the aforementioned "Y" for 1970–1971s with a 454 engine.

Four-speed manual transmissions have cast-aluminum main cases, side covers, and tail housings that are natural in color. A steel tag with a part number is affixed to the transmission with one of the side cover bolts.

Two alpha-numeric sequences are stamped into the main case on a vertical surface at the front of the right side. One of these sequences is the car's serial number. The other is a production code and the date the transmission was originally assembled.

The production code begins with a letter to indicate the source for the transmission. All Corvette four-speeds were obtained from Muncie, which is represented by the letter "P." This is followed by a number representing the last digit of the model year. Next, there is a letter indicating the month of production, followed by two numbers denoting the day of the month. Various letters are not used in denoting the month, so refer to this chart when determining assembly date:

A	January
B	February
C	March
D	April
E	May
H	June
K	July
M	August
P	September
R	October
S	November
T	December

The final character in the production code is a letter commonly called a suffix code. This letter indicates which of the three available four-speeds the unit is. For the suffix code, "A" indicates a wide-ratio M-20 with 2.52:1 first gear ratio. "B" indicates a close-ratio M-21 with a 2.20:1 first gear ratio. And "C" denotes a close-ratio M-22 "heavy-duty" transmission, which also has a 2.20:1 first gear ratio.

An example of a four-speed transmission code is "P1D18A." This identifies an M-20 wide-ratio Muncie four-speed assembled April 18, 1971.

Differential and Driveshaft

All 1970–1972 Corvettes are equipped with a Positraction limited-slip differential. The differential case and cover are both natural-colored castings and as such are a dull silvery gray.

A plastic triangular tag is attached to the differential by means of the square head oil fill plug. The

The cast-iron differential covers on 1968–1979 cars contain a casting date on the passenger side. The code "E 8 1" translates to May 8, 1971. The limited-slip lubricant tag is red with white lettering, and the blotch of paint next to the fill plug was an inspector's mark.

tag is red with white lettering that says "USE LIMITED SLIP DIFF. LUBRICANT ONLY." The fill plug is natural and has a large "W" cast into the square.

Front input yoke and side output yokes are forgings that are natural in color. Because they are forged they have a somewhat smoother surface than the case and cover, and they tend to have a slight bluish tint to their dull gray color.

Differential cases and covers both have casting numbers and a casting date that includes a letter for the month (with "A" representing January, "B" representing February, and so on), one or two numbers indicating the day of the month, and one number indicating the last digit of the year.

In addition to the cast-in dates, all cases also have a stamped-in production code. In 1970 the code begins with a number that indicates the assembly shift that built the unit. This is followed by a three-letter code indicating the gear ratio. Next comes a modified Julian date code that includes one or two numbers for the month, one or two numbers for the day, and two numbers for the

year. The final character in the 1970 production code is a letter that indicates the specific plant that built the differential.

For 1971 and 1972 the differential production code begins with two letters to indicate the gear

As with all cast-iron parts, differential housings contain a casting number. The number on this 1971 example is located on the forward passenger side.

All Corvettes were fitted with French locks under the half shaft flange mounting bolts to prevent the bolts from coming out.

ratio. This is followed by a single letter denoting the assembly plant. Then come one, two, or three numbers representing the day of the year the unit was assembled. After this there is a single letter that indicates the source for the Positraction unit (which was not necessarily the same company that assembled the differential). The final number in the sequence represents the assembly shift that built the unit.

(See Appendix E for differential gear ratio codes.)

The transmission and differential are connected by a drive shaft made from extruded steel tubing welded at each end to a forged universal joint coupling. As with the axle shafts, the drive shaft is natural in color. The center tube portion is bright silver with longitudinal extrusion lines sometimes visible and the ends are a dull silvery gray with a slight bluish hue at times.

A part number stenciled on the drive shaft tube in yellow or white paint is sometimes seen. One or two green circumferential stripes on the tube and daubs of various colors of paint on the forged ends are sometimes seen as well.

Exhaust System

All 1970–1972 Corvettes use an undercar, carbon steel exhaust system manufactured by Walker for Chevrolet. All cars equipped with a big-block engine or an LT-1 engine utilize 2 1/2-inch exhaust pipes. All other cars utilize 2-inch pipes.

Even though LT-1 engines get 2 1/2-inch pipes they still use the same 2-inch outlet exhaust manifolds as other small blocks. This is accomplished by swaging the 2 1/2-inch front engine pipes down to 2 inches at their ends.

Mufflers are galvanized on the exterior and have an embossed "W" to represent the manufacturer. At the rear of each muffler there is one welded-on bracket to which the rear hangar bolts. Mufflers are welded to the intermediate exhaust pipe, not clamped. 2 1/2-inch intermediate pipes are flattened somewhat where they pass underneath the rear camber adjustment rod bracket for additional ground clearance; 2-inch pipes are not flattened.

A rectangular, chrome-plated carbon steel exhaust tip is clamped to each muffler. There are two different tips used in 1970–1972. Tips used on 1970s assembled through approximately mid-July 1970 have a weld bead where the rectangular portion is fastened to the flat back portion. The underside of the rectangular portion does not have a weld bead or anything stamped in. It is smooth and flat.

After mid-July 1970 a second design tip began to be used. The second design tip is the same as the first except it has a weld seam on the underside of the rectangular section. Either the first or second design, or one of each, is seen on very late 1970s (cars made after mid-July 1970) and those 1971s assembled through approximately early May 1971. 1971s assembled after approximately early May 1971 and all 1972s have the second design exhaust tips.

Fuel Lines, Brake Lines, and Miscellaneous Chassis and Underbody Components.

All 1970–1972 fuel lines run along, and at times through, the right-side chassis rail. All cars except those equipped with an LT-1 engine have two fuel lines. One supplies fuel from the tank to the carburetor and the other is a return line.

In addition to the one or two fuel lines on the right side of the chassis, for all 1971s, 1972s, and those 1970s equipped with NA9 (Evaporative Emission Control, which was required for all cars delivered new in California), a vapor return line is on the left side of the chassis.

Fuel lines are galvanized carbon steel. Black rubber fuel hose connects the lines to the tank and the fuel pump. Zinc chromate–plated spring clamps are usually used to secure the hose to its line. Exceptions to this include the hoses on the fuel return line in 1970 and most of 1971, which use small, galvanized tower-style clamps.

Brake lines are galvanized carbon steel. Brake line end fittings are brass. Fittings at the master cylinder are often seen with red or blue dye, which was probably used to denote the two different sizes. In addition, daubs of yellow paint are sometimes seen on the fittings at junction blocks.

Various heat shields are affixed to the underside of the body to help insulate the passenger compartment from engine and exhaust system heat. A sheet-steel shield, which is gray phosphate plated, is mounted on the lower vertical area of the firewall on both sides. In addition, 1970s that were assembled through approximately February or March 1970 and that are equipped with a big-block engine have two more similar shields underneath the floor below the seat area.

All cars are fitted with transmission tunnel insulation. A semi-rigid foil-wrapped blanket in the shape of the tunnel is fastened above the transmission with clips riveted to the underbody.

All cars have a thick, black foam insulating pad attached to the underbody above the engine's bell-housing. A thick, white foam pad is fastened to the underbody on each side of the car just forward of the doors.

A variety of steel plates are fastened to the underbody to mount components in the passenger compartment. These components include the battery, seats, jack hold down clips, and so on. All of these plates are painted semi-gloss black and are retained by unpainted aluminum rivets.

Chapter 3

1973-1977

1973-1977 Exterior

Body Fiberglass and Body Paint

All 1973-1977 Corvette body panels are made from press molded fiberglass. The panels are smooth on both sides and are very dark gray in color. All 1973-1977 cars were painted with acrylic lacquer. Factory paint is generally smooth and shiny though some orange peel is evident throughout. Roughness and poor coverage are fairly typical along the very bottom edges of body panels. Overall paint quality was relatively poor and as consumers became more demanding the factory made a greater effort to eliminate flaws before the cars were shipped. As a result, many mid-1970s Corvettes left the St. Louis factory with considerable paint touchups. Clear coat was not used by the factory, even with metallic colors. Because clear coat was not used metallics may tend to be slightly mottled or blotchy.

Front Bumpers

All 1973-1977 Corvettes are fitted with impact-absorbing front bumper assemblies. The cover is made from urethane that is painted body color. A flex additive is mixed with the paint used on the bumper cover to discourage the paint from cracking. The flex additive often causes the paint on the bumper to be a slightly different shade than the paint on the rest of the car. The remainder of the bumper assembly, which is covered by the urethane piece, is comprised of several semi-gloss black painted steel components. Black phosphate– or silver cadmium–plated hex head bolts are used to retain the underlying bumper structure to the chassis. 1975-1977 Corvette front bumpers were redesigned to include two black rubber-tipped protrusions on either side of the license plate area. The underlying

bumper assembly was modified in 1975 to allow it to sustain minor impacts without damage.

Front Grille Area, Parking Lamps, and Front License Plate Area

In 1973 the front grille assemblies are made from cast pot metal. They are painted semi-gloss black with the leading edges of the horizontal bars chrome plated. In 1974-1977 they are made from cast aluminum instead of pot metal and are entirely semi-flat black painted with no chrome accents. Cars delivered new in states utilizing only a rear license plate also have a center grille that was placed inside the car for dealer installation. This center grille matches the two outer grilles. Cars delivered new in states requiring two license plates got a front license plate mounting assembly instead of the center grille.

For all 1973-1977 Corvettes, the front parking lamp housings are mounted in the front grilles. In 1973 the park lamp lenses are made from clear plastic with silver painted horizontal lines. In 1974-1977 they have black painted horizontal lines. All years have amber-colored bulbs.

Rectangular-shaped side marker lamps are used at all four corners in 1973-1977. The lamp housings, which can only be seen from behind the body panels, are made from diecast aluminum in 1973 and some early 1974s. Later 1974s and subsequent years have plastic-bodied side marker lamps. All front side marker lamps have amber lenses while rears have red lenses.

On those 1973-1974 cars so equipped, front license plate brackets are painted semi-gloss black and are held on by four black oxide Phillips oval head screws with integral washers. A small rubber bumper is inserted in a hole toward the bottom center of the bracket, and two white plastic nuts insert into square holes in the upper corners.

A stainless-steel license plate frame (two frames in cars delivered to states requiring two plates) was in the luggage compartment when the car was new. In addition, a small brown paper bag marked "UNIT NUMBER 3875313" across the top, "LICENSE ATTACHING" on one side, and "REAR PLATE PARTS" on the other, came in the car originally. In it were four large cadmium-plated, slotted pan head screws for the front and rear license plates.

Front Headlamps and Headlamp Bezels

All four headlamp bulbs in 1973–1977 were made by Guide and feature a Guide Power Beam logo in the glass. This logo is a circle with the word "POWER" above it and the word "BEAM" below it. Very early 1973s, assembled through approximately December 1972, may have headlamp bezels made from diecast aluminum. Later 1973 and all 1974–1977 cars have bezels made from fiberglass. All bezels are painted body color. Paint on the bezels is usually not as shiny or smooth as it is on the body. A cadmium dichromate vacuum actuator is mounted behind each headlamp assembly. A red-striped hose connects to the back of each actuator and a green-striped hose connects to the front.

Front Fenders

1973–1977 front fenders got a redesigned vent area, which features a molded-in recess in the fiberglass. In 1973–1976 both fenders have an emblem reading "Stingray" above the fender vents. The emblems are chrome with the thin stepped edge surrounding

each letter painted black. Emblems are held onto the body by a thick black adhesive strip that is visible and each has four long studs that were used for positioning only and therefore do not get nuts.

Early 1977s do not have the Stingray emblems or any other emblems on the front fenders. Later 77s have a crossed flags emblem on each fender. All 1973–1977 Corvettes are equipped with an anti-theft alarm system. In 1973 the key switch for the alarm is in the taillamp panel as before. In 1974 through mid-1977 it is located in the driver-side front fender above the forward edge of the fender vent. In mid-1977 the switch was deleted from the fender and incorporated into the driver-side door lock cylinder. For the fender-mounted alarm key switches, the bezel should be crimped over around its full circumference just like the door locks. Incorrect replacement key switches have bezels with four tabs that bend over.

Hood

All 1973–1975 cars have a functional cowl induction hood. Outside air ingested at the base of the windshield is routed through the raised area down the middle of the hood and into the carburetor. An electrically actuated solenoid under the hood vent opens a valve when the throttle is sufficiently advanced, allowing additional cold air to flow to the carburetor.

The hood vent centered at the rear of the hood's power bulge is metal that gets painted body color. Six black phosphate–plated acorn nuts on the underside of the hood retain the vent. The functional cowl induction system is eliminated in 1976 but the hood vent remains throughout the year. In 1977 the nonfunctional hood vent is eliminated.

Passenger-side hood latch details from 1977.

Hood insulation as seen in 1977.

Wiper blade inserts say "TRICO" and have various patent numbers molded in. Two raised ribs are present below all of the writing. In 1973 and 1974 the wiper blades rest against a square metal bracket when they are parked. In 1975–1977 the blades rest against a V-shaped metal bracket. The top and sides of the windshield are surrounded by stainless-steel trim. In 1973–1976 this trim is unpainted and highly polished. In 1977 the windshield trim is painted satin black.

Windshield, Door Glass, and Back Glass

All 1973–1977 Corvette windshields were manufactured by Libby-Owens-Ford (LOF) utilizing Safety Flo-Lite glass. The LOF logo, "SHADED SOFT RAY," "SAFETY FLO-LITE," "LAMINATED DOT 15 M24," and a two-letter manufacturing date code are etched into the lower right side of the windshield. In the date code, one letter represents the month and the other denotes the year. There is no discernible pattern to the letter usage, so you must refer to the glass date codes in Appendix R.

The letters "ASI" are present in the upper right portion of the windshield. These letters are white and sandwiched between the laminates of glass, not etched into the surface like the logo and date code. Both side windows are made from tinted LOF Safety Flo Lite glass that has the manufacturer's logo and a two-letter date code etched in just like the windshield. The words "Astro Ventilation" are present in white silk-screened letters in the lower forward corner of each window in 1973s and most 1974s. The designation was eliminated toward the end of the 1974 model run.

Back windows in 1973–1977 coupes, like the windshields and side glass, have the LOF logo and

There are no emblems, decals, or other markings on the hood for base-engine-equipped cars. 1973 and 1974 Corvettes fitted with a 454 engine have a "454" emblem on each side of the hood's bulge. The emblems are chrome with painted black recesses. The numbers that form each emblem are joined by a base, unlike earlier hood emblems that have individual numbers. 1975–1977 Corvettes equipped with the optional L82 engine have an "L-82" emblem on either side of the hood. Some early 1975 L82s may not have these emblems.

Windshield Wipers and Windshield Washers

Wiper arms and blade holders are dull black in color and each holder says "TRICO" on one of its ends. On those 1973s assembled through approximately mid-October 1972, a length of metal washer tubing is soldered to a small tab at the end of each wiper arm and is further retained by between one and four black plastic clips. On those 1973s assembled thereafter and all 1974–1977 cars the metal tube is replaced with rubber hose.

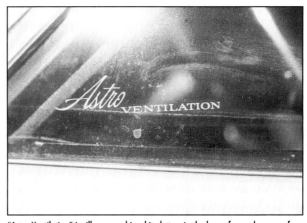

"Astro Ventilation" is silk screened in white letters in the lower forward corner of each window in 1973s and most 1974s. The designation was eliminated toward the end of the 1974 model run.

manufacturing date code etched in. Starting in 1973 back windows are no longer removable as they had been previously.

Door Mirror, Handles, and Locks

All 1973–1976 and most 1977 Corvettes have one outside rearview mirror that is mounted on the driver's door. A mounting base is held to the door by two screws and the mirror goes over the base and is held on by a black oxide Allen head screw. A thin gasket goes between the base and door and is visible when the mirror is installed.

Option D35, first available in 1977, substituted dual sport mirrors for the single chrome one. Each door got one of the sport mirrors, which were painted exterior color.

In 1973 and 1974 the mirror's rectangular head measures 3 7/8 inches high by 5 3/8 inches wide. In 1975–1977 it is 3 3/4 inches high by 6 1/4 inches wide. For all years the glass is coded with the manufacturer's symbol and a date code. The majority of 1973–1977 mirrors were supplied by Donnelly Mirror, Inc. These have "DMI" in the date code, while mirrors supplied by Ajax Mirror have "AX" in it. For example, the code in a Donnelly-supplied mirror manufactured in April 1975 would read "4-DMI-5" while the code for an Ajax-supplied mirror manufactured in February 1973 would read "2-AX-73."

All 1973–1977 door handles are a spring-loaded, press flap design. On original handles the spring action is provided by a coil spring on the hinge shaft. A butterfly spring covering a coil spring is incorrect. When the flap is depressed the spring is visible. A thin black rubber gasket is visible between the handle and door.

The door locks, which are positioned below the door handles, feature a polished stainless-steel bezel. Original bezels are retained to the cylinders by means of a continuous crimp around their entire circumference. Incorrect replacement locks may have bezels retained by four tangs. A thin, black rubber gasket is visible between the lock and door.

Side Rocker Molding

Side rocker moldings for all 1973–1977 cars are brushed aluminum with a painted 3/8-inch-wide flat black stripe along their length. They attach to the body with six black oxide Phillips oval head screws. The forward and rearmost screws are sometimes pan head instead of oval head. In addition to the six screws that go through the face toward the top edge, original rocker moldings also have a single vertical fastener that goes through a tab on the molding's lower lip near the front and into a J-nut on the body.

A single chrome-plated side view mirror mounted on the driver's door was standard in 1973–1977. Dual sport mirrors became optional in 1977. In 1973 and 1974 the mirror's rectangular head measures 3-7/8 inches high by 5-3/8 inches wide. In 1975–1977 it is 3-3/4 inches high by 6-1/4 inches wide.

A black oxide fillister head screw or a black oxide hex head screw is used at this mounting point.

Radio Antenna

A radio was still an option for Corvettes in 1973–1977 and several thousand cars were built without one. On those cars no radio antenna was installed but on all others an antenna was mounted on the driver-side rear deck. A black plastic gasket goes between the antenna base and the car's body. The base is also made of black plastic and it, along with the portion of the antenna assembly beneath the body, is retained by a chrome hex nut. A chrome cap with two flat areas for a wrench to grab holds the mast to the base.

Rear Deck Vent Grilles and Gas Fill Door

In all 1973–1975 cars two vent grilles are installed on the rear deck behind the back window (or behind the convertible top deck on convertibles). The vent

This 1976 antenna base is typical of all 1973–1977s.

Beginning in 1975 a decal reading "UNLEADED FUEL ONLY" was affixed to the gas lid door. This example is from a 1977.

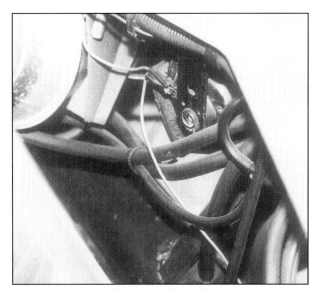

Details of the area between the radiator and front grilles in a 1977.

grilles are painted body color and are each retained by four black oxide Phillips flat head screws. The lips in the body the grilles sit on and the vent channel below are sprayed with flat black paint in varying degrees of coverage. The deck vent grilles remain open in all 1973s and in 1974s and 1975s not equipped with air conditioning. The vents exhaust passenger compartment air in non-air-conditioned cars. In 1974 and 1975 coupes equipped with air conditioning the vents are present, but get blocked with flat black painted plates. In 1974 and 1975 convertibles with air conditioning the vents are not blocked.

Gas lid doors are painted body color for all 1973–1977s. The doors in most 1973s feature a chrome and painted crossed flags emblem that is held on by cadmium acorn nuts visible with the door open. Late 1973s and all 1974s don't have any emblem on the gas lid door. 1975 and 1976 cars have a round Cloisonné emblem in the door. This emblem has a red sunburst pattern with crossed flags in the center. 1977s use a simple crossed flags emblem in the gas lid door. Beginning in 1975 a decal reading "UNLEADED FUEL ONLY" was affixed to the gas lid door. An

over-center spring integral to the hinge holds the gas lid door open. A C-shaped spring clipped to the lid holds the door closed. The door hinge is chrome plated and the door is held to the hinge with chrome-plated Phillips fillister head screws fitted with external star lock washers. The polished door bezel is held to the body with black oxide Phillips flat head screws. Two rubber bumpers insert into the bezel toward the rear of the car to cushion the door.

All 1973–1977s come with a gold irridite–plated, twist-on gas cap, not a locking cap. The locking caps, which are usually flat and chrome plated, were dealer installed or aftermarket. 1973 and 1974 caps resemble 1963–1972 units in their general appearance. Each has a handle for twisting it on and off. The handle is attached by two ears that are bent over and spot welded onto the cap. The words "OPEN SLOWLY,"

"CAUTION," and "SEALED" are stamped into the top side of the cap. The manufacturer's logo, a stylized "SM," is stamped into a circle on the cap's underside.

1975–1977 gas caps are a different design than earlier units. The twist handle is stamped into the cap from underneath rather than being a separate, welded-on piece. In addition, the outer perimeter has serrations formed in the metal. Wording stamped into the top reads "UNLEADED GASOLINE ONLY." There is also a part number stamped into the top. A black rubber boot surrounds the gas filler neck on all 1973–1977s. The boot has a plastic nipple facing the rear of the car and a rubber drain hose attaches to it. The hose, which has a metal spring inside to prevent it from collapsing, runs down behind the gas tank.

Rear Fascia, Taillamps, Bumpers, and Related Parts

In 1973 the rear body panel has "CORVETTE" spelled out in eight individual letters centered between the taillamps. Each letter is chrome plated with silver paint in its recessed face. Rear bumpers are chrome plated and are attached to the body with semi-gloss black painted brackets. Cadmium-plated hex head bolts retain the bumpers to the brackets and cadmium- and/or black oxide–plated hex head bolts hold the brackets to the chassis.

Only 1973s still have a distinct lower rear valance panel. It is painted body color but often shows poor paint quality including runs or sparse coverage along the bottom edge. It is retained to the body by four cadmium-plated, indented hex head bolts. The two outer ones utilize integral washers while the two inners have separate flat washers.

In 1974–1977 the rear body panel, chrome bumpers, and lower valance are all replaced with an impact-absorbing bumper assembly. As in the front, this assembly consists of a body-colored urethane cover fitted over a multi-piece metal understructure. In 1974 only the urethane cover is two pieces, with a vertical seam at the centerline of the car. In 1975–1977 the cover is one piece, so the seam is eliminated.

1974 and 1975 cars have "CORVETTE" spelled out in eight individual letters centered between the taillamps. 1976 and 1977 cars have "CORVETTE" spelled out in a single nameplate rather than individual letters. Earlier 1976s use a 6-inch-wide emblem and have a recess molded into the bumper for the emblem. Later 1976s and all 1977s use an 8-inch-wide emblem and do not have a recess. Recesses for taillamps and a license plate are molded into 1974–1977 rear bumper covers. 1975–1977 cars also have two black rubber-tipped protrusions toward the lower outboard corners of the rear bumper cover.

All 1973–1977 cars use a rectangular-shaped side marker. The lamp housings, which can only be seen from behind the body panels, are made from diecast aluminum for 1973s and some early 1974s. Later cars have plastic-bodied side marker lamps. All front side marker lamps have amber lenses while rears have red lenses. Note the poor front-bumper-to-body fit on this completely original 1977.

Beginning in 1974 a urethane-covered impact-absorbing bumper assembly was utilized. This example is a 1976.

Model year 1974 and 1975 Corvettes have "CORVETTE" spelled out in eight individual letters centered between the taillamps. For 1976 and 1977, "CORVETTE" is spelled out in a single emblem. Early 1976 emblems are 6 inches wide and rest in a recess molded into the bumper. Later 1976 and all 1977 emblems, as seen here, are 8 inches wide and do not rest in a recess.

In 1973 the recessed area of the body where the rear license plate mounts is covered by a diecast surround trim that is chrome plated. A lamp assembly mounts at the top of the recess behind the rear body panel and illuminates the rear license plate. A black rubber bumper is inserted into the rear valance panel centered toward the lower edge of the license plate. Two white plastic push nuts insert into square cutouts in the rear body panel for the license plate retaining screws.

In 1974–1977 the license plate recess is molded into the rear bumper cover and uses no bezel or other trim. Instead of a single light above the license plate 1974–1977 cars utilize two smaller lights, with one on either side of the plate. 1973–1977s all utilize four rear lamps. The two outer ones utilize red lenses that function as taillamps, stop lamps, and turn signals. The two inner ones utilize red lenses with clear plastic centers that function as back-up lamps. In 1973 only, taillamp lenses are separate from their housings. The lenses are rounded with a checkerboard pattern on the inside. They are retained with three black oxide Phillips pan head screws. Starting in 1974, the taillamp lenses are integral to the housings, eliminating the need for screws to hold the lens on. Each lamp has a very small moisture wick that protrudes from the bottom of the lens. The wick material resembles a cigarette filter.

All 1973–1977s originally came with undercar exhaust systems, not side pipes. For 1973 only, the exhaust tips exit the rear of the car through rectangular cutouts in the body. The cutouts are trimmed with chromed diecast bezels that are rectangular in shape but with open bottoms. The bezels are retained by chrome Phillips oval head screws. The tailpipes in 1974–1977 cars exit below the rear bumper assembly. There are no cutouts as in 1973.

Convertible Tops

1975 was the final year for the convertible body style until it was revived in 1986. 1973–1975 convertible tops are made from vinyl with a woven pattern. The convertible top is available in either white or black regardless of exterior body color. The front header roll and tack strip cover are also vinyl but have a grained pattern rather than a woven pattern. Two small stainless-steel trim pieces cover the ends of the tack strip. The trim pieces are flared around their perimeter and attach with one small, bright Phillips flat head screw. The convertible top window is clear vinyl and is heat sealed, not sewn, to the top.

The convertible top back window contains a manufacturer's logo, manufacturing date, and the words "VINYLITE, TRADE MARK, AS-6" and "DO NOT RUB DRY WASH WITH WATER SOAKED CLOTH" heat stamped in the driver-side lower corner. A paper label is sewn into the top in the corner below the heat-stamped logo and date in the window.

As an extra cost option a removable hardtop was available for convertibles in addition to the standard soft top. The hardtop is painted body color unless vinyl covered. All vinyl-covered hardtops are black. The hardtop rear window contains the LOF manufacturing logo and is date coded with two letters like the remainder of the body glass. The first letter represents the month of production and the second represents the year of production. (See Appendix R for glass date codes.)

Tires, Wheels, and Wheel Covers

1973 is the first year Corvettes came with radial tires. All 1973–1977s are equipped with size GR-70 radials. The standard tire for all years is a blackwall. Whitewalls and raised white letter tires are available as extra cost options in 1973–1976, while only raised white letter tires were available as an option in 1977. All tires are either Firestone Steel Radial 500s or Goodyear Steelgards. Raised white letter Goodyears say "Goodyear Steelgard" in block letters. Raised white letter Firestones say "Firestone Steel Radial 500" in block letters. In addition, Firestone raised white letter tires on those 1973s assembled through approximately June 1973 also have a raised, white outlined triangle with a raised white "F" in the middle.

Raised white letter Firestone Steel Radial 500 tires were available as an option in 1973–1977. The triangle with the "F" in the middle after "FIRESTONE" is also white in those 1973s assembled through approximately June 1973.

All 1973–1977 Corvettes are equipped with GR-70 radials. Raised white letter Goodyear Steelgard tires were an extra cost option. Also shown here is the optional full wheel cover.

Every 1973–1977 tire has a 10- or 11-digit "Tire Identification Number" stamped into the sidewall. The first letter of the code indicates the manufacturer, with Goodyear being represented by "M" and Firestone by "V." The second character denotes the location of the plant that manufactured the tire, with examples being "K" representing Goodyear's Union City, Tenn., plant and "N" representing Firestone's Joliette, Quebec, Canada, plant. The third and fourth digits are "U5" to indicate the tire's size, GR70-15. The following three or four letters denote the type of tire construction. The next two numbers indicate the week of the year the tire was made, with "01" being the first week of the year and "52" being the last. The final number is the last digit of the year of manufacture. Thus, a tire stamped "MKU5 FMH394" is a GR70-15 Goodyear Steelgard Radial manufactured in the Union City, Tenn., plant during the 39th week of 1974. In 1973 and 1974 Firestone recalled all of its Steel Radial 500s and replaced them with Firestone 721 Steel Belted Radials.

All 1973–1977 Corvettes are equipped with steel Rally wheels as standard equipment. They are a color called Argent Silver on the front side. The back sides are painted semi-flat black and always have silver overspray since the front side was painted silver after the black was applied to the rear. All wheels are stamped with a date code, manufacturer's logo, and size code on the front face. All 1973–1977 Corvette wheels are 15x8 inches and have the code "AZ" stamped in to indicate this. The "AZ" is adjacent to the valve stem hole.

Also adjacent to the valve stem hole is the manufacturer's logo and date code stamping. On one side

of the hole it says "K" for the wheel manufacturer, Kelsey Hayes. This is followed by a dash and a "1" that represents Chevrolet. Next comes another dash and a number to denote the last digit of the year of manufacture. This is followed by a space and one or two numbers to indicate the month of manufacture. On the other side of the valve stem hole are one or two more numbers that represent the day of manufacture. Stainless-steel trim rings and chrome center caps are standard for all cars. Original trim rings are held to the wheel by four steel clips. Center caps should read "Chevrolet Motor Division" in black painted letters.

A full wheel cover is available as an extra cost option in 1973 only. Called option PO2, this cover has a stainless-steel outer rim and closely spaced radial fins that converge outward toward a protruding ornamental disc in the center. The disc is chrome around its edge, black in the middle, and contains the Corvette crossed flags emblem. Other Chevrolet products use a similar wheel cover but those have a flat center disc instead of the protruding disc utilized for Corvettes.

Aluminum wheels were first offered as an option in 1973, but according to Chevrolet records only four cars were actually delivered with them that year. There were quality control problems with the wheels and they were not offered again until the 1976 model year. All 1973, 1976, and 1977 aluminum wheels are unpainted. Wheels on cars equipped with standard trim rings and center caps utilize black rubber valve stems that measure approximately 1-1/4 inches long. These are fitted with caps that come to a

Raised white letter Firestone Steel Radial 500 tires were an option in 1973–1977. On 1973s assembled through approximately June 1973, the Firestone logo (the "F" in the shield) after the word "Firestone" is also white. As shown here, the logo on later examples is black.

point and have longitudinal ridges around their entire perimeter. Wheels on cars equipped with optional full wheel covers have extensions threaded onto the standard valve stems. The extensions have a white-color inner shaft that is visible because they are not fitted with caps.

To ease the balancing process, steel wheels are sometimes marked with a tiny weld drop or paint dot at their highest point. This mark is lined up with an orange dot on the tire. Balance weights are the type that clamp onto the edge of the rim and are placed on the inside of the wheel only. Original balance weights usually have the letters "OEM" molded into their face. There is usually a small white or colored dot of paint on the tire adjacent to each balance weight.

All cars have a full-size spare tire and wheel. In 1973 only, those cars equipped with the optional aluminum wheel had a matching aluminum wheel for the spare. Later cars fitted with aluminum wheels, and all cars equipped with standard steel wheels, had a steel wheel for the spare. 1973 cars equipped with optional P02 full wheel covers do not have a fifth cover for the spare wheel. The spare tire and wheel are housed in a carrier bolted to the rear underbody area. The carrier is fiberglass with steel supports. The fiberglass is unpainted and the steel support is painted semi-gloss black. The tire tub portion of the carrier has a fair amount of flat to semi-gloss black paint on its outside surface applied during the blackout process. A lock covered by a black rubber boot goes over the spare tire carrier access bolt.

1973–1977 Interior
Trim Tag

Interior trim color and material, as well as exterior body color and body assembly date, are stamped into an unpainted stainless-steel plate attached to the driver's door hinge pillar by two aluminum Pop Rivets. This plate is commonly called a trim plate or trim tag.

Trim color and material is indicated in the plate by a three-digit code. For example, in 1974 trim code 413 indicates dark blue color with vinyl seat covers. (See Appendix T for interior codes.)

Exterior body paint color is indicated in the trim plate by a three-number code in 1973 and 1974, and by a two-letter code in 1975–1977. The two-letter code is followed by an "L" to indicate lacquer paint. For example, in 1976 code 33L indicates Dark Green. (See Appendix T for paint codes.)

The body build date represents the date when the painted and partially assembled body reached that point on the assembly line where the trim plate was installed. The car's final assembly date is typically one to several days after the body build date. A letter indicating the month followed by two numbers indicating the day represents the body build date. The letter "A" was assigned to the first month of production, which was August 1972 for 1973 models, August 1973 for 1974 models, October 1974 for 1975 models, August 1975 for 1976 models, and August 1976 for 1977 models. The second month of production was assigned "B," and so on. A body assembled on the sixth day of August 1975 would have "A06" stamped into the trim plate, for example, and a body built on the eleventh day of January 1975 would have "D11" stamped into its plate.

The 1977 interior was a hybrid, with new features such as the center console area, and old features such as the three-pocket storage area on the passenger-side dash.

Seats

Standard seat upholstery is a combination of very slightly grained flat vinyl with Chevrolet's "Comfort-weave" vinyl inserts sewn into the seat bottoms and backs. Vinyl seats for 1973–1977 all have vertical insert panels. 1973–1975 seats have a chrome-bordered black trim insert at the top of the seat back, while 1976 and 1977 seats do not. 1975 vinyl seats are distinguished from 1973 and 1974 by the position of the horizontal stitch seam in the lower cushion. In 1975 this seam was moved forward toward the center of the cushion.

A "Custom Interior Trim" option package was offered in 1973–1976. This package includes leather seat covers and a strip of carpet on the bottom of the door panels. All 1973–1977 leather seats have horizontal panels. 1973 and 1974 leather seats have eight stitched seams in the lower cushion while 1975–1977 seats have six seams in this cushion. Only the faces of leather-covered seats are real leather. The sides of the covers are vinyl.

In 1977 leather seat covers became standard. A combination leather and cloth upholstery was offered in 1977 as a no additional cost option. The

A combination leather and cloth upholstery was offered in 1977–1980 as a no additional cost option. As shown here in a 1977 example, the center sections of the seats are cloth with horizontal stitching, while the outer portions are leather.

131

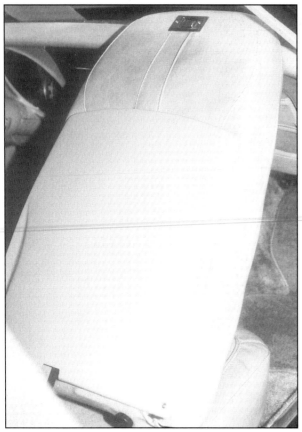

The panel on the rear of the seats is molded plastic that matches interior color. The release button and its bezel at the top of the seat are chrome plated.

center sections of the seats are cloth with horizontal stitching.

Each seat rests on two seat tracks, which allow for forward and rearward adjustment of the seat's position. The tracks are black phosphate and each is held to the floor by one black phosphate, indented hex head bolt at either end for a total of four per seat. The front bolts are covered by a flap of carpet that was cut away while the rear bolts simply pass through the carpet. The seat adjust lever is black phosphate with a chrome ball screwed onto its end.

The seat backs are made of molded plastic and match interior color. The seat back release button, its bezel, and the brackets that attach the seat back to the bottom are all chrome plated. Two bolts that allow for the adjustment of seat back position are bright silver and get a rubber cushion over their heads. Black plastic trim washers are under the seat back release bezel and adjustment bolts.

Lap and Shoulder Belts

All 1973–1977 coupes were equipped with lap and shoulder belts while 1973–1975 convertibles came with lap belts as standard and shoulder belts as an extra cost option. All 1973 and 1974 belts were manufactured by a company called Hamill, and a tag bearing that name is sewn to them. Firestone subsequently bought Hamill, and tags sewn to 1975–1977 seatbelts say "Firestone." The tag with the manufacturer's name also bears the date that particular belt was made. This date is indicated by an ink stamping with a number representing the week of the year, a letter representing the day of the week ("A" being Monday, "B" being Tuesday, and so on,), and another number representing the year. For example, a stamping of "01 D 73" means January 4, 1972, with "01" representing the first week of the year, which was the week of January 1st–5th, "D" representing the fourth day of the week, which was Thursday, January 4th, and "73" representing the year 1973.

In addition to the tag bearing the manufacturer's name and date code there is another, smaller tag sewn to both lap and shoulder belts. This second tag contains safety instructions.

All belts are made from a three-row webbing material and are the same color as the carpet. The material used for lap belts is slightly thicker than that used for shoulder belts.

Outboard belts are on a spring-loaded retractable coil for all 1973–1977 cars. The retractors are beneath each seat under a plastic cover. Inboard portions of the seatbelts are encased in a semi-rigid plastic that goes over part of the female buckles. The buckles are brushed silver in color and the black release buttons each have a rigid metallic sticker that says "GM" in silver letters on a blue background.

Door Panels and Door Hardware

All door panels are made from molded vinyl and match the interior color. With standard interiors

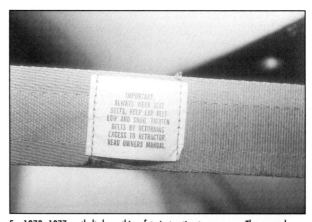

For 1973–1977 seatbelts have this safety instruction tag sewn on. The example shown is from a 1976.

Model year 1973–1976 Corvettes equipped with Custom Interior Trim, and all 1977s, have a decorative strip of carpet on the bottom of the door panel. This example is from a 1977.

(i.e., interiors with vinyl seat covers) the door panels are plain and utilize no trim. Custom interiors include fancier door panels. A piece of plush-cut pile carpet is added along the bottom of the panels and a strip of chrome trim covers the gap where the carpet meets the vinyl. In addition, custom door panels include a band of simulated walnut wood trim in the middle of the panel in 1973–1976. In 1977 a satin black insert replaces the simulated wood insert. With both standard and custom interiors, inside window felts are attached to the upper edge of the door panels with heavy staples, not Pop Rivets.

Door panels are attached to the doors by means of interlocking plastic clips fastened to the back of the panel and the door frame. Black phosphate clips at the bottom of the front and rear of the panel also hold it on. The clips insert into a cutout in the back of the panel and then get fastened to the door with black phosphate Phillips pan head screws. And finally, a chrome Phillips oval head screw with integral washer goes through the face of each panel at the upper front and rear corners.

Inside door release handles are chrome with black paint in the center knurled area. A round black emblem features the crossed flags logo. The inside lock knob is chrome with a black stripe painted in the center indent. The inside door pull is a grained vinyl handle that matches interior color. Cars equipped with standard manual windows have chrome window cranks with black plastic knobs.

Door Jambs and Door Perimeters

The door jambs and perimeter of each door are painted body color with the exception of the top front of each door, which is painted semi-gloss black. The

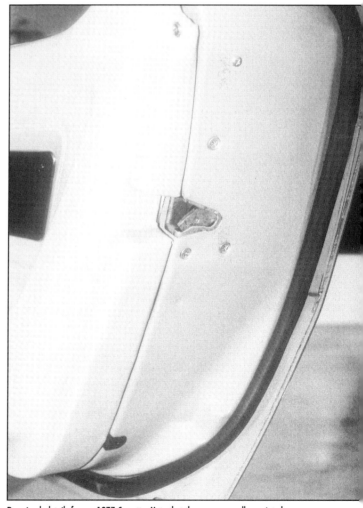

Door jamb details from a 1977 Corvette. Note that the screws are all unpainted. Also note the screw with a finishing washer holding the door panel at the top and the black phosphate clip holding it at the bottom.

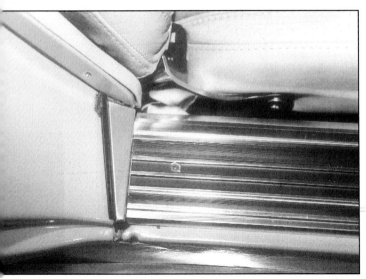

Passenger-side door jamb and sill area in a 1977. The silver item with the black rubber strip along the top is a water deflector. Note the correct black phosphate Phillips head screw holding the sill plate. Replacement screws often have too large a head.

Door jamb decals in a very late production 1977.

door striker, which is the large pin threaded into the door post, and its corresponding receiver in the door are both cadmium plated. The striker is a special indented star head design.

1973–1975 convertibles have an additional striker in the door jambs. A cone-shaped male insert is mounted to the door and a hollow cone-shaped female receiver is mounted to the body jamb. The male piece is chrome plated while the female piece is black with a brass insert.

The courtesy light pin switches and door ajar warning light/alarm system pin switches are cadmium plated and should not have any paint overspray. All pin switches have "SX," the manufacturer's logo, stamped into the head of their plunger. As with the pin switches, door strikers, and door striker receivers, the door alignment blocks and the door weather strip were added after the body was painted and should not have any body paint overspray. In 1973 the main door weather stripping is two separate pieces and typically shows a gap in the center on the bottom of the door. Starting in 1974 it is one piece and therefore does not have a gap.

The vehicle certification label glued toward the top of the rear portion of the driver's door is unpainted. It contains the car's VIN, the month and year the vehicle was produced, axle loading and gross vehicle weight ratings, and a statement that reads "THIS VEHICLE CONFORMS TO ALL APPLICABLE MOTOR VEHICLE SAFETY STANDARDS IN EFFECT ON THE DATE OF MANUFACTURE SHOWN ABOVE."

Beginning in 1974 a tire pressure sticker appears below the vehicle certification label. This sticker specifies tire pressures, tire size, and recommended vehicle capacity.

Door sills are bright aluminum with black painted ribs. Each sill is held on with four black phosphate Phillips oval head screws.

Kick Panels, Quarter Trim Panels, Pedals, and Carpet

The kick panels beneath the dash just forward of the doors are molded plastic and are interior color. On air-conditioned cars the passenger-side panel was cut by hand for increased clearance and the cut is frequently rough. One chrome Phillips head oval screw in the forward upper corner of each panel holds it in place. The panels have a bevy of small holes for the speakers that mount behind them. There is no ridge at the rear edge of the panel in 1973–1977. A ridge does appear in 1978.

The quarter trim panels just rearward of the doors are molded plastic to match the interior color.

They are each held in place by a piece of metal trim retained by four chrome Phillips oval head screws. The quarter trim panels on coupes also have one chrome Phillips oval head screw with a trim washer at their top.

In standard interiors carpet is made from an 80/20 loop pile molded material. In custom interiors it is made from plush-cut pile material. In all cases it matches interior color. A black rubber flap on the firewall insulation retains the upper edge of the front carpeting on both sides. Carpet covers the bulkhead behind the seats and has sewn-on binding on the lower edge where it overlaps the front floor carpet behind the seats. Rear storage compartment doors each have carpet under their frames. One piece of carpet covers the rear storage area floor and extends up the rear bulkhead. The edge at the top of the bulkhead is trimmed with sewn-on binding and is held by three rubber plugs. Separate pieces of untrimmed carpet cover the two wheelwells.

Carpet has a molded vinyl accelerator heel pad in the corner of the driver's foot well adjacent to the accelerator pedal. The main section of the pad is rectangular shaped and has horizontal bars molded in. Extensions come off the main section and extend up the transmission tunnel and under the accelerator pedal. In 1973–1976 a sewn-in, molded vinyl dimmer switch pad is on the carpet above the dimmer switch. As with the accelerator heel pad, the dimmer switch pad is color matched to the interior. In 1977 the dimmer switch is incorporated into the turn signal stalk, eliminating the need for a dimmer switch pad in the carpet.

Dash Pad and Dash Panels

Upper dash pad, as well as driver's and passenger's dash panels, are made of soft vinyl and match interior color. With light-color interiors the upper pad is usually a darker shade. For example, tan interiors typically have brown upper pads. The two vertical panels are attached to the upper pad by means of six Phillips oval head screws with conical washers. The screw heads are painted to match interior color. Dash pads have white stitching across their tops regardless of interior color. An interior color hard plastic grille is located in the defroster opening of the upper pad. A three-pocket storage area is inset into the passenger-side dash panel. The storage pocket assembly is made from vinyl and is the same color as the interior. The dash panel has stitching around the opening for the storage pockets. The two smaller, outboard pockets are retained to the larger one with a single chrome-plated snap. A spring-loaded retainer behind the dash holds the three-pocket assembly tight against the dash panel.

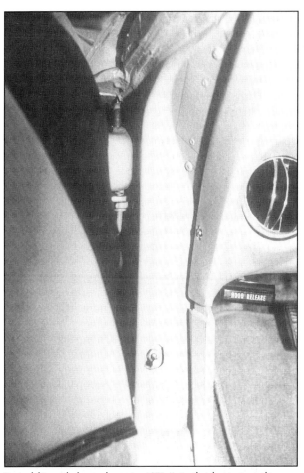

Forward driver-side door jamb area in a 1977. Notice that the trim tag in this original, unrestored car was painted over at the factory.

Interior Switches, Controls, and Related Parts

All 1973–1977 Corvettes have a headlamp switch mounted in the upper left corner of the driver-side dash pad. Headlight switch knobs are soft, black grained vinyl. The center of the knob is indented with an image of a headlamp with light rays coming out of it.

All 1973–1977 Corvettes have air vents on both sides of the dash toward the lower outboard corner. The vent mechanisms are chrome spheres that rotate to change the direction of air flow. A black push/pull knob next to each sphere controls the flow of air.

A small black T-handle pull mechanism beneath the driver-side dash on the left side releases the hood latch. The handle is black with the words "HOOD RELEASE" in white painted block letters across its face. The hood release cable is in a spiral-wound metal sheathing.

A semi-gloss black bracket beneath the steering column mounts the trip odometer reset knob and headlamp door override switch. The trip odometer reset knob has a grooved black rubber

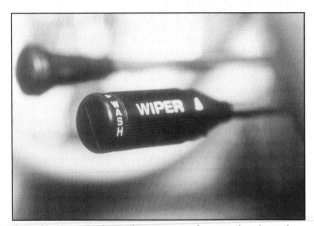

The windshield wiper/washer switch in a 1977. Cars from 1973 through 1976 have a wiper/washer switch located above the center instrument cluster.

cover. The headlamp door override switches are both vacuum switches that have dull black plastic push/pull knobs.

Steering Wheel and Steering Column

All 1973–1975 steering wheels are black regardless of interior color. These wheels have grained vinyl rims molded to a three-spoke stainless-steel hub. Each of the spokes has a brushed finish with a pattern of parallel lines extending from the center of the wheel to the outer rim. 1976 and 1977 Corvettes with standard steering columns utilize a four-spoke steering wheel. The entire wheel, including the spokes, is covered with padded vinyl that matches interior color. 1977s equipped with the optional tilt and telescoping steering column utilize a three-spoke steering wheel. The

Steering column details in a 1977. The lever in front of and below the ignition switch allows the switch to be placed in the "lock" position and ignition key to be removed.

spokes for this wheel are brushed stainless steel and the rim is covered with leather.

The standard steering column and optional tilt-telescoping column in 1973–1977 is painted whatever the interior color is in a semi-gloss finish. 1977 columns are about 2 inches shorter than earlier columns, resulting in the steering wheel being closer to the dash.

The tilt-telescoping column has a thick locking ring below the steering wheel to control the telescoping function. The ring is painted to match the rest of the column. Twisting the lever on the ring releases the locking mechanism and allows the column to telescope.

A lever similar to, but shorter than, the turn signal lever controls the tilt function of the optional steering column. The tilt lever is located between turn signal lever and dash.

All columns have a four-way flasher switch mounted on the right side. The knob for this switch is black with white lettering spelling the word "FLASHER."

1973–1976 Corvettes use a turn signal lever with a chrome-plated shaft and a dull black rubber end. The end is grained and has a single concentric groove near the tip.

Beginning in 1977, a stalk with turn signal, headlight dimmer, and windshield wiper/washer controls is mounted into the steering column. All 1973–1977 models use a textured metal horn button painted to match the interior. A crossed flags emblem is in the center of the button. In 1973–1975 the emblem is relatively large with a silver circle that cuts through the flags. In 1976 and 1977 the silver circle is eliminated and the emblem gets smaller.

1977 Corvettes were originally slated to receive brushed aluminum horn buttons, and some cars were delivered with them. They were subsequently recalled, however, because their reflectivity posed a potential safety hazard. Dealers were instructed to replace them with a button painted to match interior color.

Interior Windshield Moldings, Sun Visors, and Rearview Mirror

Three pieces of vinyl-covered molding matched to the interior color cover the inside of the windshield frame for all 1973–1977 Corvettes. The two side pieces are held on by plastic retainers attached to the reverse side. The plastic retainers are not visible when the moldings are installed. In addition, each side molding has one chrome Phillips head screw retaining it at the top. The top piece of molding is retained by black oxide, recess head Phillips screws.

All 1973–1975 steering wheels have black, grained vinyl rims molded to a three-spoke stainless-steel hub. Those 1976 and 1977 Corvettes with standard steering columns utilize a four-spoke steering wheel. The entire wheel, including the spokes, is covered with padded vinyl that matches interior color. Cars equipped with the optional tilt and telescoping steering column utilize a three-spoke steering wheel as shown here. The spokes for this wheel are brushed stainless steel and the rim is covered with leather.

Sun visors are covered with padded soft vinyl. In cars with standard interior trim they have the same Comfort-weave pattern as the vinyl seat covers. In cars with Custom Interior Trim they have a Madrid pattern in the vinyl. Each sun visor is held to the windshield frame with chrome recess head Phillips screws. In 1977 sun visor mounts are changed to allow the visors to swivel. A label describing engine starting procedures is affixed to the driver-side sun visor in 1973–1975. This label is made from a woven material in 1973 and from paper in 1974–1975. 1975 Corvettes also have a push start procedure label on the driver-side sun visor. In 1976 this label is on the passenger-side visor, and a catalytic converter label is on the driver side. In 1977 a label pertaining to the optional sport mirrors is affixed to the passenger-side visor on those cars so equipped, and a label for the sunshade sleeve is on the driver-side visor.

All 1973–1976 Corvettes have an interior day/night rearview mirror mounted to the center of the upper windshield frame. Beginning in late 1976 the mirror is mounted onto the upper windshield

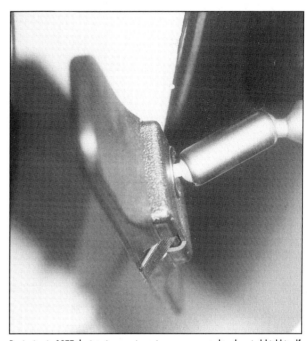

Beginning in 1977 the interior rearview mirror was mounted to the windshield itself rather than to the frame above the windshield.

All gauges, including the tachometer, have a flat-black background and straight, red needle. Tachometer redlines vary according to the engine. The example shown is from a base-engine 1976.

itself instead of the frame. In 1973 only, the mirror is 8 inches wide and is held to its mount with a slotted oval head screw. It is backed with black grained vinyl and has black rubber trim. The day/night lever is black as well, with the possible exception of some very early cars which may utilized a gray lever. Vinyl trim dyed interior color covers the mirror's mount at the windshield header.

Beginning in 1974 the interior rearview mirror is 10 inches wide. In 1973–1976 a mirror-mounted map light was offered as option UF1. This light is on the

All 1973–1977 gauges have a flat-black background and a straight, red needle. Beginning in 1975, speedometers include kilometers-per-hour markings in addition to miles-per-hour markings. This example is from a 1977.

bottom of the passenger side of the mirror. It has a clear plastic lens and a black sliding switch. A clear or black sticker with silver letters provides instructions to change the bulb.

Instruments and Radio

The center console instrument cluster housing is cast metal painted semi-gloss black. In 1973–1976 the windshield wiper/washer control switch is mounted above the center console instrument cluster housing. The wiper/washer switch moves to the steering column in 1977. All gauges, including the speedometer and tachometer, have a flat black background and a straight red needle. Tachometer redlines vary according to the engine. Beginning in 1975 speedometers include kilometers per hour markings in addition to miles per hour markings.

Beginning in 1975 fuel gauges have "UNLEADED FUEL ONLY" written below the needle. In 1973 the oil pressure gauge reads to 70 psi and the water temperature gauge is marked at 100, 210, and 250 degrees. Beginning in 1974 the pressure gauge reads to 80 psi and the temperature gauge is marked at 100, 200, and 280 degrees.

In 1977 the faces of all of the small gauges were redesigned. In addition, the ammeter gauge utilized previously was replaced with a voltmeter gauge.

All 1973–1977 Corvettes came standard without a radio. For those cars not equipped with a radio a block-off plate is fitted to the cutout where the radio would otherwise go. The block-off plate is painted semi-gloss black and has a flat face with a thin, raised chrome border around its perimeter near the edge.

As an extra cost option one of two different Delco radios could be ordered in 1973–1976. The first is an AM/FM push-button and the second is an AM/FM push-button with stereo reception. Both radios have a small slide bar above the dial that changes reception between AM and FM.

A third optional radio was offered in 1977. Dubbed option UM2, it is an AM/FM stereo with an eight-track player.

Radio knobs are dull black rubber with white-colored pictorial inserts. The on/off volume knob on the left has a musical note while the tuning knob on the right has an antenna with a radiating signal.

Beneath the main radio knobs is a secondary control, which is chrome plated. The one on the left controls tone and the one on the right, which is functional only on stereo-equipped cars, controls balance.

Center Console, Shifter, and Park Brake

All 1973–1977 center consoles are made from molded vinyl in the same color as the interior. 1973–1976 park brake lever consoles are made from rigid molded plastic and also match interior color. 1977 park brake consoles are made from a flexible vinyl material molded in the same color as the interior.

The insert in the top of the center console is painted semi-gloss black and is the same design in 1973–1976. In 1977 the entire top of the center console is redesigned, and it is also semi-gloss black. 1973–1976 cars equipped with the Custom Interior Trim option have a simulated wood insert in the top of the center console.

In 1973–1976 cars, engine specifications are stamped into the insert that is located below the shifter. These specifications include torque, compression ratio, and engine size.

In manual transmission–equipped cars the shift pattern is indicated next to the shifter. The shift pattern area is semi-gloss black and the letters and numbers are chrome. 1973–1976 cars, but not 1977s, also have a chrome border around the pattern.

The shifter boot for manual transmission cars is made from black leather and has a sewn seam toward the passenger side of the car.

Manual shifters have a chrome shaft and threaded-on black chrome ball. A T-handle integral to the shaft controls the reverse lock-out.

On those Corvettes equipped with an automatic transmission, the shift pattern is also next to the shifter. A plastic lighted band with painted letters is used to indicate shifter position. In 1973–1976 automatics shifters are surrounded by a gloss-black plastic seal that slides back and forth as the shifter is moved. In 1977 the shifter is surrounded by a boot.

Automatic shifters are made from a chrome shaft topped by a black plastic ball. The ball has a chrome, spring-loaded button in the top to release the detent and allow the shifter to be moved.

The heater/air-conditioning control assembly utilized in 1973–1976 has white letters and a fan control switch that is mounted directly behind the larger assembly, not in a separate small rectangle. A chrome lever is used to set fan speed. All air-conditioned cars use a switch with four positions in addition to "off." Switches in non-air-conditioned cars only have three positions in addition to "off."

Whether the car is equipped with air conditioning or not, in 1973–1976 its control assembly employs two large black plastic rotary thumbwheels on either side. The left-side thumbwheel controls temperature and the right-side thumbwheel controls the system setting.

Non-air-conditioned cars only have two fresh air vent controls on the center console. The controls are sliding levers made from small, black plastic balls with a flat area mounted to black oxide metal arms. The balls are shiny black on the flat face but change to dull black with a grained pattern on the rounded portion only. The word "CLOSE" in white painted letters and a white arrow appear on the balls' flat faces.

1977 Corvettes use an entirely different type of heater/air-conditioning control assembly. Instead of the previous thumbwheel-type switch assembly, the new unit relies on horizontal sliding levers to control function and temperature. A separate fan speed switch is located to the left of the control unit.

All 1973–1976s have an ashtray inset into the center console insert next to the heater/air-conditioning control assembly. All 1977s have a wider ashtray inset into the console below the heater/air-conditioning control unit. The ashtray door is semi-gloss black and slides back and forth with slight resistance. All cars are equipped with a cigarette lighter.

On those 1973–1977 Corvettes equipped with the optional rear window defogger a control switch is mounted on the left-side trim panel forward of the center console. In 1973 the switch is one speed and uses a large, round, chrome-plated knob. Thereafter it has three speeds and uses a toggle switch–type lever.

All 1973–1977 Corvettes have a park brake lever mounted between the seats. The lever's handle is made from hard, shiny black plastic with a crosshatch pattern to enhance grip. Chrome trim separates the black plastic grips in 1973 and 1974. In 1975–1977 the chrome trim is eliminated. A release button on the top of the lever is made from hard, shiny black plastic also. A chrome band separates the button from the remainder of the handle for all years.

In 1973–1976 the slotted opening in the park brake lever console is covered by a rippled, black plastic cover that slides along with the movement of the lever. In 1977 the rubber park brake console has a slit that the lever passes through.

Rear Storage Compartments
Battery, Rear Window Storage Tray

All 1973–1977s feature three enclosed storage compartments behind the seats. The lids for these compartments are made from molded fiberglass, with the exception of those found in some early 1973s, which are made from press-board. All lids are covered with carpet that matches the interior carpet. The underside of each lid is painted flat black. A white vehicle maintenance sticker is on the underside of the center compartment lid. A sticker for jacking instructions is on the underside of the passenger-side compartment lid. In 1973 and 1974 a sticker for the limited-slip differential is also on the underside of the passenger compartment lid

Each lid is surrounded by a molded plastic border that is painted to match interior color. The entire assembly of all three lids is also surrounded by a color-matched molded plastic border.

Each lid is hinged and latches with a spring-loaded mechanism. Each lid has a chrome button to release its latch and a hoop to pull it open. The hoop, which is leather in cars with leather seats and vinyl in cars with vinyl seats, is the same color as the interior and is retained to the lid by a chrome Phillips head screw.

One of the rear compartments is fitted with a locking chrome release button. The lock is usually in the passenger-side compartment door but is sometimes found in one of the other doors instead. The key for the storage compartment lid lock is the same as the keys for the anti-theft alarm and spare tire storage compartment.

The compartment directly behind the driver's seat holds the vehicle's battery. It has a thin foam seal around the perimeter of the door opening to help keep battery fumes from entering the passenger compartment.

All 1973–1977 Corvettes use a side terminal Delco battery. Different models of batteries were used for each year. In 1973–1975 the battery is called "Delco Energizer" and in 1976–1977 it's called "Delco Freedom."

In 1973, cars equipped with the standard engine or optional L82 engine use Delco model R 88ST. Those cars equipped with either a big-block engine or the heavy-duty battery option (option T60) use Delco model R 88WT.

In 1974, cars equipped with the standard engine or optional L82 engine use Delco model R 89ST. Those cars equipped with either a big-block engine or the heavy-duty battery option (option UA1) use Delco model R 89WT.

In 1975, cars equipped with the standard engine or optional L82 engine use Delco model R 89ST. Those cars equipped with the heavy-duty battery option (option UA1) use Delco model R 89WPT.

In 1976, cars equipped with the standard engine or optional L82 engine use Delco model R 87-5. Those cars equipped with the heavy-duty battery option (option UA1) use Delco model R 89WP.

In 1977, cars equipped with the standard engine or optional L82 engine use Delco model R 87-5. Those cars equipped with the heavy-duty battery option (option UA1) use Delco model R 89-5.

All of the batteries used in 1973–1975 have six cells that are covered by two plastic caps, each of which covers three cells. In those 1973s assembled through approximately January 1973, each cap has three of the Delco "split circle" logos molded into its top. The split circles are painted dark orange. The caps in those 1973s assembled after approximately January 1973, as well as in all 1974 and 1975 cars, have flat tops with no markings. In all 1973–1975 cars a black rubber vent hose runs from each of the caps through a hole in the underbody.

1973–1975 Delco Energizer batteries say "Delco Energizer" in raised letters on top of the case. A black and silver label is also on top of the case. This label reads "REPLACEMENT WITH ENERGIZER R-88 ST" (or whatever model the particular battery is).

Delco Freedom batteries used in 1976 and 1977 do not have cell caps. Instead, they have two large, raised squares in the top of the battery. One of the squares contains the "Delco Eye," a small circle of glass utilized to indicate battery condition.

The top of the Delco Freedom battery is blue and the sides are white. A caution label is affixed to the top. Also, the words "Delco Freedom Battery" are written across the top.

All 1973–1977 battery cables are side terminal–style and have a red positive end and a black negative end. The positive cable terminal has a "+" sign molded in and the negative terminal has a "-" sign molded in.

The cables themselves are both covered with black insulation that has the words "COPPER CLAD ALUMINUM" written in white block letters. The cables are retained with 5/16-inch hex head bolts.

The passenger-side storage compartment contains a removable insert. The insert, which is like a squared-off bucket, is made from grayish-black fiberboard and measures about 6-1/4 inches deep. The inside has a material called "flock." It consists of small strands of black fiber adhered to the surface, and resembles velvet.

The fiberboard insert contains an off-white cotton pouch that has a yellow drawstring. The drawstring is held on by an encasement stitched with red thread. The pouch contains eight silver washers and four oblong-shaped, gray phosphate shims that are to be used to adjust the seat backs to the occupants' preferred positions.

In addition to the seat hardware pouch, there are a number of other items in the storage insert. A small white paper envelope with the "GM mark of excellence" logo and instructions printed in black letters contains the car's keys and the key knock-outs.

A small brown paper envelope contains license plate screws. This bag is marked "UNIT NUMBER 3875313" across the top, "LICENSE ATTACHING" on one side, and "REAR PLATE PARTS" on the other side.

Another small brown paper envelope is included with those Corvettes equipped with the optional P02 Deluxe Wheel Covers. This envelope contains four extensions for the valve stems.

The final item in the storage insert is the owner's packet. This packet includes an owner's manual, warranty folder, Protect-o-plate, consumer information booklet, trim ring installation instruction card, tire warranty booklet, and radio instruction sheet (if the car has a radio). 1974 cars also had a seatbelt instruction addendum in the packet. All of these items are in a clear vinyl envelope.

The fiberboard insert in the passenger-side rear storage compartment lifts out to reveal an additional storage area beneath. A jack and jack handle are mounted to the bottom of the compartment (to the car's floor panel) with a black spring that latches onto a black hook riveted to the floor.

All jacks are painted gloss or semi-gloss black and have the letter "A" stamped in their chassis contact pad. This letter is the logo for Auto Specialties Manufacturing, the company that made the jacks.

In addition to the manufacturer's logo, all jacks contain a date code stamping. The stamping is on the jack's large side arm and contains a number for the year followed by a letter for the month, with "A" representing January, "B" representing February, and so on. For example, the date code stamping for a jack manufactured in June 1975 would say "5 F."

All jack handles are painted gloss or semi-gloss black and include a pivoting 3/4-inch boxed hex-wrench on the end to remove and install the car's lug nuts. A thick rubber ring is fitted around the hex-wrench end to prevent rattling.

In addition to the jack and jack handle, electrical relays and a flasher unit are mounted in the area underneath the fiberboard insert. These components are part of the anti-theft alarm system.

All 1973–1977 coupes have two storage bags to hold the T-tops when they are removed. Some cars have bags dyed to match interior color while others have black bags regardless of interior color. Earlier cars for each year are more likely to have a color-matched bag and later cars are more likely to have black bags.

All bags have a date code stamped inside in ink. Typical date stampings contain a month and year designation. For example, bags manufactured in October 1974 read "10-74." In addition to the date stamping, bags may also contain a logo stamping representing the manufacturer. The most common logo seen is "TEX."

All bags have a flap that closes over the opening and is retained by three chrome-plated snaps.

All 1973–1977 coupes have adjustable T-top hold down straps. Tops are held by a single harness that is attached to the rear bulkhead in the luggage area and extends to a chrome-plated anchor attached to the front bulkhead between the seats. As with the T-top bags, early cars tend to have straps dyed to match interior color and later cars tend to have black straps regardless of interior color.

All 1973–1977 coupes have molded vinyl trim mounted to the underside of the T-tops. The vinyl is the same color as the interior. Beginning in late 1976 a dome light is found in the center of the interior roof trim.

Convertible Top Frames

For 1973–1975, all convertibles top frames are painted semi-gloss black. A black fiberglass header panel is secured to the front underside of the top frame. Three chrome-plated latches secure the front top header to the windshield frame. Black rubber coats the latch levers and each latch is accompanied by an adjustable, rubber-tipped tensioning bolt.

The convertible top frame's rear bow is secured to the body deck lid with two chrome-plated pins that insert into chrome-plated receptacles affixed to the body. Chrome Phillips oval head screws hold the pins to the rear bow.

The underside of the convertible top, including the top material itself and the pads, is always black regardless of interior color.

The optional removable hardtop on those convertibles so equipped has a padded vinyl headliner color-matched to the interior. Metal trim pieces on the underside of the hardtop are also painted to match interior color. Front latches for the hardtop are chrome plated but unlike the soft top, the levers on these latches are not rubber coated.

The underside of the convertible deck lid is painted body color. Deck lid release levers, release cables, and lock mechanisms were all mounted prior to painting and should therefore also be painted body color.

The latch receptacles for the pins in the rear bow of the convertible top, as well as the rods that control the receptacles, are black. Deck lid rubber bumpers are black, as are their brackets.

1973–1977 Mechanical

Engine Blocks

The engine-block casting number for all 1973–1977 engines is located on the top rear driver side of the block, on the flange that mates to the transmission bellhousing.

Passenger-side details from a base-engine 1977. Note ripples in the vertical section of the chrome-plated ignition shielding. The dipstick, which is unpainted, is for the automatic transmission.

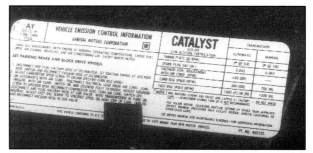

This emission control systems information label glued to the driver-side firewall is from a 1977.

Some very early 1973 small-block-equipped Corvettes utilize a block with the casting No. 3970014. All other 1973s and 1974–1977 small-block cars use a No. 3970010 block. All 1973 and 1974 big-block cars use No. 3999289 blocks.

Engine-block casting dates for all 1973–1977 small- and big-block Corvettes, with the exception of small blocks utilizing the No. 3970014 blocks, are located on the top rear passenger side of the block, on the flange that mates to the transmission bell housing. The casting date for the No. 3970014 cast block is on the top rear driver-side flange adjacent to the casting number.

The engine-block casting date for No. 3970010 small blocks and all big blocks consists of a letter for the month, one or two numbers for the day, and one number for the year. For example, a No. 3970010 block cast on June 12, 1975, would have a casting date of "F 12 5."

No. 3970014 cast small blocks found in some very early 1973s use a similar date code system, except the year is designated by two numbers rather than one. For example, a No. 3970014 block cast on August 21, 1972, would have a casting date of "H 21 72."

All 1973–1977 engines contain two distinct stampings on a machined pad located on the top of the passenger side between the cylinder head and water pump. One stamping is commonly referred to as the assembly stamping and the other is commonly called the VIN derivative stamping.

The assembly stamping begins with a prefix letter to indicate the engine assembly plant. "V" indicates the Flint plant, where all small blocks were assembled, and "T" designates the Tonawanda plant, where all big blocks were assembled. Following the prefix letter are four numbers indicating the month and day of assembly. After the numbers indicating the assembly date are three suffix letters denoting the particular engine. This suffix code is often referred to as the engine broadcast code, or simply the engine code. (Refer to Appendix C for 1973–1977 engine suffix codes.)

142

To illustrate what a typical engine assembly stamping looks like, consider the following 1977 combination; a base 350/180-horsepower engine built on April 5 and coupled to a four-speed transmission. The assembly stamping for such an engine would read "V0405CKZ."

Always remember that the engine assembly date must come after the engine-block casting date (you can't assemble an engine before the block is cast!) and both the casting date and assembly date must precede the final assembly date of the car (you can't finalize assembly on a car before the engine has been cast and assembled!) The great majority of engines were cast and assembled within a couple of weeks prior to the car's assembly date. Some engines, however, were cast and/or assembled months prior to installation in a car. Six months is generally accepted as the outer limit for the difference between an engine assembly or casting date and the final assembly date of the car it is installed into.

The VIN derivative stamping, as the name implies, is a stamping containing a portion or a derivative of the car's vehicle identification number. For 1973–1977 Corvettes the VIN derivative stamping begins with a "1" to designate the Chevrolet car line. This is followed by the final eight characters of the car's VIN. So the VIN derivative stamping in the engine for the 8,612th 1976 built would read "16S408612."

On big-block engines the assembly stamping is normally on the left and toward the rear of the pad when viewing it to read the stamping. The VIN derivative stamping is to the right and toward the front of the pad.

On small-block engines this positioning is reversed.

All 1973–1977 engine blocks are cast-iron. In 1973–1976 the blocks are painted Chevrolet Engine Orange. In 1977 they are painted blue.

Small blocks were originally painted before exhaust manifolds were installed and therefore coverage on the sides of the block behind the manifolds is good. It is believed that all or most big blocks were painted with exhaust manifolds installed. The engine stamp pad and timing tab on the timing chain cover were normally covered up when the engine was painted and therefore they normally appear unpainted.

Cylinder Heads

As with engine blocks, all 1973–1977 cylinder heads have both a casting number and a casting date. As with blocks and other cast parts, the cylinder head casting date typically has a letter to indicate month, one or two numbers to indicate the day of the month,

Forward intake manifold area details from a completely original 1977. Note the black tape holding together the vacuum hoses connected to the temperature sensors.

Driver-side view of a base-engine 1977.

and one number to indicate the year. (Refer to Appendix G for a comprehensive list of cylinder head casting numbers.)

All 1973–1977 engines utilize cast-iron cylinder heads. All cylinder heads and head bolts are painted engine color.

Intake Manifolds

All 1973–1977 intake manifolds are cast-iron that is painted engine color. As with engine blocks and cylinder heads, intake manifolds contain casting numbers and casting dates. As with other cast engine parts, the casting date consists of a letter designating the month, one or two numbers designating the day of the month, and a number denoting the year.

Casting numbers and casting dates for all manifolds are on the top surface. (Refer to Appendix H for intake manifold casting numbers.)

All 1973–1977 Corvette engines utilize an aluminum thermostat housing that is painted engine color. With the exception of some used in late 1977s, the housings do not have a hole for a temperature sending unit.

Unlike those used on earlier cars, original 1973–1977 intake manifold side gaskets do not have semicircular tabs visible sticking up between the runners for cylinders No. 3 and No. 6 and the exhaust heat crossover passage.

All intake manifolds are held on by 9/16-inch hex head bolts. The bolts do not get any type of washer.

Engine lifting brackets are attached to the engines in all 1973–1977 Corvettes. The brackets are painted engine color.

All small blocks have one bracket attached to the first and second intake manifold bolt from the front on the driver side. On four-speed cars a second bracket is attached to the rear of the engine with one of the bolts holding the bellhousing to the block. Some automatic transmission cars do not have a rear bracket and some have one attached to the rear of the intake manifold on the passenger side.

All big blocks have a front bracket that attaches to the first and second intake manifold bolts from the front on the driver side. A rear bracket is fastened to the rear of the cylinder head on the passenger side.

Distributor and Ignition Coil

All 1973 and 1974 Corvettes use a mechanical tach drive Delco Remy point distributor. All 1975–1977 cars use a Delco HEI distributor and an electronic tachometer.

All 1973 and 1974 point distributors have a thin aluminum identification band secured around the housing in a recess just above where the distributor hold down clamp rests. The identification band is natural on one side and colored on the other with a pinkish-red dye. While the majority of cars have the dye on the outside of the band, some have it on the inside, making it difficult to see when the band is installed on the distributor. The identification band has the words "DELCO REMY" stamped into it. This is followed by a seven-character part number and a date code.

All 1975–1977 HEI distributors have part numbers and date codes stamped directly into their aluminum housings. These stampings are on the driver side. (See Appendix K for distributor part numbers.)

The date code, which represents the day the distributor was assembled, consists of a number representing the year, a letter representing the month, and one or two numbers representing the day of the month. For distributor date codes the letter "A" represents January, "B" represents February, and so on. As is typical of stamped-in date codes, the letter "I" is skipped, so the month of September is represented by "J." The date code on a distributor assembled January 17, 1973, for example, would read "3 A 17."

While most distributors were made several weeks before the engine was assembled, it is entirely possible that several months can separate the two. As with most other components, six months is the generally accepted maximum.

1973 and 1974 distributor housings are painted semi-gloss black and have one of several color daubs of paint just below the distributor cap on the passenger side toward the front of the car. 1975–1977 distributor housings are unpainted.

All distributors are fitted with a vacuum advance unit. Vacuum advances have part numbers stamped into them in the bracket that mounts the vacuum canister to the distributor.

All 1973–1977 Corvettes use a black Delco Remy distributor cap. 1973 and 1974 caps have the words "Delco Remy" and a patent number molded into the top between the towers.

All 1973 and 1974 Corvettes use a separate Delco Remy ignition coil. The coil is held by a silver cadmium–plated, stamped steel bracket. The coil is clamped into the bracket with a slotted round head machine screw, and the bracket is held to the intake manifold by two hex head bolts. If the car is equipped with a radio there is a capacitor held to the coil bracket with a clamp retained by a single screw.

Coils are painted gloss black and have the last three numbers of their Chevrolet part number embossed in the housing from the inside out so they are raised up. (See Appendix L for coil numbers and applications.)

In addition to the final three numbers of the part number, ignition coils also have "B-R" embossed in their cases.

The ignition coil for 1975–1977 cars is integral to the distributor cap. It is manufactured by Delco and is black in color. It says "DELCO REMY" and "MADE IN THE USA" on the top. Also, the word "LATCH" appears on the top twice.

Ignition Shielding

All 1973–1977 Corvettes equipped with a radio are outfitted with ignition shielding. All pieces of shielding are plated with flash chrome. As such, the quality and appearance of the chrome is not very good.

All small blocks utilize a one-piece top ignition shield. A translucent plastic shield is held to the underside of the top ignition shield by four plastic rivets.

The ignition shield is held to its two support brackets by one chrome-plated wing bolt on each side. The support brackets are painted engine color and attach to the intake manifold bolts.

Small-block-equipped cars have two chrome-plated spark plug shields, each of which covers two plugs at the rear of the engine. The spark plug shields are retained to cadmium-plated brackets with chrome-plated wing bolts. The brackets are cadmium plated and have "FPM" stamped in to represent the manufacturer. Later, incorrect GM replacement brackets have the letters "CNI" stamped in.

Small blocks have four cadmium-plated spark plug heat shields, each of which covers two plugs. Each of these heat shields is retained to the engine block by means of a single silver cadmium–plated, indented hex head bolt.

All small-block-equipped cars also use a pair of boomerang or V-shaped sections of chrome-plated shielding to encapsulate the spark plug wires. The boomerang shielding runs from the bottom of the vertical shields to the area beneath the spark plugs.

Small-block cars not originally equipped with a radio still have the two main shield support brackets on the back of the intake manifold and the cadmium-plated spark plug heat shields. They do not, however, have any of the chrome shielding.

Like small blocks, 1973 and 1974 big blocks each have a one piece top ignition shield that is held to two support brackets by one chrome-plated wing bolt on each side.

However, rather than vertical spark plug wire shields and spark plug shields like small blocks, big blocks have special spark plug wires covered with braided stainless-steel wire. The braid toward the end of each wire ends in a hoop that gets fastened to the valve cover bolts to provide a ground. The four driver-side hoops are attached in two pairs to the second and fourth bolts back. The passenger side has a single hoop on both the first and second bolts, and a pair of hoops on the third bolt back. Those valve cover bolts holding the hoops are unpainted. All other valve cover bolts are painted engine color.

All big-block engines are fitted with spark plug heat shields. Each heat shield is a cadmium-plated steel tube with a welded-on tab. The tab allows each shield to be mounted to an exhaust manifold bolt.

Big-block cars not originally equipped with a radio do not have the main shield support brackets or braided steel spark plug wires, but do have the heat shields.

In addition to the external ignition shielding fitted to all 1973–1977 Corvettes equipped with a radio, 1973 and 1974 cars had an additional shield covering the ignition points beneath the distributor cap. This additional shield is called a Radio Frequency Interference (RFI) shield.

Spark Plug Wires

All 1973–1977 Corvettes use black spark plug wires manufactured by Packard Electric. All wires are ink stamped every few inches with the words "Packard T V R Suppression" and a date code. The date code indicates the quarter and the year of manufacture. For example, wires labeled "2Q-76" were made in the second quarter of 1976.

Wires for small-block engines have black boots with 90-degree bends at the spark plug end and straight black boots at the distributor end.

1973 and 1974 big-block wires have straight gray boots at the spark plug ends and gray boots with 90-degree bends at the distributor ends.

Carburetors

All 1973–1977 Corvettes have a Rochester Quadrajet carburetor. Carter was at times contracted to manufacture Rochester Quadrajet carburetors for General Motors and the Carter-built Quadrajets are almost identical to the Rochester-built ones. Carter-built Quadrajets are identified as being manufactured by Carter and use Carter's system of date coding rather than Rochester's system.

Rochester-built Quadrajets contain an alphanumeric sequence stamped into a flat, vertical area of the main body on the rear of the driver side. Either the full seven-digit GM part number or the final five digits of the part number are stamped in. Several letters, which identify the specific plant where the carburetor was made, may be stamped here as well. And finally, four numbers denoting the date of manufacture are also stamped into this area.

Rochester utilized the Julian calendar for date coding its carburetors. With this system of dating, the first three numbers represent the day of the year and the final number is the last digit of the specific year. For example, the Julian date code for a carburetor made on January 1, 1974, would read "0014." The

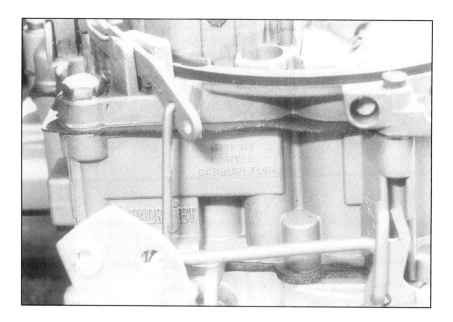

Most 1968–1972 and all 1973–1981 Corvettes have Rochester Quadrajet carburetors. Carter was at times contracted to manufacture Rochester Quadrajet carburetors for General Motors, and Carter-built Quadrajets are identified as shown here.

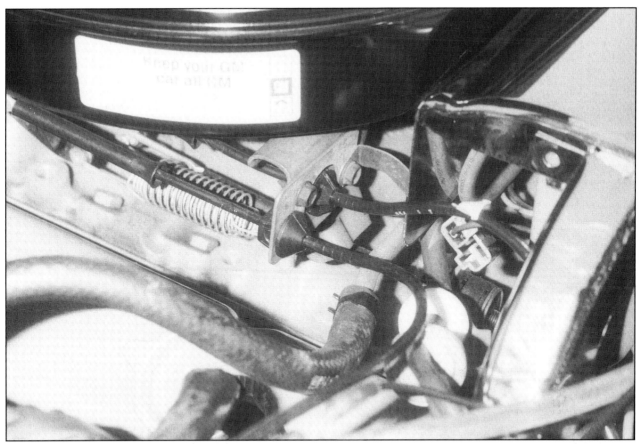

The near cable is for cruise control while the far cable is for the throttle. Note the double throttle return springs, the spring ring clamp on the hose feeding vacuum to the brake booster, and the absence of washers on the intake manifold bolts.

first three digits, "001," represent the first day of the year, and the final digit, "4," represents 1974.

One tricky element to figuring out the exact day a Julian calendar date corresponds to is remembering that leap years have an extra day.

Carter-built Quadrajets don't use a Julian calendar date coding system. Instead, they use a single letter and a single number. The letter denotes the month, with "A" indicating January, "B" indicating February, and so on. The letter "I" is not used, so September is represented by "J."

The number in the date code for Carter-built Quadrajets is the last digit for the year of manufacture. For example, a date code of "C5" indicates the carburetor was made in March 1975.

(For charts showing production codes for 1973–1977 carburetors see Appendix J.)

All carburetors are plated gold dichromate. Plating tends to be rather dark and uniform in color. All carburetors have an insulator separating them from the intake manifold.

All 1973 carburetors use a single accelerator return spring. It is natural or silver cadmium–plated

and mounts from the primary shaft bell crank to the accelerator cable mount. 1974–1977 carburetors use two accelerator return springs.

Carburetors utilize a mechanical choke controlled by a thermostatic coil. The coil is mounted in a recess on the passenger side of the intake manifold and is covered by a cadmium-plated steel housing. A rod links the coil to the choke linkage on the carburetor. The rod is secured to the linkage with a round clip that locks over a groove in the end of the rod.

Air Cleaner

All 1973–1975 Corvettes use an air cleaner design that works in conjunction with the fresh air induction hood. This design uses a housing that has two forward-facing snorkels that allow air to enter.

The housing is painted gloss black, as is the lid. There are no decals on the lid, but there is a decal on the side of the housing that reads "KEEP YOUR GM CAR ALL GM." This sticker is white with red and blue lettering.

In addition to the two forward facing snorkels, 1973–1975 air cleaners also receive air from the hood

Beginning in 1976 the air cleaner is connected to a black molded plastic plenum on top of the fan shroud by means of this type duct. The duct is made from black paper over coiled wire and is retained at each end by means of a built-in clamp that snaps into position.

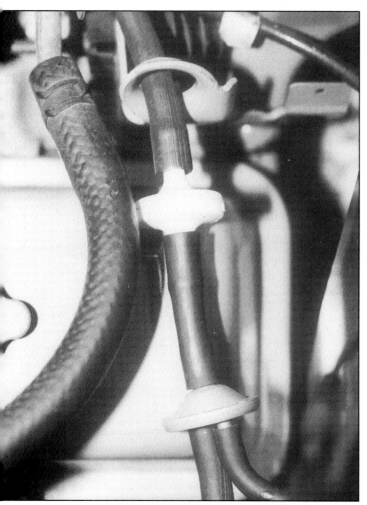

Vacuum hose details from the driver side of a 1977 base engine. The larger, textured hose on the left is for the brake booster. The smaller hoses on the right supply vacuum to a variety of components.

cowling at times. A stepped rubber gasket and steel flange sitting on the edge of the air cleaner base seals against the duct in the underside of the hood.

1976 and 1977 Corvettes use a different-design air cleaner assembly. The assembly is entirely closed and does not mate to the hood. For base-engine cars the housing has a single snorkel pointing toward the front of the car with a slight offset to the driver side. The air cleaner housing in cars equipped with an L-82 engine has two forward facing snorkels.

On base engines the snorkel is connected to a black molded plastic plenum on top of the fan shroud by means of a duct. The duct is made from black paper over coiled wire and has an accordion shape. It is retained at each end by means of a built-in clamp that snaps into position.

The snorkel has a vacuum motor that opens to permit the flow of warmed air from a metallic tube connected to the driver-side exhaust manifold. The vacuum motor is painted semi-gloss black and has the words "AUTO THERMAC" embossed on the top side.

On L-82 engines, both snorkels are connected to a molded plenum that is similar to the plenum on base-engine cars except it has two connection points.

Air cleaner assemblies have the replacement filter number and other information on a white sticker affixed to the outside of the air cleaner housing.

Original 1973–1977 air filter elements, unlike later replacements, have a fine wire screen around the outside in a vertical (and not diagonal) pattern. The horizontal and horizontal and vertical wires form rectangles with the longer measurement running vertical when the element is installed.

Some variation of this sticker is found on all 1973–1977 air cleaner housings. This example is on a 1976.

This air cleaner housing sticker is from a 1977. Note the ink-stamped date code on the bottom left.

Valve Covers

All 1973–1977 base engines are fitted with stamped steel valve covers painted engine color. These are held on with hex head bolts and metal tabs that are also painted engine color.

There are two metal wire retention clips spot welded to the passenger-side cover. This cover also has a crankcase vent intake hole. The hole gets a black rubber grommet. A tube inserts into the grommet and connects to the air cleaner base.

On base-engine cars there are two metal wire retention clips spot welded to the driver-side cover. This cover also has a PCV valve inserted into a hole fitted with a rubber grommet. A hose connects the PCV valve to the carburetor. The driver-side cover also has a provision for the oil filler cap.

Optional L82 small blocks utilize cast-aluminum valve covers with longitudinal ribs. As with the painted steel covers, a vent hose connects the passenger-side valve cover to the air cleaner base and a PCV valve is in the driver-side valve cover. Aluminum valve covers are retained by silver cadmium–plated, indented hex head bolts.

Both passenger- and driver-side aluminum valve covers are made from the same mold. The only difference between the two is that the driver-side cover has a hole for the oil fill cap that the passenger side does not have. On the passenger side, where the hole would go, there is a rigid disc with the crossed flag emblem glued on.

1973 and 1974 big-block valve covers are made from stamped steel that is painted engine color. Unlike earlier covers, they do not have internal drippers that are spot welded on.

The passenger-side cover has a hole fitted with a black rubber grommet. A long, black phosphate–plated steel tube inserts into the grommet and connects to the rear of the air cleaner housing.

The passenger-side big-block cover has a welded-on bracket at the rear to hold a plastic spark plug wire loom. Toward the top edge of the cover there are two metal brackets spot welded on. These brackets retain wires and hose. There are four individual brackets along the bottom edge of the cover to hold each of the passenger-side spark plug wires. Finally, there is another wire retention bracket welded on the bottom toward the rear.

The driver-side big-block cover has the PCV valve and a welded-on bracket at the rear to hold a plastic spark plug wire loom. The bracket has a hole to receive a clip that holds the wire to the carburetor solenoid. Toward the top edge of the cover there is a metal bracket spot welded on. This bracket also retains the wire to the carburetor solenoid. There are four individual brackets along the bottom edge of the cover to hold each of the driver-side spark plug wires. There is also a bracket welded on the bottom edge toward the middle.

The curve of the inner front corner of the driver-side big-block cover is interrupted by a small, flat indentation. The curve of the outer rear corner is recessed to provide clearance for the power brake booster.

Aluminum valve covers used on L-82 engines have chrome-plated, twist-in-style oil fill caps on the driver side. A large "S" for Stant, the manufacturer of the caps, is stamped into the center rivet.

Base engines use a steel twist-on oil fill cap in the driver-side valve cover. As with the L-82 cap, a large "S" for Stant is stamped into the center rivet. Base-engine oil fill caps are painted engine color.

1973 and 1974 big-block engines use a rubber push-in-style oil fill plug that has the word "OIL" molded into the top. Since the plug was installed before the engine was painted, it too is painted with Chevrolet Engine Orange.

Exhaust Manifolds

All 1973–1977 exhaust manifolds are cast-iron. They contain a casting number that is normally on the side facing away from the engine, and a casting date that is normally on the side facing toward the engine. (Refer to Appendix I for exhaust manifold casting numbers.)

Small-block exhaust manifold casting dates normally include a letter denoting the month and one or two numbers denoting the day of the month. Big-block exhaust manifolds normally include a letter denoting the month, one or two numbers denoting the day of the month, and two numbers denoting the year.

Small-block exhaust manifolds were not yet installed when engines were originally painted so they show no signs of overspray. Big-block manifolds were installed before the engine was painted and therefore have Chevrolet Engine Orange paint overspray.

No 1973–1977 exhaust manifolds use a gasket where they mount to the cylinder head.

Small-block manifolds use 9/16-inch hex head bolts that have two concentric rings on their heads. The front two bolts and rear two bolts on both sides of the engine get French locks with one of the two tabs bent over to prevent the bolts from loosening. In addition, the same front and rear bolts on each side get thick, flat washers that sit between the French lock and manifold. If, however, the exhaust manifold bolt also retains a bracket (such as an air-conditioning bracket) the flat washer is not used.

Bolts holding big-block manifolds have been observed with three different styles of heads. The most prevalent has two concentric rings like small-block manifold bolts. A second-design bolt, with an integral washer, recessed hex head, and the letter "A" (the manufacturer's logo) in the center of the head, is also utilized. A third variety that is sometimes seen is a simple hex head with no markings at all.

1973 and 1974 big-block exhaust manifolds do not have French locks or any type of washers used with the bolts.

Starter Motor

All 1973–1977 Corvettes use a Delco-Remy starter motor. Automatic transmission–equipped cars utilize starters with aluminum noses while starters for manual transmission–equipped cars have a cast-iron nose.

Motor housings and cast-iron noses are painted semi-gloss black. Aluminum noses are unpainted.

The starter's part number and assembly date are stamped into the side of the motor housing. The date code contains a number representing the last digit of the year, a letter denoting the month, with "A" representing January, "B" representing February, and so on. As is typical of stamped-in date codes, the letter "I" is skipped, so the month of September is represented by "J." One or two numbers indicating the day follow the letter denoting the month. For example, a date code of "7B14" indicates the starter was made February 14, 1977. (See Appendix N for starter motor part numbers.)

Starter solenoids have a black Bakelite cover for the electrical connections. Solenoid housings may be painted semi-gloss black or silver cadmium plated.

All starters use a stamped steel brace to support the forward end (the end facing toward the front of the car when the starter is installed). The brace mounts to a stud on the starter's end plate and to a threaded boss in the engine block. The brace is painted semi-gloss black.

Every starter has a heat shield to protect it from exhaust system heat. Small-block engines are fitted with a rectangular-shaped shield while big blocks get a larger, irregularly shaped shield. Small-block shields are painted semi-gloss black and big-block shields are plated with poor-quality flash chrome. Heat shields attach to the solenoid screws with barrel nuts.

Oil Filter

All 1973–1977 engines, including both small and big blocks, utilize an AC Delco spin-on-type oil filter. Earlier filters are white with a red AC logo, blue circumferential stripes, and blue lettering reading "FULL FLOW" and "TYPE PF-25." Later filters are painted dark blue with a sticker bearing the AC and GM logos.

Alternator, Power Steering Pump, and Fuel Pump

All engines are fitted with a Delco-Remy alternator mounted on the driver side. Alternator housings are made from cast aluminum and are not painted or coated with anything.

The front half of the housing has the unit's part number, amperage rating, and assembly date code stamped in. The date code contains a number for the year, and a letter for the month, with "A" representing January, "B" representing February, and so on. As is typical of stamped-in date codes, the letter "I" is skipped, so the month of September is represented by "J." The letter denoting the month is followed by one

or two numbers for the day. For example, an alternator stamped "4B11" was assembled February 11, 1974.

The alternator pulley for most small blocks is made from zinc-plated stamped steel. Some L82 engines have alternator pulleys machined from solid material.

1973 and 1974 big blocks utilize an alternator pulley with a deeper groove than that found in small-block pulleys. The center hub is machined from solid material and the pulley is silver cadmium plated.

The lower alternator bracket on all small-block-equipped 1973–1977 cars is cast metal that is painted semi-gloss black. The upper bracket is stamped steel painted semi-gloss black.

The lower alternator bracket on all 1973 and 1974 big blocks without power steering is cast and painted semi-gloss black. The bracket for big-block cars equipped with power steering is stamped steel that is painted semi-gloss black. A third bracket attaches to the lower bracket and to the water pump mount bolt underneath the brace for the A.I.R. pump. This third bracket is painted semi-gloss black.

Small-block 1973–1977 cars equipped with power steering use a semi-gloss black painted power steering pump with a neck that is the same diameter from top to bottom. The necks on 1973 and 1974 big-block pumps, in contrast, widen toward the bottom. Small-block pumps have a semi-gloss black, stamped steel belt guard bolted to the body.

Power steering pump pulleys on base-engine-impact cars are cast with open spokes. Pulleys on L82-equipped cars are semi-gloss black painted, stamped steel. All big-block-equipped cars use a double groove, open spoke, cast pulley for the power steering pump.

This small white-and-blue sticker reading "NOTICE DO NOT PRY ON RESERVOIR" and the broadcast code "BX" are on the power steering pump housing beginning in 1977.

The alternator pulley and fan are unpainted in this 1976. Note the belt guard bolted to the upper alternator brace. This was intended to protect the upper radiator hose from the belt.

All 1973–1977 power steering pumps, regardless of engine, use two semi-gloss painted, stamped steel support brackets.

All 1973–1977 Corvettes use an AC brand fuel pump. The pumps usually have "AC" cast into the top or side of the upper housing and a five-character part number stamped into the underside of the mounting flange. Pumps have a natural, dull silver, cast-aluminum body with a gold irridite–plated lower cover.

Water Pump, Engine Fan, and Fan Clutch

Early 1973 small-block cars use a water pump with an undrilled bypass hose boss. Later 1973 pumps have the boss drilled and tapped. The tapped hole is closed with a square head plug.

Unlike earlier water pumps, the snout on 1973–1977 pumps has reinforcing ribs. Small-block pumps usually have casting No. 330818 in the housing.

Very early 1973 big-block water pumps utilize casting No. 3992077 housings. Later 1973 and 1974

Original radiator hoses, such as the one shown here on a 1976, have a pronounced texture. Note the original markings on the hose and the belt guard bolted to the upper alternator support.

big blocks use casting No. 386100 water pumps. All big-block pumps utilize a bypass hose connected to a screwed-in fitting on top of the housing.

All water pump housings have a cast-in date code. The first character of the code is a letter denoting the month, with "A" representing January, "B" representing February, and so on. The second character is one or two numbers denoting the day. For small-block pumps this is followed by a single number denoting the year, and for big blocks it is followed by two numbers denoting the year.

Most water pump pulleys are painted semi-gloss black, though some originals have been observed with a black phosphate finish.

All 1973–1977 Corvettes use a thermostatically controlled, viscous coupled fan clutch. Those 1973 Corvettes assembled through approximately July 1973 use one design clutch and all cars assembled thereafter use a second design clutch.

The first design clutch uses a flat, rectangular-shaped bi-metallic strip on its front face as a thermostat. The second design uses a metallic coil instead.

Original clutches usually have a date code stamped in the flange that goes against the water pump pulley. Clutches (as well as water pump pulleys) are retained by studs and nuts that thread into the pump's front hub.

All 1973–1977 Corvettes use a gloss-black painted cooling fan that is mounted to the fan clutch. Cars equipped with air conditioning use a seven-blade fan that has a part number and date code stamped into the edge of one or more of the blades. The date code contains a letter for the month, with "A" designating January, "B" designating February, and so on. As is typical of stamped-in date codes, the letter "I" is skipped, so the month of September is represented by "J." Following the letter indicating the month are two numbers to denote the year.

Small-block air-conditioned cars use a seven-blade fan that is essentially flat along the outer edge of each blade. In contrast, the ends of the blades on big-block air-conditioned cars are irregularly shaped and come to an off-center point.

Cars not equipped with air conditioning use a five-blade fan. Five-blade fans do not have a part number or date code stamped in.

Radiator, Hoses, and Related Parts

All 1973–1977 Corvettes use a copper radiator. Radiators were manufactured by Harrison, and have that name debossed in the passenger-side radiator tank. In addition, there is a stamped steel tag containing a two-letter broadcast code and a part number

With the possible exception of 1973s assembled through approximately early October 1973, all 1973–1982s use this RC-33 radiator cap. Some very early 1973s may use an RC-29 cap. Note that the overflow hose on the radiator of this 1973 is secured by a clamp. Though difficult to see, the words "WITTEK MFG" and "CHICAGO USA" are stamped into the clamp.

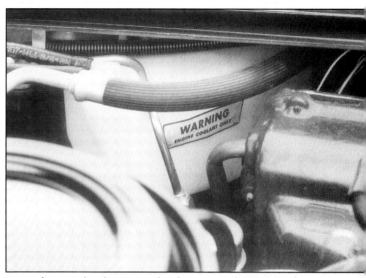

Corvettes from 1973 through 1977 use a white plastic engine coolant recovery tank like the 1976 example shown here. The tanks on 1973s have a pointed edge adjacent to the inner wheelwell whereas later tanks have a rounded edge.

attached to the passenger side. All radiators are painted semi-gloss to gloss black.

All cars use a black or dark gray plastic fan shroud. In 1973 both small- and big-block engines have the same shroud but use a different lower extension. The small-block extension is part No. 331870 and the big-block extension is part No. 336152.

1974 Corvettes use a different fan shroud than 1973s, but again both small- and big-block engines have the same shroud and use a different lower extension. The lower extensions are the same as in 1973.

All 1973–1977 cars use a white plastic coolant recovery tank. The tank for 1973 is part No. 334762. It has a pointed edge adjacent to the inner wheelwell. Starting in 1974, the tank used is part No. 339185. This second-design tank has a noticeably rounder edge where it meets the inner wheelwell.

With the possible exception of 1973s assembled through approximately early October 1973, all cars use an RC-33 radiator cap rated at 15 psi installed directly on the radiator. Some very early 1973s may use an RC-29 cap.

RC-33 caps contain the AC logo in a circle. They also contain the words "DO NOT OPEN, CHECK LEVEL IN BOTTLE, CLOSED SYSTEM, ALIGN ARROW & VENT TUBE."

RC-29 caps have a thin round disc attached to the top. The disc is silver with a blue stripe with words

that read "CLOSED SYSTEM." Above the blue stripe in red letters it reads "DO NOT OPEN." Below the stripe in blue letters it reads "ALIGN STRIPE WITH OVERFLOW TUBE." Also below the stripe, but in red letters, it reads "15lbs. RC29."

All radiator and heater hoses are molded black rubber. Stamped on radiator hoses in white ink are a part number, GM logo, and several letters that are believed to be manufacturer's codes. In addition, there is usually a colored line running the length of the hose.

In 1973 only, on air-conditioned big-block cars, the lower radiator hose is two pieces joined by a steel tube in the middle. The steel tube is painted semi-gloss black and has a small depression to provide added clearance for the engine cooling fan. 1974 big blocks use a one-piece lower hose.

Heater hoses usually contain a GM logo in white ink. They sometimes have the letters "DL" or "U" stamped on them also. Most original hoses have three or four thin ridges running lengthwise.

All cars use SURE-TITE brand stainless-steel worm drive clamps for the radiator hoses. All applications use size 28 clamps except 1973 air-conditioned big blocks, which use size 32 on the lower hose only. Original clamps have "SURE-TITE" in italics stamped into the band along their circumference. In addition, "WITTEK MFG. CO. CHI. U.S.A." is stamped into the worm screw's housing.

With the possible exception of very late 1977s, all cars use tower-style clamps for the heater hoses. The 5/8-inch heater hoses use 1-1/16-inch clamps. This size clamp has a galvanized finish and contains the size, the words "WITTEK MFG. CO. CHICAGO U.S.A.," and a date code stamped into the band. The first number of the date code denotes the quarter and the following two numbers indicate the year.

The 3/4-inch heater hose uses 1 1/4-inch clamps. These clamps have a cadmium dichromate finish that results in a translucent goldish tint as opposed to the smaller clamps' dull silver color. The larger 1 1/4-inch clamps contain the manufacturer's logo and size designation but do not have a date code. Instead, they have the letters "DCM" stamped into the band.

Brake Master Cylinder and Related Components

All master cylinders are manufactured by Delco and contain a casting number and the Delco split ring logo on the inboard side. Non–power assist master cylinders are casting No. 5455509 and power assist masters are casting No. 5480346.

In addition to the casting number, each master also contains a two-letter application code stamped in on a flat surface by the front brake line fitting. A Julian date code is also stamped in this location. The date code typically contains a number indicating the year, followed by three numbers denoting the day of the year. For example, a stamping of "3219" represents the 219th day of 1973.

Most cars with power assist brakes have "TG" stamped into the master cylinder and most without power assist have "HC" or "YA" stamped in. The entire master cylinder is semi-gloss black except for machined areas, which are natural.

All 1973 and some very early 1974 masters contain two bleeder screws above the brake line ports.

Later 1974s and 1975–1977 masters do not have bleeder screws. The bleeders are zinc-plated steel.

For all master cylinders, two steel wire bails hold the cover on. A small vinyl sticker with two letters is folded around one of the bail wires. This sticker is white with red letters, which are usually "TG" for power brake cars and "YA" or "HC" for manual brake cars.

All master cylinders use a stamped steel, cadmium dichromate–plated cover and rubber gasket. The cover has two domes that are not connected by a small ridge like later units. "SERVICE WITH DELCO PARTS" is stamped into one dome, while "USE DELCO SAE J 1703 BRAKE FLUID" or "SERVICE WITH SAE J 1703 BRAKE FLUID" is stamped into the other dome.

Power brake boosters, on cars so equipped, are painted gloss black and frequently have a spot of yellow paint somewhere. The yellow is thought to be an inspection mark or an application code.

Some boosters have a Julian date code stamped in on top opposite the vacuum valve. The code contains a number corresponding to the final number of the year and then three numbers denoting the day of the year. For example, a booster stamped "3168" was manufactured on the 168th day of 1973.

Air Conditioning and Heating System Components

All 1973–1975 and most 1976 Corvettes equipped with air conditioning utilize a model A-6 axial-type Frigidaire compressor. Starting in late 1976 and continuing in 1977, Corvettes use a radial-type Frigidaire compressor.

The broadcast code sticker on a power brake booster bears the two-letter broadcast code and date of manufacturer. This particular unit was assembled on the 193rd day of 1977.

All 1973 through late 1976 A-6-type air-conditioning compressors have a green, black, and silver foil sticker as shown. In this example, the model number "5910797" identifies it as a 1972 or 1973 unit installed on a 454 engine. The code number "061321" is actually a manufacturing date code that translates to June 13, 1972, first shift.

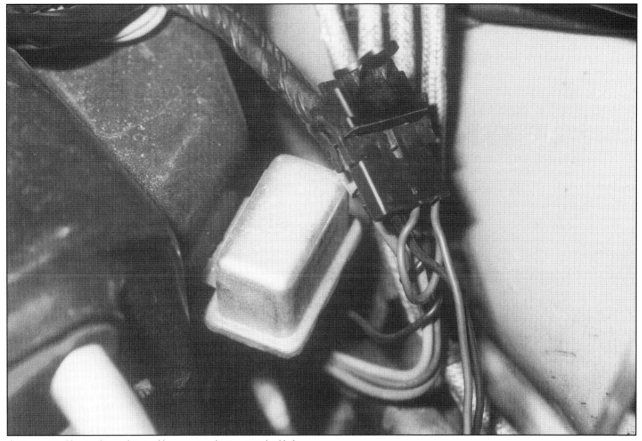

This is an original heating/air-conditioning blower motor relay in a 1973 big block.

Both types of compressors are painted semi-gloss black and have a green, black, and silver foil sticker on the top of the housing. The sticker contains, among other things, the compressor's model number and a date code. The date code contains two numbers for the month, two numbers for the day, one number for the year, and one number for the shift. For example, a date code of "031952" translates to March 19, 1975, second shift.

Unlike earlier systems that utilize a separate POA valve assembly, thermostatic expansion valve, and receiver-dehydrator, 1973–1977 systems have all of these components combined into one unit mounted beneath the heater/air-conditioning fan housing.

An unpainted, dark gray fiberglass housing covers the evaporator. There is a blue and silver Harrison foil sticker on the housing, as well as a fan relay. The relay cover is zinc or cadmium plated and does not have any words stamped in it.

Most Corvettes with air conditioning have a vacuum actuated valve spliced into the heater hose. When the air conditioning is on, this valve shuts off the flow of engine coolant to the heater core.

The blower motors for both air-conditioned and non-air-conditioned cars are painted semi-gloss to gloss black. Motors on air-conditioned cars have a rubber tube that extends from the motor housing to the evaporator housing. Motors on non-air-conditioned cars do not have this tube. Motors have a part number

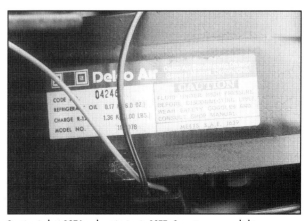

Starting in late 1976 and continuing in 1977, Corvettes use a radial-type Frigidaire compressor instead of the old A-6 axial-type. Radial compressors have this style sticker.

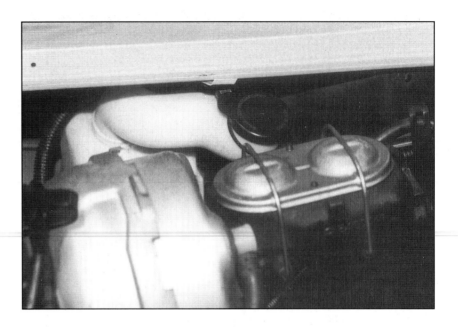

As seen in this 1977, the windshield washer fluid reservoir was tucked up underneath the driver-side inner fender area.

and date code stamped into their mounting flange. The date code contains one or two numbers to denote the month and two numbers to indicate the year.

Windshield Wiper Motor and Related Components

The wiper motor for all 1973–1977 Corvettes uses an unpainted cast-aluminum housing and transmission case. A black plastic cover goes over the wiper motor transmission assembly. A silver-colored foil sticker containing the motor's part number and date of manufacture is on the motor housing.

In 1973 the wiper motor is part No. 5044784. In 1974 it is part No. 5044811. In 1975, 1976, and part of 1977 it is part No. 5044814. Other 1977s use motor number 5044314.

Date codes for wiper motors use the Julian calendar. One, two, or three numbers indicate the day of the year. This is followed by a single number denoting the year.

The windshield washer pump utilized in 1973–1977 has three ports. The center one is an intake port that connects to the fluid reservoir and the other two feed fluid to the nozzles.

In 1973 and 1974 the washer fluid pump is integral to the wiper motor assembly. In 1975–1977 it is a separate unit mounted at the base of the fluid reservoir.

The windshield washer fluid reservoir is mounted on the engine compartment side of the left inner wheelwell. The reservoir is rigid white plastic and does not have any writing or fluid level marks on it. A long fill neck inserts in the reservoir and extends up slightly below the fender lip.

Air Injection Reactor System and other Emissions Components

Many, but not all, 1973–1977 Corvettes are equipped with an Air Injection Reactor (A.I.R.) system. In 1973 and 1974 the A.I.R. system includes black cadmium–plated tubes that thread into each of the four runners on both exhaust manifolds. In 1975 and 1976 the A.I.R. system is connected by a single tube to the passenger-side exhaust pipe below the heat riser valve. In 1977 the system is connected to the driver-side manifold with four tubes and to the passenger-side manifold with two tubes.

The A.I.R. pump body is diecast aluminum and natural in color. A semi-gloss black painted, rough textured, sand cast plate covers the back of the pump.

All pumps contain a centrifugal filter behind the pulley. This filter, which looks more like a fan, is made from black plastic.

Small-block engines use a steel spacer between the front pump pulley and centrifugal filter. Big blocks do not use a spacer. The spacer is zinc or silver cadmium plated and the pulley is gray phosphate plated or semi-gloss black painted. Pulleys used on small blocks have part No. 3917234 stamped in while those used on big blocks have part No. 330552 stamped in.

Most pumps are date coded, though the date can be difficult to see with the pump installed. It is stamped into a boss on the rear underside of the body. The sequence may begin with a letter to indicate the assembly plant or specific line. Then there are one or three numbers to indicate the day of the year on the Julian calendar. Earlier dates (prior to the 100th day) may start with two zeros or they may not.

Driver-side view of an Air Injection Reactor pump on a 1973 LS4. The ink-stamped "AC" is a broadcast code.

Passenger-side view of an A.I.R. pump on a 1973 LS4.

For example, a pump assembled on the fifth day of the year may be stamped "005" or simply "5." A fourth (or second) number follows to denote the last digit of the year. This is followed by a number indicating the shift, and a letter indicating the model of the pump.

The lower pump bracket is painted engine color and the upper bracket is semi-gloss black. For earlier small blocks, the lower bracket is cast and contains the number "3923214." Later small-block lower brackets have a casting number of 14007354. For big blocks the lower bracket is stamped steel.

The diverter valve body is natural in color, while the diaphragm cover and check valves are cadmium dichromate. The diaphragm cover has a round sticker with a two-letter broadcast code printed on it. The diverter valve muffler is plated gray phosphate. The diverter valve part number is stamped into the valve below the muffler. Check valves have a part number stamped into their center ridge.

Hoses connecting the various parts of the A.I.R. system are molded black and hose clamps are tower style. Clamps have a galvanized finish and contain the size, the words "WITTEK MFG. CO. CHICAGO U.S.A.," and a date code stamped into the band. The first number of the date code denotes the quarter and the following two numbers indicate the year.

All 1973 Corvettes were originally equipped with an A.I.R. system. All 1974s with manual transmission and all 1974s equipped with the California emissions package (option NB2) got A.I.R. systems. In 1975–1977 all cars equipped with L82, NB2, or NA6 (high-altitude emissions package) also have an A.I.R. system.

All 1973–1977 Corvettes are fitted with an Evaporative Control System. This system includes a black carbon-filled canister mounted to the lower left-side inner wheelwell.

All 1973–1977 Corvettes have a PCV valve located in the left-side valve cover. The valve has a part number stamped into it. In 1973 the valve is No. CV736C. Thereafter it is No. CV774C for the base engine and No. CV775C for the L82 engine.

Most 1973–1977 Corvettes have a Transmission Controlled Spark (TCS) system. This system includes a solenoid, timer, temperature switch, transmission switch, and vacuum advance solenoid.

The timer is usually mounted on the firewall and the temperature switch is in the passenger-side cylinder head. On small-block engines the solenoid is attached to an intake manifold stud toward the front, passenger side of the carburetor. On 1973 and 1974 big blocks it is mounted on the intake manifold to the right side of the coil bracket.

1975–1977 Corvettes are equipped with an Early Fuel Evaporation (EFE) system. With this system, a vacuum-actuated valve is mounted to the passenger-side exhaust manifold. The valve is controlled by a thermal vacuum switch mounted adjacent to the thermostat housing. This switch is later placed in the housing.

All cars have an anti-diesel solenoid that is mounted with a bracket to the carburetor base. The bracket is cadmium dichromate plated, and the solenoid housing is silver cadmium plated.

All 1973–1977 Corvettes have what is commonly called an emissions label glued to the left upper area of the firewall. This label is either white or yellow in color, and contains engine tune-up specifications as well as information about the emission control systems installed in the car.

Engine Compartment, Wiring, Horns, and Related Components

The firewall, underside of the hood, and engine compartment side of the inner wheelwells are painted semi-gloss black. The wheel side of the front and rear inner wheelwells is also painted semi-gloss black, though coverage is usually sparse. In addition, the rear areas of the wheel sides normally have some undercoating.

In all 1973–1977 cars, wire harnesses and adjacent hoses are bundled together in a row, so rather than forming a circle they are flat. The harnesses and hoses are held to each other with black plastic tie wraps.

All vacuum hose is color coded with an ink stripe that runs the length of the hose. Larger hoses have a green, red, or yellow stripe while smaller hoses usually have a white stripe.

All 1973 and 1974 Corvettes equipped with a big block have a small oil pressure line bracket on the left side of the engine block. A steel tube goes from the brass block fitting to a junction at this bracket. Then a black plastic tube continues up to the oil pressure gauge.

All 1973 small-block-equipped cars utilize black plastic tubing that goes directly from the engine block fitting to the oil pressure gauge. The plastic line has tiny white lettering and is fastened at both ends with brass fittings.

1974–1977 Corvettes are fitted with electric oil pressure gauges. A gold irridite–plated metal sending unit is threaded into the engine block above the oil filter.

In 1973 a horn relay is mounted to the driver-side inner wheelwell. It has a short, squared-off, silver cadmium cover that has nothing stamped in. The plain cover sits on a black plastic base and relies on a black plastic tab that is formed as part of the black plastic base for mounting. Starting in 1974 the horn relay is mounted under the dash adjacent to the fuse block.

1970 Corvettes have two horns, a high and a low note. The high note is part No. 9000246 and it mounts on the driver side. The low note is part No. 9000245 and it mounts on the passenger side.

In 1973, only one horn is installed, on the driver side near the headlight vacuum canister. In 1974 and 1975 a single horn is standard equipment, but a second horn is available as option U05. The second horn is a lower note than the standard one. In 1976 and 1977 dual horns are standard.

Horns have the last three digits of the part number and a manufacturing date code stamped into flat areas near the sound opening. The date code contains a number denoting the year, a letter denoting the month (with "A" representing January, "B" representing February, and so on), and another number indicating the week. For example, a horn stamped "3F2" was made the second week of June 1973.

Each horn is spot welded to a mounting bracket and the whole assembly is painted semi-gloss black.

Hood hinges are silver cadmium plated and usually have both body color and underhood black overspray on them. Hinges are usually fastened by black phosphate–plated, indented hex head bolts.

The hood support is silver cadmium plated. It has two sections that are hinged and they fold as the hood is lowered.

The hood latches are black phosphate plated and mount with black phosphate–plated hardware. The driver-side male latch has the hood release cable attached with a brass barrel cable stop that utilizes a hex bolt to lock the stop to the cable. The cable is inside a spiral-wound metal sheath.

Another cable connects the two female latches mounted to the underside of the hood. This cable is inside a black nylon sheath and its ends are secured to the latches with small clevis pins fitted with flat washers and cotter pins.

In 1977 a different-design hood latch system is employed. Hook-shaped latches replace the older pin-style latches on the firewall. A hood lift spring topped with a black rubber bumper is on either side of the firewall.

1973–1977 Chassis
Chassis

1973–1977 Corvette chassis are painted semi-gloss black. Chassis for automatic transmission–equipped cars have a removable, bolt-on center cross-member while standard transmission–equipped cars have a welded-on center cross-member. Also, cars with automatics do not have a clutch cross shaft tower welded on top of the chassis behind the left front wheel as standard transmission cars do.

In 1974 the chassis was modified in the rear with the addition of a bracket and extension to accommodate the rear impact-absorbing bumper assembly. In 1975 the chassis was again modified in the rear. The rear cross-member was made about 2 inches wider.

A pair of 1-inch-high chassis part number sequences is painted in white or yellow on the chassis with a stencil. One sequence is the A.O. Smith part number (this is the company that fabricated the chassis for GM) and the other sequence is the Chevrolet part number. These part numbers are usually found on the passenger side of the chassis behind the front wheel.

A manufacturing date code is stenciled on the rail as well. The date contains one or two numbers representing the month, one or two numbers indicating the day, and two numbers denoting the year.

Most 1973–1977 Corvettes have their serial number stamped into their chassis in two locations. It is typically found in the left-side rail slightly forward of the No. 4 body mount bracket. It is also typically found on the left-side rear kick up above the wheel area slightly forward of the No. 3 body mount bracket.

Steel shims are frequently utilized at body mount points to make up for irregularities in fit. If present, shims are usually taped to the body mount bracket with 1 1/2-inch masking tape. The number of shims needed at each body mount bracket is typically written on the chassis adjacent to the bracket with a green or white grease crayon. Unlike on earlier cars, this number is usually an actual number rather than slash marks. Also unlike earlier cars, 1973–1977 body mounts are made from rubber.

Front Suspension

Upper and lower front control arms are painted semi-gloss to gloss black. Ball joints are installed after the arms are painted and are not painted. Crushed steel rivets (not bolts) hold ball joints on and are also natural in finish.

Control arm cross shafts are painted semi-gloss black on some cars and unpainted on others. Cars with painted cross shafts typically have control arm bushing retention washers and bolts that are also painted semi-gloss black. Cars with unpainted cross shafts typically have retention washers that are gray phosphate plated and bolts that are black phosphate plated.

Front coil springs are natural in finish and sometimes have an irregular bluish cast from the manufacturing process. A green paper sticker contains two

black letters indicating the spring's broadcast code (i.e., their application) as well as a black GM part number.

Front shock absorbers are manufactured by Delco and are oil hydraulic, not gas filled. They are painted semi-gloss gray and have the words "DELCO REMY PLIACELL" and a date code stamped in around the bottom. The Julian date code contains three numbers indicating the day and two numbers denoting the year. In addition, there is a small paper sticker with a two-letter broadcast code on the side of the shock.

The upper shock mount rubber bushings are unpainted black rubber. The top upper bushing is larger in diameter than the bottom upper bushing and the upper shock washer is gray phosphate plated.

The lower shock mount rubber bushings are integral to the shock and are therefore painted along with the shock.

All 1973 and 1974 big-block Corvettes and all small-block-equipped cars with optional FE7 or Z07 suspension utilize a 15/16-inch front sway bar. All other cars utilize a 3/4-inch bar. Some cars have a semi-gloss black painted sway bar while others have a natural, unpainted finish bar.

Bushings mounting the front sway bar to the chassis, as well as bushings in the end links, are unpainted black rubber. Semi-gloss black painted, stamped steel brackets hold the bar to the chassis.

End link bolts are zinc-plated 5/16-24 SAE fine thread and usually have the manufacturer's logo, "UB" or "WB," on their heads. End link spacers are zinc plated, have a split seam, and typically have a "K" or a "C" stamped in.

Steering Box and Steering Linkage

1973–1977 Corvettes use a cast steering gear that is usually natural in color though some are painted semi-gloss black. The box cover is cast aluminum, and it is retained by three black oxide–plated hex head bolts. A daub of yellow or blue paint is frequently seen on top of the box.

A forged pitman arm links the steering box to the relay rod. The pitman arm is natural in color and is often seen with a blue or green daub of paint.

The steering relay rod and idler arm are typically natural finish. Both parts are forged and tend to have a bluish gray tint. Original idler arms do not have grease fittings.

Tie rod ends are natural finish and also typically have a bluish-gray color cast. Daubs of yellow paint are often seen on tie rod ends.

Tie rod end sleeves are painted semi-gloss black. Tie rod end clamps have two reinforcing ridges around their circumference and are sometimes painted semi-gloss black and sometimes left unpainted.

Outer tie rod ends can install into either of two holes in the steering knuckles. Cars equipped with standard, non-power steering have the outer tie rod ends installed into the rear holes while cars equipped with power steering have them in the forward holes. On those cars equipped with power steering, the unused steering knuckle hole is plugged with an aluminum plug inserted from the bottom.

On those cars so equipped, the power steering control valve and hydraulic cylinder are painted semi-gloss black. The nut and washers retaining the hydraulic cylinder's ram to the frame bracket are zinc plated. The frame bracket may be painted semi-gloss black or unpainted. Original power steering hoses typically have longitudinal ridges around their entire circumference while later replacements don't.

Rear Suspension

All 1973–1977 Corvettes equipped with standard suspension utilize a nine-leaf rear spring. Cars equipped with optional FE7 or ZO7 suspension utilize a seven-leaf spring. All springs are painted light gray and have black plastic liners between the leaves. Nine-leaf springs do not have a liner between leaf No. 6 and leaf No. 7 (with the bottom leaf being No. 1).

The center rear spring mount bracket is painted semi-gloss black. The four bolts retaining the spring to the differential typically have the manufacturer's logo, "WB," on their heads and are either black phosphate or zinc plated. The outer spring bolts and nuts are usually black phosphate–plated and the washers are typically natural.

Rear trailing arms are painted semi-gloss to gloss black. Rear wheel bearing carriers (also called spindle supports) are natural and have a part number and date code cast in. The date code has a letter representing the month, with "A" for January, "B" for February, and so on, one or two numbers for the day, and one number for the final digit of the year. The date code for a rear bearing carrier made on April 18, 1975, for example, would read "D 18 5."

All 1973 and 1974 big blocks, as well as all cars equipped with FE7 or ZO7 suspension, have a rear stabilizer bar. The bar is 9/16 inch in diameter and may be painted semi-gloss black or unpainted. It mounts to the chassis with semi-gloss black painted, stamped steel brackets. At each end the bar has a semi-gloss black painted link bracket that attaches to brackets bolted to the trailing arms. The brackets on the trailing arms have a plating that is sometimes called "pickling." It results in a brownish-olive color. These brackets attach to the trailing arm via bolts that thread into small, unpainted steel plates that slip into the rear of the arms.

Rear camber adjustment rods (also called strut rods) are usually natural and often have a bluish-gray tint. Some rods are painted semi-gloss black or are partially painted during the undercarriage blackout process. In 1973 and early 1974 the rods have 1 1/2-inch-diameter ends. Later 1974s and all 1975–1977 cars have rods with 1 3/4-inch-diameter ends.

The outboard ends of the camber adjustment rods are held to the rear wheel bearing carriers with forged L-shaped pins that also serve as the lower mounts for the rear shock absorbers. These pins, which are sometimes referred to as rear shock brackets, contain a raised part number.

The inboard ends of the camber adjustment rods attach to a semi-gloss black painted bracket with special bolts. These bolts have integral off-center washers that, when rotated, move the rods in or out and thus allow for rear wheel camber adjustment. The camber adjustment bolts are usually silver cadmium plated though they may be black phosphate plated instead.

Rear wheel toe adjustment is set with the use of shims placed on either side of the trailing arms where they mount to the chassis. The adjusting shims are unpainted rectangular pieces of steel of varying thicknesses. The shims have a slot in one end that slips over the trailing arm mount bolt. The other ends of all the shims are rotated upward so their holes all align with a corresponding hole in the chassis. A long cotter pin passes through the stacks of shims on both sides of the trailing arm and through the hole in the chassis.

Rear axle shafts (often called "half shafts") are made from forged ends welded to extruded steel tubes. The axle shafts are natural, with the tube being shiny silver and the ends being a dull gray.

U-joints do not have grease fittings and do have a raised part number on the body. They are natural and tend to have that faint bluish tint that is characteristic of forged parts.

The outboard axle shaft U-joints are pressed into a flange that is natural in color. The flange is held to the rear wheel bearing carrier by four bolts that are usually black phosphate plated. The bolts are prevented from turning out by two pairs of French locks, the tabs of which are bent over to contact the bolt heads. The French locks are zinc plated and typically have only one of the two tabs adjacent to each bolt bent over.

The inboard axle shaft U-joints are held to the differential output yokes by one of two methods: Forged caps and bolts are used on Corvettes equipped with a 454 engine, and U-shaped strap clamps with nuts are used on cars equipped with a 350 engine.

Front Wheel Assemblies

Front spindles and steering knuckles are natural and tend to have a bluish tint to their gray color. In addition, the lower portions of the spindles are frequently seen with orange or white paint as though the bottoms of the spindles were dipped into it.

Original front brake backing plates are zinc plated and then chromate dipped. This results in varying finishes ranging from gold with a faint rainbow of other colors throughout to a dull silver with only a trace of the yellowish chromate coloring. Well-preserved original backing plates typically appear dull silver, probably because the chromate dip deteriorates over time.

Front brake caliper support brackets are plated silver cadmium or cadmium dichromate, which results in a translucent gold color with varying degrees of other colors present in a rainbow-like pattern.

Cars equipped with option ZO7 have a heavy-duty brake package. This package includes front calipers that use two pins to hold the pads instead of the standard one, extra front caliper supports, semi-metallic brake pads, heat insulators on the face of all caliper pistons, and a proportioning valve mounted beneath the master cylinder.

Front brake calipers are painted semi-gloss black and frequently have blue or white daubs of paint on the side. Painting is done before the caliper halves are machined and therefore machined surfaces are unpainted. Bleeder screws are zinc plated and remain unpainted.

Caliper hoses are black rubber with gold irridite–plated end hardware. Federally mandated DOT specifications are written on the hose in red ink. In addition, there is a red longitudinal stripe put on the hoses to make it easier to see if they are twisted. Original hoses typically have raised longitudinal ridges around their entire circumference while later replacements are typically smooth.

Front brake rotors are natural in finish. The front wheel bearing carrier (also called a hub) is riveted to the rotor disc.

Rear Wheel Assemblies

As with the fronts, original rear brake backing plates are zinc plated and then chromate dipped. This results in varying finishes ranging from gold with a faint rainbow of other colors throughout to a dull silver with only a trace of the yellowish chromate coloring. Well-preserved original backing plates typically appear dull silver, probably because the chromate dip deteriorates over time.

Rear brake caliper support brackets are natural, and hence a dull gray, or on occasion painted flat to semi-flat black.

Rear brake calipers are painted semi-gloss black and frequently have blue or white daubs of paint on the side. Painting is done before the caliper halves are machined and therefore machined surfaces are unpainted. Bleeder screws are zinc plated and remain unpainted.

Rear brake rotors are natural in finish. They are riveted to the rear spindle, which is pressed into the rear wheel bearing carrier. In order to service the park brake assembly or the rear wheel bearings, the rivets are often drilled out. The wheel lug nuts retain the rotor in the absence of the rivets.

Transmission

Automatic-equipped 1973–1977 Corvettes utilize either a Turbo-Hydra-Matic 400 or a Turbo-Hydra-Matic 350. All 1973–1975 cars, as well as all 1976–1977 cars equipped with an L82 engine, use the Turbo 400. All 1976 and 1977 cars with a base engine use a Turbo 350.

For both transmissions, the main case and the tail housing are both cast aluminum with a natural finish. The fluid pan is stamped steel and is also natural.

Turbo 400 transmissions contain an identification plate riveted to the passenger side. The plate has two alpha-numeric sequences stamped in. The bottom sequence is the transmission's serial number and the top sequence is referred to as a production code. The first two numbers of this code indicate the model year. Next comes a letter that denotes the car model (in our case Corvette) and the engine. This is followed by three numbers that represent the day the transmission was assembled.

The transmission assembly date is a modified version of the Julian calendar system. The three numbers represent the day of the year, but unlike most applications of the Julian calendar system in dating Corvette components, with transmissions the count does not begin with the first day of the year. Instead, for 1973-model Corvettes it begins with January 1, 1972, and continues sequentially through calendar year 1973. Similarly, for 1974 models it begins January 1, 1973, and continues through calendar year 1974. And for 1975 models it begins January 1, 1974, and continues through calendar year 1975.

This dating system sounds confusing, but it's easy once you get the hang of it. For example, in the production code 74K018, the "74" represents the 1974 model year, "K" represents the application code (which is 1974 Corvette with base engine), and "018" represents the 18th day from when the count begins. Remember, the count begins January 1 of the preceding year, so this transmission was assembled January 18, 1973. Had that same transmission been assembled January 18, 1974, the code would read "74K383," with January 18, 1974, being 383 days after the count for the 1974 model year began.

The application codes for 1973–1977 Corvettes include "K" for all base engines, "S" for big-block engines, and "Y" for optional L82 engines in 1973 and "Z" for optional L82 engines thereafter.

Each Turbo 400 transmission also contains the final eight characters of the serial number of the car it was originally installed into. This sequence is stamped into the case on the driver-side flange adjacent to the oil pan.

The identification numbers for Turbo 350 transmissions are different than the numbers for Turbo 400s. With Turbo 350s, the identification code is on the passenger side. This code has six characters. The first is a letter that denotes the manufacturing plant. The second is a number representing the year. The third is a letter denoting the month. The third and fourth are numbers representing the day of the month. The final letter is either a "D" for day shift or "N" for night shift.

The letters designating the month of manufacture are as follows: "A" is January, "B" is February, "C" is March, "D" is April, "E" is May, "H" is June, "K" is July, "M" is August, "P" is September, "R" is October, "S" is November, and "T" is December.

In addition to the above described production code, each Turbo 350 transmission also contains the final eight digits of the serial number of the car it originally was installed into. This sequence is stamped into the case on the driver-side flange adjacent to the oil pan.

Four-speed manual transmissions manufactured by Muncie are used in 1973 and 1974 Corvettes. Beginning in mid-1974 Borg-Warner Super T-10 four-speeds are used. 1976 and 1977 Corvettes delivered new in California could not be equipped with a four-speed.

Four-speed Muncie transmissions have cast-aluminum main cases, side covers, and tail housings that are natural in color. A steel tag with a part number is affixed to the transmission with one of the side cover bolts.

Two alpha-numeric sequences are stamped into the main case on a vertical surface at the front of the right side. One of these sequences is a derivative of the car's serial number. The other is a production code and the date the transmission was originally assembled.

The production code begins with a letter to indicate the source for the transmission. All Corvette four-speeds were obtained from Muncie, which is represented by the letter "P." This is followed by a number representing the last digit of the model year. Next, there is a letter indicating the month of production followed by two numbers denoting the day of the month. Various letters are not used in denoting the month, so refer to this chart when determining assembly date;

Code	Month	Code	Month
A	January	K	July
B	February	M	August
C	March	P	September
D	April	R	October
E	May	S	November
H	June	T	December

The final character in the production code is a letter commonly called a suffix code. This letter indicates which of the three available four-speeds the unit is. The suffix code "A" indicates a wide-ratio M-20 with 2.52:1 first gear ratio. "B" indicates a close-ratio M-21 with a 2.20:1 first gear ratio. And "C" denotes a close-ratio M-22 "heavy-duty" transmission, which also has a 2.20:1 first gear ratio.

An example of a four-speed transmission code is "P3M18A." This identifies an M-20 wide-ratio Muncie four-speed assembled August 18, 1973.

With Borg-Warner four-speeds, the car's serial number derivative, as well as the production code and assembly date, are stamped into the main case on the driver-side flange adjacent to where the tail housing attaches.

In the production code, the first letter is "W" to indicate Borg-Warner. The next letter indicates the month of production, with "A" representing January, "B" representing February, and so on to "L" representing December. The month code is followed by one or two numbers denoting the day. Next comes a single number to indicate the year. And finally, the last number indicates whether the transmission is a close- or wide-ratio unit.

For example, a code of WG2761 translates to a Borg-Warner four-speed, built on July 27, 1976. The final "1" indicates that it is a wide-ratio unit. (See Appendix D for transmission codes.)

Differential and Driveshaft

All 1973–1977 Corvettes are equipped with a Positraction limited-slip differential. The differential case and cover are both natural-colored castings and as such are a dull silvery gray.

A plastic triangular tag is attached to the differential by means of the square head oil fill plug. The tag is red with white lettering that says "USE LIMITED SLIP DIFF. LUBRICANT ONLY." The fill plug is natural and often has a large "W" cast into the square.

Front input yoke and side output yokes are forgings that are natural in color. Because they are forged they have a somewhat smoother surface than the case and cover, and they tend to have a slight bluish tint to their dull gray color.

Differential cases and covers both have casting numbers and a casting date that includes a letter for the month (with "A" representing January, "B" representing February, and so on), one or two numbers indicating the day of the month, and one number indicating the last digit of the year.

In addition to the cast-in dates, all cases also have a stamped-in production code. The production code is on the bottom rear edge of the case adjacent to where it meets the cover. The differential production code begins with two letters to indicate the gear ratio. This is followed by a single letter denoting the assembly plant. Then come one, two, or three numbers representing the day of the year the unit was assembled. After this there is a single letter that indicates the source for the Positraction unit (which was not necessarily the same company that assembled the differential). The final number in the sequence represents the assembly shift that built the unit.

(See Appendix E for differential gear ratio codes.)

The transmission and differential are connected by a drive shaft made from extruded steel tubing welded at each end to a forged universal joint coupling. As with the axle shafts, the drive shaft is natural in color. The center tube portion is bright silver with longitudinal extrusion lines sometimes visible, and the ends are a dull silvery gray with a slight bluish hue at times.

A part number stenciled on the drive shaft tube in yellow or white paint is sometimes seen. One or two green circumferential stripes on the tube and daubs of various colors of paint on the forged ends are sometimes seen as well.

Exhaust System

All 1973–1977 Corvettes use an undercar, carbon steel exhaust system manufactured by Walker for Chevrolet. All cars equipped with a big-block engine or an L82 engine utilize 2-1/2-inch exhaust pipes. All other cars utilize 2-inch pipes.

Even though L82 engines get 2-1/2-inch pipes they still use the same 2-inch outlet exhaust manifolds as other small blocks. This is accomplished by swaging the 2-1/2-inch front engine pipes down to 2 inches at their ends.

Mufflers are galvanized on the exterior and may have an embossed "W" to represent the manufacturer. In addition, an embossed part number is sometimes found on each muffler. At the rear of each muffler there is one welded-on bracket to which the rear hangar bolts. Mufflers are welded to the intermediate exhaust pipe, not clamped. 2-1/2-inch intermediate pipes are flattened somewhat where they pass underneath the rear camber adjustment rod bracket for additional ground clearance. 2-inch pipes are not flattened.

Beginning in 1974 small resonators are in each exhaust pipe beneath the seat area. Beginning in 1975 all Corvettes are equipped with a catalytic converter.

The exhaust pipes connecting the converter to the engine are stainless steel.

A rectangular, chrome-plated carbon steel exhaust tip is clamped to each muffler in 1973. Unlike some earlier tips, those used in 1973 each have a weld seam on the underside of the rectangular section. 1974–1977 mufflers do not have separate tips.

Fuel Lines, Brake Lines, and Miscellaneous Chassis and Underbody Components.

All 1973–1977 fuel lines run along, and at times through, the right-side chassis rail. Most cars have two fuel lines. One supplies fuel from the tank to the carburetor and the other is a return line.

In addition to the one or two fuel lines on the right side of the chassis, all cars have a vapor return line on the appendix of the chassis. This line is part of the Evaporative Emission Control system.

Fuel lines are galvanized carbon steel. Black rubber fuel hose connects the lines to the tank and the fuel pump. Zinc chromate–plated spring clamps are usually used to secure the hose to its line.

Brake lines are galvanized carbon steel. Brake line end fittings are brass. Fittings at the master cylinder are often seen with red or blue dye, which was probably used to denote the two different size fittings. In addition, daubs of yellow paint are sometimes seen on the fittings at junction blocks.

Various heat shields are affixed to the underside of the body to help insulate the passenger compartment from engine and exhaust system heat. A sheet-steel shield, which is gray phosphate plated, is mounted on the lower vertical area of the firewall on both sides.

All cars are fitted with transmission tunnel insulation. A semi-rigid foil-wrapped blanket in the shape of the tunnel is fastened above the transmission with clips riveted to the underbody.

All cars have a thick, black foam insulating pad attached to the underbody above the engine's bellhousing. A thick, white foam pad is fastened to the underbody on each side of the car just forward of the doors.

A variety of steel plates are fastened to the underbody to mount components in the passenger compartment. These components include the battery, seats, jack hold down clips, and so on. All of these plates are painted semi-gloss black and are retained by unpainted, aluminum rivets.

Chapter 4

1978-1982

1978–1982 Exterior
Body Fiberglass and Body Paint
All 1978–1982 Corvette body panels are made from press-molded fiberglass. The panels are smooth on both sides and are dark gray in color. Though it improved somewhat in these later cars, the same relatively poor body panel alignment and fit seen in earlier Corvettes is seen in 1978–1982 models as well.

The quality of the fit of all ancillary body components such as doors, hood, and headlamp doors also varies and is, at times, poor. Factory assembly manuals call for the gap between most adjacent panels to be between 1/8 inch and 3/16 inch wide. The manuals also specify that any differential in height be no more than 1/8 inch. The hood gap should be equal side-to-side within 1/16 inch and the headlamp door gap should be equal side-to-side within 1/32 inch.

Hood height is regulated in part by the use of small, rectangular rubber blocks placed in the inner fender drip rails. The number and location of these blocks varies and some cars don't have them at all.

All 1978–1980 cars were painted with acrylic lacquer. All 1981s assembled in the old St. Louis, Missouri, Corvette factory were also painted with acrylic lacquer. During production of the 1981 models, Corvette assembly was moved to a new factory in Bowling Green, Kentucky. All 1981s assembled in Bowling Green, as well as all 1982s, were painted with an acrylic enamel base coat/clear coat system.

On Corvettes assembled in St. Louis, factory paint is generally smooth and shiny, though some

The year 1978 was the first in which Corvette was selected to pace the Indy 500, and 6,502 Pace Car Replicas were sold that year.

Many of the 1978 Indy Pace Car Replicas have been preserved by collectors rather than driven by enthusiasts. This L82/four-speed example has traveled just a little over 400 miles since new.

orange peel is evident throughout. Roughness and poor coverage are fairly typical along the very bottom edges of body panels. Clear coat was not used by the St. Louis factory, even with metallic colors. Because clear coat was not used, metallics may tend to be slightly mottled or blotchy.

The new base coat/clear coat paint used on 1981s assembled in Bowling Green and all 1982s generally resulted in a better-quality finish than the old lacquer paint system. As the name implies, clear coat was applied over the base or color coat. As a result, metallics do not typically exhibit the mottling sometimes seen on cars painted with lacquer.

Front Bumpers

All 1978–1982 Corvettes are fitted with impact-absorbing front bumper assemblies. The cover is made from urethane that is painted body color. A flex additive is mixed with the paint used on the bumper cover to discourage the paint from cracking. The flex additive often causes the paint on the bumper to be a slightly different shade than the paint on the rest of the car.

The remainder of the bumper assembly, which is covered by the urethane piece, is comprised of several semi-gloss black painted steel components. Black phosphate- or silver cadmium–plated hex head bolts are used to retain the underlying bumper structure to the chassis.

In 1978 and 1979, the front bumper fascias are the same as previous Corvettes. In 1980–1982 the bumper fascias are a different design. They feature a noticeably revised shape that includes an integral spoiler. The new bumper design reduces drag coefficient from .503 to .443, plus increases air flow to the radiator by as much as 50 percent for improved cooling

In 1978–1979, a black plastic air deflector is bolted to the underneath of the front bumper fascia toward the rear. Black oxide, hex head bolts with integral flat washers secure the deflector. On those cars equipped with option V01, a heavy-duty radiator, or the optional L82 engine, an additional air deflector is attached to the front of the first air deflector. This additional deflector is made from black rubber and is attached with eight aluminum Pop Rivets. A two-piece reinforcement, made from gloss-black painted steel strips, is placed behind the second deflector.

The 1980–1982 cars use a two-piece air deflector extension bolted to reinforcements in the front bumper fascia underneath and toward the rear. These extensions are made from unpainted black rubber.

The front bumper impact-absorbing assembly is held to the car's chassis by semi-gloss black painted steel brackets. In addition to the steel brackets, the front bumper is also held in place with fiberglass braces along each side. These braces are usually a raw, dark gray color, though some have been observed painted semi-gloss black. Because of production variances, shims were frequently used to adjust the fit of the bumpers to the car. These shims, which are typically found between the bumper brackets and the chassis, are plated silver cadmium.

The tubular cross-member included in the front bumper assembly also serves as the vacuum reservoir for the front headlamp system.

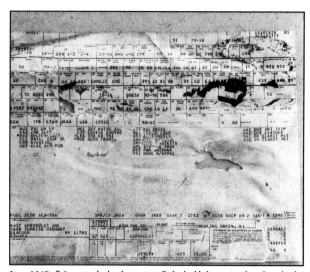

Since 1967 all Corvettes had a document called a build sheet or tank sticker glued to the gas tank. Though the appearance changed somewhat over time, all contain a lot of the same basic information. This example is from a 1982. Later tank stickers, like the one shown, contain more details than earlier versions.

Paperwork that shows how a Corvette was originally equipped and various other information is always of interest to collectors and restorers. This is the original window sticker from a 1982.

Bolts retaining the front bumper brackets to the chassis are typically black oxide or gray phosphate in finish.

Front Grille Area, Parking Lamps, and Front License Plate Area

In 1978–1982, the left and right front grilles are made from black plastic. They are each one piece and are held to the car with black oxide Phillips screws in 1978 and 1979, and with black oxide, hex head bolts in 1980–1982.

Cars built in 1978 and 1979 have a front license plate mount bracket that is painted semi-gloss black. A single black rubber bumper is pressed into a hole toward the bottom center of the bracket and two white plastic push nuts are in the upper corners to receive the license plate screws.

In addition, 1980–1982 cars have a recess for the front license plate molded into the front bumper cover. Square holes are cut near the bottom corners of the recess. A black phosphate–plated "J" nut is installed into each cutout to receive the license plate mount screws.

For 1978 and 1979, fenders have a crossed flags emblem above the vent area. The emblems used for early 1978 cars have a white square in the upper right corner of the checkered flag (as seen here), while later cars have emblems with a black square in this position. The "LIMITED EDITION" decal is unique to 1978 Pace Cars.

This is the 1982-only crossed flags nose emblem. The fleur-de-lis symbol found in the left-side flag for decades was replaced with the Chevrolet "bow tie."

This is the Chevrolet dealer's copy of a document called the car shipper. This example is for a 1982.

License plate mount screws are large, slotted-head units with coarse threads. In 1978–1981, they are silver cadmium plated and in 1982 they are dark cadmium plated. The screws came in a small brown paper bag marked "UNIT NUMBER 3875313" across the top, "LICENSE ATTACHING" on one side, and "REAR PLATE PARTS" on the other. The bag was placed inside the car in a storage compartment behind the seats.

In 1978, the front nose emblem and gas filler door emblem feature a design that commemorates the 25th anniversary of the Corvette. This special emblem features the traditional crossed flags in a circle with "CORVETTE" around the top edge and "1953 ANNIVERSARY 1978" around the bottom. Also, a "25" is above the crossed flags.

In 1979, the crossed flags alone are utilized for the front nose emblem and gas filler door emblem.

In 1980, the crossed flags emblem was redesigned and this newer version is on the nose in 1980 and 1981 cars. In 1980, the staffs for the crossed flags are chrome plated, and in 1981 they are black.

In 1982, the crossed flags nose emblem was again redesigned. The fleur-de-lis symbol found in the left-side flag for decades was replaced with the Chevrolet "bow tie."

The 1982 Collector Edition Corvettes use special cloisonné emblems. With this emblem design, the crossed flags are surrounded by a black ring with the words "CORVETTE COLLECTOR EDITION" in gold letters.

In 1978 and 1979 the front park lamp lenses are made from clear plastic with black painted horizontal lines that correlate to the lines in the front grilles. The lenses attach with black oxide Phillips head screws. In 1980–1982 the lenses are made from amber plastic and also have black painted horizontal lines. They attach with black oxide Torx head screws. All years have amber-colored bulbs in the parking lamps.

Rectangular-shaped side marker lamps are used at all four corners in 1978 and 1979. The lamp housings are made from plastic and are bordered with chrome strips around the outer perimeter. All front side marker lamps have amber lenses, while rears have red lenses.

In addition to side marker lamps, 1980–1982 cars also have front cornering lamps that activate when the turn signal is turned on. Cornering lamp lenses are clear. Front side marker / cornering lamp assemblies are bordered by black plastic trim that is painted body color. As in 1978 and 1979, the rear side marker lamps used in 1980–1982 are bordered by chrome trim.

Front Headlamp Doors, Headlamps, and Headlamp Bezels

Headlamp housings are made from cast metal. The entire assemblies are painted body color. They typically show a dull or slightly rough paint finish except for the top of the housing, which should be consistent with the remainder of the exterior.

All low beam headlamp bulbs in 1978–1982 were made by Guide and feature a Guide Power Beam logo in the glass. This logo is a circle with the word "POWER" above it and the word "BEAM" below it. High beam bulbs in 1978 and those 1979 cars assembled through approximately November 1979 are also Guide Power Beams. High beam bulbs in those 1979s assembled after approximately November 1979 and

A cadmium dichromate vacuum actuator is mounted behind each headlamp assembly. Actuators are usually stamped with a Julian date code. This example was made on the 87th day of 1978.

all 1980–1982 cars are General Electric Halogen Sealed Beams. They say "HALOGEN" in a rectangle in the center of the lens and "SEALED BEAM" near the bottom. "GENERAL ELECTRIC" also appears near the bottom.

All 1978–1982 cars have headlamp bezels made from fiberglass. All bezels are painted body color. On

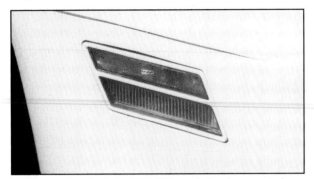

In addition to side marker lamps, 1980–1982 cars also have front cornering lamps that activate when the turn signal is put on. Side marker/cornering lamp assemblies are bordered by plastic trim that is painted body color.

This "cross-fire injection" emblem above the fender vents was used in 1982 only. It has chrome-plated letters on a black base.

St. Louis–built cars especially, paint on the bezels is usually not as shiny or smooth as it is on the body. Bezels are retained by four chrome-plated Phillips oval head screws. The two on the sides are fitted with integral, countersunk washers and the two on the front are not.

A cadmium dichromate vacuum actuator is mounted behind each headlamp assembly. A red-striped hose connects to the back of each actuator and a green-striped hose connects to the front.

Front Fenders

The 1978 and 1979 front fenders feature a molded-in recess as in previous years. The 1980–1982 front fenders got a redesigned vent area, which features an insert in the molded-in recess. The insert is black plastic and the area behind it is painted semi-gloss black. The insert is held in place by black oxide–plated Torx screws.

In 1978 and 1979, both fenders have a crossed flags emblem above the vent area. The emblems used for early 1978 cars have a white square in the upper right corner of the checkered flag. Later 1978 and most 1979 cars have a black square in the upper right corner.

The 1978 Indy Pace Car replicas have a unique decal on each front fender below the crossed flags emblem. This decal is clear with white lettering that reads "LIMITED EDITION."

Crossed-flags emblems are not used on the front fenders of 1980-82 Corvettes. In 1980, cars equipped with an L82 engine have an emblem that says "L-82" above the fender vents. This emblem utilizes chrome-plated characters on a black base. In 1982, an emblem reading "CROSS-FIRE INJECTION" is above the fender vents. This emblem also has chrome-plated letters on a black base.

Hood

All 1978 and 1979 cars have the same hood design seen in preceding years.

The 1980–1982 Corvettes have a revised hood design. This new hood design has a relatively subdued wind split in the middle rather than the "power bulge" seen in previous years.

The 1978 and 1979 Corvettes equipped with the optional L82 engine have an "L-82" emblem on either side of the hood. These emblems feature red paint between the chrome-plated characters. Hood emblems were not used on 1980–1982 Corvettes.

Windshield Wipers and Windshield Washers

Wiper arms and blade holders are dull black in color. Both arms and blades typically say "TRICO"

Most 1975s and all 1976–1979 Corvettes equipped with the optional L82 engine have an "L-82" emblem on either side of the hood. This example is on a 1978 Pace Car.

Rear window molding utilized on 1978s assembled through approximately mid-October 1977 is typically unpainted along the outer edge and painted satin black along the inner edge. The moldings on cars assembled from approximately mid-October 1977 through approximately the end of November 1977 are sometimes half painted and sometimes unpainted. Those 1978s assembled after the end of November 1977 are typically seen half painted. All 1978 Pace Cars, as well as all 1979–1982 Corvettes, use rear window molding that is completely painted. Note how sloppy the paint edge is on this original 1978.

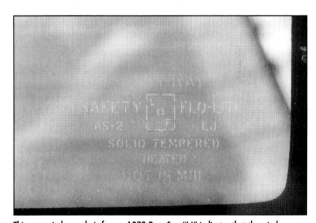

This rear window code is from a 1978 Pace Car. "LJ" indicates that the window was made in March 1978.

on one of the ends. Some cars are equipped with blade holders manufactured by Anco instead of Trico. Anco blade holders are more prevalent in 1978–1980 than in 1981 or 1982.

A length of rubber hose serves to convey washer fluid along the arms up to the windshield washer nozzles.

Windshield, Door Glass, and Back Glass

All 1978–1982 Corvette windshields were manufactured by Libby-Owens-Ford (LOF) utilizing Safety Flo-Lite glass. The LOF logo, "SHADED SOFT-RAY," "SAFETY FLO LITE," "LAMINATED DOT 15 M24," and a two-letter manufacturing date code are etched into the lower right side of the windshield. In the date code, one letter represents the month and the other denotes the year. There is no discernible pattern to the letter usage, so you must refer to the glass date codes in Appendix R.

The letters "ASI" are present in the upper right portion of the windshield. These letters are white and sandwiched between the laminates of glass, not etched into the surface like the logo and date code.

All windshields are painted on the interior side along the bottom edge and along the side edges with black paint. For all 1978–1982 cars the exterior top and sides of the windshield are surrounded by stainless-steel trim. This trim is painted satin black.

In 1978–1982 both side windows are made from tinted LOF Safety Flo Lite, Soft-Ray tinted glass that has the manufacturer's logo and a two-letter date code etched in just like the windshield.

All 1978–1982 Corvettes use a dramatically restyled back window area. Instead of the notch-back design introduced in 1968 and used through 1977, these newer cars use a fastback design. Like the other

glass in the cars, all back windows have the LOF logo and manufacturing date code etched in.

The 1982 Collector Edition Corvettes utilize a back window that opens up. No other 1978–1982 Corvettes have this feature. The hardware and hinges for the functional hatch found on the 1982 Collector Edition are semi-gloss black.

Rear window surround molding is stainless steel in all 1978–1982 Corvettes. The moldings utilized on those 1978 cars assembled through approximately mid-October 1977 are typically unpainted and polished along the outer edge and painted satin black along the inner edge. The moldings on cars assembled from approximately mid-October 1977 through approximately the end of November 1977 are sometimes as in earlier cars and sometimes entirely unpainted and polished. The 1978s assembled after approximately the end of November 1977 are typically seen with unpainted outer edges and black satin painted inner edges as with earlier cars. All 1978 Pace Cars, as well as all 1979–1982 Corvettes, use rear-window molding that is completely painted satin black.

Door Mirror, Handles, and Locks

One chrome-plated, outside rearview mirror mounted on the driver's door is standard in 1978 and most of 1979. In 1978 and early 1979, option D35 substituted dual sport mirrors for the single chrome one. Each door got one of the sport mirrors, which were painted body color. The 1978 Pace Cars, 1978 Silver Anniversary models, late 1979s, and all 1980–1982s have dual sport mirrors as standard equipment.

For all years, the mirror glass is shaded and is coded with the manufacturer's symbol and a date code. The majority of 1978–1982 mirrors were supplied by Donnelly Mirror, Inc. These have "DMI" in the date code, while mirrors supplied by Ajax Mirror have "AX" in it. For example, the code in a Donnelly-supplied mirror manufactured in April 1979 would read "4-DMI-9" while the code for an Ajax-supplied mirror manufactured in February 1980 would read "2-AX-80."

All 1978–1982 door handles are a spring-loaded, press flap design. On original handles the spring action is provided by a coil spring on the hinge shaft. A butterfly spring covering a coil spring is incorrect. When the flap is depressed the spring is visible. No gasket is utilized between the handle and door.

The door locks, which are positioned below the door handles, feature a polished stainless-steel bezel. Original bezels are retained to the cylinders by means of a continuous crimp around their entire circumference. Incorrect replacement locks may have bezels retained by four tangs.

Side Rocker Molding

Side rocker moldings for all 1978–1982 cars are brushed aluminum. All 1978–1980 models except 1978 Pace Cars have moldings painted semi-flat black with a thin strip of unpainted aluminum along the top. The rocker moldings for 1978 Pace Cars are unpainted except for a painted 3/8-inch-wide, semi-flat black stripe along their length. The moldings for 1981 and 1982 cars are completely painted semi-flat black.

Rocker moldings attach to the body with six black oxide–plated Phillips oval head screws. The forward two and rearmost screws use a hex nut with an integral washer. The middle three screws go into nut plates in the body. The forward two and rearmost screws are sometimes pan head instead of oval head.

Original 1978–1982 rocker moldings do not have a tab on the molding's lower lip near the front like earlier moldings.

Radio Antenna

On those 1978–1982 cars assembled without a radio, no radio antenna was installed. On all others an antenna was mounted on the driver-side rear deck.

A fixed-mast antenna was standard equipment on all 1978–1982 Corvettes fitted with a radio. A power antenna was available as an extra cost option for all years.

For fixed-mast antennas, a black plastic gasket goes between the antenna base and the car's body.

The 1978 Silver Anniversary Paint option included a thin double stripe toward the quarter panel and fender peaks.

In 1978 and early 1979 option D35 substituted dual sport mirrors for the standard single chrome one. The 1978 Pace Cars, 1978 Silver Anniversary models, late 1979s, and all 1980–1982s have dual sport mirrors as standard equipment. This passenger-side example was made by Donnelly Mirror, Inc. in February 1978 (2 DMI 8).

The base is also made of black plastic. A chrome cap (with two flat areas for a wrench to grab) secures the mast to the base. The ball at the tip of the antenna is .300 inches in diameter in the vast majority of cars. Later GM service replacement masts have a .250-inch-diameter ball. It is possible that some original antennas have the smaller ball.

The optional power antenna utilizes a black plastic bezel on very early 1978 models. Later 1978s and early 1979s use a chrome-plated bezel. Later 1979s and 1980–1982 cars do not use a bezel. The antenna mounting nut for all cars is chrome plated and has four flat areas for a wrench.

The 1978–1982 cars equipped with the optional CB radio have a unique antenna. It has what is called a loading coil that is part of the antenna mast. The loading coil is cylindrical in shape and has a diameter that is slightly larger than the mast.

The antenna mounting area of the rear deck on all 1978 and those 1979 cars assembled through approximately late-February 1979 is flat and even with the remainder of the deck. The mounting area on 1979 Corvettes assembled after approximately late-February 1979 and on all 1980–1982 cars has a recess molded in. This recess allows the antenna to mount horizontally rather than on a slight angle.

Gas Lid Door and Gas Cap

Gas lid doors are painted body color for all 1978–1982 cars. The doors for all years are fitted with a crossed flags emblem that is secured by acorn nuts visible with the door open. Some very early 1978 cars use chrome-plated acorn nuts, while all remaining cars use black oxide–plated nuts.

The gas lid door bezel used on 1978 cars assembled through approximately July 1978 is chrome plated. Thereafter, all gas lid door bezels are painted semi-gloss black. Both the chrome-plated and painted bezels are retained by four black oxide–plated Phillips head screws in 1978 and 1979. In 1980–1982, the bezel is retained by four black oxide–plated Posidriv screws.

The gas lid door hinge is chrome plated and the door is held to its bezel with chrome-plated Phillips fillister head screws fitted with external star lock washers. Two black rubber bumpers with the letters "ABC" molded in support the gas lid door when it is closed.

In 1978 through early 1981, a straight decal reading "UNLEADED FUEL ONLY" with black outlined silver letters was used. On Pace Cars and those 1979 cars equipped with the optional RPO D80 spoilers, the decal was affixed to the spoiler, near the notch for the gas lid door. On all other 1978 and 1979 cars, it

In 1978 through early 1981 this decal reading "UNLEADED FUEL ONLY" was used. On all cars except Pace Cars and 1979s equipped with the optional spoilers (option D80), the decal was affixed to the deck surface immediately behind the door as shown.

On Pace Cars and those 1979 cars equipped with the optional spoilers (option D80), the "UNLEADED FUEL ONLY" decal was affixed to the spoiler as shown.

was affixed to the deck surface immediately behind the door.

Later-1981 and all 1982 Corvettes do not have an "UNLEADED FUEL ONLY" decal. Instead, their bezels are stamped with the words "UNLEADED FUEL ONLY" on the right side and "ESSENCE SANS PLOMB SEULEMENT" on the left side.

The 1978 and 1979 Corvettes use a gold irridite–plated, twist-on metal gas cap. The letters "NDH" and the numbers "559346" are stamped in around a recess in the center of the cap.

The 1980 Corvettes also use gold irridite–plated, twist-on metal gas caps. The caps were manufactured by Stant and the company's logo—as well as the number "22503147"—are stamped in.

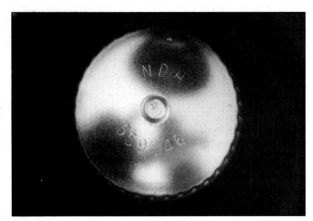

This gold irridite–plated, twist-on metal gas cap was used in 1978 and 1979.

The 1978–1982 cars all have "CORVETTE" spelled out in a single nameplate affixed to the rear bumper cover. The stylized lowercase letters are chrome plated and rest on a semi-gloss black base.

Recesses for taillamps are molded into the rear bumper cover. All 1978–1982 cars utilize four rear lamps. The two outer lamps have red lenses that function as taillamps, stop lamps, and turn signals. The two inner lamp assemblies have red lenses with clear plastic centers that function as back-up lamps.

In 1978 and 1979, the taillamps each have a stainless-steel ring around the outer perimeter and another stainless-steel ring around the center portion of the lens.

In 1980–1982, the taillamp lenses each have a concentric groove molded in. Unlike earlier years, they do not have stainless-steel rings around the perimeter or the center of each lens.

Each lamp has a very small moisture wick that protrudes from the bottom of the lens. The wick material resembles a cigarette filter.

The rear bumper cover has a molded-in recess for a license plate in all years. A lamp with a plastic cover is mounted in a cutout above the license plate. The lamp assembly is held by chrome-plated Phillips head screws.

Silver cadmium–plated steel brackets for mounting the rear license plate are held to the bumper cover by Pop Rivets. Two white plastic push nuts insert into the brackets and receive the license plate retaining screws. As with the front, 1978–1981 license plate screws are plated silver cadmium and 1982 screws are plated dark gray cadmium.

In 1981 and 1982, Corvettes use an off-white-color plastic gas cap instead of the previous metal design. These caps were also manufactured by Stant and have a Stant logo molded in.

A black rubber boot surrounds the gas filler neck on all 1978–1982 cars. The boot has a plastic nipple facing the rear of the car. A rubber drain hose attaches to the nipple. The hose, which has a metal spring inside to prevent it from collapsing, runs down behind the gas tank and exits behind the license plate area.

Rear Fascia, Taillamps, Bumpers, and Related Parts

All 1978–1982 Corvettes utilize an impact-absorbing rear bumper assembly. As in the front, this assembly consists of a body-colored urethane cover fitted over a multi-piece metal understructure.

The 1978 Silver Anniversary Paint (option BZ2) included a thin, dark silver stripe around the perimeter of the car. Note the correct light lenses and rear bumper.

The quarter panel decal found on 1978 Indy Pace Cars. Thin, black and silver stripes separating the two-tone black/silver body paint are actually a decal, not painted on.

Door decals on a 1978 Indy Pace Car. Pace Car decals were not installed onto the cars at the factory. Instead, they were placed inside the car for dealer installation if the buyer wanted them installed.

This style rear bumper emblem was used in 1978–1982.

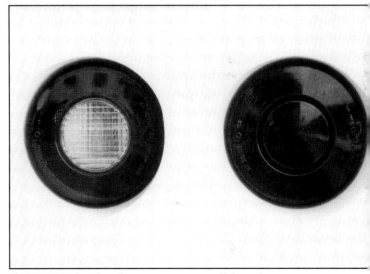

All 1980–1982 taillamp lenses have a concentric groove molded in as shown in these 1982 examples.

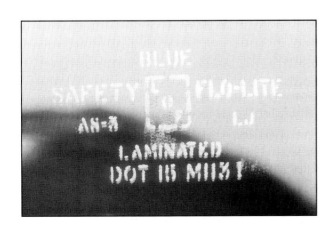

Glass T-tops are standard on 1978 Pace Cars and 1982 Collector Editions, and are optional on all other 1978–1982 Corvettes. "LOF" is the manufacturer's logo for Libby-Owens-Ford. "LJ" is the date code, indicating this top was made March 1978. Glass tops on all 1978–1980s and those 1981 Corvettes assembled in St. Louis are "Laminated," while tops on 1981s assembled in Bowling Green and all 1982s are "Solid Tempered." Laminated tops have a bluish tint and say "blue," as seen here, while Solid Tempered tops have a grayish tint. Collector Edition tops have a bronze tint. By the way, this photo is not blurry; the etching is sloppy.

T-Tops

All 1978–1982 Corvettes except 1978 Pace Cars and 1982 Collector Editions come standard with fiberglass T-tops painted body color. In 1978, the tops are fitted with unpainted stainless-steel trim. In 1979–1982, the stainless trim is painted semi-gloss black.

Glass T-tops are standard on 1978 Pace Cars and 1982 Collector Editions, and are optional on all other 1978–1982 Corvettes. Instead of stainless steel, glass tops are trimmed with black plastic.

All glass T-tops were manufactured by the Libby-Owens-Ford Company (LOF) and have the "LOF" manufacturer's logo etched in. As with the other glass in the car, glass T-tops have a two-letter date code indicating when they were made. (See Appendix R for glass date codes.)

Glass tops on all 1978–1980 and those 1981 Corvettes assembled in St. Louis are "Laminated." Glass tops on 1981s assembled in Bowling Green and all 1982s are "Solid Tempered." Laminated tops have a bluish tint while Solid Tempered tops

have a grayish tint. Collector Edition tops have a bronze tint.

Tires, Wheels, and Wheel Covers

All 1978–1982 Corvettes were equipped with Goodyear Polysteel P225/70R15 blackwall radials as standard equipment. These same tires with raised white letters were available as an extra cost option. The optional version says "GOODYEAR" and "POLYSTEEL RADIAL" in raised white block letters on the sidewall.

Also available as an extra cost option was a larger-size Goodyear radial tire. This tire—sized at P255/60R15—was available only in a raised white letter configuration. The raised white letters say "GOODYEAR" and "GT RADIAL" in 1978 through very early 1980. The optional larger tires in later-1980 models and subsequent cars say "GOODYEAR" and "EAGLE GT." In 1978 and 1979, these larger tires necessitated trimming the front and rear lower edges of the front fenders for clearance.

Every 1978–1982 tire has a 10- or 11-character "Tire Identification Number" stamped into the sidewall. The first character of the code indicates the manufacturer. The second character denotes the location of the plant that manufactured the tire. The third and fourth characters indicate the tire's size. The following three or four letters denote the type of tire construction. The next two numbers indicate the week of the year the tire was made, with "01" being the first week of the year and "52"

GOODYEAR POLYSTEEL RADIAL raised white letter tires were available as an extra cost option in 1978–1982.

A larger Goodyear radial tire, sized at P255/60R15, was available as an option in 1978–1982 only in raised white letter configuration. The GOODYEAR GT RADIAL was used in 1978 through very early 1980, and the GOODYEAR EAGLE GT was used in later cars. In 1978 and 1979 the larger tires necessitated trimming the front and rear lower edges of the front fenders for clearance. This example is on a 1978 Pace Car wheel. Compared with those used on other Corvettes, Pace Car aluminum wheels are more highly polished, do not have black painted center areas or black painted hubcaps, are painted black in the inside edges of the rectangular slots, and have a red stripe painted around the outer edge.

being the last. The final number is the last digit of the year of manufacture.

All 1978–1982 Corvettes are equipped with steel Rally wheels, finished in Argent Silver on the front side, as standard equipment. The back sides are painted semi-flat black and always have silver over-spray, since the front side was painted silver after the black was applied to the rear.

All wheels are stamped with a date code, manufacturer's logo, and size code on the front face. All 1978–1982 Corvette wheels are 15x8 inches and are stamped with the code "AZ" to indicate this. The "AZ" is adjacent to the valve stem hole.

Also adjacent to the valve stem hole is the manufacturer's logo and date code stamping. On one side of the hole it says "K" for the wheel manufacturer, Kelsey Hayes. This is followed by a dash and a "1" that represents Chevrolet. Next is another dash and a number to denote the last digit of the year of manufacture. This is followed by a space and one or two numbers to indicate the month of manufacture. On the other side of the valve stem hole are one or two more numbers that represent the day of manufacture.

Stainless-steel trim rings and chrome center caps are standard for all cars. Original trim rings are held to the wheel by four steel clips. Center caps should read "CHEVROLET MOTOR DIVISION" in black painted letters.

Aluminum wheels were offered as an option in 1978–1982. In 1978 and 1979, the aluminum wheels on all Corvettes except Pace Cars have semi-gloss black painted center sections and small chrome-plated hub caps with semi-gloss black painted centers. Also, the 1978 and 1979 aluminum wheels are unpainted inside the edges of the rectangular slots, and are not clear coated.

The aluminum wheels used on Pace Cars are more highly polished overall, do not have black painted center areas nor black painted hub caps, but are painted black in the inside edges of the rectangular slots. In addition, Pace Car wheels each have a red stripe painted around the outer edge.

Aluminum wheels used in 1980–1982, except on 1982 Collector Edition cars, are essentially the same as those fitted to 1978 Pace Cars, with the exception of the red stripe. The 1980–1982 wheels are highly polished overall, do not have black painted center areas or caps, and are painted black in the inside edges of the rectangular slots. Unlike earlier versions, 1980–1982 aluminum wheels are clear coated. All 1978–1982 aluminum wheels are retained by chrome-plated lug nuts.

The 1982 Collector Edition wheels are made from aluminum but differ in design from the regular

All 1978–1982 Corvettes use this space-saver spare tire manufactured by Goodyear. Regardless of whether the car is fitted with standard Rally or optional aluminum wheels, the spare tire is mounted to a semi-black painted 15X5 inch stamped steel rim. Some very early 1978s have a rim that is painted bright yellow instead of black.

production option aluminum wheels. These wheels utilize a center hub to cover the chrome-plated lug nuts. The center of the hub is fitted with a silver disc containing the 1982 crossed flags logo.

All 1978–1982 wheels, including both standard steel Rallys and optional aluminum wheels, utilize black rubber valve stems that measure approximately 1 1/4 inches long. These are fitted with caps that come to a point and have longitudinal ridges around their entire perimeter.

To ease the balancing process, steel wheels are sometimes marked with a tiny weld drop or paint dot at their highest point. This mark is lined up with an orange dot on the tire. Balance weights are the type that clamp onto the edge of the rim and are placed on the inside of the wheel only. Original balance weights usually have the letters "OEM" molded into their face. There is usually a small white or colored dot of paint on the tire, adjacent to each balance weight.

All aluminum wheels are fitted with balance weights attached to the inside of the rim only.

All 1978–1982 Corvettes are equipped with a space-saver spare tire manufactured by Goodyear. This tire was called "Polyspare" by Goodyear and is sized at P195/80D15. The words "GOODYEAR," "TEMPORARY USE ONLY," and "MAX. SPEED 50 M.P.H." appear on the black sidewall.

Regardless of what type of wheels the car is fitted with the space-saver spare tire is mounted to a

15x5-inch stamped steel rim that is painted semi-gloss black. Some very early 1978 Corvettes have a spare tire rim that is painted very bright yellow instead of black.

Spare tire wheels are all stamped with "YA," which is the size designation. They are also stamped with the manufacturer's logo, a code for the manufacturing plant, and a number to indicate the year of production. A typical stamping reads "K39" with "K" indicating the manufacturer, Kelsey-Hayes, "3" indicating the plant where the wheel was made, and "9" indicating that the wheel was made in 1979.

The spare tire and wheel are housed in a carrier bolted to the rear underbody area. The carrier is fiberglass with steel supports. The fiberglass is unpainted and the steel support is painted semi-gloss black. The tire tub portion of the carrier has a fair amount of flat to semi-gloss black paint on its outside surface applied during the blackout process. A lock covered by a black rubber boot goes over the spare tire carrier access bolt.

1978–1982 Interior

Trim Tag

Interior trim color and material, as well as exterior body color and body assembly date, are stamped into a stainless-steel plate attached to the driver's door hinge pillar by two aluminum Pop Rivets. This plate is commonly called a trim plate or trim tag.

The trim tag for 1978–1980 and those 1981 Corvettes assembled in St. Louis was installed before the body painting process was completed and were painted over. Tags on 1981 Corvettes assembled in Bowling Green and all 1982s were installed after the painting process was completed and therefore are unpainted.

Trim color and material is indicated in the plate by a three-digit code. For example, in 1978 trim code "12C" indicates Oyster White color with cloth and leather seat covers.

Exterior body paint color is indicated in the trim plate by a three-character code. For example, in 1980

This is a 1982 interior. The four-way toggle switch between the power window switches controls adjustment for the optional sport mirrors. The small rocker switch below the toggle switch alternates the control between the right and left mirrors.

178

code "52L" indicates yellow. (See Appendix T for paint and interior trim codes.)

The body build date represents the date when the painted and partially assembled body reached that point on the assembly line where the trim plate was installed. The car's final assembly date is typically one to several days after the body build date.

For 1978–1980 and those 1981 Corvettes assembled in St. Louis, a letter indicating the month followed by two numbers indicating the day represents the body build date. The letter "A" was assigned to the first month of production, which was September 1977 for 1978 models, August 1978 for 1979 models, October 1979 for 1980 models, and August 1980 for 1981 models. The second month of production was assigned "B," and so on. A body assembled on the sixth day of August 1978 would have "A06" stamped into the trim plate, for example, and a body built on the eleventh day of January 1980 would have "D11" stamped into its plate.

The body build date code for those 1981 Corvettes assembled in Bowling Green and all 1982 cars is different. It begins with a letter to designate the year, with "B" denoting 1981 and "C" denoting 1982. The letter is followed by two numbers that indicate the month, with "01" representing January, "02" representing February, and so on. The final character is a letter denoting the week of the month, with "A" representing the first week, "B" representing the second week, and so on.

A body build code for a Bowling Green–assembled Corvette that reads "C 05 B" translates to a 1982 assembled the second week of May.

Seats

All 1978 Corvettes except Pace Car replicas utilize the same high-back-style seat as was used in previous years. Pace Cars and all 1979–1982 Corvettes use a completely revised seat design featuring deeper recesses and additional protrusions for side bolster support. With the new design, seatbacks tilt forward at a point that is higher than their predecessors. This permits the back to move much farther forward and thus gives improved access to the rear storage area.

Standard seat upholstery is leather for all 1978–1982 Corvettes. All 1978–1982 leather seats have horizontal panels, though the pattern is noticeably different in the new seat design fitted to 1978 Pace Cars and all 1979–1982s. In all cars except the 1982 Collector Edition, only the faces of leather-covered seats are real leather. The sides of the covers are vinyl. The seat covers in 1982 Collector Editions are all leather.

A combination leather and cloth upholstery was optional in 1978–1980 at no additional cost. The center

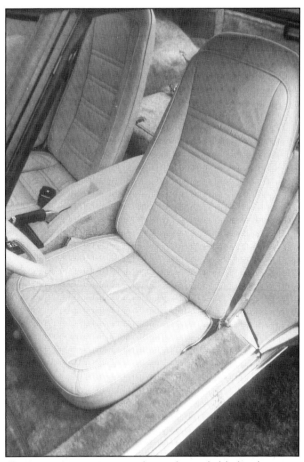

All 1978 Corvettes except Pace Car Replicas use the same high back–style seats as were used in previous years. The square, black item on the passenger's seat is the microphone for the optional CB radio this 1978 Silver Anniversary is equipped with.

sections of the seats are cloth with horizontal stitching. An all-cloth seat upholstery was available in 1981 and 1982.

Each seat rests on two seat tracks, which allow for forward and rearward adjustment of the seat's position. The tracks are black phosphate and each is held to the floor by one black phosphate, indented hex head bolt at either end for a total of four per seat. The front bolts are covered by a flap of carpet that was cut away. The carpet was usually trimmed away where the rear bolts pass through the floor, though in some cars the rear bolts simply pass through the carpet. The flaps of carpet are usually glued over the front seat bolts. The seat adjustment lever is black phosphate with a plastic knob on its end. The knob has a grained texture and is the same color as the interior.

For all 1978s other than Pace Cars, the seatbacks are made of molded plastic and match interior color. The seatback release button, its bezel, and the brackets that attach the seatback to the bottom are all chrome

A completely revised seat design is used on 1978 Pace Car Replicas and all 1979–1982 cars; it features deeper recesses and additional protrusions for side bolster support.

plated. Two bright silver bolts allow for adjustment of seatback position and get a rubber cushion over their heads. Black plastic trim washers are under the seatback release bezel and adjustment bolts.

The second-design seat, introduced with the 1978 Pace Cars, uses a molded plastic shell for both the top and bottom sections of the seat. The shells are color matched to the interior and the back of the top shell

has a carpet insert that is also color keyed to the interior. The 1978 Pace Cars and some very early 1979 Corvettes have a vinyl border around the seatback carpet insert. Subsequent cars do not have this border.

The second-design seats do not have any release hardware to tilt the seatback forward. Instead, the backs simply move forward and an inertial mechanism locks them in place in the event of a sudden stop. There is no means of adjusting seatback angle with these seats.

Beginning in 1981, a six-way power driver-side seat became optional. Externally, this seat appears essentially identical to the standard seat, with the exception of three switches mounted in the front left side of the seat bottom.

With the old design seats found in all 1978s except Pace Car Replicas, the backing is molded plastic that matches interior color. The seatback release button and its bezel are chrome plated.

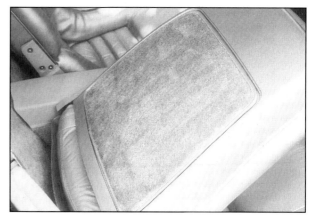
The new-design seatbacks used in 1978 Pace Car Replicas and all 1979–1982 cars tilt forward at a higher point than did their predecessors. This permits the back to move much farther forward and thus gives improved access to the rear storage area. There is no release button for these seatbacks. Instead, an inertia system locks them in place in the event of a sudden deceleration.

A six-way power driver-side seat was optional in 1981 and 1982. Externally, this seat appears identical to the standard seat with the exception of these three control switches mounted in the front left side of the seat bottom.

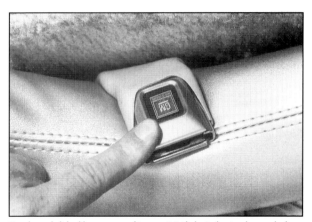

Female seatbelt buckles are encased in a semi-rigid plastic that is color-matched to the interior. The buckle housings are chrome plated with a brushed silver cover.

Lap and Shoulder Belts

All 1978–1982 Corvettes are equipped with combination lap and shoulder belts. All belts were manufactured by Firestone and tags sewn to the belts say "Firestone."

In addition to the manufacturer's name, the large tags sewn on lap and shoulder belts also indicate the model number and bear the date that that particular belt was made. The model number for all 1978–1982 Corvette belts is "C 75."

The lap and shoulder belt date is indicated by an ink stamping with a number representing the week of the year, a letter whose meaning is not yet understood, and another number representing the year. For example, a stamping of "01 E 81" indicates the belt was made in January 1981. The majority of 1978–1980 belts have the letter "E" in the date code, while the majority of 1981 and 1982 belts have the letter "L."

In addition to the tag bearing the manufacturer's name and date code, there is another, smaller tag sewn to both lap and shoulder belts. This second tag contains safety instructions.

All belts are made from a four- or five-row webbing material and are the same color as the carpet. The outboard portion of each belt is on a spring-loaded retractable coil.

Inboard portions of the seatbelts are encased in a semi-rigid plastic that goes over part of the female buckles. The plastic is color matched to the interior. The buckles have a chrome housing with a brushed silver cover. The release buttons each have the "GM" logo.

Door Panels and Door Hardware

Most 1978–1982 door panels are made from molded vinyl with carpet along the bottom. The

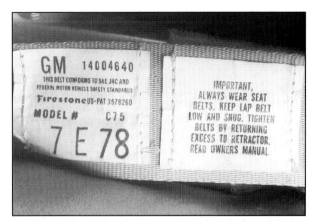

Seatbelts for 1978–1982 have these two tags sewn to them. The date code for this belt, which is in a 1978 Silver Anniversary, indicates that it was made the 7th week of 1978.

1978–1980 cars equipped with cloth seats have a cloth insert above the armrest. The 1982 Collector Editions have leather material on the door panels in place of vinyl. For all door panels, inside window felts are attached to the upper edge of the door panels with heavy staples, not Pop Rivets.

The forward, lower section of all door panels has a storage pocket that is covered with a section of carpet. The carpet is bound with vinyl trim and held shut with two Velcro-type fasteners.

Door panels are attached to the doors by means of interlocking plastic clips fastened to the back of the panel and the door frame. Black phosphate clips at the bottom of the front and rear of the panel also hold it on. The clips insert into a cutout in the back of the panel and then get fastened to the door with black phosphate Phillips pan head screws. Finally, three chrome Phillips head screws with integral washers help retain the door panel. One, with a pan head, goes through the face of each panel at the upper rear and the two others, with oval heads, go through the carpeted area at the bottom.

Inside door release handles are chrome. They protrude from a rectangular plastic escutcheon molded in the same color as the interior.

The inside door pull is integral to the armrest. The armrest is molded vinyl and is held to the door with three, black oxide–plated Phillips head screws.

Power windows were an option in 1978 and most of 1979 and became standard in May 1979. Cars equipped with standard manual windows have chrome window cranks with black plastic knobs.

Door Jambs and Door Perimeters

The door jambs and perimeter of each door are painted body color with the exception of the top front of each door, which is painted semi-gloss black. The door striker, which is the large pin threaded into the door post, and its corresponding receiver in the door are both cadmium plated. The striker is a special, indented-star head design.

Attached to the rear door jamb, toward the bottom, is a strip of aluminum and black rubber. This assembly is supposed to channel water outward.

The main door weather stripping is one piece and therefore does not have a gap. It is held on with yellowish adhesive that is often sloppily applied. In addition to the adhesive, three Phillips pan head screws also retain the weather strip, one at the forward end and two at the rearward end. In 1978 and early 1979, these screws tend to be silver cadmium plated on the driver's door and black oxide plated on the passenger's door. Later

This 1978 door panel is typical of most 1978–1982 panels. Those 1978–1980 cars fitted with cloth seats have a cloth insert above the armrest, and 1982 Collector Editions have panels covered with leather material rather than vinyl.

Pin switches in the door jambs utilize white-colored plastic tips.

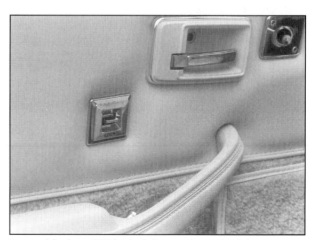

Door panel details in a 1979 fitted with the optional power door locks

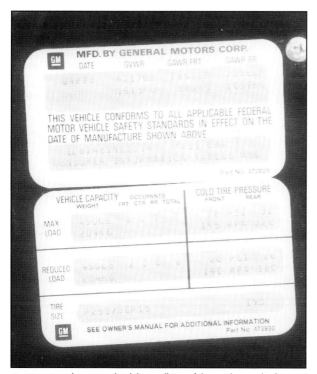

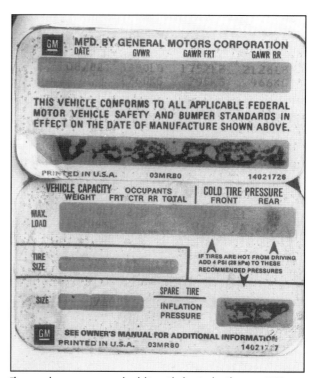

Government regulations mandated the installation of these stickers on the driver-side door. These examples are on a 1978 Pace Car.

These are the government-mandated driver-side door jamb stickers on a 1982.

cars tend to have black oxide–plated screws on both doors.

The vehicle certification label, glued toward the top of the rear portion of the driver's door, is unpainted. It contains the car's VIN, the month and year the vehicle was produced, axle loading and gross vehicle weight ratings, plus a statement that the vehicle conforms to all applicable motor vehicle safety standards in effect on the date of manufacture.

In addition to the vehicle certification label, a tire information sticker appears on the rear of the driver's door. This sticker specifies tire pressures, tire size, and recommended vehicle capacity.

Door sills consist of a thin bright aluminum strip.

Kick Panels, Quarter Trim Panels, Pedals, and Carpet

The kick panels beneath the dash, just forward of the doors, are molded plastic and are interior color. On air-conditioned cars, the passenger-side panel was cut by hand for increased clearance and the cut is frequently rough.

Kick panels are secured by an interference fit with the vertical door frame and by one chrome-plated Phillips head oval screw in the forward upper corner.

The panels have a bevy of small holes for the speakers that mount behind them. Unlike 1977 and

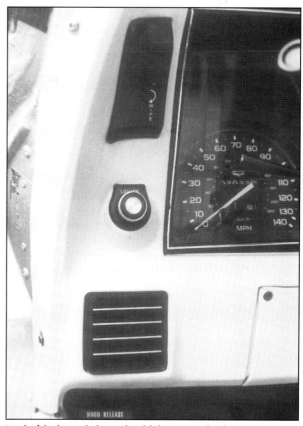

Details of the driver-side door jamb and dash area. Note that the trim tag was originally painted over on this 1978 and all 1978–1981 St. Louis–built cars.

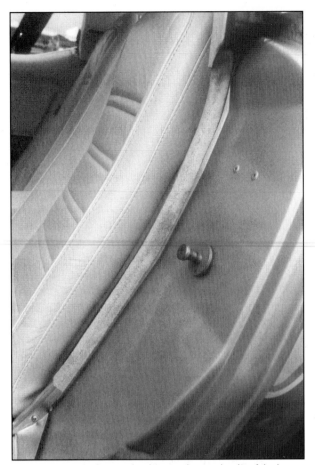

Beginning in 1978 this fuzzy pinch welt was used to trim the edge of the door jamb area.

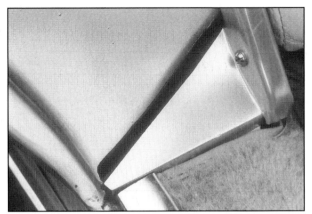

The bright silver, triangular-shaped piece with the strip of black rubber on the top edge in this 1978 is a water deflector that was installed at the bottom of the rear door jamb area. Note the unusual screw in the upper right of the photo. Also note the thin strip of aluminum in place of the previously used wide sill plates.

Horizontally ribbed black rubber pedals are typical of 1978–1982 production. These examples are from a 1978.

The original carpet heel pad in 1978–1982 is sewn to the carpet with a thread that resembles fishing line.

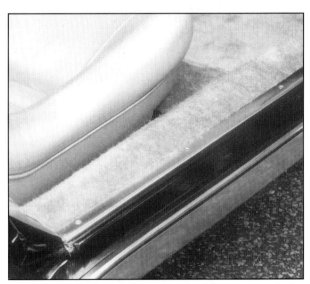

Beginning in 1978 this thin strip of aluminum replaced the previously used wide sill plates.

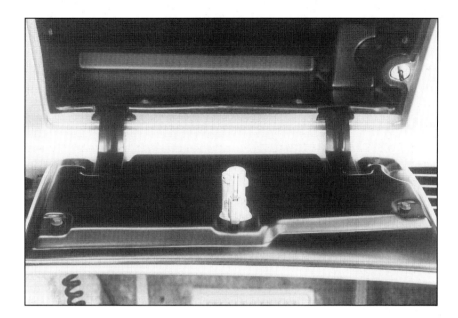

The reverse side of the glove box door. The lock/release mechanism is unpainted, as are the hex head screws holding the face of the door to the back.

earlier kick panels, there is a ridge at the rear edge of 1978–1982 panels. Also unlike earlier panels, there is a carpet insert stapled to the kick panels. This insert matches the car's floor carpeting.

In all 1978–1982 Corvettes, carpet is made from plush-cut-pile material. In all cases it matches interior color.

A black rubber flap on the firewall insulation retains the upper edge of the front carpeting on both sides.

Carpet covers the bulkhead behind the seats and has sewn-on binding on the lower edge where it overlaps the front floor carpet behind the seats. Rear storage compartment doors each have carpet under their frames. One piece of carpet covers the rear storage area floor and extends up the rear bulkhead. The edge at the top of the bulkhead is trimmed with sewn-on binding, while the edges at the tops of the wheelwells are not trimmed. The only exception to this is carpet in 1978 Pace Cars, which is trimmed with vinyl on the edge above each wheelwell.

Carpet has a molded vinyl accelerator heel pad in the corner of the driver's foot well, adjacent to the accelerator pedal. The main section of the pad is rectangular shaped and has horizontal bars molded in. Extensions come off the main section and extend up the transmission tunnel and under the accelerator pedal. The heel pad is sewn to the carpet with a thread that resembles fishing line.

Dash Pad and Glove Box

The upper dash pad is made of soft vinyl and matches interior color along the edge closest to the steering wheel. The remainder of the upper pad is flat black.

Details of the glove box lamp in this 1978 are typical of all 1978–1982 cars. One of the black oxide–plated Phillips head screws that holds the liner in place also retains a small black metal shield over the lamp.

A glove box door is inset into the passenger-side dash panel where a three-pocket storage area was placed in previous years. The door matches the dash panel in both texture and color. The door is released by means of a chrome-plated latch knob, which incorporates a key lock. The latch mechanism is made from unpainted pot metal components.

Two hinges are spot welded to the inside of the door. The hinges, as well as the back side of the door, are painted flat black.

A small lamp is mounted on the right side of the glove box. It is activated by a plunger-type switch that utilizes a black plastic button surrounded by a chrome-plated bezel.

The glove box is formed from a black plastic liner that is retained by six black oxide–plated Phillips pan head screws. One of the liner screws also secures a metal shield for the glove box lamp.

On those cars equipped with a cassette or eight-track player, a tape rack is installed in the glove box. This rack is made from black plastic.

The glove box contains a clear plastic envelope with no writing on it. Inside this envelope are the owner's manual, tire guide and warranty folder, maintenance folder, consumer information booklet, battery information card, vehicle and emissions warranty folder, CB radio manual (if the car is so equipped), and ETR radio manual (if the car is so equipped).

Interior Switches, Controls, and Related Parts

All 1978–1982 Corvettes have a headlamp switch mounted in the upper left corner of the driver-side dash pad. In 1978–1980, headlamp switch knobs are chrome plated with a black inner ring and chrome-plated center.

The 1981 and 1982 knobs are made from glossy black plastic with a thin chrome ring. The center of the knob is black with a symbol for headlamps in white.

All the 1978–1982 cars have a windshield wiper and washer switch mounted in the dash below the headlamp switch. In 1978 and 1979 intermittent wipers were an option. The knob for the windshield wiper/washer switch is plain black plastic on cars that are not equipped with intermittent

All 1978–1982 Corvettes have a headlamp switch mounted in the upper left corner of the driver-side dash pad. This is a 1978–1980-style switch knob.

This is the 1981–1982-style light switch knob. It is made from glossy black plastic with a thin chrome ring. The bezel behind the knob is the same as on 1978–1982s.

This is a 1978–1980 windshield wiper and washer switch. In 1981 and 1982 the switch was the same but the plastic bezel around it was interior color rather than black.

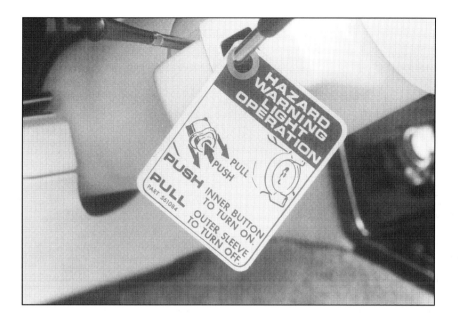

This hazard warning light instructional card was hung on the turn signal lever.

wipers. On those 1978 and 1979 cars equipped with intermittent wipers and on all 1980–1982 cars the knob has a white-colored arc and arrow. In 1978–1980, the wiper switch bezel is black and in 1981–1982 it is the same color as the interior.

All 1978–1982 headlamp knobs have a black plastic bezel on the dash. The word "LIGHTS" appears in the bezel in white letters.

The 1978–1982 Corvettes have square-shaped air-conditioning vents on both sides of the dash toward the lower, outboard corner. The black plastic vent mechanisms swivel to change the direction of air flow. A grouping of movable slats is also utilized to control the direction of air flow. The slats are made from black plastic and have chrome edges.

On non-air-conditioned cars, the vents on either side of the dash allow outside air to enter the passenger compartment. Controls for these fresh air vents are positioned underneath the dash.

A small, black T-handle pull mechanism beneath the driver-side dash on the left side releases the hood latch. The handle is black with the words "HOOD RELEASE" in white painted block letters across its face. The hood release cable is in a smooth, black plastic sheathing.

The trip odometer reset knob for all 1978–1982 cars is in the lower left area of the speedometer lens. The knob is made from glossy black plastic and is square in shape.

The headlamp door override switch is mounted beneath the plastic fill panel underneath the steering column. It is a flat-black, plastic pull-type switch.

Steering Wheel and Steering Column

All 1978 and 1979 cars equipped with a standard steering column have a four-spoke steering wheel that is completely covered in molded vinyl that matches interior color. Those 1978 and 1979 cars equipped with the optional tilt-telescopic steering column, and all 1980–1982 cars, utilize a three-spoke steering wheel. The spokes for this wheel are brushed stainless steel and the rim is covered with leather dyed to match interior color.

The standard steering column and optional tilt-telescoping column in 1978–1982 are painted whatever the interior color is in a semi-gloss finish. The column-mounted ignition switch is chrome plated. A notch in the switch aligns with the word "LOCK" that is cast into the column housing when the switch is in the locked position. All 1978–1982 columns have a key release lever located slightly forward of and below the ignition switch.

The tilt-telescoping column has a thick locking ring below the steering wheel to control the telescoping function. The ring is painted to match the rest of the column. Twisting the lever on the ring releases the locking mechanism and allows the column to telescope.

A lever similar to, but shorter than, the turn signal lever controls the tilt function of the optional tilt-telescopic steering column. The tilt lever is located between the turn signal lever and dash.

All columns have a four-way flasher switch mounted on the right side. This switch consists of a push button inside of a sleeve. The sleeve has the word "HAZARD" written on it with white letters in two locations.

Details of a turn signal lever and tilt/telescopic steering column release lever in a 1978.

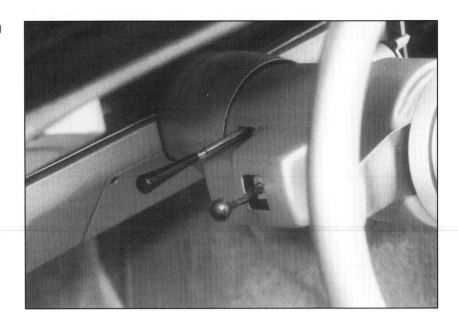

For all years, a stalk with turn signal and head-light dimmer is mounted into the steering column.

With the exception of 1982 Collector Editions, all 1978–1982 models use a textured metal horn button painted to match the interior. Collector Editions use a horn button covered with leather dyed to match interior color. A crossed flags emblem is in the center of the button.

Interior Windshield Moldings, Sun Visors, and Rearview Mirror

Three pieces of vinyl-covered molding, matched to the interior color, cover the inside of the windshield frame for all 1978–1982 Corvettes. The two side pieces are each held on by one chrome-plated Phillips head screw at the top and two chrome-plated Phillips head screws on the vertical section. The top piece of molding is retained by chrome-plated, recess head Phillips screws fitted with countersunk washers.

Sun visors are covered with padded soft vinyl. The pattern of the vinyl used for the sun visors matches the pattern in the vinyl used for seat covers. Each sun visor is held to the windshield frame with chrome-plated, recess head Phillips screws. Sun

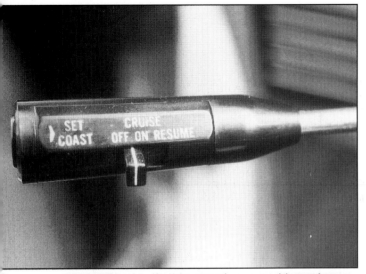

Cruise control was optional in 1978–1982. When so equipped the controls were incorporated into the end of the turn signal lever. This example is from a 1982.

With the exception of 1982 Collector Editions, which use a horn button covered with leather dyed to match interior color, all 1978–1982 horn buttons are painted to match interior color. This example is from a 1978 Pace Car, and hence it is silver.

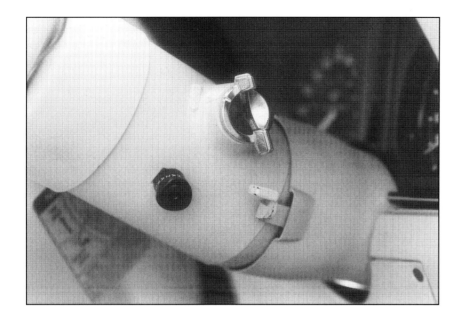

visor mounts allow the visors to swivel toward the side windows.

In 1978–1980 Corvettes and those 1981 cars assembled in St. Louis, a sleeve-type label describing operation of the turn signal and headlamp dimmer switches, ignition key removal procedure, and proper adjustment procedures for the optional dual sport mirrors is slid over the driver-side sun visor.

Another sleeve-type label describing proper adjustment procedures for glass T-tops is slid over the passenger-side sun visor in those cars equipped with glass tops.

Those 1978 and early 1979 cars equipped with the Convenience Group option (option ZX2) have a vanity mirror mounted to the passenger-side sun visor.

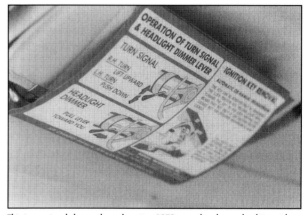

This instructional sleeve, shown here in a 1978, was placed over the driver-side sun visor.

The convenience group option (ZX2) offered in 1978 and 1979 included this vanity mirror mounted to the top of the passenger-side sun visor.

All 1978–1982 Corvettes use this style interior day/night rearview mirror. The mirror's mounting arm is usually flat black as seen here, though some cars have a dull silver arm.

An AM/FM stereo with integral CB radio was an available option in 1978–1982. This example is from a 1978.

Late 1979 and all 1980–1982 Corvettes all have a vanity mirror on the passenger-side sun visor. Also beginning in late 1979, the driver-side sun visor mount allows the visor to telescope in and out for a greater range of adjustment.

All 1978–1982 Corvettes have an interior day/night rearview mirror mounted directly onto the upper windshield.

All mirrors are in a black, grained plastic housing. The day/night lever is black plastic as well, with horizontal ribs to enhance grip.

The mirror is fastened to a small mounting pad by means of an Allen screw. The pad is glued to the windshield with special adhesive. The mirror's

mounting arm is usually flat black, though some cars have a dull silver arm.

Instruments and Radio

Both the speedometer and tachometer in all 1978–1982 Corvettes have flat black faces and white numerals. A secondary scale on the speedometer face indicates kilometers per hour. This scale is blue in 1978 and in those 1979s assembled through approximately July 1979, and yellow in subsequent 1979s and in all 1980–1982 cars.

All 1978 and most 1979 cars are fitted with 140-mile-per-hour speedometers. Those 1979s assembled after approximately July 1979 and all 1980–1982 cars have 85 mile-per-hour speedometers.

All 85-mile-per-hour speedometers have white numerals with the exception of those indicating 55 miles per hour. The 55-mile-per-hour designation is orange.

Beginning in 1982, speedometers read in 5-mile-per-hour increments instead of the previously used 10-mile-per-hour increments.

In 1978 and 1979 the cumulative and trip odometer drums are black with white numerals in all positions except tenths, which are yellow with black numerals. In 1980–1982 the trip odometer drums are yellow with black numerals in all positions except tenths, which are white with black numerals.

Tachometer redlines vary according to the engine and, at times, whether the car is equipped with air conditioning. In 1978, those cars equipped with an L48 engine, or an L82 engine and air conditioning, have a 5,300 rpm redline. Those cars equipped with an L82 engine but without air conditioning have a 5,600 rpm

This 1978 cigarette lighter and ashtray are typical of all 1977–1982s.

In all 1978–1982 Corvettes the center console instrument cluster housing is semi-gloss black. With the exception of the clock, all gauges have a flat-black background, white numerals, and a straight, white needle. The clock has white hour and minute hands but a red second hand.

Those 1981–1982s fitted with an electronically tuned receiver (ETR) do not have a clock in the central instrument cluster since a clock is included in the ETR radio's display. An oil temperature gauge is substituted for the clock.

All 1978 and most 1979 cars feature 140-mile-per-hour speedometers. Those 1979s assembled after approximately July 1979 and all 1980–1982 cars have 85-mile-per-hour speedometers. In 1978s and 1979s through July 1979 production, the inner circle of smaller numbers, which represent kilometers per hour, are pale blue. Also in 1978s and 1979s through July 1979 production, the tenths position on the trip odometer is pale orange with a black numeral.

redline. In 1979, L48s have a 5,300 rpm redline and all L82s have a 5,600 rpm redline. In 1980, LG4s and L48s have a 5,300 rpm redline and L82s have a 6,000 rpm redline. In 1981 and 1982 the only available engine got a 5,300 rpm redline.

The center console instrument cluster housing is semi-gloss black. All secondary gauges have a flat-black background, white numerals, and a straight white needle. The only exception to this is the clock, which has a red second hand in conjunction with white hour and minute hands.

Cars fitted with an electronically tuned receiver (ETR) do not have a clock since a clock is included in the ETR radio's display. An oil temperature gauge is substituted for the clock in the center instrument cluster.

1978 was the last year Corvettes came standard without a radio. Four different radios were offered that year as extra cost options. These included an AM/FM monaural, an AM/FM stereo, an AM/FM stereo with 8-track player, and an AM/FM stereo with CB.

In 1979, the monaural radio became standard equipment. For additional cost it could be replaced in 1979 and 1980 with a stereo, a stereo with a CB, a stereo with an 8-track, or a stereo with a cassette player.

In 1981, the optional radio selection was expanded to include ETRs and combinations of stereo reception, CB, and either a cassette or 8-track

This is the 85-mile-per-hour speedometer used in 1979s assembled after approximately July 1979 and all 1980–1982s. The inner circle of smaller numbers representing kilometers per hour is yellow, as are the first three drums of the trip odometer. As seen here, in 1982 only the speedometer reads in 5-mile-per-hour increments. Prior speedometers read in 10 mile-per-hour increments.

Tachometer redlines varied according to engine and, in 1978 and 1979, whether the car was air conditioned. As seen in this example, 1978-1980 cars equipped with the optional L-82 engine have "L-82" below the needle.

In 1982 the tachometer was revised to look like this. Note the "cross-fire injection" designation below the needle. The rectangle below and to the left of the "RPM/100" designation is a choke warning light. All tachometers used since July 1979 (when the 85-mile-per-hour speedometer appeared) have this light in the tachometer.

player. In 1982, the 8-track could no longer be had in combination with the CB.

All non-ETR radios have a small slide bar above the dial that changes reception between AM and FM. With these radios, a small stereo indicator light comes on when an FM signal is received.

Center Console, Shifter, and Park Brake

All 1978–1982 center consoles have carpeted sides that match the remainder of the car's carpeting. With the exception of 1982 Collector Editions, all cars have a semi-gloss black painted console trim plate accented by a chrome stripe around the outside perimeter. Collector Editions have a console trim plate painted dark bronze.

Park brake consoles for 1978–1982 cars are made from a flexible vinyl material molded in the same color as the interior. The park brake lever has a textured handle molded in black plastic. The lever is

This type of air-conditioning/heater control assembly was used 1977–1982. Minor changes are seen between earlier and later examples. This one is in a 1978.

This air-conditioning/heater control assembly is from a 1982. Minor changes from earlier assemblies include the addition of symbols for the defroster and fan.

A CB radio integral to the AM/FM stereo was an option in 1978–1982. The CB's microphone latched onto the passenger-side dash between the glove box and center instruments when not in use.

chrome plated, as is the bezel around the release button. The button is molded from gloss-black plastic.

In cars equipped with a manual transmission, the shift pattern is indicated next to the shifter. The shift pattern area is semi-gloss black and the letters and numbers are white.

The shifter boot for manual transmission cars is made from black leather and has a sewn seam toward the passenger side of the car.

Manual shifters have a chrome-plated shaft and threaded-on black chrome ball. A chrome-plated T-handle integral to the shaft controls the reverse lock-out.

On those Corvettes equipped with an automatic transmission, the shift pattern is also next to the shifter. A white pointer in a plastic lighted band with white painted letters is used to indicate shifter position. Like their manual counterparts, automatic shifters are surrounded by a black leather boot with a sewn seam facing the passenger side.

Automatic shifters are made from a chrome shaft topped by a black plastic ball. The ball has a chrome, spring-loaded button in the top to release the detent and allow the shifter to be moved.

All 1978–1982 Corvettes use a similar heater/air-conditioning control assembly. It has two horizontal sliding levers, one to control function and another to control temperature. A separate toggle switch is mounted in the left side of the control unit to regulate blower fan speed. The switch in 1978 and 1979 air-conditioned cars has four positions, and in non-air-conditioned cars it has three positions. In 1980–1982, air conditioning was standard and therefore only the four-position switch is used.

All 1978–1982 cars have an ashtray inset into the console below the heater/air-conditioning control unit. The ashtray door is semi-gloss black in all cars

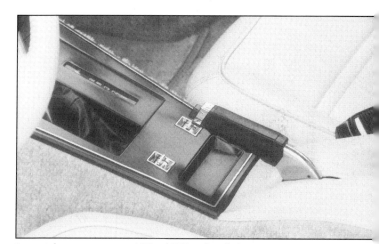

Power windows were an option in 1978 and 1979, and standard in 1980–1982. Switches and their bezels are chrome plated.

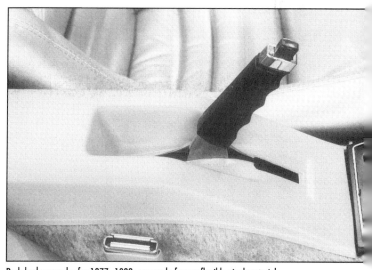

Park brake consoles for 1977–1982s are made from a flexible vinyl material molded in the same color as the interior. This example is from a 1978.

except 1982 Collector Editions and slides back and forth with slight resistance. The ashtray door is dark bronze in Collector Editions. The small tab inside the ashtray has a round hole.

All cars are equipped with a cigarette lighter. The lighter has a gloss-black plastic knob with a white circle and ridges around the outer portion. The lighter's element for all years is usually stamped "78 CASCO 12V."

On those 1978–1982 Corvettes equipped with the optional rear window defogger a control switch is mounted on the left side of the heater/air-conditioning control unit. In 1978 and 1979, the switch has a black handle and black bezel with white letters. When the defogger is on the indicator light is green.

In late 1980 through 1982 the rear window defogger switch is modified slightly so its bezel is below the surface of the console rather than above it as before. The indicator light is amber and the bezel has a symbol to represent a heating element.

Rear Storage Compartments and Their Contents

All 1978 and the great majority of 1979 cars feature three enclosed storage compartments behind the seats. During the last few weeks of 1979 production in September 1979 some cars were fitted with two enclosed storage compartments as in 1980–1982.

The lids for the rear storage compartments found in all 1978–1982 cars are made from molded black fiberglass. All lids are covered with carpet that matches the interior carpet.

Each lid is surrounded by a molded plastic border that is painted to match interior color. The entire assembly of all of the lids is also surrounded by a color-matched molded plastic border. With the three-door assembly used in 1978 and most of 1979, the plastic trim around each door is held on with glue. With the two-door assembly used from very late 1979 through 1982, the trim is retained by rivets.

With both the three- and two-door assemblies, the doors are held to their hinges by black phosphate–plated hex head bolts with integral flat washers. The hinges attach to the assembly's frame with rivets. The frame attaches to the car's body with chrome-plated or black oxide–plated Phillips oval head screws fitted with integral washers.

Each lid latches with a spring-loaded mechanism. Each lid has a chrome button to release its latch. Three-door assemblies use a metal lift handle painted to match interior color on each door. Two compartment door assemblies use a color-matched plastic handle on each door.

Beginning in mid-1980, thin, black plastic–coated cables are attached to the outer edges of both doors and to the compartment frame. The cables prevent the doors from opening far enough to damage the hinges or hinge areas.

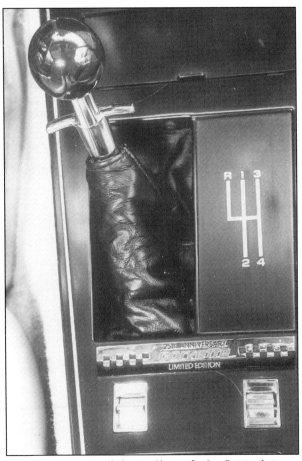

The "25th Anniversary Limited Edition" emblem was fitted to all 1978 Indy Pace Car Replicas. The remainder of the console is typical of 1977–1982 cars. Note the shifter boot, which is made from black leather and has a sewn seam toward the passenger side of the car.

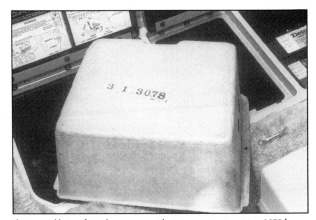

The removable tray from the passenger-side storage compartment in a 1978 has a date code stamped in black ink.

Three rear storage compartment doors were used on Corvettes through the very end of 1979 production. Some very late 1979s and all 1980–1982s have two compartments.

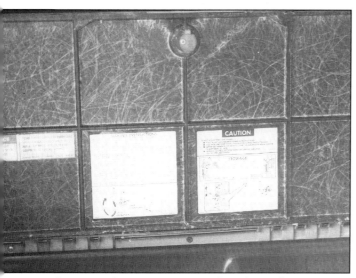

The passenger-side rear storage compartment door in this 1982 has instructional/warning decals placed underneath. The small one on the left pertains to the fiberglass rear leaf spring and the other two provide jacking and wheel stowage instructions.

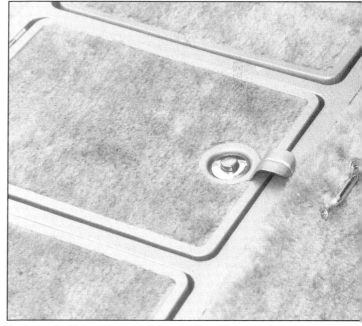

The chrome-plated bar screwed into the bulkhead in front of the storage door is the forward anchor point for the strap that holds the T-tops down when they are not in use.

These instruction labels were glued to the underside of the door for the passenger-side interior storage compartment.

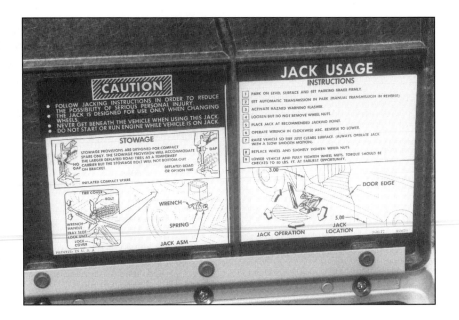

With both the two- and three-door assemblies the compartment behind the passenger's seat is equipped with a lock in the push-button release. The key for the storage compartment lid lock is the same as the key for the anti-theft alarm, spare tire storage compartment, and doors.

In 1978 and 1979, a sticker for jacking instructions is on the underside of the passenger-side compartment lid. In 1980–1982 a sticker pertaining to the aluminum wheels is under the lid on those cars equipped with aluminum wheels. In 1981 and 1982, cars equipped with standard suspension also have a

The Y-shaped strap is to hold down the T-tops when they are not in use. In the upper center of this photo is one of the two rear speakers with which this car is equipped. Dual rear speakers were an option from 1978 through 1980. This example is from 1980.

sticker under the lid with information about the fiberglass rear spring. And finally, 1982 Collector Editions have a sticker on the underside of the lid describing the proper procedure for hubcap removal.

The compartment directly behind the driver's seat holds the vehicle's battery. It has a thin foam seal around the perimeter of the door opening to help keep battery fumes from entering the passenger compartment.

All 1978–1982 Corvettes use a side terminal Delco Battery. In 1978–1980, two different models of batteries were used. Both are called "Delco Freedom Batteries." The standard battery is a model 87-5, and the optional heavy-duty battery is a model 89-5.

Delco Freedom Batteries used in 1978–1980 have two large raised squares in the top of the battery. One of the squares contains the "Delco Eye," a small circle of glass utilized to indicate battery condition.

The top of the Delco Freedom Battery is blue and the sides are white. A caution label is affixed to the top. Also, the words "Delco Freedom Battery" are written across the top.

Beginning in 1981, the Delco Freedom Battery was replaced with the Delco Freedom II Battery. The Delco Freedom II used in 1981 and 1982 Corvettes is model number 695. It is essentially the same in appearance as the Delco Freedom Battery it replaced, until late 1982, when the top went from blue to black.

All 1978–1982 battery cables are side terminal–style and have a red positive end and a black negative end. The positive cable terminal has a "+" sign molded in and the negative terminal has a "-" sign molded in.

The cables themselves are both covered with black insulation that has the words "COPPER CLAD

ALUMINUM" written in white block letters. The cables are retained with 5/16-inch hex head bolts.

With the three-door assembly used in 1978 and most of 1979, the passenger-side storage compartment contains a removable insert. The insert, which is like a squared-off bucket, is made from grayish-black fiberboard and measures about 5 inches deep. The inside has a material called "flock." It consists of small strands of black fiber adhered to the surface and resembles velvet.

The fiberboard insert contains a small brown paper envelope containing license plate screws. This bag is marked "UNIT NUMBER 3875313" across the top, "LICENSE ATTACHING" on one side, and "REAR PLATE PARTS" on the other side.

The center storage compartment found in three-door assemblies used in 1978 and most of 1979 has a black flocking like the passenger-side insert tray. A light is not used in this center compartment.

With the two-door assembly used in very late 1979 through 1982s, the passenger-side storage compartment contains a removable tray made from smooth black plastic. On the plastic it says "MADE IN CANADA" and the part number "14007098."

For all 1978–1982 cars, the insert in the passenger-side rear storage compartment lifts out to reveal an additional storage area beneath. A jack and jack handle are mounted to the bottom of the compartment (to the car's floor panel) with a black spring that latches onto a black hook riveted to the floor.

All jacks are painted gloss or semi-gloss black and contain a date code stamping. For 1978 cars, the date code stamping is on the head of one of the rivets on the jack's base. The code contains three numbers, the first indicating the year and the subsequent two indicating the week of production. For example, a 1978 jack with the code "811" was made the 11th week of 1978.

Beginning in 1979, and continuing through 1982, both the location and designation for the jack's date code changed. Rather than on a rivet head, the code in 1979 and later cars is stamped into the cross-member at the end where the jack is cranked. The date code begins with a number denoting the year. This is followed by a letter denoting the month, with "A" representing January, "B" representing February, and so on. The code ends with two numbers denoting the day of the month. For example, a jack with a date code of "1E17" was manufactured May 17, 1981.

All jack handles are painted gloss or semi-gloss black and include a pivoting, 3/4-inch, boxed hex-wrench on the end to remove and install the car's lug nuts. A thick rubber ring is fitted around the hex-wrench end to prevent rattling.

All 1978–1982 Corvettes have two storage bags to hold the T-tops when they are removed. These bags are made from a vinyl material and are usually black. The bags in some cars are very dark green rather than black.

Most T-top storage bags have a date code stamped inside in ink. Typical date stampings contain a month and year designation. For example, bags manufactured in October 1979 read "10-79." In addition to the date stamping, bags may also contain a logo stamping representing the manufacturer. The most common logo seen is "TEX."

All bags have a flap that closes over the opening and is retained by three chrome-plated snaps.

All 1978–1982 cars have adjustable T-top hold down straps. Tops are held by a single harness with a "Y" configuration that is attached to the rear bulkhead in the luggage area and extends to a chrome-plated anchor attached to the front bulkhead between the seats. Most cars have straps dyed to match interior color, though black straps are seen occasionally in cars that don't have black interiors.

All 1978–1982 Corvettes have molded vinyl trim mounted to the underside of the T-tops. The vinyl is the same color as the interior. A dome light is found in the center of the interior roof trim.

1978–1982 Mechanical
Engine Blocks

The engine-block casting number for all 1978–1982 engines is located on the top rear driver side of the block, on the flange that mates to the transmission bellhousing.

Most 1978 Corvettes utilize a block with the casting No. 3970010. Some 1978s may use a block with casting No. 376450 or 460703. All 1980 Corvettes equipped with a 350 engine use either a No. 3970010 or a No. 14010207 block. The 1980 cars equipped with an LG4 305 engine use a No. 4715111 block. All 1981 and 1982 Corvettes use a No. 14010207 block.

Engine-block casting dates for all 1978–1982 Corvettes are located on the top rear passenger side of the block, on the flange that mates to the transmission bellhousing.

The engine-block casting date consists of a letter for the month, one or two numbers for the day, and one number for the year. For example, a No. 3970010 block cast on June 12, 1978, would have a casting date of "F 12 8."

All 1978–1982 engines contain two distinct stampings on a machined pad located on the top of the passenger side between the cylinder head and water pump. One stamping is commonly referred to

Driver-side view of a 1978 L82 engine compartment.

Passenger-side view of a 1978 L82 engine compartment.

as the assembly stamping and the other is commonly called the VIN derivative stamping.

While the great majority of 1978–1982 cars have the VIN derivative stamping on the machined pad described above, a small number of cars have it in a different location. With these cars, it is stamped into an area on the side of the block just above and toward the rear of the oil filter mount. This area of the block is not machined and therefore retains a rough cast texture.

The assembly stamping begins with the prefix letter "V" to indicate the Flint engine assembly plant. Following the prefix letter are four numbers indicating the month and day of assembly. After the numbers indicating the assembly date are three suffix letters denoting the particular engine. This suffix code is often referred to as the engine broadcast code, or simply the engine code. (Refer to Appendix C for 1978–1982 engine suffix codes.)

To illustrate what a typical engine assembly stamping looks like, consider the following 1981 combination: a base 350/190-horsepower engine built on April 5 and coupled to a four-speed transmission. The assembly stamping for such an engine would read "V0405ZAM."

Always remember that the engine assembly date must come after the engine-block casting date (you can't assemble an engine before the block is cast!), and both the casting date and assembly date must precede the final assembly date of the car (you can't

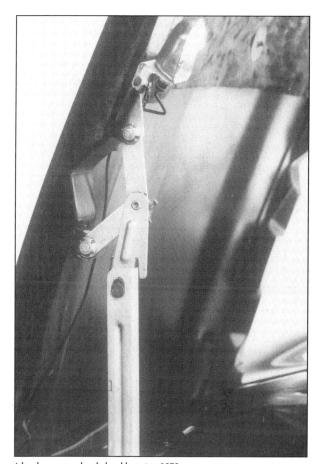

A hood support and underhood lamp in a 1979.

Driver-side view of a 1982 engine compartment.

Passenger-side view of a 1982 engine compartment.

finalize assembly of a car before the engine has been cast and assembled). The great majority of engines were cast and assembled within a couple of weeks prior to the car's assembly date. Some engines, however, were cast and/or assembled months prior to installation in a car. Six months is generally accepted as the outer limit for the difference between an engine assembly or casting date and the final assembly date of the car in which it was installed.

The VIN derivative stamping, as the name implies, is a stamping containing a portion or a derivative of the car's vehicle identification number. For all 1978 Corvettes except Pace Cars, the VIN derivative stamping begins with "18S4." The "1" designates the Chevrolet car line, the "8" is for model year 1978, "S" is for St. Louis, which is where all 1978 Corvettes were assembled, and "4" is thought to be a place holder. The VIN derivative for all 1978 Pace Cars begins with "18S9."

The VIN derivative for all 1979 Corvettes begins with "19S4." For all 1980 cars, it begins with "1AS4." For 1981s built in St. Louis, the VIN derivative begins with "1BS4," while for 1981s built in Bowling Green it begins with "1B51." For all 1982 Corvettes, the derivative begins with "1C51."

For all 1978–1982 Corvettes, the first four characters of the VIN derivative are followed by the final five characters of the particular car's VIN or serial number. For example, the VIN derivative stamping in the engine for the 9,411th 1978 built would read "18S409411."

All 1978–1982 engine blocks are cast-iron. All 1978–1981 and most 1982 engines are painted GM "Corporate Blue." Beginning in approximately August 1982, engine color was changed to black.

Engines were originally painted before exhaust manifolds were installed and therefore coverage on the sides of the block behind the manifolds is good. The engine stamp pad and timing tab on the timing chain cover were normally covered up when the engine was painted and therefore they normally appear unpainted.

Cylinder Heads

As with engine blocks, all 1978–1982 cylinder heads have both a casting number and a casting date. As with blocks and other cast parts, the cylinder head casting date typically has a letter to indicate month, one or two numbers to indicate the day of the month, and one number to indicate the year. (Refer to Appendix G for a comprehensive list of cylinder head casting numbers.)

All 1978–1982 engines utilize cast-iron cylinder heads. All cylinder heads and head bolts are painted engine color.

Intake Manifolds

The 1978 and 1979 base engines use a cast-iron intake manifold, while 1978 and 1979 L82 engines use an aluminum intake. All 1980–1982 engines, including base engines, L82s, LG4 California 305s, and 1982 cross-fire injection engines, use an aluminum intake manifold.

As with engine blocks and cylinder heads, intake manifolds contain casting numbers and casting dates. As with other cast engine parts, the casting date consists of a letter designating the month, one or two numbers designating the day of the month, and a number denoting the year.

Casting numbers and casting dates for all cast-iron intake manifolds are on the top surface. Casting numbers for aluminum intakes are on the top surface, but casting dates are on the underside. (Refer to Appendix H for intake manifold casting numbers.)

Cast-iron intake manifolds are painted engine color. Aluminum intake manifolds are painted dull silver.

All 1978–1982 Corvette engines utilize an aluminum thermostat housing that is painted the same color as the intake manifold.

In 1978–1981, each intake manifold bolt gets a flat washer unless it also holds on a bracket. Intake bolts that also retain a bracket typically do not have a washer. In 1982, intake bolts have a washer-style head and do not use an additional washer.

All 1978–1982 engines use side intake manifold gaskets made from a metal core covered with a fiber composition. No gaskets are used on the ends of the intake. Instead, a light-reddish RTV sealant is used on the ends.

Engine lifting brackets are attached to the engines in all 1978–1982 Corvettes. The brackets are painted engine color if a cast-iron intake manifold is utilized and silver if an aluminum intake is used.

All engines have one bracket attached to the first and second intake manifold bolt from the front on the driver side. A second bracket is attached to the rear of the intake on the passenger side with one bolt.

Distributor and Ignition Coil

All 1978–1982 cars use a Delco HEI distributor and an electronic tachometer. All HEI distributors have a part number and date code stamped directly into the aluminum housing. These stampings are on the driver side when the distributor is correctly installed in the car. (See Appendix K for distributor part numbers.)

The distributor date code, which represents the day the distributor was assembled, consists of a number representing the year, a letter representing the month, and one or two numbers representing the day of the month. For distributor date codes, the letter "A" represents January, "B" represents February, and so on. As is typical of stamped-in date codes, the letter "I" is skipped, so the month of September is represented by "J." The date code on a distributor assembled January 12, 1979, for example, would read "9 A 12."

Shown here are details of the passenger-side rear intake manifold area of a 1978 L82. Note the bright silver cadmium plating on the vacuum advance, the small blotch of yellow paint on the breather tube coming out of the valve cover (an inspection mark), and the routing of various hoses and wires.

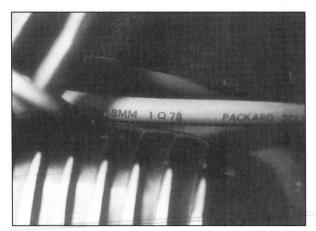

All 1978–1982 Corvettes use gray 8 millimeter spark plug wires manufactured by Packard Electric. All wires are ink stamped every few inches with the words (partially seen here) "PACKARD DELCORE ELECTRONIC SUPPRESSION 8MM." The date code "1 Q 78" indicates that this wire was manufactured during the first quarter of 1978.

While most distributors were made several weeks before the engine was assembled, it is entirely possible that several months can separate the two. As with most other components, six months is the generally accepted maximum.

All distributors are fitted with a vacuum advance unit. Vacuum advances have part numbers stamped into them in the bracket that mounts the vacuum canister to the distributor

All 1978–1982 Corvettes use a black Delco Remy distributor cap. The ignition coil is integral to the distributor cap on all cars. It is manufactured by Delco and is black in color. It says "DELCO REMY" and "MADE IN THE USA" on the top. Also, the word "LATCH" appears on the top twice. A white sticker with a black UPC bar code is present on some coils.

Ignition Shielding

All 1978–1982 Corvettes equipped with a radio are outfitted with ignition shielding. The top shield, which goes over the distributor, is made from black plastic. It has a grainy texture on the outside and an aluminum foil liner on the inside. The shield is unchanged from 1978–1981. It is very similar for 1982, except it was shortened on the passenger side.

In addition to the top ignition shield, all radio-equipped cars also have side shielding, V-shaped lower shielding, and spark plug shields. These pieces are plated with "flash chrome" and, as such, the quality of the plating is not very good.

Ignition shielding and firewall details from a 1982.

The chrome-plated side shielding and V-shaped sections of shielding encapsulate the spark plug wires. The V-shaped shielding runs from the bottom of the vertical shields to the area beneath the spark plugs.

The spark plug shields cover only the rear two spark plugs on either side of the engine. The passenger-side spark plug shield used on 1978–1980 L82 engines has a hole in it for passage of the wire to the temperature sending unit.

The spark plug shields are retained to cadmium-plated brackets with chrome-plated wing bolts or silver cadmium–plated hex head bolts. The brackets are silver cadmium plated and may have "FPM" stamped in to represent the manufacturer.

All engines also have a silver cadmium–plated spark plug heat shield on the right side of the engine only. The heat shield is retained to the engine block by means of a single silver cadmium–plated indented hex head bolt.

Spark Plug Wires

All 1978–1982 Corvettes use 8 millimeter spark plug wires manufactured by Packard Electric. The wires are gray in color with black boots at both ends.

All spark plug wires are ink stamped every few inches with the words "PACKARD DELCORE ELECTRONIC SUPPRESSION." In addition, all wires are stamped with a date code. The date code indicates the quarter and the year of manufacture. For example, wires labeled "3Q-81" were made in the third quarter of 1981.

Carburetors and Throttle Body Injection

All 1978–1981 Corvettes have a Rochester Quadrajet carburetor. Carter was at times contracted to manufacture Rochester Quadrajet carburetors for General Motors and the Carter-built Quadrajets are almost identical to the Rochester-built ones. Carter-built Quadrajets are identified as being manufactured by Carter and may use Carter's system of date coding rather than Rochester's system.

Rochester-built Quadrajets contain an alphanumeric sequence stamped into a flat, vertical area of the main body on the rear of the driver side. Either the full seven-digit GM part number or the final five digits of the part number are stamped in. Several letters, which identify the specific plant where the carburetor was made, may be stamped here as well. And finally, four numbers denoting the date of manufacture are also stamped into this area.

Rochester utilized the Julian calendar for date coding its carburetors. With this system of dating the first three numbers represent the day of the year and

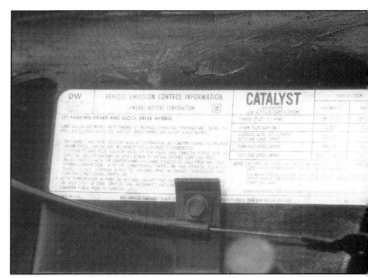

The emission control system information label glued to the top of the driver-side firewall in a 1978. Note the small clamp holding the hood release crossover cable in place.

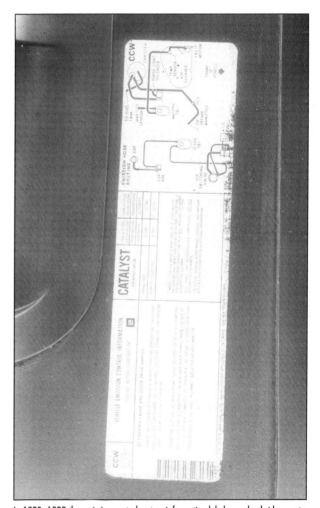

In 1980–1982 the emission control system information label was glued sideways to the underside of the hood on the driver side. This example is from 1982.

the final number is the last digit of the specific year. For example, the Julian date code for a carburetor made on January 1, 1978, would read "0018" The first three digits, "001," represent the first day of the year, and the final digit, "8," represents 1978.

One tricky element to figuring out the exact day a Julian calendar date corresponds to is remembering that leap years have an extra day.

With the possible exception of some later units, Carter-built Quadrajets generally don't use a Julian calendar date coding system. Instead, they use a single letter and a single number. The letter denotes the month, with "A" indicating January, "B" indicating February, and so on. The letter "I" is not used, so September is represented by "J."

The number in the date code for Carter-built Quadrajets is the last digit for the year of manufacture. For example, a date code of "D9" indicates the carburetor was made in April 1979.

All carburetors are plated gold dichromate. Plating tends to be rather dark and uniform in color. All carburetors have an insulator separating them from the intake manifold. (See Appendix J for carburetor numbers.)

In 1982 only, Corvettes use a Throttle Body Injection system instead of a carburetor. Each throttle body injection unit is stamped with a model number, but not a date code. The model number is stamped into a vertical area on the flange adjacent to a rear mounting bolt.

Air Cleaner

All 1978–1981 Corvettes are equipped with an air cleaner design that is closed to the engine compartment and receives fresh air from ducting and a plenum assembly on top of the fan shroud.

For 1978 base-engine cars, the housing has a single snorkel pointing toward the front of the car with a slight offset to the driver side. The snorkel is connected to a black molded plastic plenum on top of the fan shroud by means of a duct. The duct is made from black paper over coiled wire and has an accordion shape. It is retained at each end by means of a built-in clamp that snaps into position.

The snorkel has a vacuum motor that opens to permit the flow of warmed air from a metallic tube connected to the driver-side exhaust manifold. The

Details of the rear, driver side of a 1978 L48 engine. The half-black, half-silver component in the center is part of the optional cruise control. Note the routing of the vacuum hoses, the double throttle return spring, and the selective use of one clamp on the hoses toward the left that supply vacuum to the brake booster.

Some variation of this sticker is found on all 1973–1981 air cleaner housings. This example is on a 1980. The sticker utilized on early 1978s reads "KEEP YOUR GM CAR ALL GM." Later 1978s and subsequent cars use this sticker, which says "KEEP YOUR GM VEHICLE ALL GM."

vacuum motor is painted semi-gloss black and has the words "AUTO THERMAC" embossed on the top side.

The air cleaner housing in 1978 models equipped with an L-82 engine, and on all 1979–1981 cars, has two forward facing snorkels. Both snorkels are connected to a molded plenum that is similar to the plenum on base-engine cars, except that it has two connection points.

The air cleaner housing utilized in 1978–1981 is painted gloss black. The air cleaner lid in 1978–1980 is also painted gloss black, but in 1981 it is chrome plated. There are no decals on any of the lids, but there is a decal on the side of the housings. The sticker utilized on early 1978s reads "KEEP YOUR GM CAR ALL GM." Later 1978s and subsequent cars use a sticker that says "KEEP YOUR GM VEHICLE ALL GM."

In addition to the above admonition, the air cleaner sticker also contains logos for AC, GM, and Delco, various part numbers and codes, and the replacement filter number. The sticker is white with red and blue lettering.

Original 1978–1981 air filter elements, unlike later replacements, have a fine wire screen around the outside in a vertical (and not diagonal) pattern. The horizontal and vertical wire forms rectangles with the longer measurement running vertical when the element is installed.

All 1978–1981 Corvettes use an AC A348C air cleaner element. The element says "BEST WAY TO PROTECT YOUR ENGINE REPLACE WITH AC TYPE 348C" in white along the horizontal perimeter.

The 1982 Corvettes utilize a uniquely designed air cleaner assembly for the Cross-Fire Injection system. It mounts diagonally across both throttle body

When a vacuum motor in the air cleaner snorkel in this 1978 is open, this accordion-shaped metallic tube channels warm air from the driver-side exhaust manifold up into the incoming engine air. Note the top screw clamp at the top of the tube, the hose bracket attached to the alternator, and the black tape holding the alternator wires and two of the vacuum hoses together.

injection units. The top of the assembly has a black, wrinkle finish and a "Cross-Fire Injection" emblem. Metal knobs that are painted black retain the air cleaner assembly cover.

Inside the main air cleaner housing are two smaller air cleaners for the two throttle body injectors. These two smaller air cleaners have semi-gloss black painted covers, and use AC A824C paper filter elements.

The Cross-Fire Injection air cleaner housing has a thermostatic vacuum motor assembly in the intake snorkel. The snorkel is linked to the exhaust manifold

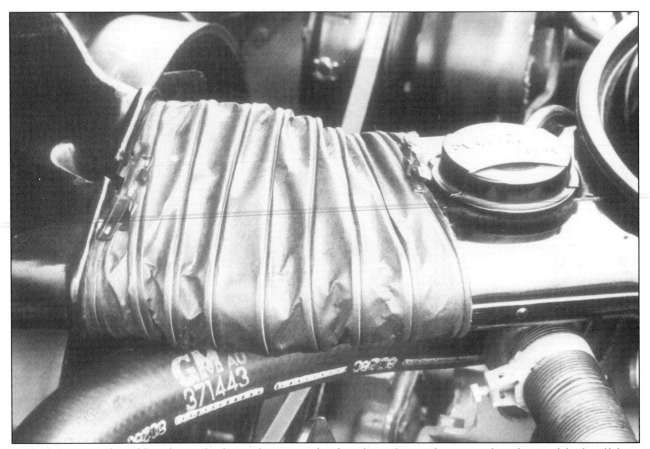

Note the GM logo, part number, and date code stamped on this original 1978 upper radiator hose. Also note the correct duct connecting the air cleaner snorkel to the molded plastic plenum above the fan shroud.

by a gloss-black metal heat riser tube. An unpainted aluminum PCV tube extends from a black rubber grommet in the passenger-side valve cover toward the PCV filter in the air cleaner housing. The tube connects to the filter with a short length of black rubber hose.

Valve Covers

All 1978–1980 base engines, as well as the 1980 California-only LG4 engines, are fitted with stamped steel valve covers painted engine color. These are held on with hex head bolts and metal tabs that are also painted engine color.

There are two metal wire retention clips spot welded to the passenger-side cover. This cover also has a crankcase vent intake hole. The hole gets a black rubber grommet. A tube inserts into the grommet and connects to the air cleaner base.

On base-engine cars there are two metal wire retention clips spot welded to the driver-side cover. This cover also has a PCV valve inserted into a hole fitted with a rubber grommet. A hose connects the PCV valve to the carburetor. The driver-side cover also has a provision for the oil filler cap.

The 1978–1980 optional L82 engines utilize cast-aluminum valve covers with longitudinal ribs. All 1981 and 1982 cars are equipped with the same design covers, but they are made from cast magnesium rather than aluminum.

As with the painted steel covers, a vent hose connects the passenger-side alloy valve cover to the air cleaner base and a PCV valve is in the driver-side valve cover. Alloy valve covers are retained by silver cadmium–plated, indented hex head bolts. These bolts frequently have an "M" in the head.

Both passenger- and driver-side alloy valve covers are made from the same mold. The only difference between the two is that the driver-side cover has a hole for the oil fill cap that the passenger-side cover does not have. On the passenger side, where the hole would go, there is a rigid disc with the crossed-flags emblem glued on.

The passenger-side cover has a hole fitted with a black rubber grommet. A long, black phosphate–plated steel tube inserts into the grommet and connects to the rear of the air cleaner housing.

Alloy valve covers used on 1978–1980 L-82

engines and all 1981 and 1982 engines have chrome-plated twist-in-style oil fill caps on the driver side. A large "S" for Stant, the manufacturer of the caps, is stamped into the center rivet.

Painted steel valve covers use a steel twist-on oil fill cap in the driver-side valve cover. In 1978 a large "S" for Stant is stamped into the domed center rivet of the cap. In 1979 and 1980 the design of the cap used in painted steel valve covers changes. Instead of a round, domed head, the center rivet is crushed in such a way that four distinct quadrants are formed. Also, this cap design has "ENGINE OIL FILL" and "AC FC 2" stamped in around the center rivet.

In 1982 only, the oil fill cap twists onto an extension tube that mounts into the driver-side valve covers. This is necessary in order to clear the Cross-Fire Injection air cleaner assembly.

All engine oil fill caps used in conjunction with steel valve covers are painted engine color.

This is the underhood duct that mates with the cross-fire injection air cleaner in 1982. It is part of the hood louver control system used that year.

This is the EGR valve in a 1978. "ON" is the broadcast code. Beneath the part number "ON17056495" is a date code.

All 1968–1982 Corvettes utilize a Delco Remy starter motor that contains a part number and date code stamped into the housing. This No. 1998241 motor is dated "2F21," which translates to June 21, 1982.

Exhaust Manifolds

All 1978–1980 exhaust manifolds, except those utilized on 1980 LG4 305 California engines, are cast-iron. Exhaust manifolds used on LG4 engines, as well as all 1981 and 1982 engines, are tubular stainless steel.

All cast-iron exhaust manifolds contain a casting number that is normally on the side facing away from the engine, and a casting date that is normally on the side facing toward the engine. (Refer to Appendix I for exhaust manifold casting numbers.)

Stainless-steel tubular exhaust manifolds used on 1980 LG4 and all 1980–1981 engines are stamped with a part number. Left-side manifolds are stamped "GM 14037671-W" and right-side manifolds are stamped "GM 14037672-W."

Exhaust manifolds were not yet installed when engines were originally painted, so they show no signs of overspray. This applies to both cast-iron and tubular stainless-steel manifolds.

Cast-iron exhaust manifolds use 9/16-inch hex head bolts in all positions except for the forward-most passenger-side spot. In that spot a stud with an integral nut is used. The integral nut tightens the stud and retains the manifold, while the protruding portion of the stud is used to fasten the air-conditioning compressor bracket.

Exhaust manifold bolts typically have two concentric rings on their heads. The front two bolts and rear two bolts on both sides of the engine get French locks with one of the two tabs bent over to prevent the bolts from loosening.

The heads on bolts for tubular stainless-steel exhaust manifolds have six lines that radiate out from a small circle in the center.

Exhaust manifolds do not use a gasket where they mount to the cylinder head.

Starter Motor

All 1978–1982 Corvettes use a Delco-Remy starter motor. Automatic transmission–equipped cars utilize starters with aluminum noses, while starters for manual transmission–equipped cars have a cast-iron nose.

Some motor housings and cast-iron noses are painted semi-gloss black, while others are unpainted. Aluminum noses are unpainted.

The starter's part number and assembly date are stamped into the side of the motor housing. The date code contains a number representing the last digit of the year, a letter denoting the month, with "A" representing January, "B" representing February, and so on. As is typical of stamped-in date codes, the letter "I" is skipped, so the month of September is represented by "J." One or two numbers indicating the day follow the letter denoting the month. For example, a date code of "2B10" indicates the starter was made February 10, 1982. (See Appendix N for starter motor part numbers)

Starter solenoids have a black or brown Bakelite cover for the electrical connections. Solenoid housings may be painted semi-gloss black or silver cadmium plated.

Starters use a stamped steel brace to support the forward end (the end facing toward the front of the car when the starter is installed). The brace mounts to a stud on the starter's end plate and to a threaded boss in the engine block. The brace is painted semi-gloss black.

Every starter has a heat shield to protect it from exhaust system heat. The shield is rectangular in shape, and is painted semi-gloss black. The shield attaches to the solenoid screws with barrel nuts.

A black phosphate–plated spring steel clip is snapped over the starter motor solenoid. This clip holds the wires going to the solenoid in place so they don't burn against the exhaust manifold.

Oil Filter

All 1978–1982 engines utilize an AC Delco PF-25 spin-on-type oil filter. Filters are painted dark blue with a dark blue sticker bearing the AC and GM logos. The sticker has a white border and white lettering, and contains the part number "6438261." Original stickers do not say "DURAGUARD" as do the stickers on current AC Delco PF-25 filters.

Alternator, Power Steering Pump, and Fuel Pump

All engines are fitted with a Delco-Remy alternator mounted on the driver side. Alternator housings are made from cast aluminum and are not painted or coated with anything.

In 1978 and 1979 the front half of the alternator housing has the unit's part number, amperage rating, and assembly date code stamped in. The date code contains a number for the year, and a letter for the month, with "A" representing January, "B" representing February, and so on. As is typical of stamped-in date codes, the letter "I" is skipped, so the month of September is represented by "J." The letter denoting the month is followed by one or two numbers for the day. For example, an alternator stamped "8F22" was assembled June 22, 1978.

Beginning in 1980 and continuing through 1982, a different design of alternator is used. With this new design the assembly date code is different. The first character is either a number or letter to represent the month. The numbers "1" through "9" represent January through September, the letter "O" represents October, the letter "N" represents November, and the letter "D" represents December. The first character is followed by two numerals that denote the day of the month. The final numeral is the last digit of the year. For example, a date code stamping of "5292" indicates the alternator was manufactured May 29, 1982.

An example of a 1979 alternator. The body is unpainted, cast aluminum. The "WP" stamped on the side in black ink is a broadcast code.

The alternator pulley is made from zinc-plated, stamped steel. Some earlier L82 engines have alternator pulleys machined from solid material.

The lower alternator bracket on all cars is cast metal that is painted semi-gloss black. The upper bracket is stamped steel painted semi-gloss black.

Most 1978–1982 alternators are ink stamped with a one- or two-letter code called a broadcast code. Commonly seen codes are "LP," "WP," and "RK." (See Appendix M for alternator codes.)

All 1978–1982 Corvettes are equipped with power steering. The system uses a semi-gloss black painted power steering pump with a neck that is the same diameter from top to bottom. All pumps have a semi-gloss black, stamped steel belt guard bolted to the body. A small white and blue sticker reading "NOTICE DO NOT PRY ON RESERVOIR" and the broadcast code "BX" is on the pump housing.

Power steering pump pulleys on all cars are machined from steel stock and feature a raised edge in the front to aid removal with a puller. All pulleys are painted semi-gloss black.

All pumps use a semi-gloss black painted, stamped steel support to mount to the engine.

All 1978-1981 Corvettes use an AC brand fuel pump. The pumps usually have "AC" cast into the top or side of the upper housing and a five-character part number stamped into the underside of the mounting flange. Pumps have a natural dull silver, cast-aluminum body with a gold irridite–plated lower cover.

In 1982 the mechanical, engine-mounted fuel pump is replaced with an electric unit mounted inside the fuel tank. The opening in the fuel pump mount area of the engine block is closed with a block-off plate. The block-off plate is held with hex head bolts and a stud that goes in the forward upper position. This stud retains a small clip that holds the fuel line.

The 1978-1981 Corvettes did not use an external fuel filter. They have a small filtration device inside the carburetor at the point where the fuel line enters. In 1982 an external fuel filter is used. It is spliced into the fuel line and is mounted inside the passenger-side frame rail in the area below the forward portion of the passenger-side door.

Water Pump, Engine Fan, and Fan Clutch

All 1978-1982 Corvettes use a cast-iron water pump with a boss on top. The boss is drilled and tapped. The tapped hole is closed with a square head plug. A daub of yellow paint is frequently seen on this plug.

The snout on all water pumps has reinforcing ribs that are part of the casting. Pumps usually have casting No. 330818 in the housing.

All water pump housings have a cast-in date code. The first character of the code is a letter denoting the month, with "A" representing January, "B" representing February, and so on. The second character is one or two numbers denoting the day. This is followed by a single number denoting the year.

Most water pump pulleys are painted semi-gloss black, though some originals have been observed with a black phosphate finish. On 1978 and 1979 cars equipped with an Air Injection Reactor pump, the water pump pulley that drives the pump has the number "3991425BX" stamped in. Cars not equipped with A.I.R. use a water pump pulley with the numbers "3991423BW" stamped in. In 1980, the water pump pulley that drives the A.I.R. pump is stamped with the number "188072DE." In 1981 and 1982 this same pulley is stamped with the number "14023158CW."

All 1978-1982 Corvettes use a thermostatically controlled, viscous coupled fan clutch. The clutch uses a metallic coil on the front face as a thermostat. The clutch body is aluminum while the shaft and mounting flange are steel. Most fan clutches are unpainted, though occasionally some are painted dull aluminum.

Original clutches usually have a date code stamped in the flange that goes against the water pump pulley. Clutches (as well as water pump pulleys) are retained by studs and nuts that thread into the pump's front hub. The mounting flange on the clutch has holes rather than slots for the studs to pass through.

All 1978–1982 Corvettes use a cooling fan that is painted gloss black and mounted to the fan clutch with hex head bolts.

The 1978 and 1979 cars equipped with a base engine but not equipped with air conditioning use a five-blade engine cooling fan that is 17.5 inches in diameter. The 1978 and 1979 cars equipped with a base engine and air conditioning, and 1980–1982 cars equipped with air conditioning, heavy-duty cooling, or the optional LG4 California 305-ci engine, use a seven-blade fan that is 18.5 inches in diameter. All 1978–1980 cars equipped with an L82 engine, as well as all 1981 and 1982 cars not equipped with air conditioning, use a five-blade fan that is 18.5 inches in diameter.

An electric engine cooling fan in addition to the regular cooling fan was fitted to 1979 and 1980 cars equipped with an L82 engine and air conditioning. It is mounted on the engine side of the radiator with semi-gloss black painted brackets that attach to the fan shroud. The electric fan motor is painted gloss black. The fan is made from black plastic.

Radiator, Hoses, and Related Parts

All 1978–1982 Corvettes use a copper radiator. Radiators were manufactured by Harrison, and have that name embossed in the passenger-side radiator tank. In addition, there is a stamped steel tag containing a two-letter broadcast code and a part number attached to the passenger side of the radiator. All radiators are painted semi-gloss to gloss black.

All cars use a black or dark gray plastic fan shroud. Shrouds in 1979 and 1980 cars equipped with air conditioning and an L82 engine have an opening at the bottom. This opening has a hinged door that opens when additional cooling is required. A sticker that reads "CAUTION FAN" is on the top of the shroud. Cars equipped with an auxiliary electric cooling fan have a second copy of the same sticker toward the bottom of the shroud as well.

All 1978–1982 cars use a white plastic coolant recovery tank. The tank is mounted underneath the passenger-side fender. It has a black plastic cap that has a blue, white, and black sticker on the top. The sticker says "NOTICE" in white letters and "ENGINE COOLANT ONLY" in black letters. All coolant recovery tanks are fitted with a black overflow hose. The hose is marked "3/8" and has various other numbers as well as letters written in yellow ink.

All 1978–1982 Corvettes use an RC-33 radiator cap rated at 15 psi installed directly on the radiator. RC-33 caps contain the AC logo in a circle. They also contain the words "DO NOT OPEN, CHECK LEVEL IN BOTTLE, CLOSED SYSTEM, ALIGN ARROW & VENT TUBE."

All radiator and heater hoses are molded black rubber. Stamped on the radiator hoses in white ink are a part number, GM logo, and several letters that are believed to be manufacturer's codes. In addition, there is usually a colored line running the length of the hose.

Heater hoses usually contain a GM logo in white ink. They sometimes have the letters "DL" or "U" stamped on them also. Most original hoses have three or four thin ridges running lengthwise.

All cars use stainless-steel worm-drive clamps for the radiator hoses. All applications use size 28 clamps. Most cars use SURE-TITE brand clamps, though at least one other supplier originally provided clamps to the factory. Original SURE-TITE clamps have "SURE-TITE" in italics stamped into the band

All 1978–1982 cars use a white plastic engine coolant recovery tank mounted underneath the passenger-side fender. This example is from a 1979.

along their circumference. In addition, "WITTEK MFG. CO. CHI. U.S.A." is stamped into the worm screw's housing. Radiator clamps do not have date codes stamped in as some heater hoses do.

Most cars use stainless-steel worm-drive clamps for the heater hoses. On occasion, however, tower-style clamps are used for heater hoses. Tower-style clamps are much more likely to be seen on earlier 1978–1982 cars than on later ones.

The 5/8-inch heater hoses use 1 1/16-inch clamps. This size clamp typically has a galvanized finish with the size, the words "WITTEK MFG. CO. CHICAGO U.S.A.," and a date code stamped into the band. The first number of the date code denotes the quarter and the following two numbers indicate the year.

The 3/4-inch heater hose uses 1 1/4-inch clamps. These clamps have a cadmium-dichromate finish that results in a translucent goldish tint, as opposed to the smaller clamps' dull silver color. The larger 1 1/4-inch clamps contain the manufacturer's logo and size designation, but do not have a date code. Instead, they have the letters "DCM" stamped into the band.

Brake Master Cylinder and Related Components

All master cylinders are manufactured by Delco and contain a casting number and the Delco split-ring logo on the inboard side.

In addition to the casting number, each master also contains a two-letter application code stamped in on a flat surface by the front brake line fitting. Master cylinders in early 1978 cars utilize the code "DM." Later 1978 and all 1979–1982 cars use the code "YC."

In addition to the two-letter application code, a Julian date code is also stamped in the flat, machined area adjacent to where the front brake line attaches. The date code typically contains a number indicating the year, followed by three numbers denoting the day of the year. For example, a stamping of "9214" represents the 214th day of 1979.

The entire master cylinder is semi-gloss black except for machined areas, which are natural. No 1978–1982 masters are fitted with bleeder screws.

For all master cylinders, two steel wire bails hold the cover on. A small vinyl sticker with two letters is folded around one of the bail wires. This sticker is white with the two-letter application code in red. Beginning in 1981 a second sticker is applied to the outboard side of the master cylinder. This sticker is white with black letters and a black bar code.

All master cylinders use a stamped steel, cadmium dichromate–plated cover and rubber gasket. The cover has two domes that are connected by a small ridge. "WARNING CLEAN FILLER CAP

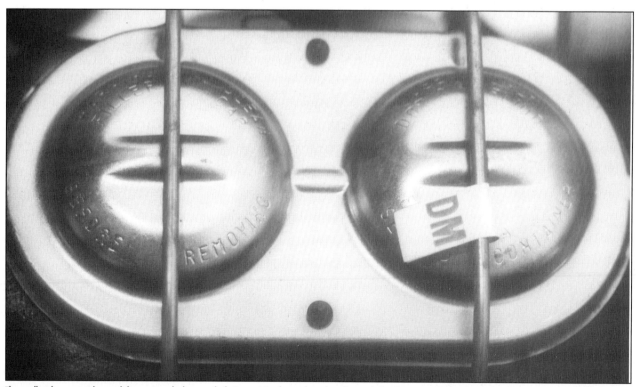

The small sticker wrapped around the master cylinder cover bail wire contains the two-letter broadcast code for the master. "DM" indicates that this is an early 1978 car. Later 1978s and all 1979–1982 cars use the code "YC."

Master cylinder and booster details from a 1978. A broadcast code sticker on the booster bears the two-letter broadcast code "YB" and the date of manufacturer. This unit was made on the 75th day of 1978.

BEFORE REMOVING" and "USE ONLY DOT 3 FLUID FROM A SEALED CONTAINER" are stamped into the cover.

All 1978–1982 Corvettes are equipped with power brakes. Power brake boosters are cadmium dichromate plated.

Power boosters have a broadcast code as well as a Julian date code stamped in on top. For 1978 Corvettes, the broadcast code is "YB." For 1979 and 1980 cars the code is "RL." For 1980–1982 cars the code is "NR."

The Julian date code stamped into the power booster contains a number corresponding to the final number of the year and then three numbers denoting the day of the year. For example, a booster stamped "1168" was manufactured on the 168th day of 1981.

Besides being stamped into the top of the power booster, the two-letter broadcast code and Julian date code are also found on a white sticker affixed to the front of the unit.

Air Conditioning and Heating System Components

All 1978–1982 Corvettes use a Delco Air–type R-4 radial-style air-conditioning compressor. It is painted semi-gloss black and has a yellow, black, and silver foil sticker on the top of the housing. The sticker contains, among other things, the compressor's model number and a date code. The date code contains two numbers for the month, two numbers for the day, one number for the year, and one number for the shift. For example, a date code of "031922" translates to March 19, 1982, second shift.

The 1978 and 1979 Corvettes use a model No. 1131078 air-conditioning compressor. The 1980–1982 Corvettes use a model No. 1131198 compressor.

An unpainted, dark gray fiberglass housing covers the evaporator. There is a blue and silver Harrison foil sticker, as well as a fan relay on the housing. The relay cover is zinc or cadmium plated and does not have any words stamped in it.

Most Corvettes with air conditioning have a vacuum actuated valve spliced into the heater hose. When the air conditioning is on, this valve shuts off the flow of engine coolant to the heater core.

The blower motors for both air-conditioned and non-air-conditioned cars are painted semi-gloss to gloss black. Motors on air-conditioned cars have a rubber tube that extends from the motor housing to the evaporator housing. Motors on non-air-conditioned cars do not have this tube. Motors have a part number and date

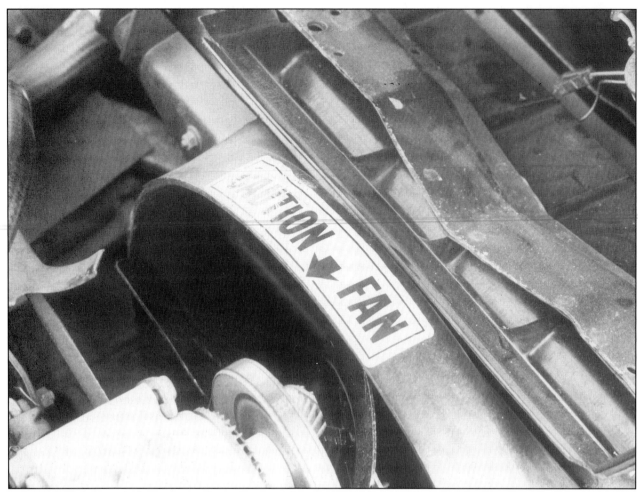

Those 1979s and 1980s equipped with an L82 engine and air conditioning, and all 1981–1982s have this bright yellow "CAUTION FAN" sticker glued to the top of the fan shroud. The same sticker is also glued to the bottom of the shroud.

This is the sticker on a 1982 R-4 radial-style air-conditioning compressor. The code number "080222" is the manufacturing date. It translates to August 2, 1982, second shift.

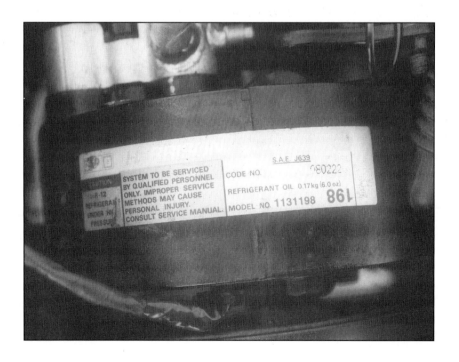

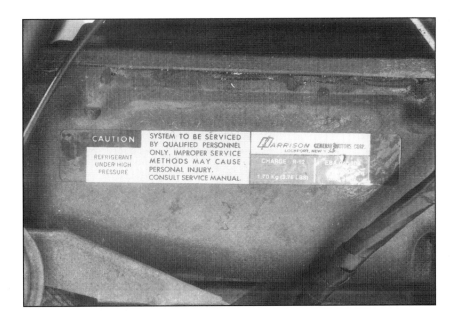

This foil sticker is on the air-conditioning evaporator housing in 1982.

code stamped into their mounting flange. The date code contains one or two numbers to denote the month and two numbers to indicate the year.

Windshield Wiper Motor and Related Components

The wiper motor for all 1978–1982 Corvettes uses an unpainted cast-aluminum housing and transmission case. A black plastic cover goes over the wiper motor transmission assembly. A silver-colored foil sticker containing the motor's part number and date of manufacture is on the motor housing.

In early 1978, the wiper motor is part No. 5044814. Later 1978 and all 1979–1982 cars use a wiper motor that is part No. 5044907.

Date codes for wiper motors use the Julian calendar. One, two, or three numbers indicate the day of the year. This is followed by a single number denoting the year.

The windshield washer pump utilized in 1978–1982 is mounted at the base of the fluid reservoir. The motor for the pump is contained in a silver cadmium–plated metal housing, and the pump has a white plastic covering.

The windshield washer fluid reservoir is mounted toward the rear of the driver's inner wheelwell. The reservoir is rigid white plastic and does not have fluid level marks on it. The tank does, however, have "5045644 ASM" and "4961311" in its side in 1978–1981. In 1982, these numbers changed to "14047109 ASM" and "22020937."

In all years, a long fill neck inserts in the reservoir and extends up slightly below the fender lip. The name "DONLEE" and the part number "344810" appear on the long fill neck.

Air Injection Reactor System and Other Emissions Components

In 1978 and 1979, an Air Injection Reactor (A.I.R.) system is included with all cars equipped with an L82, option NB2 (California emissions), or option NA6 (high-altitude emissions). All 1980–1982 Corvettes are equipped with an A.I.R. system.

The A.I.R. system includes two tube assemblies that thread into the exhaust manifolds. In 1978–1980, the system is connected to the driver-side manifold with four tubes (one to each manifold runner) and to the passenger-side manifold with two tubes (one to the front runner and one to the rear runner).

In 1978 and early 1979 the A.I.R. tube assemblies are black cadmium plated. The tubes in later 1979 and all 1980–1982 cars are cadmium dichromate plated.

The A.I.R. pump body is diecast aluminum and natural in color. A semi-gloss black painted, rough-textured, sand cast plate covers the back of the pump. In 1978–1980, this plate bears casting No. 7817872. In 1981 and 1982 it bears casting No. 7836920.

All pumps contain a centrifugal filter behind the pulley. This filter, which looks more like a fan, is made from black plastic.

The 1978 and 1979 Corvettes use a steel spacer between the front pump pulley and centrifugal filter. The spacer is zinc or silver cadmium plated. In 1980–1982, the spacer is unplated aluminum.

For all years, the front pump pulley is gray phosphate plated or painted semi-gloss black. Pulleys are not stamped with a part number.

Most pumps are date coded, though the date can be difficult to see with the pump installed. It is stamped into a boss on the rear underside of the

Passenger-side view of a 1979 Air Injection Reactor pump. Note the tower-style hose clamps and dark-colored centrifugal filter in back of the pulley.

body. The sequence may begin with a letter to indicate the assembly plant or specific line. Then there are one or three numbers to indicate the day of the year on the Julian calendar. Earlier dates (prior to the 100th day) may start with two zeros or they may not. For example, a pump assembled on the fifth day of the year may be stamped "005" or simply "5." A fourth (or second) number follows to denote the last digit of the year. This is followed by a number indicating the shift, and a letter indicating the model of the pump.

In 1978, most diverter valve bodies are metal, but later in the year they are molded plastic. The diaphragm cover and check valves are cadmium dichromate. The diverter valve muffler is plated gray phosphate. The diverter valve part number is stamped into the valve below the muffler. Check valves have a part number stamped into their center ridge.

Hoses connecting the various parts of the A.I.R. system are molded black rubber and most hose clamps are tower style. Clamps have a galvanized finish and have their size, the words "WITTEK MFG.

CO. CHICAGO U.S.A.," and a date code stamped into the band. The first number of the date code denotes the quarter and the following two numbers indicate the year.

All 1978–1982 Corvettes are fitted with an Evaporative Control System. This system includes a black carbon-filled canister mounted to the front lower-left-side inner wheelwell.

All 1978–1982 Corvettes have a Positive Crankcase Ventilation (PCV) valve located in the left-side valve cover. The PCV valve has a part number stamped into it. In 1978–1980 Corvettes equipped with an L48 or LG4 engine, and all 1981 cars, the valve is No. CV774C. In those 1978–1980 Corvettes equipped with an L82 engine, the valve is No. CV775C. In all 1982 cars the valve is No. CV853C.

Many but not all 1978–1982 Corvettes have a Transmission Controlled Spark (TCS) system. This system includes a thermal vacuum switch that is mounted on the side of the thermostat housing.

The 1978–1982 Corvettes are equipped with an Early Fuel Evaporation (EFE) system. With this

Passenger-side view of a 1982 Air Injection Reactor pump.

Driver-side view of a 1982 Air Injection Reactor pump.

system, a vacuum-actuated valve is mounted to the passenger-side exhaust manifold. The valve is controlled by a thermal vacuum switch mounted in the thermostat housing.

All 1978–1980 Corvettes equipped with air conditioning and an automatic transmission have an anti-diesel idle solenoid that is mounted with a bracket to the carburetor base. The bracket is cadmium dichromate plated and the solenoid housing is silver cadmium plated.

All 1978–1982 Corvettes are fitted with an Exhaust Gas Recirculation (EGR) system. The heart of the system is an EGR valve mounted on the passenger side of the intake manifold. The EGR valve is manufactured by Rochester Products Division and that company's logo is stamped into the valve's housing.

The EGR valve housing is cadmium dichromate plated, and the lower portion of the valve is unpainted and unplated cast-iron. A part number, date code, and broadcast code are stamped into the valve housing. The date code typically consists of five numbers. The first three represent the day of the year, the fourth is the last digit of the year, and the fifth is the shift during which that valve was made. For example, a date code of "15192" indicates the valve was made the 151st day of 1979, during the second shift.

Beginning with 1980 Corvettes equipped with an LG4 engine, and continuing in all 1981 and 1982 cars, something called a Computer Command Control (CCC) system is installed. An electronic control module (ECM) mounted in the battery compartment behind the driver's seat controls the functions of this system. The ECM is fed data from various devices located in different parts of the car. These devices include a Manifold Absolute Pressure (MAP) sensor, oxygen sensor, Vehicle Speed Sensor (VSS), Throttle Position Sensor (TPS), and Electronic Spark Timing (EST) sensor.

All 1978–1982 Corvettes have what is commonly called an emissions label glued to the left upper area of the firewall. This label is either white or yellow in color, and contains engine tune-up specifications as well as information about the emission control systems installed in the car.

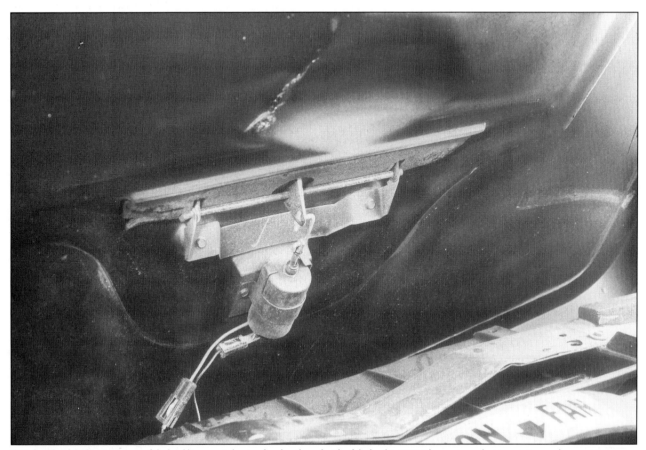

This solenoid and mechanism are part of the hood louver control system found on the underside of the hood in 1982. When engine coolant temperature reaches a certain point and the throttle is sufficiently advanced, the louver opens up to allow additional outside air to enter the air cleaner assembly.

Engine Compartment, Wiring, Horns, and Related Components

The firewall, underside of the hood, and engine compartment side of the inner wheelwells are painted semi-gloss black. The wheel side of the front and rear inner wheelwells are also painted semi-gloss black, though coverage is usually sparse. In addition, the rear areas of the wheelwells normally have some undercoating.

In all cars, wire harnesses and adjacent hoses are bundled together in a row, so rather than forming a circle they are flat. The harnesses and hoses are held to each other with black plastic tie wraps.

All vacuum hose is color coded with an ink stripe that runs the length of the hose. Larger hoses have a green, red, or yellow stripe, while smaller hoses usually have a white stripe.

In 1978 and 1979, the underside of the hood is fitted with a fiberglass insulation mat. It is held on with six metal spring clips. No insulation is used under the hood for 1980–1982 cars.

In 1982 only, the underside of the hood is fitted with a Hood Louver Control system. This system allows additional fresh air to enter the engine's induction system when engine coolant is hot and the throttle is at or near its fully open position.

The 1978–1982 Corvettes are fitted with an electric oil pressure gauge. A gold irridite–plated metal sending unit is threaded into the engine block above the oil filter.

Dual horns are standard for all years. They are mounted behind the front grille area. From 1978 through mid-1981 horns are mounted inboard of the headlight assemblies. In late 1981 and all of 1982, they are mounted farther apart on the outboard sides of the headlights.

Horns have the last three digits of the part number and a manufacturing date code stamped into flat areas near the sound opening. In 1978 and 1979, the low note horn is No. 9000144 and the high note horn is No. 9000143. In 1980 and early 1981, the low note horn is the same but the high note horn is changed to No. 9000192. In late 1981 and all of 1982, the low note horn is No. 9000176 and the high note horn is No. 9000203.

The date code in each horn contains a number denoting the year, a letter denoting the month (with "A" representing January, "B" representing February, and so on), and another number indicating the week. For example, a horn stamped "0F2" was made the second week of June 1980.

Each horn is spot welded to a mounting bracket and the whole assembly is painted semi-gloss black.

Hood hinges are silver cadmium–plated and usually have both body color and underhood black overspray on them. Hinges are usually fastened by black phosphate–plated, indented hex head bolts.

The hood support is silver cadmium–plated. It has two sections that are hinged and they fold as the hood is lowered.

The hood latches are black phosphate plated and mount with black phosphate–plated hardware. The driver-side male latch has the hood release cable attached with a brass barrel cable stop that utilizes a hex bolt to lock the stop to the cable. The cable is inside a smooth, black plastic sheath.

Another cable connects the two female latches mounted to the underside of the hood. This cable is inside a black nylon sheath and its ends are secured to the latches with small clevis pins fitted with flat washers and cotter pins. The cable is secured to the distributor ignition shield with two clips.

1978–1982 Chassis

Chassis

Corvette chassis built between 1978 and 1982 are painted semi-gloss black. Chassis for automatic transmission–equipped cars have a removable, bolt-on center cross-member while cars equipped with a standard transmission have a welded-on center cross-member. Also, cars with automatics do not have a clutch cross shaft tower welded on top of the chassis, behind the left front wheel, as do standard transmission cars.

In 1978 and 1979, the chassis cross-member that supports the rear differential is made from steel that is painted semi-gloss black. In 1980–1982, this cross-member is made from unpainted aluminum.

A pair of 1-inch-high chassis part number sequences is painted in white or yellow on the chassis with a stencil. One sequence is the A.O. Smith part number (this is the company that fabricated the chassis for GM), and the other sequence is the Chevrolet part number. These part numbers are usually found on the passenger side of the chassis behind the front wheel.

A manufacturing date code is stenciled on the rail as well. The date contains one or two numbers representing the month, one or two numbers indicating the day, and two numbers denoting the year.

Most 1978–1982 Corvettes have their serial number stamped into their chassis in two locations. It is typically found in the left-side rail slightly forward of the No. 4 body mount bracket. It is also typically found on the left-side rear kick up above the wheel area slightly forward of the No. 3 body mount bracket.

Steel shims are frequently utilized at body mount points to make up for irregularities in fit. If present, shims are usually taped to the body mount bracket with 1 1/2-inch-wide masking tape. The number of shims needed at each body mount bracket is typically written on the chassis adjacent to the bracket with a green, yellow, or white grease crayon. The 1978–1982 body mount cushions are made from molded black rubber.

Front Suspension

Upper and lower front control arms are painted semi-gloss to gloss black. Ball joints are installed after the arms are painted and are therefore not painted. Crushed steel rivets (not bolts) hold ball joints on and are also natural in finish. On some control arms, the area surrounding the ball joint is unpainted. This is more prevalent on later cars.

Control arm cross shafts are painted semi-gloss black on some cars and unpainted on others. Cars with painted cross shafts typically have control arm bushing retention washers and bolts that are also painted semi-gloss black. Cars with unpainted cross shafts typically have retention washers that are gray phosphate plated and bolts that are black phosphate plated.

Front coil springs are natural in finish and sometimes have an irregular bluish cast from the manufacturing process. A green paper sticker contains two black letters indicating the spring's broadcast code (i.e., their application) as well as a black GM part number.

Front shock absorbers are manufactured by Delco. They are painted semi-gloss black and have the words "DELCO REMY PLIACELL" and a date code stamped in around the bottom. The Julian date code contains three numbers indicating the day and two numbers denoting the year. In addition, there is a small paper sticker with a two-letter broadcast code on the side of the shock.

The upper shock mount rubber bushings are unpainted black rubber. The top upper bushing is larger in diameter than the bottom upper bushing and the upper shock washer is gray phosphate plated or raw steel.

The lower shock mount rubber bushings are integral to the shock and are therefore painted along with the shock.

All 1978–1982 Corvettes utilize a front stabilizer bar. Cars with standard suspension use a .875-inch bar while cars with optional FE7 suspension utilize a 1.12-inch bar. Some cars have a semi-gloss black painted stabilizer bar while others have a natural, unpainted bar.

Front stabilizer bar chassis mount bushings—as well as bushings in the end links—are unpainted black rubber. Stamped steel brackets painted semi-gloss black secure the bar to the chassis.

End link bolts are zinc-plated 5/16-24 SAE fine thread and usually have the manufacturer's logo, "UB" or "WB," on their heads. End link spacers are zinc plated, have a split seam, and typically have a "K" or a "C" stamped in.

Steering Box and Steering Linkage

The 1978–1982 Corvettes use a cast steering gear case that is either natural in color or painted semi-gloss black. The box cover is cast aluminum, and it is retained by three black oxide–plated hex head bolts. The letters "WZ" are usually stamped on the box in yellow ink. A five-character date code is cast into the side of the box next to the manufacturer's logo. The first three digits represent the day of the year and the last two digits represent the year. For example, a date code of "19381" indicates the box was cast on the 193rd day of 1981.

A forged pitman arm links the steering box to the relay rod. The pitman arm is natural in color and is often seen with a blue or green daub of paint.

The steering relay rod and idler arm are typically natural finish. Both parts are forged and tend to have a bluish-gray tint. Original idler arms do not have grease fittings.

Tie rod ends are natural finish and also typically have a bluish-gray color cast. Daubs of yellow paint are often seen on tie rod ends.

Tie rod end sleeves are painted semi-gloss black. Tie rod end clamps have two reinforcing ridges around their circumference and are sometimes painted semi-gloss black and sometimes left unpainted.

The power steering control valve and hydraulic cylinder are painted semi-gloss black. The nut and washers retaining the hydraulic cylinder's ram to the frame bracket are zinc plated. The frame bracket may be painted semi-gloss black or unpainted. Original power steering hoses typically have longitudinal ridges around their entire circumference, while later replacements do not.

Rear Suspension

All 1978–1980 Corvettes, plus all 1981 cars with four-speed manual transmission that are equipped with standard suspension, utilize a nine-leaf steel rear spring. In 1978 and 1979, there are no retaining bands on the rear spring. Beginning in 1980, a retaining band is used around the lower six leaves of the spring. The standard nine-leaf steel springs used in all 1978–1980 cars, and all 1981 cars equipped with a four-speed, are painted light gray and have black plastic liners between the leaves. Since the liners were installed when the springs were painted, they too are painted light gray.

The 1981 Corvettes equipped with automatic transmission and standard suspension, and all 1982 cars equipped with standard suspension, utilize a monoleaf fiberglass rear spring. This fiberglass spring is dark gray in color.

The 1978 and 1979 cars equipped with optional FE7 suspension utilize a six-leaf steel spring pack. The 1980–1982 Corvettes equipped with FE7 suspension use a nine-leaf steel spring pack. Both configurations of the FE7 rear spring are painted light gray. Unlike the standard steel spring, however, the black plastic liners used in the FE7 spring are not painted.

The center rear spring mount bracket is painted semi-gloss black. The four bolts retaining the spring to the differential typically have the manufacturer's logo, "WB," on their heads and are either black phosphate or zinc plated. The outer spring bolts and nuts are usually black phosphate plated and the washers are typically natural.

The six-leaf FE7 rear spring used in 1978 and 1979 is 2 1/4 inches wide while the standard suspension rear spring is 2 1/2 inches wide. To compensate for the decreased width, FE7 springs mount to the bottom of the differential cover with two spacers, one in front and the other in back.

Rear trailing arms are painted semi-gloss to gloss black. Rear wheel bearing carriers (also called spindle supports) are painted semi-gloss black and have a part number and date code cast in. The date code has a letter representing the month, with "A" for January, "B" for February, and so on, one or two numbers for the day, and one number for the final digit of the year. The date code for a rear bearing carrier made on April 18, 1980, for example, would read "D 18 0."

All 1978–1982 cars equipped with FE7 suspension have a rear stabilizer bar. The bar is 9/16 inch in diameter and may be painted semi-gloss black or unpainted. It mounts to the chassis with stamped steel brackets painted semi-gloss black. Each end of the bar has a semi-gloss black painted link bracket that attaches to a bracket bolted to the trailing arm. The brackets on the trailing arms have a plating that is sometimes called "pickling." This type of plating results in a brownish-olive color. These brackets attach to the trailing arm via bolts that thread into small, unpainted steel plates that slip into the rear of the arms.

Rear camber adjustment rods (also called strut rods) are usually natural and often have a bluish-gray tint. Some rods are painted semi-gloss black or are partially painted during the undercarriage blackout process. All 1978–1982 cars have rods with 1 3/4-inch outside diameter ends.

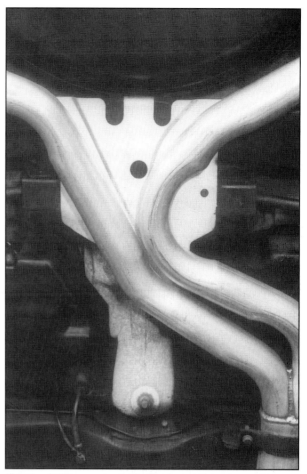

All 1981 and 1982 cars equipped with a fiberglass rear leaf spring use a heat shield between the spring and exhaust pipes.

The outboard ends of the camber adjustment rods are held to the rear wheel bearing carriers with forged L-shaped pins that also serve as the lower mounts for the rear shock absorbers. These pins, which are sometimes referred to as rear shock brackets, contain a raised part number.

The inboard ends of the camber adjustment rods attach to a semi-gloss black painted bracket with special bolts. These bolts have integral off-center washers that, when rotated, move the rods in or out and thus allow for rear wheel camber adjustment. The camber adjustment bolts are usually silver cadmium plated though they may be black phosphate plated instead.

Rear wheel toe adjustment is set with the use of shims placed on either side of the trailing arms where they mount to the chassis. The adjusting shims are unpainted rectangular pieces of steel of varying thicknesses. The shims have a slot in one end that slips over the trailing arm mount bolt. The other ends of all the shims are rotated upward so their holes all align with a corresponding hole in the chassis. A long cotter pin passes through the stacks of shims on both sides of the trailing arm and through the hole in the chassis.

Rear axle shafts (often called "half shafts") are made from forged ends welded to extruded steel tubes. The axle shafts are natural, with the tube a shiny silver and the ends a dull gray.

U-joints do not have grease fittings and do have a raised part number on the body. They are natural and tend to have that faint bluish tint that is characteristic of forged parts.

The outboard axle shaft U-joints are pressed into a flange that is natural in color. The flange is held to the rear wheel bearing carrier by four bolts that are usually black phosphate plated. The bolts are prevented from loosening by two pairs of French locks, the tabs of which are bent over to contact the bolt heads. The French locks are zinc plated and typically have only one of the two tabs adjacent to each bolt bent over.

Front Wheel Assemblies

Front spindles and steering knuckles are natural and tend to have a bluish tint to their gray color. In addition, the lower portions of the spindles are frequently seen with orange or white paint as though the bottoms of the spindles were dipped into it.

Original front brake backing plates are zinc plated and then chromate dipped. This results in varying finishes ranging from gold with a faint rainbow of other colors throughout to a dull silver with only a trace of the yellowish chromate coloring. Well-preserved original backing plates typically appear dull silver, probably because the chromate dip deteriorates over time.

Front brake caliper support brackets are plated silver cadmium or cadmium dichromate, which results in a translucent gold color with varying degrees of other colors present in a rainbow-like pattern.

Front brake calipers are painted semi-gloss black and frequently have blue or white daubs of paint on the side. Painting is done before the caliper halves are machined and therefore machined surfaces are unpainted. Bleeder screws are zinc plated and remain unpainted.

Caliper hoses are black rubber with gold irridite–plated end hardware. Federally mandated DOT specifications are written on the hose in red ink. In addition, there is a red longitudinal stripe put on the hoses to make it easier to see if they are twisted. Original hoses typically have raised longitudinal ridges around their entire circumference while later replacements are typically smooth.

Front brake rotors are natural in finish. The front wheel bearing carrier (also called a hub) is riveted to the rotor disc.

Rear Wheel Assemblies

As with the fronts, original rear brake backing plates are zinc plated and then chromate dipped. This results in varying finishes ranging from gold with a faint rainbow of other colors throughout to a dull silver with only a trace of the yellowish chromate coloring. Well-preserved original backing plates typically appear dull silver, probably because the chromate dip deteriorates over time.

Rear brake caliper support brackets are natural, and hence a dull gray, or on occasion they are painted flat to semi-flat black.

Rear brake calipers are painted semi-gloss black and frequently have blue or white daubs of paint on the side. Painting is done before the caliper halves are machined and therefore machined surfaces are unpainted. Bleeder screws are zinc plated and remain unpainted.

Rear brake rotors are natural in finish. They are riveted to the rear spindle, which is pressed into the rear wheel bearing carrier. In order to service the park brake assembly or the rear wheel bearings, the rivets are drilled out. The wheel lug nuts retain the rotor in the absence of the rivets.

Transmission

Those 1978–1981 Corvettes equipped with an automatic transmission utilize a Turbo-Hydra-Matic 350. All 1982 cars equipped with an automatic use a Turbo-Hydra-Matic 700-R4. For both transmissions, the main case and the tail housing are cast aluminum with a natural finish.

The identification code for a Turbo 350 transmission is stamped in a vertical surface on the passenger side. This code has six characters. The first is a letter that denotes the manufacturing plant. The second is a number representing the year. The third is a letter denoting the month. The third and fourth are numbers representing the day of the month. The final letter is either a "D" for day shift or "N" for night shift.

The letters designating the month of manufacture are as follows: A is January, B is February, C is March, D is April, E is May, H is June, K is July, M is August, P is September, R is October, S is November, and T is December.

In addition to the above described production code, each Turbo 350 transmission also contains the final eight digits of the serial number of the car in which it was originally installed. This sequence is stamped into the case on the driver-side flange adjacent to the oil pan.

The Turbo-Hydra-Matic 700-R4 used in 1982 is a four-speed overdrive automatic. It contains a transmission code stamping on the passenger-side oil pan rail. The code begins with the number "9" to indicate the 1982 model year. This is followed by the letters "YA," which represent the application code. Next come three numbers that denote the day of the year the transmission was built. The final character is either a "D" or an "N" to indicate either the day or night shift.

Four-speed manual transmissions used in all 1978–1981 Corvettes are Borg-Warner Super T-10 units. With these Borg-Warner four-speeds, the car's serial number derivative, as well as the production code and assembly date, are stamped into the main case on the driver-side flange adjacent to where the tail housing attaches.

In the production code, the first letter is "W" to indicate Borg-Warner. The next letter indicates the month of production, with "A" representing January, "B" representing February, and so on to "L" representing December. The month code is followed by one or two numbers denoting the day. Next comes a single number to indicate the year. And finally, the last number indicates whether the transmission is a close- or wide-ratio unit.

For example, a code of "WG2791" translates to a Borg-Warner four-speed, built on July 27, 1979. The final "1" indicates that it is a wide-ratio unit.

Differential and Driveshaft

All 1978–1982 Corvettes are equipped with a Positraction limited-slip differential. In 1978 and 1979, the differential case and cover are both natural-colored steel castings and as such are a dull silvery gray. In 1980–1982, the differential case and cover are both natural-colored aluminum castings.

A plastic triangular tag is attached to the differential by means of the oil fill plug. The tag is red with white lettering that says "USE LIMITED SLIP DIFF. LUBRICANT ONLY" or "LIMITED SLIP LUBE ONLY."

The front input yoke and side output yokes are forgings that are natural in color. Because they are forged they have a somewhat smoother surface than the case and cover, and they tend to have a slight bluish tint to their dull gray color.

Differential cases and covers both have casting numbers and a casting date that includes a letter for the month (with "A" representing January, "B" representing February, and so on), one or two numbers

indicating the day of the month, and one number indicating the last digit of the year.

In addition to the casting date, all cases also have a stamped-in production code. The production code is on the bottom rear edge of the case adjacent to where it meets the cover. The differential production code typically begins with two letters to indicate the gear ratio. This is usually followed by a single letter denoting the assembly plant. Then come one, two, or three numbers representing the day of the year the unit was assembled. After this there is a single letter that indicates the source for the Positraction unit (which was not necessarily the same company that assembled the differential). The final number in the sequence represents the assembly shift that built the unit.

(See Appendix E for differential gear ratio and production source codes.)

The transmission and differential are connected by a drive shaft made from extruded steel tubing welded at each end to a forged universal joint coupling. As with the axle shafts, the drive shaft is natural in color. The center tube portion is bright silver with longitudinal extrusion lines sometimes visible, and the ends are a dull silvery-gray with a slight bluish hue at times.

A part number stenciled on the drive shaft tube in yellow or white paint is sometimes seen. One or two green circumferential stripes on the tube and daubs of various colors of paint on the forged ends are sometimes seen as well.

Exhaust System

All 1978–1982 Corvettes use an undercar carbon steel exhaust system manufactured by Walker for Chevrolet. In 1978, cars equipped with an L48 engine use 2-inch pipes throughout the system. The 1978s equipped with an L82 and all 1979–1982 cars use 2-inch pipes from the manifolds to a junction where they join, and then 2 1/2-inch pipes for the remainder of the system.

All 1978–1982 Corvettes are equipped with a catalytic converter in the exhaust system. The housing of the converter is made from galvanized steel. A pressed-in, round steel plug closes the hole in the underside of the converter that allows it to be filled with the catalyst material. A galvanized steel heat shield is fitted between the converter and the floor. All 1978–1981 converters look the same. The 1982 converters are somewhat longer and narrower than their predecessors. In 1981 and 1982, a pipe from the A.I.R. system is connected to the converter.

Mufflers are galvanized on the exterior and typically have an embossed "W" to represent the manufacturer. In addition, an embossed part number and date code are usually found on each muffler. The date code includes a number for the month and two numbers for the year.

Muffler part numbers for 1978 Corvettes equipped with an L48 engine are 458963 for the driver side and 458964 for the passenger side. Muffler part numbers for 1979 Corvettes equipped with an L48 engine are 476875 for the driver side and 476876 for the passenger side.

For 1978 and 1979 cars with an L82 engine the mufflers are No. 473035 for the driver side and No. 473036 for the passenger side. For 1980 Corvettes, the driver-side muffler is No. 14011289 and the passenger-side muffler is No. 14011290. For 1981 Corvettes the driver-side muffler is No. 14033965 and the passenger-side muffler is No. 14033965. Later 1981 and all 1982 cars use muffler No. 14033701 on the driver side and muffler No. 14033702 on the passenger side.

Fuel Lines, Brake Lines, and Miscellaneous Chassis and Underbody Components.

All 1978–1982 fuel lines run along, and at times through, the right-side chassis rail. All cars have two fuel lines. One supplies fuel from the tank to the carburetor and the other is a return line.

In addition to the two fuel lines on the right side of the chassis, all cars have a vapor return line on the left side of the chassis. This line is part of the Evaporative Emission Control system.

Fuel lines are galvanized carbon steel. Black rubber fuel hose connects the lines to the tank and the fuel pump. Zinc chromate–plated spring clamps are usually used to secure the hose to its line.

Brake lines are galvanized carbon steel. Brake line end fittings are brass. Fittings at the master cylinder are often seen with red or blue dye, which was probably used to denote the two different size fittings. In addition, daubs of yellow paint are sometimes seen on the fittings at junction blocks.

Various heat shields are affixed to the underside of the body to help insulate the passenger compartment from engine and exhaust system heat. A sheet-steel shield, which is gray phosphate plated, is mounted on the lower vertical area of the firewall on both sides.

All cars are fitted with transmission tunnel insulation. A semi-rigid, foil-wrapped blanket in the shape of the tunnel is fastened above the transmission with clips riveted to the underbody.

A variety of steel plates are fastened to the underbody to mount components in the passenger compartment. These components include the battery, seats, jack hold down clips, and so on. All of these plates are painted semi-gloss black and are retained by unpainted aluminum rivets.

Appendices

Appendix A
Production Totals and Vehicle Identification Numbers

Production Totals

Year	Coupes	Convertibles	Total
1968	9,936	18,630	28,566
1969	22,129	16,633	38,762
1970	10,668	6,648	17,316
1971	14,680	7,121	21,801
1972	20,496	6,508	27,004
1973	25,521	4,943	30,464
1974	32,028	5,474	37,502
1975	33,836	4,629	38,465
1976	46,567		
1977	49,213		
1978	Regular Production: 40,274		
1978	Indy Pace Car Replicas: 6,502		
1979	53,807		
1980	40,614		
1981	40,606		
1982	Regular Production: 18,648		
1982	Collector Editions: 6,759		

Vehicle Identification Numbers

1968	194378S400001–194378S428566
1969	194379S700001–194379S738762
1970	194370S400001–194370S417316
1971	194371S100001–194371S121801
1972	1Z37K2S500001–1Z37K2S527004
1973	1Z37J3S400001–1Z37J3S434464
1974	1Z37J4S400001–1Z37J4S437502
1975	1Z37J5S400001–1Z37J5S438465

(Vehicle Identification Numbers cont.)

1976	1Z37L6S400001–1Z37L6S446558
1977	1Z37L7S400001–1Z37L7S449213
1978	1Z87L8S400001–1Z87L8S440274
1978	1Z87L8S900001–1Z87L8S906502 (Indy Pace Cars)
1979	1Z8789S400001–1Z8789S453807
1980	1Z878AS400001–1Z878AS440614
1981	1G1AY8764BS400001– 1G1AY8764BS431611 (St. Louis, Missouri, Corvette Assembly Plant)
1981	1G1AY8764B5100001– 1G1AY8764B5108995 (Bowling Green, Kentucky, Corvette Assembly Plant)
1982	1G1AY8786C5100001– 1G1AY8786C5125407

In 1968–1971 the fourth character is a "6" for convertibles.

In 1972–1975 the third character is a "6" for convertibles.

In 1970–1980 the fifth character indicates what engine was originally installed into the car:

1972	"K" indicates base engine, "L" indicates LT-1, and "W" indicates 454.
1973– 1974	"J" indicates base engine, "T" indicates L82, and "Z" indicates 454.
1975	"J" indicates base engine and "T" indicates L82.
1976– 1977	"L" indicates base engine and "X" indicates L82.
1978	"L" indicates base engine and "4" indicates L82.
1979	"8" indicates base engine and "4" indicates L82.
1980	"8" indicates base engine, "L" indicates L82, and "H" indicates LG4 305-ci California engine.

Appendix B
Option Prices and Production Quantities

1968

Code	Item	Number Produced	Price
19437	Corvette Sport Coupe:	9,936	$4,663.00
19467	Corvette Convertible:	18,630	$4,320.00
A01	Tinted Glass	17,635	$15.80
A02	Tinted Windshield	5,509	$10.55
A31	Power Windows	7,065	$57.95
A82	Head Restraints	3,197	$42.15
A85	Custom Shoulder Harness	350	$26.35
C07	Auxiliary Hardtop	8,735	$231.75
C08	Auxiliary Hardtop Vinyl Covering	3,050	$52.70
C50	Rear Window Defroster	693	$31.60
C60	Air Conditioning	5,664	$412.90
F41	Special Performance Suspension	1,758	$36.90
G81	Positraction Rear Axle	27,008	$46.35
J50	Vacuum Power Brakes	9,559	$42.15
J56	Heavy-Duty Brakes	81	$384.45
K66	Transistor Ignition	5,457	$73.75
L30	327/300 Horsepower Engine	5,875	base engine
L36	427/390 Horsepower Engine	7,717	$200.15
L68	427/400 Horsepower Engine	1,932	$305.50
L71	427/435 Horsepower Engine	2,898	$437.10
L79	327/350 Horsepower Engine	9,440	$105.35
L88	427/430 Horsepower Engine	80	$947.90
L89	427/435 Horsepower Engine with Aluminum Cylinder Heads	624	$805.75
M20	Four-Speed Wide-Ratio Manual Transmission	10,760	$184.35
M21	Four-Speed Close-Ratio Manual Transmission	12,337	$184.35
M22	Four-Speed Heavy-Duty Manual Transmission	80	$263.30
M40	Turbo-Hydra-Matic Transmission	5,063	$226.45
N11	Off Road Exhaust	4,695	$36.90
N36	Telescopic Steering Column	6,477	$42.15
N40	Power Steering	12,364	$94.80
PT6	F70-15 Red Stripe Tires	11,686	$31.30
PT7	F70-15 White Stripe Tires	9,692	$31.30
PO1	Wheel Trim Covers	8,971	$57.95
UA6	Horn Alarm System	388	$26.35
U15	Speed Warning Indicator	3,453	$10.55
U69	AM-FM Radio	27,920	$172.75
U79	Stereo Equipment	3,311	$278.10
—	Leather Interior Trim	2,429	$79.00

1969

Code	Item	Number Produced	Price
19437	Corvette Sport Coupe:	22,129	$4,763.00
19467	Corvette Convertible:	16,633	$4,420.00
A01	Tinted Glass	31,270	$16.90
A31	Power Windows	9,816	$63.20
A82	Head Restraints	38,762	$17.95
A85	Custom Shoulder Harness	600	$42.15
C07	Auxiliary Hardtop	7,878	$252.80
C08	Auxiliary Hardtop Vinyl Trim	3,266	$57.95
C50	Rear Window Defroster	2,485	$32.65
C60	Air Conditioning	11,859	$428.70
F41	Special Performance Suspension	1,661	$36.90
G81	Positraction Rear Axle	36,965	$46.35
J50	Vacuum Power Brakes	16,876	$42.15
J56	Heavy-Duty Brakes	115	$384.45
K05	Engine Block Heater	824	$10.55
K66	Transistor Ignition	5,702	$81.10
L36	427/390 Horsepower Engine	10,531	$221.20
L46	350/350 Horsepower Engine	12,846	$131.65
L68	427/400 Horsepower Engine	2,072	$326.55
L71	427/435 Horsepower Engine	2,722	$437.10
L88	427/430 Horsepower Engine	116	$1,032.15
L89	427/435 Horsepower Engine with Aluminum Cylinder Heads	390	$832.05
MA6	Heavy-Duty Clutch	102	$—
M20	Four-Speed Wide-Ratio Manual Transmission	16,507	$184.80
M21	Four-Speed Close-Ratio Manual Transmission	13,741	$184.80
M22	Four-Speed Heavy-Duty Manual Transmission	101	$290.40
M40	Turbo-Hydra-Matic Transmission	8,161	$221.80

(M40 Turbo-Hydra-Matic automatic with L71, L88, or L89 engine option cost $290.40)

Code	Item	Number Produced	Price
N14	Side Mounted Exhaust	4,355	$147.45
N37	Tilt and Telescopic Steering Column	10,325	$84.30
N40	Power Steering	22,866	$105.35
PT6	F70-15 Red Stripe Tires	5,210	$31.30
PT7	F70-15 White Stripe Tires	21,379	$31.30
PU9	F70-15 White Lettered Tires	2,398	$33.15
PO2	Deluxe Wheel Trim Covers	8,073	$57.95
UA6	Horn Alarm System	12,436	$26.35
U15	Speed Warning Indicator	3,561	$11.60
U69	AM-FM Radio	37,985	$172.75
U79	Stereo Equipment	4,114	$278.10
ZL1	Special Aluminum 427 Engine	2	$3,000
ZQ3	350/300 Horsepower Engine	10,083	base engine
—	Leather Interior Trim	3,729	$79.00

1970

Code	Item	Number Produced	Price
19437	Corvette Sport Coupe:	10,668	$5,192.00
19467	Corvette Convertible:	6,648	$4,849.00
A31	Power Windows	4,813	$63.20
A85	Custom Shoulder Harness	475	$42.15
C07	Auxiliary Hardtop	2,556	$273.85
C08	Auxiliary Hardtop Vinyl Trim	832	$63.20
C50	Rear Window Defroster	1,281	$36.90
C60	Air Conditioning	6,659	$447.65
G81	Optional Positraction Axle Ratio	2,862	$12.65
J50	Vacuum Power Brakes	8,984	$47.40
L46	350/350 Horsepower Engine	4,910	$158.00
LS5	454/390 Horsepower Engine	4,473	$289.65
LT1	350/370 Horsepower Engine	1,287	$447.60
M21	Four-Speed Close-Ratio Manual Transmission	4,383	no charge
M22	Four-Speed Heavy-Duty Manual Transmission	25	$95.00
M40	Turbo-Hydra-Matic Transmission	5,102	no charge
NA9	California Emissions Equipment	—	$36.90
N37	Tilt and Telescopic Steering Column	5,803	$84.30
N40	Power Steering	11,907	$105.35
PT7	F70-15 White Stripe Nylon Tires	6,589	$31.30
PU9	F70-15 White Letter Nylon Tires	7,985	$33.15
PO2	Deluxe Wheel Trim Covers	3,467	$57.95
T60	Heavy-Duty Battery	165	$15.80
UA6	Horn Alarm System	6,727	$31.60
U69	AM-FM Radio	16,991	$172.75
U79	Stereo Equipment	2,462	$278.10
ZR1	Special Purpose 350 Engine Package*	25	$968.95
ZQ3	350/300 Horsepower Engine	6,646	base engine
ZW4	Four-Speed Wide-Ratio Manual Transmission	7,806	no charge
—	Leather Interior Trim	3,191	$158.00

* Option ZR1 is a road-racing package that includes an LT1 engine, stiffer front and rear springs, heavy-duty shock absorbers, a special Harrison aluminum radiator (part No. 3007436), an M22 four-speed transmission, and a heavy-duty brake package. The brake package includes twin pin front calipers, an extra support for each front caliper, a proportioning valve, and metallic brake pads. N40 power steering, A31 power windows, PO2 wheel covers, C50 rear window defroster, and C60 air conditioning could not be ordered with the ZR1 package.

1971

Code	Item	Number Produced	Price
19437	Corvette Sport Coupe:	14,680	$5,496.00
19467	Corvette Convertible:	7,120	$5,259.00
A31	Power Windows	6,192	$79.00
A85	Custom Shoulder Harness	677	$42.00
C07	Auxiliary Hardtop	2,619	$274.00
C08	Auxiliary Hardtop Vinyl Trim	832	$63.00
C50	Rear Window Defroster	1,598	$42.00
C60	Air Conditioning	11,481	$459.00
J50	Vacuum Power Brakes	13,558	$47.00
LS5	454/365 Horsepower Engine	5,079	$295.00

1971 cont.

Code	Item	Number Produced	Price
LS6	454/425 Horsepower Engine	188	$1,221.00
LT1	350/330 Horsepower Engine	1,949	$483.00
M21	Four-Speed Close-Ratio Manual Transmission	2,387	no charge
M22	Four-Speed Heavy-Duty Manual Transmission	130	$100.00
M40	Turbo-Hydra-Matic Transmission	10,060	no charge

with small-block engine, $100.00 extra when car is equipped with LS5 or LS6 engine.

Code	Item	Number Produced	Price
N37	Tilt and Telescopic Steering Column	8,130	$84.30
N40	Power Steering	17,904	$115.90
PT7	F70-15 White Stripe Nylon Tires	6,711	$28.00
PU9	F70-15 White Letter Nylon Tires	12,449	$42.00
PO2	Deluxe Wheel Trim Covers	3,007	$63.00
T60	Heavy-Duty Battery	1,455	$15.80
U69	AM-FM Radio	21,509	$178.00
U79	Stereo Equipment	3,431	$283.00
ZQ1	Rear Axle Selection	2,395	$13.00
ZQ3	350/300 Horsepower Engine	14,547	base engine
ZR1	350/330 Horsepower Engine—Special*	8	$1,010.00
ZR2	454/425 Horsepower Engine—Special*	12	$1,747.00
ZW4	Four-Speed Wide-Ratio Manual Transmission	9,224	no charge
—	Leather Interior Trim	2,602	$158.00

* Options ZR1 and ZR2 are both road-racing packages. The ZR1 package includes an LT1 engine and the ZR2 package includes an LS6 engine. Both packages also include stiffer front and rear springs, heavy-duty shock absorbers, a special Harrison aluminum radiator (part No. 3007436), and a heavy-duty brake package. The brake package includes twin pin front calipers, an extra support for each front caliper, a proportioning valve, and metallic brake pads. N40 power steering, A31 power windows, PO2 wheel covers, C50 rear window defroster, and C60 air conditioning could not be ordered with the ZR1 package. The ZR1 package could only be ordered with an M22 four-speed transmission while the ZR2 could be ordered with either an M22 or an M40 automatic.

1972

Code	Item	Number Produced	Price
19437	Corvette Sport Coupe:	20,496	$5,533.00
19467	Corvette Convertible:	6,508	$5,296.00
AV3	Three-Point Seatbelts	17,693	—
A31	Power Windows	9,495	$85.35
A85	Deluxe Shoulder Harness	749	$42.15
C05	Folding Top Color	6,507	standard
C07	Auxiliary Hardtop	2,646	$273.85
C08	Auxiliary Hardtop Vinyl Trim	811	$158.00
C50	Rear Window Defroster	2,221	$42.15
C60	Air Conditioning	17,011	$464.50
F41	Special Suspension	20	
	(included with ZR1 option package.)		
GS4	3.70 Axle Type A	985	no charge
GV3	3.08 Axle Type B	15,845	no charge
GV4	3.36 Axle Type A	8,676	no charge
GV5	3.36 Axle Type B	466	no charge

1972 cont.

Code	Item	Number Produced	Price
GV7	3.55 Axle Type B	670	no charge
GV8	4.11 Axle Type B	356	no charge
J50	Vacuum Power Brakes	18,770	$47.40
J56	Heavy-Duty Brakes	20	
	(included with ZR1 option package.)		
K19	Air Injection Reactor	3,912	no charge
LS5	454/270 Horsepower Engine	3,913	$294.90
LT1	350/255 Horsepower Engine	1,741	$483.45
M21	Four-Speed Close-Ratio Manual Transmission	1,638	no charge
M22	Four-Speed Heavy-Duty Manual Transmission	20	
	(included with ZR1 option package.)		
M40	Turbo-Hydra-Matic Transmission	14,543	

(no charge with small-block engine, $100.35 extra when car is equipped with LS5 engine)

Code	Item	Number Produced	Price
NB2	Exhaust Emission Control	1,766	no charge
N37	Tilt and Telescopic Steering Column	12,992	$84.30
N40	Power Steering	23,794	$115.90
PT1	F70-15 Blackwall Tires	3,716	no charge
PT7	F70-15 White Stripe Nylon Tires	6,666	$30.35
PU9	F70-15 White Letter Nylon Tires	16,623	$43.65
PO2	Deluxe Wheel Trim Covers	3,593	$63.20
T60	Heavy-Duty Battery	2,969	$15.80
UL5	Radio Delete	292	no charge
U69	AM-FM Radio	26,669	$178.00
U79	Stereo Equipment	5,832	$283.35
VJ9	Exhaust Emission Label	1,968	no charge
V78	Certificate of Compliance Delete*	64	no charge
YE2	Special Axle Ratio	1	$12.65
YF5	California Emissions	1,967	$15.80
YF6	Delete California Emissions	1,805	no charge
ZP2	Color and Trim Override	654	no charge
ZP3	Special Paint	48	no charge
ZQ1	Rear Axle Selection	1,986	$12.65
ZQ3	350/200 Horsepower Engine	21,352	base engine
ZR1	350/255 Horsepower Engine—Special**	20	$1,010.05
ZR5	Three-Point Shoulder Belts	2	no charge
ZR7	Factory Delivery	16	no charge
ZV1	Statement of Origin	135	no charge
ZW4	Four-Speed Wide-Ratio Manual Transmission	10,804	no charge
ZX1	Export Preparation	290	price unknown
ZY5	Export Tire Tax	8	price unknown
ZY6	Taxable Tax Status	246	price unknown
ZY7	Non-Taxable Tax Status	133	price unknown
Z49	Canadian Base Equipment	1,234	price unknown

* For those cars exported outside the United States, option V78 deleted the Certificate of Compliance sticker required by federal law.

** *Option ZR1 is a road-racing package that includes an LT1 engine, stiffer front and rear springs, heavy-duty shock absorbers, a special Harrison aluminum radiator (part number 3007436), an M22 four-speed transmission, and a heavy-duty brake package. The brake package includes twin pin front calipers, an extra support for each front caliper, a proportioning valve, and metallic brake pads. N40 power steering, A31 power windows, PO2 wheel covers, C50 rear window defroster, and C60 air conditioning could not be ordered with the ZR1 package. In 1972 (but not in 1970 or 1971) ZR1-equipped cars do not have a fan shroud.*

1973

Code	Item	Number Produced	Price
1YZ37	Corvette Sport Coupe:	25,521	$5,561.50
1YZ67	Corvette Convertible:	4,943	$5,398.50
A31	Power Windows	14,024	$83.00
A85	Deluxe Shoulder Harness	788	$41.00
C07	Auxiliary Hardtop	1,328	$267.00
C08	Auxiliary Hardtop Vinyl Trim	323	$62.00
C50	Rear Window Defroster	4,412	$41.00
C60	Air Conditioning	21,578	$452.00
J50	Vacuum Power Brakes	24,168	$46.00
LS4	454/275 Horsepower Engine	4,412	$250.00
L48	350/190 Horsepower Engine	20,342	standard
L82	350/250 Horsepower Engine	5,710	$299.00
M20	Standard Four-Speed Manual Transmission	8,833	no charge
M21	Four-Speed Close-Ratio Manual Transmission	3,704	no charge
M40	Turbo-Hydra-Matic Transmission	17,927	no charge

with small-block engine, $97.00 extra when car is equipped with LS4 or L82 engine.

Code	Item	Number Produced	Price
N37	Tilt and Telescopic Steering Column	17,949	$82.00
N40	Power Steering	27,872	$113.00
PO2	Deluxe Wheel Trim Covers	1,739	$62.00
QRM	GR70-15 White Stripe Radial Tires	19,903	$32.00
QRN	GR70-15 Blackwall Radial Tires	6,020	no charge
QRZ	GR70-15 White Letter Radial Tires	4,541	$45.00
T60	Heavy-Duty Battery	4,912	$15.00
U58	AM-FM Stereo Radio	12,482	$276.00
U69	AM-FM Radio	17,598	$173.00
UF1	Map Lite	8,186	$5.00
UL5	Radio Delete	384	no charge
YF5	California Emissions	3,008	$15.00
YJ8	Aluminum Wheels	4	$175.00
—	Rear Axle Ratio Selection	1,791	$12.00
—	Custom Interior With Leather Trim	13,434	$154.00

1974

Code	Item	Number Produced	Price
1YZ37	Corvette Sport Coupe:	32,028	$6,001.50
1YZ67	Corvette Convertible:	5,474	$5,765.50
A31	Power Windows	23,940	$86.00
A85	Deluxe Shoulder Harness	618	$41.00
C07	Auxiliary Hardtop	2,612	$267.00
C08	Auxiliary Hardtop With Vinyl Trim	367	$329.00
C50	Rear Window Defroster	9,322	$43.00

1974 cont.

Code	Item	Number Produced	Price
C60	Air Conditioning	29,397	$467.00
FE7	Gymkhana Suspension	1,905	$7.00
J50	Vacuum Power Brakes	33,306	$49.00
LS4	454/270 Horsepower Engine	3,494	$250.00
L48	350/195 Horsepower Engine	27,318	standard
L82	350/250 Horsepower Engine	6,690	$299.00
M20	Standard Four-Speed Manual Transmission	8,862	no charge
M21	Four-Speed Close-Ratio Manual Transmission	3,494	no charge
M40	Turbo-Hydra-Matic Transmission	25,146	no charge

with small-block engine, earlier in year $97.00 extra when car is equipped with LS4 or L82 engine.Later in year charge increased to $103.00

Code	Item	Number Produced	Price
N37	Tilt and Telescopic Steering Column	27,700	$82.00
N41	Power Steering	35,944	$117.00
QRM	GR70-15 White Stripe Radial Tires	9,140	$32.00
QRN	GR70-15 Blackwall Radial Tires	4,260	no charge
QRZ	GR70-15 White Letter Radial Tires	24,102	$45.00
U05	Dual Horns	5,258	$4.00
T60	Heavy-Duty Battery	4,912	$15.00
U58	AM-FM Stereo Radio	19,581	$276.00
U69	AM-FM Radio	17,374	$173.00
UA1	Heavy-Duty Battery	9,169	$15.00
UF1	Map Lite	16,101	$5.00
UL5	Radio Delete	547	no charge
YF5	California Emissions	—	$20.00
Z07	Off-Road Suspension and Brakes*	47	$400.00
—	Rear Axle Ratio Selection	1,219	$12.00
—	Custom Interior With Leather Trim	19,959	$154.00

Z07 Off-Road Suspension and Brakes is an option package available with LS4 or L82 only. It includes stiffer front and rear springs, heavy-duty shock absorbers, twin pin front calipers, an extra support for each front caliper, a proportioning valve, and metallic brake pads.

1975

Code	Item	Number Produced	Price
1YZ37	Corvette Sport Coupe:	33,836	$6,810.10
1YZ67	Corvette Convertible:	4,629	$6,550.10
A31	Power Windows	28,745	$93.00
A85	Deluxe Shoulder Harness	646	$41.00
C07	Auxiliary Hardtop	2,407	$267.00
C08	Auxiliary Hardtop With Vinyl Trim	279	$350.00
C50	Rear Window Defroster	13,760	$46.00
C60	Air Conditioning	31,914	$490.00
FE7	Gymkhana Suspension	3,194	$7.00
J50	Vacuum Power Brakes	35,842	$50.00
L48	350/165 Horsepower Engine	36,093	standard
L82	350/205 Horsepower Engine	2,372	$336.00
M20	Standard Four-Speed Manual Transmission	8,935	no charge
M21	Four-Speed Close-Ratio Manual Transmission (available with L82 only)	1,057	no charge
M40	Turbo-Hydra-Matic Transmission	28,473	no charge

with L48 engine, $120.00 extra when car is equipped with L82 engine.

Code	Item	Number Produced	Price
N37	Tilt and Telescopic Steering Column	31,830	$82.00
N41	Power Steering	37,591	$129.00
QRM	GR70-15 White Stripe Radial Tires	5,233	$35.00
QRN	GR70-15 Blackwall Radial Tires	2,825	no charge
QRZ	GR70-15 White Letter Radial Tires	30,407	$48.00
U05	Dual Horns	22,011	$4.00
U58	AM-FM Stereo Radio	24,701	$284.00
U69	AM-FM Radio	12,902	$178.00
UA1	Heavy-Duty Battery	16,778	$15.00
UF1	Map Lite	21,676	$5.00
UL5	Radio Delete	862	no charge
YF5	California Emissions	3,037	$20.00
Z07	Off-Road Suspension and Brakes*	144	$400.00
—	Rear Axle Ratio Selection	1,969	$12.00
—	Custom Interior With Leather Trim	—	$154.00

Z07 Off-Road Suspension and Brakes is an option package available with L82 only. It includes stiffer front and rear springs, heavy-duty shock absorbers, twin pin front calipers, an extra support for each front caliper, a proportioning valve, and metallic brake pads.

1976

Code	Item	Number Produced	Price
1YZ37	Corvette Sport Coupe:	46,558	$7,604.85
A31	Power Windows	38,700	$107.00
C49	Rear Window Defroster	24,960	$78.00
C60	Air Conditioning	40,787	$523.00
FE7	Gymkhana Suspension	5,368	$35.00
J50	Vacuum Power Brakes	46,558	$59.00
L48	350/180 Horsepower Engine	40,838	standard
L82	350/210 Horsepower Engine	5,720	$481.00
M20	Standard Four-Speed Manual Transmission	7,845	no charge
M21	Four-Speed Close-Ratio Manual Transmission (available with L82 only)	2,088	no charge
M40	Turbo-Hydra-Matic Transmission	36,625	no charge

with base L48 engine, $134.00 extra when car is equipped with L82 engine.

Code	Item	Number Produced	Price
N37	Tilt and Telescopic Steering Column	41,797	$95.00
N41	Power Steering	46,385	$151.00
QRM	GR70-15 White Stripe Radial Tires	3,992	$37.00
QRN	GR70-15 Blackwall Radial Tires	2,643	no charge
QRZ	GR70-15 White Letter Radial Tires	39,923	$51.00
U58	AM-FM Stereo Radio	34,272	$281.00
U69	AM-FM Radio	11,083	$187.00
UA1	Heavy-Duty Battery	25,909	$16.00
UF1	Map Lite	35,361	$10.00
UL5	Radio Delete	1,203	no charge
YF5	California Emissions	3,527	$50.00
YJ8	Aluminum Wheels	6,253	$299.00
—	Rear Axle Ratio Selection	1,371	$13.00
—	Custom Interior With Leather Trim	—	$164.00

1977

Code	Item	Number Produced	Price
1YZ37	Corvette Sport Coupe:	49,213	$8,647.65
A31	Power Windows	44,341	$116.00

1977 cont.

Code	Item	Number Produced	Price
B32	Floor Mats	36,763	$22.00
C49	Electro-Clear Rear Defogger	30,411	$84.00
C60	Air Conditioning	45,249	$553.00
D35	Sport Mirrors	20,206	$36.00
FE7	Gymkhana Suspension	7,269	$38.00
G95	Rear Axle Ratio Selection	972	$14.00
K30	Cruise-Master Speed Control	29,161	$88.00
L48	350/180 Horsepower Engine	43,065	standard
82	350/210 Horsepower Engine	6,148	$495.00
M20	Standard Four-Speed Manual Transmission	5,922	no charge
M21	Four-Speed Close-Ratio Manual Transmission (available with L82 only)	2,060	no charge
M40	Turbo-Hydra-Matic Transmission with base L48 engine, $146.00 extra when car is equipped with L82 engine.	41,231	no charge
NA6	High Altitude Emissions	—	$22.00
N37	Tilt and Telescopic Steering Column	46,487	$165.00
QRN	GR70-15 Blackwall Radial Tires	2,986	no charge
QRZ	GR70-15 White Letter Radial Tires	46,227	$57.00
U58	AM-FM Stereo Radio	18,483	$281.00
U69	AM-FM Radio	4,700	$187.00
UM2	AM-FM Stereo with 8-Track	24,603	$414.00
UA1	Heavy-Duty Battery	32,882	$17.00
UL5	Radio Delete	1,427	no charge
Y54	Luggage and Roof Carrier	—	$73.00
YF5	California Emissions	—	$70.00
YJ8	Aluminum Wheels	12,646	$321.00
ZN1	Trailer Package	289	$83.00
ZX2	Convenience Package	40,872	$22.00

1978

Code	Item	Number Produced	Price
1YZ87	Corvette Sport Coupe:	40,274	$9,351.89
A31	Power Windows	39,931	$130.00
AU3	Power Door Locks	12,187	$120.00
BZ2	25th Anniversary Paint	15,283	$399.00
CC1	Removable Glass Roof Panels	972	$349.00
C49	Electro-Clear Rear Defogger	30,912	$95.00
C60	Air Conditioning	37,638	$605.00
D35	Sport Mirrors	38,405	$40.00
FE7	Gymkhana Suspension	12,590	$41.00
G95	Rear Axle Ratio Selection	382	$15.00
K30	Cruise-Master Speed Control	31,608	$99.00
L48	350/185 Horsepower Engine	34,037	standard
L82	350/220 Horsepower Engine	12,739	$525.00
M20	Standard Four-Speed Manual Transmission	4,777	no charge
M21	Four-Speed Close-Ratio Manual Transmission (available with L82 only)	3,385	no charge
M38	Turbo-Hydra-Matic Transmission	38,614	no charge
NA6	High Altitude Emissions	—	$33.00
N37	Tilt and Telescopic Steering Column	37,858	$175.00
QBS	P255/60R15 White Letter Radial Tires	18,296	$216.00

1978 cont.

Code	Item	Number Produced	Price
QGQ	P225/70R15 Blackwall Radial Tires	2,277	no charge
QGR	P225/70R15 White Letter Radial Tires	26,203	$51.00
U58	AM-FM Stereo Radio	10,189	$286.00
U69	AM-FM Radio	2,057	$199.00
U75	Power Antenna	23,069	$49.00
U81	Dual Rear Speakers	12,340	$49.00
UM2	AM-FM Stereo with 8-Track	20,899	$419.00
UP6	AM-FM Stereo with CB	7,138	$638.00
UA1	Heavy-Duty Battery	28,243	$18.00
YF5	California Emissions	—	$70.00
YJ8	Aluminum Wheels	28,008	$340.00
ZN1	Trailer Package	972	$89.00
ZX2	Convenience Group	37,222	$84.00
Z78	Limited Edition Pace Car	6,502	$13,653.21

1979

Code	Item	Number Produced	Price
1YZ87	Corvette Sport Coupe:	53,807	$10,220.23
A31	Power Windows	20,631	$141.00
AU3	Power Door Locks	9,054	$131.00
CC1	Removable Glass Roof Panels	14,480	$365.00
C49	Electro-Clear Rear Defogger	41,587	$102.00
C60	Air Conditioning	47,136	$635.00
D35	Sport Mirrors	48,211	$45.00
D80	Front and Rear Spoilers	6,853	$265.00
F51	Heavy-Duty Shock Absorbers	2,164	$33.00
FE7	Gymkhana Suspension	12,321	$49.00
G95	Rear Axle Ratio Selection	428	$19.00
K30	Cruise-Master Speed Control	34,445	$113.00
L48	350/195 Horsepower Engine	39,291	standard
L82	350/225 Horsepower Engine	14,516	$565.00
M20	Standard Four-Speed Manual Transmission	8,291	no charge
M21	Four-Speed Close-Ratio Manual Transmission (available with L82 only)	4,062	no charge
M38	Turbo-Hydra-Matic Transmission	41,454	no charge
NA6	High Altitude Emissions	—	$35.00
N37	Tilt and Telescopic Steering Column	47,463	$190.00
N90	Aluminum Wheels	33,741	$380.00
QBS	P255/60R15 White Letter Radial Tires	17,920	$226.20
QGQ	P225/70R15 Blackwall Radial Tires	6,284	no charge
QGR	P225/70R15 White Letter Radial Tires	29,603	$55.00
U58	AM-FM Stereo Radio	9,256	$90.00
U69	AM-FM Radio	6,523	$199.00
U75	Power Antenna	35,730	$52.00
U81	Dual Rear Speakers	37,754	$52.00
UM2	AM-FM Stereo with 8-Track	21,435	$228.00
UN3	AM-FM Stereo with Cassette	12,110	$234.00
UP6	AM-FM Stereo with CB	4,483	$439.00
UA1	Heavy-Duty Battery	3,405	$21.00
YF5	California Emissions	—	$83.00
ZN1	Trailer Package	1,001	$98.00
ZQ2	Power Windows and Door Locks	28,465	$272.00
ZX2	Convenience Group	41,530	$94.00

1980

Code	Item	Number Produced	Price
1YZ87	Corvette Sport Coupe:	40,614	$13,140.24
AU3	Power Door Locks	32,692	$140.00
CC1	Removable Glass Roof Panels	19,695	$391.00
C49	Electro-Clear Rear Defogger	36,589	$109.00
F51	Heavy-Duty Shock Absorbers	1,695	$35.00
FE7	Gymkhana Suspension	9,907	$55.00
K30	Cruise-Master Speed Control	30,821	$123.00
L48	350/195 Horsepower Engine	32,324	standard
L82	350/225 Horsepower Engine	5,069	$595.00
M18	Four-Speed Manual Transmission	5,726	no charge
M33	Turbo-Hydra-Matic Transmission (California)	—	no charge
MV4	Turbo-Hydra-Matic Transmission	34,838	no charge
N90	Aluminum Wheels	34,128	$407.00
QGQ	P225/70R15 Blackwall Radial Tires	1,266	no charge
QGR	P225/70R15 White Letter Radial Tires	26,208	$62.00
QXH	P255/60R15 White Letter Radial Tires	13,140	$426.16
U58	AM-FM Stereo Radio	6,138	$46.00
U69	AM-FM Radio	985	no charge
U75	Power Antenna	32,863	$56.00
U81	Dual Rear Speakers	36,650	$52.00
UA1	Heavy-Duty Battery	1,337	$22.00
UL5	Radio Delete (Credit)	201	-$126.00
UM2	AM-FM Stereo with 8-Track	15,708	$155.00
UN3	AM-FM Stereo with Cassette	15,148	$168.00
UP6	AM-FM Stereo with CB	2,434	$391.00
V54	Roof Panel Carrier	3,755	$125.00
YF5	California Emissions	3,221	$250.00
ZN1	Trailer Package	796	$105.00

1981

Code	Item	Number Produced	Price
1YY87	Corvette Sport Coupe:	40,606	$16,258.52
AU3	Power Door Locks	36,322	$145.00
A42	Power Driver Seat	29,200	$183.00
CC1	Removable Glass Roof Panels	20,095	$414.00
C49	Electro-Clear Rear Defogger	36,893	$119.00
D84	Custom Two-Tone Exterior Paint	5,352	$399.00
DG7	Electric Sport Mirrors	13,567	$117.00
F51	Heavy-Duty Shock Absorbers	1,128	$37.00
FE7	Gymkhana Suspension	7,803	$57.00
G92	Performance Axle Ratio	2,400	$20.00
K35	Cruise Control	32,522	$155.00
L81	350/190 Horsepower Engine	40,606	standard
M18	Four-Speed Manual Transmission	5,757	no charge
MX3	Turbo-Hydra-Matic Transmission	34,849	no charge

1981 cont.

Code	Item	Number Produced	Price
N90	Aluminum Wheels	36,485	$428.00
QGQ	P225/70R15 Blackwall Radial Tires	663	no charge
QGR	P225/70R15 White Letter Radial Tires	21,939	$72.00
QXH	P255/60R15 White Letter Radial Tires	18,004	$491.92
U58	AM-FM Stereo Radio	5,145	$95.00
U69	AM-FM Radio	851	no charge
U75	Power Antenna	32,903	$55.00
UL5	Radio Delete (Credit)	315	-$118.00
UM4	AM-FM Stereo ETR Radio with 8-Track	8,262	$386.00
UM5	AM-FM Stereo ETR Radio with 8-Track and CB	792	$712.00
UM6	AM-FM Stereo ETR Radio with Cassette	22,892	$423.00
UN5	AM-FM Stereo ETR Radio with Cassette and CB	2,349	$750.00
V54	Roof Panel Carrier	3,303	$135.00
YF5	California Emissions	4,951	$46.00
ZN1	Trailer Package	916	$110.00

1982

Code	Item	Number Produced	Price
1YY87	Corvette Sport Coupe:	18,648	$18,290.07
1YY07	Collector Edition Hatchback	6,759	$22,537.59
AG9	Power Driver Seat	22,585	$197.00
AU3	Power Door Locks	23,936	$155.00
CC1	Removable Glass Roof Panels	14,763	$443.00
C49	Electro-Clear Rear Defogger	16,886	$129.00
D84	Custom Two-Tone Exterior Paint	4,871	$428.00
DG7	Electric Sport Mirrors	20,301	$125.00
FE7	Gymkhana Suspension	5,457	$61.00
K35	Cruise Control	24,313	$165.00
L83	350/200 Horsepower Engine	25,407	standard
MD8	Turbo-Hydra-Matic Transmission	25,407	no charge
N90	Aluminum Wheels	16,844	$458.00
QGQ	P225/70R15 Blackwall Radial Tires	405	no charge
QGR	P225/70R15 White Letter Radial Tires	5,932	$80.00
QXH	P255/60R15 White Letter Radial Tires	19,070	$542.52
U58	AM-FM Stereo Radio	1,533	$101.00
U75	Power Antenna	15,557	$60.00
UL5	Radio Delete (Credit)	150	-$124.00
UM4	AM-FM Stereo ETR Radio with 8-Track	923	$386.00
UM6	AM-FM Stereo ETR Radio with Cassette	20,355	$423.00
UN5	AM-FM Stereo ETR Radio with Cassette and CB	1,987	$755.00
	($695.00 with Collector Edition Hatchback)		
V08	Heavy-Duty Cooling	6,006	$57.00
V54	Roof Panel Carrier	1,992	$144.00
YF5	California Emissions	4,951	$46.00

Appendix C
Engine Codes

1968

Code	Item	Description
HE	327/300	Base engine with Rochester Q-Jet and manual transmission
HO	327/300	Base engine with Rochester Q-Jet and automatic transmission
HP	327/300	Base engine with Rochester Q-Jet, a/c, p/s, and manual transmission
HT	327/350	L79 with Rochester Q-Jet, special camshaft, and four-speed
IL	427/390	L36 with Rochester Q-Jet, hydraulic lifters, and four-speed
IQ	427/390	L36 with Rochester Q-Jet, hydraulic lifters, and automatic transmission
IM	427/400	L68 with Holley 3x2 carburetors, hydraulic lifters, and four-speed
IO	427/400	L68 with Holley 3x2 carburetors, hydraulic lifters, and automatic transmission
IR	427/435	L71 with Holley 3x2 carburetors, mechanical lifters, and four-speed
IU	427/435	L89 with Holley 3x2 carburetors, mechanical lifters, aluminum cylinder heads, and four-speed
IT	427/430	L88—heavy-duty engine with Holley four-barrel, mechanical lifters, and M22 four-speed

1969

Code	Item	Description
HY	350/300	Base engine with Rochester Q-Jet and manual transmission
HZ	350/300	Base engine with Rochester Q-Jet and automatic transmission
HW	350/350	L46 with Rochester Q-Jet, special camshaft, and four-speed
HX	350/350	L46 with Rochester Q-Jet, special camshaft, a/c, and four-speed
GD	350/350	L46 with Rochester Q-Jet, special camshaft, a/c, K66, and four-speed
LM	427/390	L36 with Rochester Q-Jet, hydraulic lifters, and four-speed
LL	427/390	L36 with Rochester Q-Jet, hydraulic lifters, and automatic transmission
LQ	427/400	L68 with Holley 3x2 carburetors, hydraulic lifters, and four-speed
LN	427/400	L68 with Holley 3x2 carburetors, hydraulic lifters, and automatic transmission
LO	427/430	L88—heavy-duty engine with Holley four-barrel, mechanical lifters, and M22 four-speed
LV	427/430	L88—heavy-duty engine with Holley four-barrel, mechanical lifters, and automatic transmission
LR	427/435	L71 with Holley 3x2 carburetors, mechanical lifters, and four-speed
LX	427/435	L71 with Holley 3x2 carburetors, mechanical lifters, and automatic
LP	427/435	L89 with Holley 3x2 carburetors, mechanical lifters, aluminum cylinder heads, and four-speed
LW	427/435	L89 with Holley 3x2 carburetors, mechanical lifters, aluminum cylinder heads, and automatic
LT	427/435	L71 with Holley 3x2 carburetors, mechanical lifters, MA6, and four-speed
LU	427/435	L89 with Holley 3x2 carburetors, mechanical lifters, aluminum cylinder heads, MA6, and four-speed
ME	427/430	ZL1 performance package, aluminum block, heavy-duty engine with Holley four-barrel, mechanical lifters, and M22
MG	427/430	ZL1 performance package, aluminum block, heavy-duty engine with Holley four-barrel, mechanical lifters, and automatic transmission
MH	427/390	L36 with Rochester Q-Jet, hydraulic lifters, K66, and four-speed

1970

Code	Item	Description
CTL	350/300	Base engine with Rochester Q-Jet and four-speed (earlier base-engine code)
CTD	350/300	Base engine with Rochester Q-Jet and four-speed (later base-engine code)
CTM	350/300	Base engine with Rochester Q-Jet and automatic transmission (earlier base-engine code)
CTG	350/300	Base engine with Rochester Q-Jet and automatic transmission (later base-engine code)
CTN	350/350	L46 with Rochester Q-Jet, special camshaft, and four-speed (earlier L46 code)
CTH	350/350	L46 with Rochester Q-Jet, special camshaft, and four-speed (later L46 code)
CTO	350/350	L46 with Rochester Q-Jet, special camshaft, a/c, and four-speed (earlier L46 code)
CTJ	350/350	L46 with Rochester Q-Jet, special camshaft, a/c, and four-speed (later L46 code)
CTP	350/350	L46 with Rochester Q-Jet, special camshaft, a/c, and four-speed
CTQ	350/350	L46 with Rochester Q-Jet, special camshaft, a/c, K66, and four-speed
CTU	350/370	LT1 with Holley four-barrel, mechanical lifters, K66, and four-speed (earlier LT1 code)
CTK	350/370	LT1 with Holley four-barrel, mechanical lifters, K66, and four-speed (later LT1 code)
CTV	350/370	ZR1 performance package, LT1 engine, and M22
CZU	454/390	LS5 with Rochester Q-Jet, hydraulic lifters, and four-speed
CGW	454/390	LS5 with Rochester Q-Jet, hydraulic lifters, and automatic transmission
CRI	454/390	LS5 with Rochester Q-Jet, hydraulic lifters, K66, and four-speed
CRJ	454/390	LS5 with Rochester Q-Jet, hydraulic lifters, K66, and automatic transmission

1971

Code	Item	Description
CJL	350/270	Base engine with Rochester Q-Jet and four-speed
CGT	350/270	Base engine with Rochester Q-Jet and automatic transmission (earlier base-engine code)
CJK	350/270	Base engine with Rochester Q-Jet and automatic transmission (later base-engine code)
CGZ	350/330	LT1 with Holley four-barrel, mechanical lifters, and four-speed
CGY	350/330	ZR1 performance package, LT1 engine, and M22
CPH	454/365	LS5 with Rochester Q-Jet, hydraulic lifters, and four-speed
CPJ	454/365	LS5 with Rochester Q-Jet, hydraulic lifters, and automatic transmission
CPW	454/425	LS6 with Holley four-barrel, mechanical lifters, aluminum cylinder heads, and M22 four-speed
CPX	454/425	LS6 with Holley four-barrel, mechanical lifters, aluminum cylinder heads, and automatic

1972

Code	Item	Description
CKW	350/200	Base engine with Rochester Q-Jet and four-speed
CDH	350/200	Base engine with Rochester Q-Jet, NB2, and four-speed
CKX	350/200	Base engine with Rochester Q-Jet and automatic
CDJ	350/200	Base engine with Rochester Q-Jet, NB2, and automatic
CKY	350/255	LT1 with Holley four-barrel, mechanical lifters, and four-speed
CRT	350/255	LT1 with Holley four-barrel, mechanical lifters, K19, and four-speed
CKZ	350/255	ZR1 performance package, LT1 engine, and M22
CPH	454/270	LS5 with Rochester Q-Jet, hydraulic lifters, and four-speed
CPJ	454/270	LS5 with Rochester Q-Jet, hydraulic lifters, and automatic transmission
CSR	454/270	LS5 with Rochester Q-Jet, hydraulic lifters, K19, and four-speed
CSS	454/270	LS5 with Rochester Q-Jet, hydraulic lifters, K19, and automatic transmission

1973

Code	Item	Description
CKZ	350/190	L48 with four-speed
CLA	350/190	L48 engine with automatic
CLB	350/190	L48 engine with four-speed (California)
CLC	350/190	L48 engine with automatic (California)
CLD	350/250	L82 with automatic
CLH	350/250	L82 engine with automatic (California)
CLR	350/250	L82 engine with four-speed
CLS	350/250	L82 engine with four-speed (California)
CWM	454/275	LS4 with four-speed
CWR	454/275	LS4 with automatic
CWS	454/275	LS4 with automatic (California)
CWT	454/275	LS4 with four-speed (California)

1974

Code	Item	Description
CKZ	350/195	L48 with four-speed
CLA	350/195	L48 engine with automatic
CLB	350/195	L48 engine with four-speed (California)
CLC	350/195	L48 engine with automatic (California)
CLD	350/250	L82 with automatic (federal & some California)
CLH	350/250	L82 engine with automatic (California)
CLR	350/250	L82 engine with four-speed (federal and some California)
CLS	350/250	L82 engine with four-speed (California)
CWM	454/270	LS4 with four-speed (federal & some California)
CWR	454/270	LS4 with automatic
CWS	454/270	LS4 with automatic (California)
CWT	454/270	LS4 with four-speed (California)

1975

Code	Item	Description
CHA	350/165	L48 with four-speed (federal)
CHB	350/165	L48 engine with automatic (federal)
CHC	350/205	L82 with four-speed (federal)
CHR	350/205	L82 engine with automatic (federal & California)
CHU	350/165	L48 with four-speed (federal)
CHZ	350/165	L48 engine with automatic (federal)
CKC	350/205	L82 engine with automatic (federal)
CRJ	350/165	L48 with four-speed (federal)
CRK	350/165	L48 engine with automatic (federal)
CRL	350/205	L82 with four-speed (federal)
CRM	350/205	L82 engine with automatic (federal)
CUA	350/165	L48 with four-speed (federal)
CUB	350/165	L48 with four-speed (federal)
CUD	350/205	L82 with four-speed (federal)
CUT	350/205	L82 with four-speed (federal)

1976

Code	Item	Description
CHC	350/210	L82 with four-speed (federal)
CKC	350/210	L82 engine with Turbo-Hydra-Matic 400 (federal)
CKW	350/180	L48 with four-speed (federal)
CKX	350/180	L48 engine with Turbo-Hydra-Matic 350 (federal)
CLM		(Unverified usage)
CLR		(Unverified usage)
CLS	350/180	L48 engine with Turbo-Hydra-Matic 350 (California)

1977

Code	Item	Description
CHD	350/180	L48 with Turbo-Hydra-Matic 350 (California)
CKD	350/180	L48 with Turbo-Hydra-Matic 350 (high altitude)
CKZ	350/180	L48 with four-speed (federal)
CLA	350/180	L48 engine with Turbo-Hydra-Matic 350 (federal)
CLB	350/180	L48 with Turbo-Hydra-Matic 350 (high altitude) (used in early production)
CLC	350/180	L48 with Turbo-Hydra-Matic 350 (California) (used in early production)
CLD	350/210	L82 engine with four-speed (federal)
CLF	350/210	L82 engine with Turbo-Hydra-Matic 400 (federal)

1978

Code	Item	Description
CHW	350/185	L48 with four-speed (federal)
CLM	350/185	L48 with Turbo-Hydra-Matic 350 (federal)
CLR	350/175	L48 with Turbo-Hydra-Matic 350 (California)
CLS	350/175	L48 with Turbo-Hydra-Matic 350 (high altitude)
CMR	350/220	L82 engine with four-speed (federal)
CMS	350/220	L82 engine with Turbo-Hydra-Matic 350 (federal)
CUT	350/185	L48 with Turbo-Hydra-Matic 350 (federal)

1979

Code	Item	Description
ZAA	350/195	L48 with four-speed (federal) (early)
ZAB	350/195	L48 with Turbo-Hydra-Matic 350 (federal) (early)
ZAC	350/195	L48 with Turbo-Hydra-Matic 350 (California) (early)
ZAD	350/195	L48 with Turbo-Hydra-Matic 350 (high altitude)
ZAF	350/195	L48 engine with four-speed (federal)
ZAH	350/195	L48 with Turbo-Hydra-Matic 350 (federal)
ZAJ	350/195	L48 with Turbo-Hydra-Matic 350 (California)
ZBA	350/225	L82 engine with four-speed (federal)
ZBB	350/225	L82 engine with Turbo-Hydra-Matic 350(federal)

1980

Code	Item	Description
ZAK	350/190	L48 with Turbo-Hydra-Matic 350 (federal)
ZAM	350/190	L48 with four-speed (federal)
ZBC	350/230	L82 engine with Turbo-Hydra-Matic 350 (federal)
ZBD	350/230	L82 engine with four-speed (federal)
ZCA	305/180	LG4 with Turbo-Hydra-Matic 350 (California)

1981

Code	Item	Description
ZDA	350/190	L81 with four-speed (federal)
ZDB	350/190	L81 with Turbo-Hydra-Matic 350 (California)
ZDC	350/190	L81 engine with four-speed (California)
ZDD	350/190	L81 engine with Turbo-Hydra-Matic 350 (federal)

1982

Code	Item	Description
ZBA	350/200	L83 engine with Turbo-Hydra-Matic 700-R4 (federal)
ZBC	350/200	L83 with Turbo-Hydra-Matic 700-R4 (California) (early)
ZBN	350/200	L83 with Turbo-Hydra-Matic 700-R4 (California)

Appendix D
Transmission Codes

1968

Code	Description
S	Saginaw three-speed
P	Muncie four-speed
K	Turbo-Hydra-Matic 400 with 327 engines
L	Turbo-Hydra-Matic 400 with 427 engines

1969

Code	Description
S	Saginaw three-speed
P	Muncie four-speed
A	M20 Muncie four-speed with wide-gear ratio
B	M21 Muncie four-speed with close-gear ratio
C	M22 Muncie heavy-duty four-speed with close-gear ratio
K	Turbo-Hydra-Matic 400 with 350 engines
L	Turbo-Hydra-Matic 400 with hydraulic lifter 427 engines
Y	Turbo-Hydra-Matic 400 with mechanical lifter 427 engines

1970

Code	Description
P	Muncie four-speed
A	M20 Muncie four-speed with wide-gear ratio
B	M21 Muncie four-speed with close-gear ratio
C	M22 Muncie heavy-duty four-speed with close-gear ratio
K	Turbo-Hydra-Matic 400 with 350 engines
S	Turbo-Hydra-Matic 400 with 454 engines

1971

Code	Description
P	Muncie four-speed
A	M20 Muncie four-speed with wide-gear ratio
B	M21 Muncie four-speed with close-gear ratio
C	M22 Muncie heavy-duty four-speed with close-gear ratio
K	Turbo-Hydra-Matic 400 with 350 engines
S	Turbo-Hydra-Matic 400 with LS5 454 engines
Y	Turbo-Hydra-Matic 400 with LS6 454 engines

1972

Code	Description
P	Muncie four-speed
A	M20 Muncie four-speed with wide-gear ratio
B	M21 Muncie four-speed with close-gear ratio
C	M22 Muncie heavy-duty four-speed with close-gear ratio
K	Turbo-Hydra-Matic 400 with 350 engines
S	Turbo-Hydra-Matic 400 with 454 engines

1973

Code	Description
P	Muncie four-speed
A	M20 Muncie four-speed with wide-gear ratio
B	M21 Muncie four-speed with close-gear ratio
CK	Turbo-Hydra-Matic 400 with L48 350 engine
CY	Turbo-Hydra-Matic 400 with L82 350 engines
CS	Turbo-Hydra-Matic 400 with 454 engines

1974

Code	Description
P	Muncie four-speed
A	M20 Muncie four-speed with wide-gear ratio
B	M21 Muncie four-speed with close-gear ratio
W	Warner four-speed
CK	Turbo-Hydra-Matic 400 with L48 350 engines
CZ	Turbo-Hydra-Matic 400 with L82 350 engines
CS	Turbo-Hydra-Matic 400 with 454 engines

1975

Code	Description
W	Warner four-speed
CK	Turbo-Hydra-Matic 400 with L48 350 engines
CZ	Turbo-Hydra-Matic 400 with L82 350 engines

1976

Code	Description
W	Warner four-speed
AM	Turbo-Hydra-Matic 350 with L48 350 engines
XH	Turbo-Hydra-Matic 350 with L48 350 engines
CZ	Turbo-Hydra-Matic 400 with L82 350 engines

1977

Code	Description
W	Warner four-speed
AM	Turbo-Hydra-Matic 350 with L48 350 engines
CB	Turbo-Hydra-Matic 400 with L82 350 engines

1978

Code	Description
S6	Warner four-speed, wide ratio (2.85:1 first gear)
ZU	Warner four-speed, wide ratio (2.64:1 first gear)
ZW	Warner four-speed, close ratio (2.43:1 first gear)
5WB	Turbo-Hydra-Matic 350
5TL	Turbo-Hydra-Matic 350

1979

Code	Description
UH	Warner four-speed, wide ratio (2.64:1 first gear)
UK	Warner four-speed, close ratio (2.43:1 first gear)
TB	Turbo-Hydra-Matic 350
WB	Turbo-Hydra-Matic 350

1980

Code	Description
ZJ	Warner four-speed, wide ratio (2.88:1 first gear)
JC	Turbo-Hydra-Matic 350 with LG4 305 engines
TW	Turbo-Hydra-Matic 350 with 350 engines

1981

Code	Description
CC	Warner four-speed, wide ratio (2.88:1 first gear)
8JD	Turbo-Hydra-Matic 350

1982

Code	Description
YA	Turbo-Hydra-Matic 700-R4

Appendix E
Differential Codes

1968s and 1969s
Manufactured through Approximately August 1969

Code	Ratio	Type
AK	3.36:1	Standard non-Positraction with 327 and 350
AL	3.08:1	Positraction with 327 and 350
AM	3.36:1	Positraction with 327 and 350
AN	3.55:1	Positraction with 327 and 350
AO	3.70:1	Positraction with 327 and 350
AP	4.11:1	Positraction with 327 and 350
AS	3.70:1	Standard non-Positraction with 327 and 350
AT	3.08:1	Heavy-duty Positraction with 427
AU	3.36:1	Heavy-duty Positraction with 427
AV	3.08:1	Positraction with 427
AW	3.08:1	Heavy-duty Positraction with 427
AY	2.73:1	Heavy-duty Positraction with 427 and automatic
AZ	3.55:1	Heavy-duty Positraction with 427
FA	3.70:1	Heavy-duty Positraction with 427
FB	4.11:1	Heavy-duty Positraction with 427
FC	4.56:1	Heavy-duty Positraction with 427

1969s
Manufactured After Approximately August 1969 and 1970

Code	Ratio	Type
CAK	3.36:1	Standard non-Positraction with 350
CAL	3.08:1	Standard non-Positraction with 350
CAM	3.36:1	Positraction with 350
CAN	3.55:1	Standard non-Positraction with 350
CAO	3.70:1	Positraction with 350
CAP	4.11:1	Standard non-Positraction with 350
CAS	3.70:1	Standard non-Positraction with 350
CAT	3.08:1	Heavy-duty Positraction with 454
CAU	3.36:1	Heavy-duty Positraction with 454
CAV	3.08:1	Standard non-Positraction with 454

1969s cont.

Code	Ratio	Type
CAW	3.08:1	Standard non-Positraction with 454
CAX	3.36:1	Heavy-duty Positraction with 454
CAY	2.73:1	Heavy-duty Positraction with 454 and automatic
CAZ	3.55:1	Heavy-duty Positraction with 454
CFA	3.70:1	Positraction with 454
CFB	4.11:1	Heavy-duty Positraction with 454
CFC	4.56:1	Heavy-duty Positraction with 454
CLR	3.36:1	Standard non-Positraction with 454

1971

Code	Ratio	Type
AA	3.55:1	Positraction
AB	3.70:1	Positraction
AC	4.11:1	Positraction
AD	4.56:1	Positraction
AW	3.08:1	Positraction
AX	3.36:1	Positraction
LR	3.36:1	Positraction

1972

Code	Ratio	Type
AA	3.55:1	Positraction
AB	3.70:1	Positraction
AC	4.11:1	Positraction
AX	3.36:1	Positraction
LR	3.36:1	Positraction

1973 and 1974

Code	Ratio	Type
AA	3.55:1	Positraction
AB	3.70:1	Positraction

1974 cont.

Code	Ratio	Type
AC	4.11:1	Positraction
AW	3.08:1	Positraction
AX	3.36:1	Positraction
LR	3.36:1	Positraction

1975

Code	Ratio	Type
AA	3.55:1	Positraction
AB	3.70:1	Positraction
AC	4.11:1	Positraction
AY	2.73:1	Positraction
AW	3.08:1	Positraction
AX	3.36:1	Positraction
LR	3.36:1	Positraction

1976 and 1977

Code	Ratio	Type
0A	3.08:1	Positraction
0D	3.36:1	Positraction
LR	3.36:1	Positraction
0B	3.55:1	Positraction
0C	3.70:1	Positraction

1978

Code	Ratio	Type
0K	3.08:1	Positraction
0M	3.36:1	Positraction
0H	3.55:1	Positraction
0J	3.70:1	Positraction

1979

Code	Ratio	Type
0M	3.36:1	Positraction
0H	3.55:1	Positraction
0J	3.70:1	Positraction

1980

Code	Ratio	Type
0F	3.07:1	Positraction
0H	3.07:1	Positraction

1981

Code	Ratio	Type
0J	2.87:1	Positraction with automatic
0K	2.72:1	Positraction with four-speed

1982

Code	Ratio	Type
0A	2.72:1	Positraction with standard wheels
0F	2.87:1	Positraction with aluminum wheels

Appendix F
Engine-Block Casting Numbers

1968

Casting Number	Description
3914460	early 327/300
3914678	327
3916321	early 427
3935439	late 427

1969

Casting Number	Description
3932386	very early 350
3932388	possible 350 usage
3956618	mid-year 350
3970010	late 350
3935439	early 427
3955270	early 427
3963512	late 427
3946052	ZL1 aluminum block

1970 and 1971

Casting Number	Description
3970010	350
3963512	454

1972-1974

Casting Number	Description
3970010	350
3970014	late 1972 and early 1973 350
3999289	454

1975-1977

Casting Number	Description
3970010	350

1978

Casting Number	Description
3970010	350
376450	350
460703	350

1979

Casting Number	Description
3970010	350
14016379	late 350

1980

Casting Number	Description
3970010	350
14010207	350
4715111	LG4 California 305

1981 and 1982

Casting Number	Description
14010207	350

Appendix G
Cylinder Head Casting Numbers

1968

Casting Number	Description
3917291	327/300 and 327/350
3917292	327/350
3917215	427/390 and 427/400
3919840	427/435
3919842	Aluminum L89 427/435 and L88 427/430

1969

Casting Number	Description
3927186	350/300 and 350/350
3927187	350/350
3947041	350/300
3931063	427/390 and 427/400
3919840	427/435
3919842	Aluminum L89 427/435
3946074	Aluminum ZL1 427/430 and L88 427/430

1970

Casting Number	Description
3927186	350/300, 350/350, and 350/370
3927187	350/350
3973414	350/370
3964290	454

1971

Casting Number	Description
3973487	350
3993820	454/365
3994026	LS6 454/425
3946074	LS6 454/425

1972

Casting Number	Description
3998993	350/200
3998916	350/255
3973487(x)	later 350/200 and 350/255
3999241	454

1973

Casting Number	Description
3998993	L48 350
333881	L48 350
333882	L48 350
330545	L82 350
353049	454

1974

Casting Number	Description
333881	L48 350
333882	L48 350
333882	L82 350
336781	454

1975 and 1976

Casting Number	Description
333882	350

1977

Casting Number	Description
376450	L48 350
333882	L48 350 and L82 350

1978-1982

Casting Number	Description
462624	350
14914416	1980 LG4 California 305

Appendix H
Intake Manifold Casting Numbers

1968

Casting Number	Description
3919803	327, cast-iron
3919849	427/390, aluminum
3919850	Early 427/400, aluminum
3937795	Late 427/400, aluminum
3885069	L88 427/430, aluminum (possible usage)
3933198	L88 427/430, aluminum (possible usage)
3919852	Early 427/435, aluminum
3937797	Late 427/435, aluminum

1969

Casting Number	Description
3927184	350, cast-iron
3947801	427/390, aluminum
3937795	427/400, aluminum
3937797	427/435, aluminum
3933198	L88 427/430 and ZL1 427/430, aluminum

1970

Casting Number	Description
3965577	350/300 and 350/350, cast-iron
3972110	LT1 350/370, aluminum
3955287	454/390, aluminum
3969802	454/390, aluminum

1971

Casting Number	Description
3973469	350/270, cast-iron
3959594	LT1 350/330, aluminum
3955287	454/365, cast-iron
3967474	LS6 454/425, aluminum
3963569	LS6 454/425, aluminum

1972

Casting Number	Description
6263751	350/200, cast-iron
3959594	LT1 350/255, aluminum
6263753	454/270, cast-iron

1973

Casting Number	Description
3997770	L48 350/190, cast-iron
3997771	L48 350/190 and L82 350/250, cast-iron
353015	454, cast-iron

1974

Casting Number	Description
340261	L48 350/195 and L82 350/250, cast-iron
353015	454, cast-iron
336789	454, cast-iron

1975-1977

Casting Number	Description
346249	350, cast-iron

1978

Casting Number	Description
346249	L48 350, cast-iron
458520	L82 350, aluminum

1979

Casting Number	Description
14007376	L48 350, cast-iron
14014433	Late L48 350, cast-iron
458520	Early L82 350, aluminum
14007378	Late L82 350, aluminum

1980

Casting Number	Description
14014432	L48 350, L82 350, and LG4 305, aluminum

1981

Casting Number	Description
14033058	L81 350, aluminum

1982

Casting Number	Description
14031372	L83 350, aluminum

Appendix I
Exhaust Manifold Casting Numbers

1968

Left Side Casting No.	Right Side Casting No.	Description
3872765	3872778	327
3880827	3880828	427

1969

Left Side Casting No.	Right Side Casting No.	Description
3872765	3932461	350
3880827	3880828	427

1970

Left Side Casting No.	Right Side Casting No.	Description
3846559	3932465	Early 350/300 and 350/350
3846559	3989036	Late 350/300 and 350/350
3872765	3932461	LT1 350/370
3969869	3880828	454

1971

Left Side Casting No.	Right Side Casting No.	Description
3846559	3989036	350/270
3872765	3932461	LT1 350/330
3880869	3880828	LS5 454/365 and LS6 454/425
3969869	3880828	LS5 454/365 and LS6 454/425

1972

Left Side Casting No.	Right Side Casting No.	Description
3932461	3989036	Early 350/200
3932461	3932461	Late 350/200 and LT1 350/255
386711	386711	LT1 350/255
3969869	3880828	454

1973–1974

Left Side Casting No.	Right Side Casting No.	Description
3932461	3932461	350
3969869	3880828	454

1975–1979

Left Side Casting No.	Right Side Casting No.	Description
3932461	3932461	350

1980

Left Side Casting No.	Right Side Casting No.	Description
3932461	3932461	L48 350/190 and L82 350/230
14037671-W	14037672-W	LG4 305 (tubular stainless steel)

1981–1982

Left Side Casting No.	Right Side Casting No.	Description
14037671-W	14037672-W	350 (tubular stainless steel)

Appendix J
Carburetors and Cross-Fire Injection Part Numbers

1968

Description	Manufacturer No.	Chevrolet No.
327/300, four-speed	Rochester MV4	7028207
327/300, automatic	Rochester MV4	7028208
327/350, four-speed	Rochester MV4	7028219
427/390, four-speed	Rochester MV4	7028209
427/390, automatic	Rochester MV4	7028216
Early 427/400, four-speed, center	Holley R4055A	3925517
Late 427/400, four-speed, center	Holley R4055-1A	3940929
427/400, four-speed, ends	Holley R3659A	3902353
Early 427/400, automatic, center	Holley R4056A	3902516
Late 427/400, automatic, center	Holley R4055-1A	3940930
427/400, automatic, ends	Holley R3659A	3902353
Early L71 and L89 427/435, center	Holley R4055A	3925517
Late L71 and L89 427/435, center	Holley R4055-1A	3940929
L71 and L89 427/435, ends	Holley R3659A	3902353
L88 427/430	Holley R4054A	3925519

1969

Description	Manufacturer No.	Chevrolet No.
350/300, four-speed	Rochester MV4	7029203
350/300, automatic	Rochester MV4	7029202
350/350, four-speed	Rochester MV4	7029207
427/390, four-speed	Rochester MV4	7029215
427/390, automatic	Rochester MV4	7029204
427/400, four-speed, center	Holley R4055-1A	3940929
427/400, four-speed, ends	Holley R3659A	3902353
427/400, automatic, center	Holley R4055-1A	3940930
427/400, automatic, ends	Holley R3659A	3902353
L71 and L89 427/435, center	Holley R4055-1A	3940929
L71 and L89 427/435, ends	Holley R3659A	3902353
L88 427/430	Holley R4054A	3925519

1970

Description	Manufacturer No.	Chevrolet No.
Early 350/300, four-speed	Rochester MV4	7040203
Late 350/300, four-speed	Rochester MV4	7040213
Early 350/300, automatic	Rochester MV4	7040202
Late 350/300, automatic	Rochester MV4	7040212
Early 350/300, four-speed with ECS	Rochester MV4	7040503
Late 350/300, four-speed with ECS	Rochester MV4	7040513
350/300, automatic with ECS	Rochester MV4	7040502
350/350, four-speed	Rochester MV4	7029207
350/350, four-speed with ECS	Rochester MV4	7029507
LT1 350/370, four-speed	Holley R4555A	3972121
LT1 350/370, four-speed with ECS	Holley R4489A	3972123
454/390, four-speed	Rochester MV4	7040205
454/390, automatic	Rochester MV4	7040204

1970 cont.

Description	Manufacturer No.	Chevrolet No.
454/390, four-speed with ECS	Rochester MV4	7040505
454/390, automatic with ECS	Rochester MV4	7040504

1971

Description	Manufacturer No.	Chevrolet No.
350/270, four-speed	Rochester MV4	7040213
350/270, automatic	Rochester MV4	7040212
LT1 350/330, four-speed	Holley R4801A	3989021
454/365, four-speed	Rochester MV4	7040205
454/365, automatic	Rochester MV4	7040204
LS6 454/425, four-speed	Holley R4803A	3986195
LS6 454/425, automatic	Holley R 4802A	3986196

1972

Description	Manufacturer No.	Chevrolet No.
350/200, four-speed	Rochester MV4	7042203
350/200, four-speed with NB2	Rochester MV4	7042903
350/200, automatic	Rochester MV4	7042202
350/200, automatic with NB2	Rochester MV4	7042902
LT1 350/255, four-speed	Holley R6239A	3999263
454, four-speed	Rochester MV4	7042217
454, automatic	Rochester MV4	7042216

1973

Description	Manufacturer No.	Chevrolet No.
350/190, four-speed	Rochester MV4	7043203
350/190, automatic	Rochester MV4	7043202
350/250, four-speed	Rochester MV4	7043213
350/250, automatic	Rochester MV4	7043212
454, four-speed	Rochester MV4	7043201
454, automatic	Rochester MV4	7043200

1974

Description	Manufacturer No.	Chevrolet No.
350/195, four-speed	Rochester MV4	7044207
350/195, automatic	Rochester MV4	7044206
350/250, four-speed	Rochester MV4	7044211
350/250, automatic (California)	Rochester MV4	7044506
350/250, four-speed (California)	Rochester MV4	7044507
350/250, automatic	Rochester MV4	7044210
454, four-speed	Rochester MV4	7044221
454, automatic	Rochester MV4	7044225
454, automatic (California)	Rochester MV4	7044505

1975

Description	Manufacturer No.	Chevrolet No.
350/165, four-speed	Rochester M4MC	7045223
350/165, automatic	Rochester M4MC	7045222
350/205, four-speed	Rochester M4MC	7045211
350/205, automatic	Rochester M4MC	7045210

1976

Description	Manufacturer No.	Chevrolet No.
350/180, four-speed	Rochester M4MC	17056207
350/180, automatic	Rochester M4MC	17056208
350/180, four-speed (California)	Rochester M4MC	17056507
350/180, automatic (California)	Rochester M4MC	17056506
350/210, four-speed	Rochester M4MC	17056211
350/210, automatic	Rochester M4MC	17056210
350/210, automatic with a/c	Rochester M4MC	17056506

1977

Description	Manufacturer No.	Chevrolet No.
350/180, four-speed	Rochester M4MC	17057203
350/180, automatic	Rochester M4MC	17057202
350/180, automatic with a/c	Rochester M4MC	17057204
350/180, automatic (California)	Rochester M4MC	17057502
350/180, auto, a/c (California)	Rochester M4MC	17057504
350/180, automatic and NA6	Rochester M4MC	17057582
350/180, automatic, a/c and NA6	Rochester M4MC	17057584
350/210, four-speed	Rochester M4MC	17057211
350/210, automatic	Rochester M4MC	17057210
350/210, automatic with a/c	Rochester M4MC	17057228
350/210, automatic (California)	Rochester M4MC	17057510

1978

Description	Manufacturer No.	Chevrolet No.
350/185, four-speed	Rochester M4MC	17058203
350/185, automatic	Rochester M4MC	17058202
Early 350/180, auto with a/c	Rochester M4MC	17058204
Late 350/180, auto with a/c	Rochester M4MC	17058206
350/175, automatic (California)	Rochester M4MC	17058502
350/175, auto, a/c (California)	Rochester M4MC	17058504
350/175, automatic and NA6	Rochester M4MC	17058582
350/175, automatic, a/c and NA6	Rochester M4MC	17058584

1978 cont.

Description	Manufacturer No.	Chevrolet No.
350/220, four-speed	Rochester M4MC	17058211
350/220, automatic	Rochester M4MC	17058210
350/220, automatic with a/c	Rochester M4MC	17058228

1979

Description	Manufacturer No.	Chevrolet No.
350/195, four-speed	Rochester M4MC	17059203
350/195, automatic	Rochester M4MC	17059217
350/195, automatic	Rochester M4MC	17059202
350/195, automatic (California)	Rochester M4MC	17059502
350/195, auto with a/c	Rochester M4MC	17059216
350/195, auto, a/c (California)	Rochester M4MC	17059504
350/195, auto, a/c (California)	Rochester M4MC	17059507
350/195, automatic and NA6	Rochester M4MC	17059582
350/195, automatic, a/c and NA6	Rochester M4MC	17059584
350/225, four-speed	Rochester M4MC	17059211
350/225, automatic	Rochester M4MC	17059210
350/225, automatic with a/c	Rochester M4MC	17059228

1980

Description	Manufacturer No.	Chevrolet No.
350/190, four-speed	Rochester M4ME	17080207
350/190, automatic	Rochester M4ME	17080204
350/180, automatic (California)	Rochester E4ME	17080504
350/180, automatic (California)	Rochester E4ME	17080517
350/230, four-speed	Rochester M4ME	—
350/230, automatic	Rochester M4ME	17080228

1981

Description	Manufacturer No.	Chevrolet No.
350/190, four-speed	Rochester E4ME	17081217
350/190, automatic (California)	Rochester E4ME	17081218
350/190, automatic	Rochester E4ME	17081228

1982

Description	Manufacturer No.	Chevrolet No.
Cross-Fire Injection	Front Rochester 400	17082053
Cross-Fire Injection	Rear Rochester 400	17082052

Appendix K
Distributor Part Numbers

1968

Part Number	Description
1111194	327/300
1111293	427/390 and 427/400
1111294	427/390 and 427/400 with K66
1111295	L88 427/430 with K66
1111296	L71 and L89 427/435 with K66
1111438	327/350
1111441	Early 327/350 with K66
1111475	Late 327/350 with K66

1969

Part Number	Description
1111490	350/300
1111491	350/350 with K66
1111493	350/350
1111926	427/390 and 427/400
1111927	L88 427/430 with K66
1111928	L71 and L89 427/435 with K66
1111954	427/390 and 427/400 with K66

1970

Part Number	Description
1111490	Early 350/300
1112020	Late 350/300
1111491	LT1 350/370 with K66
1111493	Early 350/350
1112021	Late 350/350
1111464	454/390

1971

Part Number	Description
1112050	350/270
1112038	LT1 350/330 with K66
1111493	Early 350/350
1112051	454/365
1112053	LS6 454/425 with automatic and K66
1112076	LS6 454/425 with four-speed and K66

1972

Part Number	Description
1112050	350/200
1112101	LT1 350/255 with K66
1112051	454/270

1973

Part Number	Description
1112098	350/190
1112130	L82 350/250 with four-speed

1973 cont.

Part Number	Description
1112150	L82 350/250 with automatic
1112051	454/270

1974

Part Number	Description
1112247	L48 350/195
1112544	L48 350/195 with four-speed and YF5
1112850	L48 350/195 with four-speed and YF5
1112851	L48 350/195 with automatic and YF5
1112150	L82 350/250 with four-speed
1112853	L82 350/250 with automatic
1112526	454/270
1112114	454/270

1975

Part Number	Description
1112888	L48 350/165
1112880	L48 350/165 with YF5
1112883	Early L82 350/205
1112979	Late L82 350/205

1976

Part Number	Description
1112888	L48 350/180
1112905	L48 350/180 with automatic and YF5
1103200	L82 350/210 with four-speed
1112979	L82 350/210 with automatic

1977

Part Number	Description
1103246	L48 350/180
1103248	L48 350/180 with automatic and YF5
1103256	L82 350/210

1978

Part Number	Description
1103337	L48 350/185 with four-speed
1103353	L48 350/185 with automatic
1103285	L48 350/175 with YF5
1103291	L82 350/220

1979

Part Number	Description
1103302	L48 350/195 with four-speed
1103353	L48 350/195 with automatic
1103285	L48 350/195 with YF5
1103291	L82 350/225

1980

Part Number	Description
1103287	L48 350/190 with four-speed
1103352	L48 350/190 with automatic
1103353	L48 350/190 with auto/high altitude emissions
1103285	L48 305/180 with automatic and YF5
1103291	L82 350/230 with four-speed
1103435	L82 350/230 with automatic

1981

Part Number	Description
1103443	L81 350/190

1982

Part Number	Description
1103479	L83 350/200

Appendix L
Ignition Coil Part Numbers

1968

Part Number	Description
1115270	327/300 and 327/350 with standard ignition
1115207	Early 327/350 with K66
1115272	327/350 with K66
1115287	427/390 and 427/400 with standard ignition
1115263	427 with K66

1969

Part Number	Description
1115270	350 with standard ignition
1115272	350 with K66
1115287	427/390 and 427/400 with standard ignition
1115263	427 with K66

1970

Part Number	Description
1115270	350/300 and 350/350 with standard ignition
1115272	350/350, 350/370, and 454/390 with K66
1115287	454/390 with standard ignition

1971

Part Number	Description
1115270	350/270 with standard ignition
1115272	350/330 with K66
1115287	454/365 with standard ignition
1115263	454/425 with K66

1972–1974

Part Number	Description
1115270	350
1115287	454

Appendix M
Alternator Part Numbers

1968

Part Number	Description
1100693	37 amp, all cars without K66 or C60
1100696	42 amp, all engines with K66
1100750	61 amp, all cars with C60

1969

Part Number	Description
1100859	42 amp, all 350s without K66 or C60
1100833	42 amp, all 427s without K66 or C60
1100825	61 amp, all cars with C60 or K66
1100884	61 amp, 350/300 with C60
1100882	61 amp, L88 and L89 with K66

1970

Part Number	Description
1100901	42 amp, 350/300 without C60
1100900	42 amp, 350/350 and 454/390 without C60
1100884	61 amp, 350/370 and all cars with C60

1971

Part Number	Description
1100950	42 amp, 350/330 and 350/270 without C60
1100543	42 amp, 454/425 and 454/365 without C60
1100544	61 amp, all cars with C60

1972

Part Number	Description
1100950	42 amp, 350/330 and 350/200 without C60
1100543	42 amp, 454/270 without C60
1100544	61 amp, all cars with C60

1973

Part Number	Description
1100950	42 amp, L48 and L82 without C60, and LS4 without N40
1102353	42 amp, LS4 with N40
1100544	61 amp, all cars with C60

1974

Part Number	Description
1102394	37 amp, L48 (possible usage)
1100950	42 amp, L48 and L82 without C60, and LS4 without N40
1102353	42 amp, LS4 with N40
1100544	61 amp, all cars with C60 or UA1

1975

Part Number	Description
1102483	37 amp, early L48 (possible usage)
1102394	37 amp, later L48 (possible usage)
1100950	42 amp, L48 and early L82 without C60
1102484	42 amp, later L82
1100544	61 amp, early cars with C60
1100597	61 amp, early cars with UA1
1102474	61 amp, later cars with C60
1102480	61 amp, later cars with UA1

1976

Part Number	Description
1102484	42 amp, all cars without C60
1102474	61 amp, all cars with C60

1977

Part Number	Description
1102394	37 amp, L48 (possible usage)
1102484	42 amp, L48 and L82 without C60
1102474	61 amp, early cars with C60 or C49
1102909	63 amp, mid-production with C60 or C49
1102908	63 amp, later cars with C60 or C49

1978

Part Number	Description
1102394	37 amp, L48 (possible usage)
1102484	42 amp, L48 and L82 without C60
1102908	63 amp, all cars with C60 or C49

1979

Part Number	Description
1102394	37 amp, L48 (possible usage)
1102484	42 amp, L48 and L82 without C60
1102474	61 amp, all cars with C60 but without C49 and UA1
1102908	63 amp, all cars with C60 or C49
1101041	70 amp, all cars with C60 and C49 or UA1

1980

Part Number	Description
1102474	61 amp, early cars with C60 but without C49 and UA1
1103122	63 amp, mid-production cars with C60 but without C49 and UA1
1103103	63 amp, late cars with C60 but without C49 and UA1
1101041	70 amp, early cars with C60 and C49 or UA1
1101075	70 amp, later cars with C60 and C49 or UA1

1981

Part Number	Description
1103103	63 amp, all cars with C60 but without C49
1101075	70 amp, all cars with C60 and C49

1982

Part Number	Description
1103103	63 amp, all coupes with C60 but without C49
1103091	63 amp, all coupes with C60 but without C49 (possible usage)
1101071	70 amp, all hatchbacks and coupes with C60 and C49 (possible usage)
1101075	70 amp, all hatchbacks and coupes with C60 and C49

Appendix N
Starter Motor Part Numbers

1968

Part Number	Description
1108361	327 with manual transmission
1108338	327 with automatic
1107365	All 427 except L88
1108351	Early L88 with M22 four-speed
1108400	Later L88 with M22 four-speed

1969

Part Number	Description
1108361	Early 350 with manual transmission
1108338	350 with manual transmission
1108427	350 with automatic
1107365	Early 427 (possible usage)
1108351	427 with M22 four-speed
1108400	427 except L88 with M22 four-speed

1970

Part Number	Description
1108338	350 with four-speed
1108381	ZR1 with M22 four-speed
1108418	350 with four-speed (possible usage)
1108430	350 with automatic
1108400	454 with four-speed
1108429	454 with automatic

1971

Part Number	Description
1108338	Early 350 with four-speed
1108418	Later 350 with four-speed
1108381	ZR1 with M22 four-speed
1108430	350 with automatic
1108400	454 with four-speed
1108429	454 with automatic

1972

Part Number	Description
1108418	350 with four-speed
1108381	ZR1 with M22 four-speed
1108430	350 with automatic
1108400	454 with four-speed
1108429	454 with automatic

1973–1974

Part Number	Description
1108418	350 with four-speed
1108430	350 with automatic
1108400	454 with four-speed
1108429	454 with automatic

1975

Part Number	Description
1108418	Early 350 with four-speed
1108430	Early 350 with automatic
1108775	Later 350 with four-speed
1108776	Later 350 with automatic

1976

Part Number	Description
1108775	350 with four-speed
1108776	350 with automatic

1977

Part Number	Description
1108775	Early 350 with four-speed
1109052	350 with automatic
1109059	Later 350 with four-speed

1978

Part Number	Description
1109052	Early 350 with automatic
1109059	Early 350 with four-speed
1109065	Later 350 with automatic
1109067	Later 350 with four-speed

1979

Part Number	Description
1109065	Early 350 with automatic
1109067	350 with four-speed
1998217	Later 350 with automatic

1980

Part Number	Description
1109059	350 with four-speed
1998222	350 with automatic (possible usage)
1998225	350 with four-speed (possible usage)
1998217	350 with automatic

1981

Part Number	Description
1109067	350 with four-speed
1998217	350 with automatic

1982

Part Number	Description
1998241	350 with automatic

Appendix O
Horn and Horn Relay Part Numbers

Year	Low-Note Part No.	High-Note Part No.	Relay No.	Year	Low-Note Part No.	High-Note Part No.	Relay No.
1968 (early)	9000245	9000246	1115837	1975 (early)	9000049	9000038	344813
1968 (late)	9000245	9000246	1115862	1975 (late)	9000033	9000106	344813
1969 (early)	9000245	9000246	1115862	1976	9000144	9000143	344813
1969 (late)	9000245	9000246	1115890	1977	9000144	9000143	344813
1970	9000245	9000246	1115890	1978	9000144	9000143	344813
1971	9000245	—	1115889	1979	9000144	9000143	344813
1972	9000032	—	3996283	1980	9000144	9000192	344813
1973	9000032	—	3996283	1981	9000144	9000192	25505674
1974 (early)	9000032	—	329820	1982	9000176	9000203	25505674
1974 (late)	9000049	9000038	344813				

Appendix P
Windshield Wiper Motor Numbers

Year	Part No.
1968	5044683
1969	5044731
1970	7044758
1971	7044758
1972	5044780
1973	5044784
1974	5044811
1975	5044814
1976	5044814
1977	5044814
1978	5044814 (standard)
1978	5044907 (pulse)
1979	5044814 (standard)
1979	5044907 (pulse)
1980	5044907
1981	5044907
1982	5044907

Appendix Q
Air Conditioning Compressor Part Numbers

Year	Part No.
All 1968 and early 1969 small block	5910645
1969 small block	5910741
1969 big block	5910740
1970 small block	5910741
1970 big block	5910740
Early 1971 small block	5910741
Late 1971 small block	5910778
1971 big block	5910740
1972 small block	1131002
1972 big block	5910797
1973 small block	1131002
1973 big block	5910797
1974 small block	5910741
1974 big block	5910740
1975	5910741
1976 A-6 axial type	5910741
1976 R-4 radial type	1131078
1977	1131078
1978	1131078
1979	1131078
1980	1131198
1981	1131198
1982	1131198

Appendix R
Glass Date Codes

All 1968–1982 Corvette glass was manufactured by Libby Owens Ford (LOF). The date code contains a letter for the month and a second letter for the year.

LOF Month	Code	LOF Month	Code
January	N	July	U
February	X	August	T
March	L	September	A
April	G	October	Y
May	J	November	C
June	I	December	V

LOF Calendar Year	Code	LOF Calendar Year	Code
1	Z	9	I
2	X	10	C
3	V	11	G
4	T	12	J
5	N	13	A
6	Y	14	Z
7	U	15	X
8	L	16	V

Appendix S
Body Build Date Codes

1968
Code	Date
A	August 1967
B	September 1967
C	October 1967
D	November 1967
E	December 1967
F	January 1968
G	February 1968
H	March 1968
I	April 1968
J	May 1968
K	June 1968
L	July 1968
M	August 1968

1969
Code	Date
A	August 1968
B	September 1968
C	October 1968
D	November 1968
E	December 1968
F	January 1969
G	February 1969
H	March 1969
I	April 1969
J	May 1969
K	June 1969

1969 cont.
Code	Date
L	July 1969
M	August 1969
N	September 1969
O	October 1969
P	November 1969
Q	December 1969

1970
Code	Date
A	January 1970
B	February 1970
C	March 1970
D	April 1970
E	May 1970
F	June 1970
G	July 1970

1971
Code	Date
A	August 1970
B	September 1970
C	October 1970
D	November 1970
E	December 1970
F	January 1971
G	February 1971
H	March 1971

1971 cont.
Code	Date
I	April 1971
J	May 1971
K	June 1971
L	July 1971

1972
Code	Date
A	August 1971
B	September 1971
C	October 1971
D	November 1971
E	December 1971
F	January 1972
G	February 1972
H	March 1972
I	April 1972
J	May 1972
K	June 1972
L	July 1972

1973
Code	Date
A	August 1972
B	September 1972
C	October 1972
D	November 1972
E	December 1972

1973 cont.
Code	Date
F	January 1973
G	February 1973
H	March 1973
I	April 1973
J	May 1973
K	June 1973
L	July 1973

1974
Code	Date
A	August 1973
B	September 1973
C	October 1973
D	November 1973
E	December 1973
F	January 1974
G	February 1974
H	March 1974
I	April 1974
J	May 1974
K	June 1974
L	July 1974
M	August 1974
N	September 1974

1975

Code	Date
A	October 1974
B	November 1974
C	December 1974
D	January 1975
E	February 1975
F	March 1975
G	April 1975
H	May 1975
I	June 1975
J	July 1975

1976

Code	Date
A	August 1975
B	September 1975
C	October 1975
D	November 1975
E	December 1975
F	January 1976
G	February 1976
H	March 1976
I	April 1976
J	May 1976
K	June 1976
L	July 1976
M	August 1976

1977

Code	Date
A	August 1976
B	September 1976
C	October 1976
D	November 1976

1977 cont.

Code	Date
E	December 1976
F	January 1977
G	February 1977
H	March 1977
I	April 1977
J	May 1977
K	June 1977
L	July 1977
M	August 1977

1978

Code	Date
A	September 1977
B	October 1977
C	November 1977
D	December 1977
E	January 1978
F	February 1978
G	March 1978
H	April 1978
I	May 1978
J	June 1978
K	July 1978
L	August 1978

1979

Code	Date
A	August 1978
B	September 1978
C	October 1978
D	November 1978
E	December 1978
F	January 1979

1979 cont.

Code	Date
G	February 1979
H	March 1979
I	April 1979
J	May 1979
K	June 1979
L	July 1979
M	August 1979
N	September 1979

1980

Code	Date
A	October 1979
B	November 1979
C	December 1979
D	January 1980
E	February 1980
F	March 1980
G	April 1980
H	May 1980
I	June 1980
J	July 1980
K	August 1980

1981

(Cars Assembled in St. Louis)

Code	Date
A	August 1980
B	September 1980
C	October 1980
D	November 1980
E	December 1980
F	January 1981
G	February 1981

1981 cont.

Code	Date
H	March 1981
I	April 1981
J	May 1981
K	June 1981
L	July 1981

1981

(Cars Assembled in Bowling Green)

Code	Date
B05	May 1981
B06	June 1981
B07	July 1981
B08	August 1981
B09	September 1981
B10	October 1981

1982

Code	Date
C10	October 1981
C11	November 1981
C12	December 1981
C01	January 1982
C02	February 1982
C03	March 1982
C04	April 1982
C05	May 1982
C06	June 1982
C07	July 1982
C08	August 1982
C09	September 1982
C10	October 1982

Appendix T

Exterior Paint Color Codes, Interior Trim Color Codes, and Available Combinations

1968

Interior Color/Trim Codes

STD	Black vinyl
402	Black leather
1	Red vinyl
2	Red leather
414	Medium Blue vinyl
415	Medium Blue leather
411	Dark Blue vinyl
425	Dark Orange vinyl
426	Dark Orange leather
435	Tobacco vinyl

Interior Color/Trim Codes, 1968 cont.

436	Tobacco leather
442	Gunmetal vinyl

Exterior Color Codes and Available Trim Combinations

900	Tuxedo Black (available with all interior colors)
1	Polar White (available with all interior colors)
974	Rally Red (STD, 402, 407, 408)
1	LeMans Blue (STD, 402, 414, 415, 411)
2	International Blue (STD, 402, 414, 415, 411)
3	British Green (STD, 402)

Exterior Color Codes and Available Trim Combinations, 1968 cont.

4	Safari Yellow (STD, 402)	
5	Silverstone Silver (STD, 402, 442)	
988	Cordovan Maroon (STD, 402,)	
1	Corvette Bronze (STD, 402, 425, 426, 435, 436)	

1969
Interior Color/Trim Codes

STD	Black vinyl
ZQ4	Black vinyl
402	Black leather
407	Red vinyl
408	Red leather
411	Bright Blue vinyl
1	Bright Blue leather
427	Green vinyl
428	Green leather
420	Saddle vinyl
421	Saddle leather
416	Gunmetal vinyl
417	Gunmetal leather

Exterior Color Codes and Available Trim Combinations

900	Tuxedo Black (available with all interior colors)
1	Can-Am White (available with all interior colors)
974	Monza Red (STD, ZQ4, 402, 407, 408, 420, 421)
976	LeMans Blue (STD, ZQ4, 402, 411, 412)
980	Riverside Gold (STD, ZQ4, 402, 420, 421)
983	Fathom Green (STD, ZQ4, 402, 427, 428, 420, 421)
984	Daytona Yellow (STD, ZQ4, 402)
986	Cortez Silver (available with all interior colors)
988	Burgundy (STD, ZQ4, 402, 420, 421)
990	Monaco Orange (STD, ZQ4, 402)

1970
Interior Color/Trim Codes

400	Black vinyl
403	Black leather
407	Red vinyl
411	Blue vinyl
422	Green vinyl
418	Saddle vinyl
424	Saddle leather
414	Brown vinyl

Exterior Color Codes and Available Trim Combinations

972	Classic White (available with all interior colors)
974	Monza Red (400, 403, 407, 418, 424, 414)
1	Marlboro Maroon (400, 403, 418, 424, 414)
976	Mulsanne Blue (400, 403, 411)
979	Bridgehampton Blue (400, 403, 411)
982	Donnybrooke Green (400, 402, 422, 418, 424, 414)
984	Daytona Yellow (400, 403, 422)
986	Cortez Silver (available with all interior colors)
992	Laguna Gray (available with all interior colors)
1	Corvette Bronze (400, 403)

1971
Interior Color/Trim Codes

400	Black vinyl
403	Black leather
407	Red vinyl
412	Dark Blue vinyl
423	Dark Green vinyl
417	Saddle vinyl
420	Saddle leather

Exterior Color Codes and Available Trim Combinations

905	Nevada Silver (400, 403, 407, 412, 423)
912	Sunflower Yellow (400, 403, 423, 417, 420)
972	Classic White (available with all interior colors)
973	Mille Miglia Red (400, 403, 407)
976	Mulsanne Blue (400, 403, 412)
979	Bridgehampton Blue (400, 403, 412)
983	Brands Hatch Green (400, 403, 423)
987	Ontario Orange (400, 403, 423, 417, 420)
988	Steel Cities Gray (400, 403, 417, 420)
1	War Bonnet Yellow (400, 403, 423, 417, 420)

1972
Interior Color/Trim Codes

400	Black vinyl
404	Black leather
407	Red vinyl
412	Blue vinyl
417	Saddle vinyl
421	Saddle leather

Exterior Color Codes and Available Trim Combinations

924	Pewter Silver (available with all interior colors)
912	Sunflower Yellow (400, 404, 417, 421)
972	Classic White (available with all interior colors)
973	Mille Miglia Red (400, 404, 407, 417, 421)
945	Bryar Blue (400, 404,)
979	Targa Blue (400, 404, 412)
946	Elkhart Green (400, 404, 421, 417)
987	Ontario Orange (400, 404, 417, 421)
988	Steel Cities Gray (400, 404, 407, 417, 421)
1	War Bonnet Yellow (400, 404, 417, 420)

1973
Interior Color/Trim Codes

400	Black vinyl
404	Black leather
425	Dark Red vinyl
413	Dark Blue vinyl
415	Medium Saddle vinyl
1	Medium Saddle leather
418	Dark Saddle vinyl
422	Dark Saddle leather

910	Classic White (available with all interior colors)
914	Silver Metallic (available with all interior colors)
976	Mille Miglia Red (available with all interior colors)
922	Medium Blue Metallic (400, 404, 413, 415, 416)
927	Dark Blue Metallic (400, 404, 413, 415, 416, 425)
947	Elkhart Green Metallic (400, 404, 415, 416)
980	Orange Metallic (400, 404, 413, 415, 416, 418, 422)
953	Yellow Metallic (400, 404, 413)
952	Bright Yellow (400, 404, 413, 418, 422)
945	Blue-Green Metallic (400, 404, 415, 416, 418, 422, 425)

1974

Interior Color/Trim Codes

400	Black vinyl
404	Black leather
425	Dark Red vinyl
413	Dark Blue vinyl
415	Medium Saddle vinyl
416	Medium Saddle leather
406	Silver vinyl
407	Silver leather
408	Neutral vinyl

Exterior Color Codes and Available Trim Combinations

910	Classic White (available with all interior colors)
914	Silver Mist Metallic (400, 404, 406, 407, 413, 415, 416, 425)
976	Mille Miglia Red (400, 404, 406, 407, 408, 415, 416, 425)
922	Medium Blue Metallic (400, 404, 406, 407, 413)
948	Dark Green Metallic (400, 404, 406, 407, 408, 415, 416)
980	Orange Metallic (400, 404, 406, 407, 408, 415, 416)
956	Bright Yellow (400, 404, 406, 407, 408, 415, 416)
968	Dark Brown Metallic (400, 404, 406, 407, 408, 415, 416)
917	Corvette Gray Metallic (available with all interior colors)
1	Medium Red Metallic (400, 404, 406, 407, 408, 415, 416, 425)

1975

Interior Color/Trim Codes

19V	Black vinyl
192	Black leather
73V	Dark Red vinyl
732	Dark Red leather
26V	Dark Blue vinyl
262	Dark Blue vinyl
65V	Medium Saddle vinyl
652	Medium Saddle leather
14V	Silver vinyl
142	Silver leather
60V	Neutral vinyl

10	Classic White (available with all interior colors)
13	Silver Metallic (19V, 192, 73V, 732, 26V, 262, 65V, 652, 14V, 142)
76	Mille Miglia Red (19V, 192, 73V, 732, 60V, 65V, 652, 14V, 142)
22	Bright Blue Metallic (19V, 192, 26V, 262, 14V, 142)
27	Steel Blue Metallic (19V, 192, 26V, 262, 14V, 142)
42	Bright Green Metallic (19V, 192, 65V, 652, 14V, 142, 60V)
70	Orange Flame (19V, 192, 65V, 652, 60V)
56	Bright Yellow (19V, 192, 65V, 652, 60V)
67	Medium Saddle Metallic (19V, 192, 65V, 652, 60V)
74	Dark Red Metallic (19V, 192, 65V, 652, 14V, 142, 60V, 73V, 732)

1976

Interior Color/Trim Codes

19V	Black vinyl
192	Black leather
71V	Dark Firethorn vinyl
712	Dark Firethorn leather
322	Blue-Green leather
152	Smoke-Gray leather
64V	Light Buckskin vinyl
642	Light Buckskin leather
15V	White vinyl
112	White leather
692	Dark Brown leather

Exterior Color Codes and Available Trim Combinations

10	Classic White (available with all interior colors)
13	Silver Metallic (19V, 192, 71V, 712, 322, 15V, 112, 152, 64V, 642)
72	Corvette Red (19V, 192, 71V, 712, 64V, 642, 15V, 112, 152)
22	Bright Blue Metallic (19V, 192, 152)
33	Dark Green Metallic (19V, 192, 64V, 642, 15V, 112, 152, 322)
70	Orange Flame (19V, 192, 64V, 642, 692)
56	Bright Yellow (19V, 192, 692)
64	Light Buckskin (15V, 112, 19V, 192, 64V, 642, 692, 71V, 712)
69	Dark Brown Metallic (19V, 192, 64V, 642, 15V, 112, 692)
1	Mahogany Metallic (19V, 192, 71V, 712, 15V, 112, 152, 64V, 642)

1977

Interior Color/Trim Codes

19C	Black cloth
192	Black leather
72C	Medium Red cloth
722	Medium Red leather
15C	Smoke-Gray cloth
152	Smoke-Gray leather
64C	Buckskin cloth
642	Buckskin leather
112	White leather
27C	Dark Blue cloth

Interior Color/Trim Codes, 1977 cont.

272	Dark Blue leather
69C	Dark Brown cloth
692	Dark Brown leather

Exterior Color Codes and Available Trim Combinations

10	Classic White (available with all interior colors)
13	Silver Metallic (112, 19C, 192, 72C, 722, 27C, 272, 15C, 152)
19	Black (112, 19C, 192, 72V, 722, 64C, 642, 15C, 152)
26	Light Blue Metallic (112, 19C, 192, 15C, 152)
28	Dark Blue (112, 19C, 192, 15C, 152, 27C, 272, 64C, 642)
41	Chartreuse (19C, 192)
66	Orange Metallic (19C, 192, 64C, 642, 69C, 692)
52	Corvette Yellow (19C, 192, 69C, 692) (code No. changed from 52 to 56 mid-year)
80	Tan Buckskin (112, 19C, 192, 64C, 642, 69C, 692, 72C, 722)
83	Dark Red (19C, 192, 64C, 642, 15C, 152)
72	Medium Red (112, 19C, 192, 72C, 722, 15C, 152, 64C, 642)

1978

Interior Color/Trim Codes

15C	Silver cloth (Pace Car Replica only)
152	Silver leather (Pace Car Replica only)
19C	Black cloth
192	Black leather
72C	Medium Red cloth
722	Medium Red leather
76C	Saffron cloth
762	Saffron leather
59C	Light Doeskin cloth
592	Light Doeskin leather
12C	Oyster White cloth
122	Oyster White leather
29C	Dark Blue cloth
292	Dark Blue leather
69C	Dark Brown cloth
692	Dark Brown leather

Exterior Color Codes and Available Trim Combinations

10	Classic White (available with all interior colors)
13	Silver Metallic (12C, 122, 19C, 192, 72C, 722, 29C, 292, 76C, 762)
19	Black (12C, 122, 19C, 192, 72C, 722, 59C, 592, 76C, 762)
52	Yellow (19C, 192, 69C, 692, 12C, 122)
59	Frost Beige (19C, 192, 72C, 722, 29C, 292, 76C, 762, 59C, 592, 69C, 692)
72	Red (19C, 192, 72V, 722, 59C, 592, 12C, 122)
83	Dark Blue Metallic (122, 12C, 19C, 192, 72C, 722, 59C, 592, 29C, 292)
66	Orange Metallic (19C, 192, 64C, 642, 69C, 692)
82	Mahogany Metallic (122, 12C, 19C, 192, 76C, 762, 59C, 592)
1	Dark Brown Metallic (122, 12C, 19C, 192, 59C, 592, 69C, 692)
07M	Silver Anniversary (12C, 122, 19C, 192, 72C, 722, 29C, 292, 76C, 762)
47M	Pace Car Replica (15C, 152)

1979

Interior Color/Trim Codes

192	Black leather
722	Medium Red leather
59C	Light Doeskin cloth
592	Light Doeskin leather
12C	Oyster White cloth
122	Oyster White leather
29C	Dark Blue cloth
292	Dark Blue leather
49C	Dark Green cloth
492	Dark Green leather

Exterior Color Codes and Available Trim Combinations

10	Classic White (available with all interior colors)
13	Silver Metallic (12C, 122, 192, 722, 29C, 292, 49C, 492)
19	Black (12C, 122, 192, 722, 59C, 592)
28	Frost Blue (192, 29C, 292, 12C, 122)
52	Yellow (192, 59C, 592, 12C, 122)
58	Dark Green Metallic (192, 59C, 592, 49C, 492, 12C, 122)
59	Frost Beige (192, 722, 29C, 292, 49C, 492, 59C, 592)
1	Hilton Brown Metallic (192, 59C, 592, 12C, 122) (also appears as code 82)
72	Red (192, 722, 59C, 592, 12C, 122)
83	Dark Blue Metallic (122, 12C, 192, 722, 59C, 592, 29C, 292)

1980

Interior Color/Trim Codes

192	Black leather
722	Medium Red leather
59C	Light Doeskin cloth
592	Light Doeskin leather
12C	Oyster White cloth
122	Oyster White leather
29C	Dark Blue cloth
292	Dark Blue leather
492	Dark Green leather
79C	Claret cloth
792	Claret leather

Exterior Color Codes and Available Trim Combinations

10	Classic White (available with all interior colors)
13	Silver Metallic (12C, 122, 192, 722, 29C, 292, 79C, 792, 492)
19	Black (12C, 122, 192, 722, 59C, 592)
28	Dark Blue Metallic (192, 722, 59C, 592, 29C, 292, 12C, 122)
52	Yellow (192, 12C, 122)
58	Dark Green Metallic (192, 59C, 592, 492, 12C, 122)
59	Frost Beige (192, 122, 12C, 29C, 292)
47	Hilton Brown Metallic (available with all interior colors)
83	Medium Red (192, 722, 59C, 592, 12C, 122)
1	Dark Claret Metallic (122, 12C, 192, 59C, 592, 79C, 792)

1981

Interior Color/Trim Codes

19C	Charcoal cloth
192	Charcoal leather
722	Medium Red leather
64C	Camel cloth
642	Camel leather
29C	Dark Blue cloth
292	Dark Blue leather
152	Silver leather
67C	Medium Cinnabar cloth
672	Medium Cinnabar leather

Exterior Color Codes and Available Trim Combinations

06	Mahogany Metallic (64C, 642, 67C, 672)
10	Classic White (19C, 192, 722, 64C, 642, 29C, 292, 67C, 672)
13	Silver Metallic (19C, 192, 722, 152, 29C, 292)
19	Black (19C, 192, 722, 64C, 642, 152, 67C, 672)
24	Bright Blue Metallic (19C, 192, 152, 64C, 642, 29C, 292)
28	Dark Blue Metallic (722, 64C, 642, 29C, 292, 152)
52	Yellow (19C, 192, 64C, 642)
59	Frost Beige (722, 64C, 642, 29C, 292, 67C, 672)
75	Red (19C, 192, 722, 64C, 642, 152)
79	Maroon Metallic (19C, 192, 722, 64C, 642, 152)
84	Charcoal Metallic (19C, 192, 722, 64C, 642, 152)
33/38	Silver/Dark Blue (29C, 292, 152)
33/39	Silver/Charcoal (19C, 192, 152, 67C, 672)
50/74	Beige/Dark Bronze (64C, 642)
80/98	Red/Dark Claret (64C, 642, 152, 67C, 672)

1982

Interior Color/Trim Codes

592	Collector Edition Hatchback Silver Beige leather
132	Silver Gray leather
182	Charcoal leather
74C	Dark Red cloth
742	Dark Red leather
64C	Camel cloth
642	Camel leather
22C	Dark Blue cloth
222	Dark Blue leather
402	Silver Green leather

Exterior Color Codes and Available Trim Combinations

10	Classic White (available with all interior colors)
13	Silver Metallic (132, 182, 74C, 742, 22C, 222)
19	Black (132, 182, 74C, 742, 64C, 642, 402)
24	Silver Blue Metallic (132, 182, 64C, 642)
26	Dark Blue Metallic (132, 64C, 642, 22C, 222)
31	Bright Blue Metallic (132, 182, 64C, 642, 22C, 222)
39	Charcoal Metallic (132, 182, 74C, 742)
40	Silver Green Metallic (182, 402)
56	Gold Metallic (132, 64C, 642)
59	Silver Beige Metallic (592)
70	Red (132, 182, 74C, 742, 64C, 642)
99	Dark Claret Metallic (132, 74C, 742, 64C, 642)
13/99	Silver/Dark Claret (132, 74C, 742)
24/26	Silver Blue/Dark Blue (22C, 222)
13/39	Silver/Charcoal (132, 182)
10/13	White/Silver (132, 182)

Appendix U
Final Monthly Serial Numbers

1968

Date	Serial Number
September 1967	400905
October 1967	403410
November 1967	405682
December 1967	407922
January 1968	410386
February 1968	412647
March 1968	415000
April 1968	417676
May 1968	420928
June 1968	423978
July 1968	unknown
August 1968	428566

1969

Date	Serial Number
September 1968	703041
October 1968	706272
November 1968	709159
December 1968	711742
January 1969	714695
February 1969	717571
March 1969	720543
April 1969	721315
May 1969	no cars built
June 1969	723374
July 1969	725875
August 1969	728107
September 1969	730963
October 1969	734067
November 1969	736798
December 1969	738762

1970

Date	Serial Number
January 1970	402261
February 1970	405183
March 1970	407977
April 1970	408314
May 1970	410652
June 1970	413829
July 1970	417316

1971

Date	Serial Number
August 1970	101212
September 1970	102226
October 1970	no cars built
November 1970	102675
December 1970	105269
January 1971	108230
February 1971	110886
March 1971	113626
April 1971	115983
May 1971	118223
June 1971	120686
July 1971	121801

1972

Date	Serial Number
August 1971	501344
September 1971	503697
October 1971	506050
November 1971	508406
December 1971	510310
January 1972	512661
February 1972	515020
March 1972	517613
April 1972	519993
May 1972	522611
June 1972	525226
July 1972	527004

1973

Date	Serial Number
August 1972	401138
September 1972	403539
October 1972	406054
November 1972	408696
December 1972	410679
January 1973	413600
February 1973	416301
March 1973	419253
April 1973	421933
May 1973*	428892
June 1973	431731
July 1973	434464

*The May 1973 production total includes 4,000 serial numbers from 424001 through 428000 that were not utilized

1974

Date	Serial Number
August 1973	401250
September 1973	404111
October 1973	407605
November 1973	410813
December 1973	412830
January 1974	416184
February 1974	419258
March 1974	422367
April 1974	425751
May 1974	429602
June 1974	433257
July 1974	no cars built
August 1974	no cars built
September 1974	437502

1975

Date	Serial Number
October 1974	402385
November 1974	406180
December 1974	409110
January 1975	413159
February 1975	417112
March 1975	420856
April 1975	425228
May 1975	429379
June 1975	433474
July 1975	438465

1976

Date	Serial Number
August 1975	401602
September 1975	405693
October 1975	409982
November 1975	413481
December 1975	416696
January 1976	420568
February 1976	424370
March 1976	428760
April 1976	432805
May 1976	436656
June 1976	440830
July 1976	444767
August 1976	446558

1977

Date	Serial Number
August 1976	402287
September 1976	406337
October 1976	410547
November 1976	414216
December 1976	417551

1977 cont.

Date	Serial Number
January 1977	421118
February 1977	424662
March 1977	429041
April 1977	433057
May 1977	437029
June 1977	441233
July 1977	445179
August 1977	449213

1978 Regular Production

Date	Serial Number
September 1977	403186
October 1977	407401
November 1977	411316
December 1977	414695
January 1978	418154
February 1978	422503
March 1978	425280
April 1978	no cars built
May 1978	428833
June 1978	433131
July 1978	436848
August 1978	440274

1978 Pace Car Production

Date	Serial Number
March 1978	901675
April 1978	905766
May 1978	906502

1979

Date	Serial Number
August 1978	400770
September 1978	404612
October 1978	409292
November 1978	413389
December 1978	416891
January 1979	421182
February 1979	425115
March 1979	429500
April 1979	433259
May 1979	437626
June 1979	441770
July 1979	445884
August 1979	450434
September 1979	453807

1980

Date	Serial Number
September 1979	400011
October 1979	404267
November 1979	408343
December 1979	411652
January 1980	416198
February 1980	420057
March 1980	424380
April 1980	427800
May 1980	431152
June 1980	434509
July 1980	438049
August 1980	440614

1981 St. Louis–Assembled Cars

Date	Serial Number
August 1980	400775
September 1980	404136
October 1980	408594
November 1980	412124
December 1980	415234
January 1981	418399
February 1981	421392
March 1981	424742
April 1981	426422
May 1981	428003
June 1981	429775
July 1981	431611

1981 Bowling Green–Assembled Cars

Date	Serial Number
June 1981	100692
July 1981	103155
August 1981	105025
September 1981	106896
October 1981	108995

1982*

Date	Serial Number
October 1981	100515
November 1981	100590
December 1981	102647
January 1982	105004
February 1982	107287
March 1982	110060
April 1982	112598
May 1982	115020
June 1982	117686
July 1982	120227
August 1982	121889
September 1982	124433
October 1982	125408

*Though the final serial number is 25,408, actual 1982 production totaled 25,407. The discrepancy is attributed to the loss of one serial number

Index